THE PRINCETON ANTHOLOGY OF WRITING

The Princeton Anthology of Writing *Favorite Pieces by the Ferris/McGraw*

Writers at Princeton University

John McPhee AND **Carol Rigolot**

EDITORS

810.
8
P957

PRINCETON UNIVERSITY PRESS   PRINCETON AND OXFORD

Copyright © 2001 by Princeton University Press
Published by Princeton University Press, 41 William Street,
Princeton, New Jersey 08540
In the United Kingdom: Princeton University Press, 3 Market Place,
Woodstock, Oxfordshire OX20 1SY

All Rights Reserved

Library of Congress Catalog Card Number 2001089961

ISBN 0-691-08680-X (cloth)
ISBN 0-691-08681-8 (alk. paper)

This book has been composed in Berkeley

Designed by Jan Lilly
Composed by Gretchen Oberfranc

Printed on acid-free paper: ∞

www.pup.princeton.edu

Printed in the United States of America

10 9 8 7 6 5 4 3 2 1

10 9 8 7 6 5 4 3 2 1
(Pbk.)

PREFACE

One morning in 1957, Edgar Gemmell, an administrative vice-president of Princeton University, telephoned Willard Thorp, chairman of the English Department. He said, "Willard, I wonder if you'd stop in here on your way to the faculty meeting this afternoon. Something has come up." Gemmell's office was in Nassau Hall, the school's oldest and principal building, and so is the Faculty Room. When Thorp showed up, Gemmell told him that the owner and founding editor of the *Scranton Times* had died, and, more recently, the widow of the owner and founding editor of the *Scranton Times* had died, and now the Girard Trust Corn Exchange Bank of Philadelphia had informed the university that 92 percent of the resulting estate had been left to Princeton specifically to establish and maintain a professorship in journalism.

Thorp was a man of exquisite words, each highly selected. He had built a broad critical platform underlying the whole of American literature. He was large of heart and girth. To Gemmell he said, "Over my dead body."

Gemmell looked out the window and up through the canopies of dying elms. Offhandedly, he mentioned that the will said that if Princeton were to refuse the bequest it was to go to the Society of the Home for Friendless Women and Children of the City of Scranton. Then he said, "Willard, the amount of this bequest is . . ."

He named a sum that translates into twenty-first-century money as five million dollars.

Right back, without a flicker, Thorp said, "What this university has long needed is deeper insight into contemporary communication."

The deeper insight came first from Irving Dilliard, formerly of the *St. Louis Post-Dispatch*, who held the Ferris professorship for fourteen years. Thereafter, as Princeton's Council of the Humanities gradually broadened the themes of Ferris seminars—under titles like *Politics and the Press*, *The Literature of Fact*, *Workshop in Scientific Writing*, etc.—the number of Ferris professors grew exponentially, and, for several decades now, different figures from the world of journalism have appeared every year to teach directly from their writing experience.

In 1984, Harold W. McGraw, Jr., of the Princeton Class of 1940, created a closely analogous professorship—with seminars called, for example, *Writing about Films and Theater*, *Writing about the Economy*, *Writing about Nature*—that engaged even more working journalists in dialogue with Princeton students. As the twentieth century was fading out, nearly sixty journalists had served as Ferris or McGraw professors. Examples of their own journalistic prose—chosen by them—are the contents of this book.

The contents are long, short, individual, and idiosyncratic. They represent so many aspects of magazine and newspaper writing, not to mention television and the Internet, that it seems uninviting to attempt to present them in fabricated compartments—e.g., Foreign Correspondence, Domestic Ruminations, Other. Instead, we spread out all the pieces and then put them together in a freelance manner that we hoped would enhance the pleasure of the whole. We saw juxtapositions of association, and went for them, but not always. We tried juxtapositions of dissociation if, for example, somebody's act was hard to follow in kind. Uncharitably, this could be described as magnetic structuring done with black-and-white Scotty dogs. But it seemed vastly preferable to an alphabetical list or a chronological list or a set of earnest chambers like named hotel rooms.

When I was an undergraduate at Princeton, one of my favorite professors was Willard Thorp. In the English Department, we did not study contemporary journalistic prose. In the conversation, nonfiction was not yet a term, let alone a literary term. Its synonyms were tainted by the fish they had wrapped. Even as late as 1973, a Harvard anthology purporting to represent all the important writing done in the United States since the Second World War did not include a single nonfiction example. As this book splendidly attests, factual writing has found its place in the regard of the academy, to the great pleasure of all of us who are represented here.

CONTENTS

JOHN McPHEE *Preface*   v

DAVID K. SHIPLER *Beauty for Ashes*   3

JONATHAN SCHELL *A View of Mountains*   9

HAYNES JOHNSON *The Boat*   11

JANE KRAMER *Joséphine Guezou*   18

ROBERT DONOVAN *Twentieth-Century Odyssey*   22

DON OBERDORFER *A Farewell to Hue*   29

LESLIE COCKBURN *Looking for Trouble*   36

KARL E. MEYER *The Forthright Estate: In Praise of the
                Newspaper Column*   41

ROGER MUDD *Code of Ethics*   46

PAUL TAYLOR *Father of His Country*   51

STUART S. TAYLOR JR. *Workplace Discrimination*   59
                *Harassment by Kids: Are More
                Lawsuits the Answer?*   62

LARRY L. KING *Driver's Education*   66

IRVING DILLIARD *People and Character*   72

VICTOR NAVASKY *Saving* The Nation   75

RICHARD GILMAN *Faith, Sex, Mystery*   87

RICHARD STENGEL *My Own Vox Pop*   94
                Stardom? They'd Rather Pass   95
                Space Invaders   97

CHARLOTTE GRIMES *The Country Is at Crisis Point*   99
                *Memo to Conservatives: Family Ties Are
                the Strongest Values of All*   104

BARBARA CROSSETTE *All Sentient Beings* 107

RONALD STEEL *When Worlds Collide* 114

ISABEL WILKERSON *First Born, Fast Grown: The Manful Life of Nicholas, 10* 117

NANCY GIBBS *Massacre at Columbine High School* 123

DEBORAH TANNEN *Gender in the Classroom* 126

JONATHAN ALTER *Cop-Out on Class: Why Private Schools Are Today's Draft Deferments* 131
It's a Wonderful Legacy 133
The Era of Bad Feeling 134

JIM HOAGLAND *Two of a Kind* 137
Truly a Nation . . . 139
A Little Homer at the Beach 140

LAWRENCE WESCHLER *Why I Can't Write Fiction* 143

BLAIR CLARK *On Robert Lowell* 147

ALICE STEINBACH *The Miss Dennis School of Writing* 151

MILTON VIORST *Meeting Mahfouz* 156

RICHARD EDER *Critic's Notebook* 163

TERRENCE RAFFERTY *L'Atalante* 166

JEREMY BERNSTEIN *Annie of Corsica* 170

JOHN DARNTON *Two Deaths—One Then, One Now: On Losing a Father, a Newspaperman* 176

GEOFFREY WOLFF *Heavy Lifting* 179

CHRISTOPHER WREN *Lenin Peak* 193

JONATHAN WEINER *From So Simple a Beginning* 198

JOHN NOBLE WILFORD *Pioneer 10 Pushes Beyond Goals, Into the Unknown* 204
Get Set to Say Hi to the Neighbors 207

MALCOLM W. BROWNE *Left the Light On, But Nobody
                     Came* 209
                     The Invisible Flying Cat 210
                     At Least the Monsters Survive 212
                     Beauty, as Scientists Behold It 213

JAMES GLEICK *Manual Labor* 216
               Maintenance Not Included 218

GINA KOLATA *At Last, Shout of "Eureka!" in Age-Old Math
              Mystery* 221
              *Scientist Reports First Cloning Ever of Adult
              Mammal* 223

WALTER SULLIVAN *What If We Succeed?* 225

HARRISON E. SALISBURY *Deus Conservat Omnia* 234

JEAN STROUSE *Introduction to* Morgan, American
               Financier 242

ROBERT K. MASSIE *Down Twenty-Three Steps* 249

DAVID REMNICK *The Forest Coup* 252

JONATHAN SANDERS *Pictures from the Rubble Patch* 259

SERGE SCHMEMANN *A Corner of Russia* 264

GLORIA EMERSON *Goodbye to Rafah* 268

WILLIAM GREIDER *Mock Democracy* 272

LANDON Y. JONES JR. *The Big Barbecue* 281

SAMUEL G. FREEDMAN *The Rope Line* 289

FRANCINE DU PLESSIX GRAY *Nixonland* 298

WALTER GUZZARDI *Consultants: The Men Who Came to
                  Dinner* 306

JEREMY TREGLOWN *Class Act* 316

JOHN HERBERS *The New American Heartland* 321

CONTENTS

CHARLES KAISER *The 1950s*   325

NAT HENTOFF *Jazz: Music Beyond Time and Nations*   330

LUCINDA FRANKS *Miracle Kid*   335

JOHN McPHEE *Travels of the Rock*   351

Acknowledgments   369

Author Index   373

The McGraw Professors in Writing, 1984–1999

Malcolm W. Browne

Samuel G. Freedman

Richard Gilman

James Gleick

William Greider

Landon Y. Jones Jr.

Karl E. Meyer

Terrence Rafferty

Harrison E. Salisbury

Alice Steinbach

Walter Sullivan

Deborah Tannen

Stuart S. Taylor Jr.

Jonathan Weiner

John Noble Wilford

The Ferris Professors of Journalism, 1963–1999

Jonathan Alter

Jeremy Bernstein

Blair Clark

Leslie Cockburn

Barbara Crossette

John Darnton

Irving Dilliard

Robert Donovan

Richard Eder

Gloria Emerson

Lucinda Franks

Nancy Gibbs

Francine du Plessix Gray

Charlotte Grimes

Walter Guzzardi

Nat Hentoff

John Herbers

Jim Hoagland

Haynes Johnson

Charles Kaiser

Larry L. King

Gina Kolata

Jane Kramer

Robert K. Massie

John McPhee

Roger Mudd

Victor Navasky

Don Oberdorfer

David Remnick

Jonathan Sanders

Jonathan Schell

Serge Schmemann

David K. Shipler

Ronald Steel

Richard Stengel

Jean Strouse

Paul Taylor

Jeremy Treglown

Milton Viorst

Lawrence Weschler

Isabel Wilkerson

Geoffrey Wolff

Christopher Wren

THE PRINCETON ANTHOLOGY OF WRITING

David K. Shipler, a Pulitzer Prize–winning author, reported from 1968–88 for the *New York Times* from New York, Saigon, Moscow, Jerusalem, and Washington. His books include *Russia: Broken Idols, Solemn Dreams* and *Arab and Jew: Wounded Spirits in a Promised Land.* This piece comes from *A Country of Strangers: Blacks and Whites in America* (Knopf, 1997).

Beauty for Ashes

If you deprive a man of who he is, you can make him anything that you want him to be. But if you teach him his heritage and his culture, he will aspire to be greater than those before him.

Maj. H. L. Barner, a descendant of slaves

It is a September Saturday on the plantation. People are gathering for a day of reunion, and yellow ribbons are tied around the thick trunks of the cypresses planted two centuries ago by their enslaved ancestors. Families stroll in clusters, toward the mansion, up the walkway of red bricks laid by those who went before, along the dirt carriage path that borders the narrow canal. The earth smells of ripeness and age.

The canal is soothing, and it strikes a chill. The placid water moves lazily in the late summer shade, and harbors suffering in its murkiness. A double image shimmers beneath the towering trees. One is for those who do not consider the history; beauty shrouds the shame. The other is for those who recognize that they have come upon the site of a great crime and can feel a shiver of remembrance.

To drain a North Carolina swamp so that timber could be cut and rice could be grown, the canal was dug by slaves through two stifling summers and two raw winters in the 1780s; it ran twenty feet wide and six miles from Lake Phelps to the Scuppernong River, among tangled roots and swarms of black-flies and mosquitoes. Imagine the whistle of the whip, the ebony bodies glistening with sweat, the groan and cadence of the melancholy work songs. African-Americans too exhausted to return to their shacks at the end of the day were left behind, to be found dead at dawn. The canal they created is a lovely river of sorrow; it marks the divide in America between those who see the beauty and those who feel the chill.

The gathering today is of those who try to do both, who have traced their family lines back, back into slavery in this very place, on this particular ground, and who now stand on the same soil, pained and proud, reconciling themselves with history. Across the plantation drift the notes of a spiritual

3

sung by two male voices, then the beat of four African drummers, then the sad and sour blues of a harmonica, like fragments of reminiscence.

The land is flat and the soil is rich, and the fields are deep in cotton and tobacco. Most of the back roads are paved now, slender traces of blacktop through the tranquil North Carolina countryside. With the arrival of air conditioning and television, folks don't sit out on their porches much anymore to watch the gentle summer evenings settle over the woods and farms; many of the houses are bunched in suburban enclaves, where lawns are carefully mowed and azaleas lovingly fertilized so that they bloom in pastel reds and pinks in the springtime.

Near the little town of Creswell, the main road to the coast passes a small supermarket, a tiny restaurant, a Mobil station, and an historic marker that was finally erected a few years ago to acknowledge that human beings other than white planters had lived here and helped build the nation:

> Somerset Place
> Antebellum plantation of Josiah Collins III,
> who grew rice and corn. Home in 1860
> to 328 slaves. Located six miles south

If you're white, you probably don't stop to think that the road you're driving may have been first cut by slaves, that the field you're passing may have been first cleared by slaves. Americans, especially white Americans, have short memories. We are impatient with the past, always hurrying into the future, moving on, getting beyond, not dwelling, leaving behind. "That's history," we say dismissively. Whatever reverence our European ancestors had for the power of history has been lost in the frontier culture of this continent; whatever deference later immigrants felt for the age-old rhythms of their homelands in Asia, the Middle East, Latin America, and elsewhere has not been transplanted well into the soil of the United States.

Although some whites appreciate the durability of the past in shaping the present, the sense of continuity held by other cultures has not found its way into the American mainstream. History here begins the day you are born: To most of white America, slavery is an evil long gone, the segregation of Jim Crow is deeply buried, and the civil rights movement has wiped the slate clean. Our ethic is practical, and problems are for solving; we do not easily admit to those that we cannot fix. Wrongs have been righted, the residue of guilt erased—this is the current creed of many whites, especially those too young to have seen those pictures of white girls' faces twisted in hatred as they screamed at little black children who were integrating their schools.

Some blacks acquire this habit of historical amnesia, but black America generally lives with a different memory, one that feels the reverberations of slavery, yearns for roots, searches for pride, and reaches back to grasp at ancient uncertainties. Present events occur in context, not in isolation, so they are interpreted according to what has gone before. Hence, in the eyes of many blacks, elements of the complex relationships of slavery are constantly being reenacted—between bosses and workers, between blacks and whites sexually, between African-Americans of lighter and darker skin, among blacks who suppress dissent within their ranks. Slavery is a permanent metaphor.

Rosanne Katon-Walden, for example, a passionate advocate of interracial adoption, engages in frequent combat with black social workers who oppose placing black children with white parents. And when she wants to explain why her fellow blacks are uncomfortable having this dispute in public, she reaches for old patterns: "You don't rat to the massah about what's going on in the slave quarters," she says.

A black policewoman in Baltimore, noting that white women are almost never assigned with black men in patrol cars, sees a policy with distant origins. "It's a thing that goes all the way back to slavery," she says. "The white slave owners didn't want their wives to associate too much with the black slaves, and sometimes the wives were attracted to them, you know, white females were attracted to black males."

Understandably, some of the finest literature by African-Americans is haunted by the ghosts of slavery. Toni Morrison's *Beloved* and August Wilson's *The Piano Lesson* lay bare the wrenching struggles that blacks have with themselves over how to coexist with that past—whether to bury it, fear it, despise it, deny it, revise it, memorialize it, or somehow to absorb and face it and take nourishment from the sorrow and the survival. . . . August Wilson's piano, purchased by a slaveowner in exchange for the heroine's father and grandmother, stands at the pivot point of family, memory, history, and revenge. It is an unplayed instrument, a commodity, a shrine, an artifact of inner suffering.

Blacks and whites who manage to engage each other successfully across the racial line often do so by achieving concord in the historical dimension: Whites who are accepted by blacks are frequently those for whom black history has resonance. Blacks who are accepted by whites may tend toward the ahistorical, observing events in a vacuum and activating less white guilt as they put aside the prism of slavery and segregation.

More often, however, the black regard and the white disdain for history foster a collision of memories. Bearing the burden of history in its own manner, each group hears different echoes, tells a different story, creates a complete universe of perception that separates and disconnects. We need to listen to each other's echoes.

SOMERSET is in a mood of warm celebration, not mourning. Quite a crowd has now assembled, mostly of blacks, who are hugging relatives on the lawn near the old mansion, filling the grounds with laughter and joyous greetings.

On a makeshift stage, with the lake in the background, one of the musicians gets up from his African drums and approaches the microphone. "We're gathered here in recognition of our ancestors," he declares. "We're here on hallowed ground, where our ancestors lived in the physical world at one time. But they're still here spiritually. We're going to call our ancestors to come and be with us this morning." A hush moves across the crowd. "We'll follow the African tradition of pouring libation."

He instructs all those gathered to close their eyes and breathe deeply. Silence has settled over the plantation. "We ask that our ancestors, those who were left on the African continent, who go back to time immemorial, we ask that you come to be with us." He pours a little water from a green goblet onto the ground. "Ancestors, those who died in the middle passage, whose bones are buried beneath the Atlantic Ocean, all the way to the shores of North America, South America, the Caribbean islands, we ask you to come and be with us." The goblet is tipped again. "Ancestors, those who were in bondage in North America, South America, and the Caribbean islands, and those, in particular, here at Sunset Plantation"—there are a few titters as he misstates the name—"we ask that you come and be with us." Another splash of water into the soil.

Dorothy Spruill Redford is dressed as a slave might have been, in a skirt and blouse the color of burlap, her hair in a head wrap the color of field cotton. . . . Born a few miles from Somerset in 1943, she first encountered the enslavement of her ancestors by averting her eyes. "My parents were not much for history, for talking about the old days. But they did reminisce now and then," she wrote in her 1988 book, *Somerset Homecoming*. "Slavery was never mentioned around our house. The first time I heard the word, I thought some shame was attached to you if you even uttered it. I told myself it was just another thing about this place that had nothing to do with me. It was some kind of distant stain, something deep in the soul of the South. . . . When they talked about slavery in school, I was puzzled to think that an entire people could allow themselves to be enslaved—as puzzled as I was to see my parents allow little white children to call them by their first names."

This vague belief that the victims were somehow responsible for their own suffering has haunted other black families as well. Just as some Jewish survivors of the Holocaust have not talked of their trials to their children, some black grandparents have never spoken of their parents' or grandparents' lives as slaves.

THERE is something delicious about seeing the bright blues and reds and oranges of men's African dashikis against the bland, buttermilk-colored mansion. There is some satisfying justice in feeling the beat of African drums thundering across this ground. Here, at the genesis of America's racial divide, blacks are recapturing a bit of what was stolen from them.

A brisk breeze comes off the lake and eases the midday heat. People are sitting around on folding chairs, eating traditional foods: fried chicken, black-eyed peas, mashed potatoes, and okra. They are talking about gathering strength from this reunion, seeing their ancestors as the true role models, as heroes who had the vigor, the dignity, the ingenuity to survive slavery.

Clara Small, a young history professor from Maryland, is in a reflective mood about this place of her ancestors, judging it a kind of neutral ground where people are searching for understanding. She smiles slightly. It is an interesting concept: neutral ground. Once, she notes, it was anything but neutral. Now it is acknowledged as a place that the whites owned but the blacks built. A curious equilibrium has been achieved, and with it a sense of calm that suspends Somerset in a temper of contentment. The moment is strange and intricate, tenuous and clean, for embracing the reality of the past creates an island of unreal harmony in the present. Surrounded by turbulence, isolated from the larger, contentious society, Somerset's tranquillity today is a lesson in the therapy of honest history.

A spirit of remarkable charity pervades this place today. Oscar Bennett captures it directly. "I don't hold no madness against nobody, cause you didn't do nothing to me," he says. "Those people who done that is dead and gone. I don't hold you responsible for something somebody else did. That's the way I feel about it. I think we all should live together and be as one."

On the shady lawn, Cathy Collins Gowing is standing in a bright, flowered dress, her dark hair straight and long and framing a beatific smile as she gazes around her. She and the several other Collins descendants—including her little girl, Amber, who is clinging to her skirts—are incidental to this day, and that seems right to her. "I think it's great," she says softly. "Oh, this is theirs. This is their place." She laughs. "It's wonderful. It means redemption. It means hope." She has come all the way from Oregon to be here.

Only in a vague, undefined way was the history of Somerset transmitted to her by her relatives, and the gauzy images were so abstract that they never encouraged her to think about her ancestors as the owners of slaves. "I knew it was here," she says, "but I didn't know any of the background. I knew that eventually it traced back to Somerset, England, but that's about all I knew." Here, too, a certain silence had descended over the generations.

"I was an anti-war activist by the time I was fourteen," she explains, "and became a revolutionary by the time I was seventeen. I organized May Day marches and lived in Paris working with the North Vietnamese. I was very concerned about racism and very angry." She laughs again. "Lots of marches, and lots of getting beat over the head with sticks and Mace and all of that. I gave my father Bobby Seale's book when I was seventeen—*Seize the Time*—and he read it." Her father would "always raise us saying, 'Never lose the common touch.' He was a humble man. So he challenged us to have open hearts. And I challenged him, too."

She looks out over the grounds. "This is just excellent. I care about it being redeemed."

She pauses for a moment, listening to a spiritual being played over the loudspeakers, then hums along for a while before speaking again, her voice so low that it is nearly lost in the strains of the music. "I went home and I thought, What's the verse for this? And it's Isaiah," and then she paraphrases Isaiah 61:3: "To appoint unto them that mourn in Zion, to give unto them beauty for ashes, the oil of joy for mourning, the garment of praise for the spirit of heaviness; that they might be called trees of righteousness, the planting of the Lord, that he might be glorified."

Over the music, family names are still being called for photographs. How does she feel the descendants of slaves are seeing her? "Well, I would understand it if they despised me. That's all right. But most people haven't. So, if I expect that, then everything else is a bonus." And what is she feeling, what is she thinking? "I pray for forgiveness for all that's gone on here. You know, there's deep roots of wrong that my family has carried out that needs to be redeemed, that needs to be healed. I think that this is an excellent place for that to happen."

The day is coming to an end at Somerset Place. By 6:00, most people have departed, blacks with blacks and whites with whites, into separateness once again, abandoning the plantation to the lengthening shadows cast by the towering cypresses and sycamores. The sun sinks toward the lake, and the breeze off the water seems a little cooler.

Clusters of conversation are thinning out. The remaining descendants of slaves drift gently away, down the brick paths that slaves built, slowly saying farewells with handshakes and hugs and bursts of hearty laughter. Some pull the yellow ribbons, the symbols of homecoming, from around the tree trunks to take as pieces of memory.

In the deepening shade beneath the old, thick trees where families sat and talked, empty chairs are left in ragged circles on the lawn. Beauty for ashes.

Jonathan Schell is the author of *The Village of Ben Sue* and *The Fate of the Earth*. He was a writer for the *New Yorker* from 1967–87 and a columnist for *Newsday* from 1990–96. He teaches at Wesleyan University and the New School, and is the Harold Willens Peace Fellow at The Nation Institute. This is the epilogue from his book *The Gift of Time: The Case for Abolishing Nuclear Weapons Now* (Henry Holt & Co., 1998).

A View of Mountains

On August 9, 1945, the day the atomic bomb was dropped on Nagasaki, Yosuke Yamahata, a photographer serving in the Japanese army, was dispatched to the destroyed city. The hundred or so pictures he took the next day constitute the fullest photographic record of nuclear destruction in existence. Hiroshima, destroyed three days earlier, had largely escaped the camera's lens in the first days after the bombing. It was therefore left to Yamahata to record, methodically—and, as it happens, with a great and simple artistry—the effects on a human population of a nuclear weapon only hours after it had been used. Some of Yamahata's pictures show corpses charred in the peculiar way in which a nuclear fireball chars its victims. They have been burned by light—technically speaking, by the "thermal pulse"—and their bodies are often branded with the patterns of their clothes, whose colors absorb light in different degrees. One photograph shows a horse twisted under the cart it had been pulling. Another shows a heap of something that once had been a human being hanging over a ledge into a ditch. A third shows a girl who has somehow survived unwounded standing in the open mouth of a bomb shelter and smiling an unearthly smile, shocking us with the sight of ordinary life, which otherwise seems to have been left behind for good in the scenes we are witnessing. Stretching into the distance on all sides are fields of rubble dotted with fires, and, in the background, a view of mountains. We can see the mountains because the city is gone. That absence, even more than the wreckage, contains the heart of the matter. The true measure of the event lies not in what remains but in all that has disappeared.

It took a few seconds for the United States to destroy Nagasaki with the world's second atomic bomb, but it took fifty years for Yamahata's pictures of the event to make the journey back from Nagasaki to the United States. They were shown for the first time in this country in 1995, at the International Center for Photography in New York. Arriving a half-century late, they are still news. The photographs display the fate of a single city, but their meaning is universal, since, in our age of nuclear arms, what happened to Nagasaki can, in a flash, happen to any city in the world. In the photographs, Nagasaki comes into its own. Nagasaki has always been in the shadow of Hiroshima, as if the human imagination had stumbled to exhaustion in the wreckage of the first ruined city without reaching even the outskirts of the second. Yet the bombing of Nagasaki is in certain respects the fitter symbol of the nuclear danger that still hangs over us. It is proof that, having once used nuclear weapons, we can use them again. It introduces the idea of a series—the series that, with tens of thousands of nuclear weapons remaining in existence, continues to threaten everyone. (The unpredictable, open-ended character of this series is suggested by the fact that the second bomb originally was to be dropped on the city of Kokura, which was spared Nagasaki's fate only because bad weather protected it from view.) Each picture therefore seemed not so much an image of something that happened a half-century ago as a window cut into the wall of the photography center showing what soon could easily happen to New York. Wherever the exhibit might travel, moreover, the view of the threatened future from these "windows" would be roughly accurate, since, although every intact city is different from every other, all cities that suffer nuclear destruction will look much the same.

Yamahata's pictures afford a glimpse of the end of the world. Yet in our day, when the challenge is not just to apprehend the nuclear peril but to seize a God-given opportunity to dispel it once and for all, we seem to need, in addition, some other picture to counterpoise against ruined Nagasaki—one showing not what we would lose through our failure but what we would gain by our success. What might that picture be, though? How do you show the opposite of the end of the world? Should it be Nagasaki, intact and alive, before the bomb was dropped—or perhaps the spared city of Kokura? Should it be a child, or a mother and child, or perhaps the Earth itself? None seems adequate, for how can we give a definite form to that which can assume infinite forms, namely, the lives of all human beings, now and in the future? Imagination, faced with either the end of the world or its continuation, must remain incomplete. Only action can satisfy.

Once, the arrival in the world of new generations took care of itself. Now, they can come into existence only if, through an act of faith and collective will, we ensure their right to exist. Performing that act is the greatest of the responsibilities of the generations now alive. The gift of time is the gift of life, forever, if we know how to receive it.

Haynes Johnson was awarded the Pulitzer Prize in 1966 for his reporting on the civil rights crisis in Selma, Alabama. He is the author of thirteen books, and currently holds the Knight Chair in Journalism at the University of Maryland. The following is an excerpt from Johnson's book *The Bay of Pigs* (Norton, 1964), describing what happened to some of the survivors of the disastrous 1961 invasion of Cuba after they desperately swam to a sailboat at the invasion beachhead to avoid capture by victorious Castro forces advancing on them. They had been secretly trained, financed, and put ashore by the American CIA and led to believe they would easily liberate Cuba from the Castro regime.

The Boat

They were twenty-two men on a twenty-two-foot sailboat. In the few hours before dark they sailed toward the American destroyers, away from Girón and away from the sound of battle. The wind was south and they were heading straight toward the larger ships on the horizon. Night came. They never saw the destroyers again.

Most of them were paratroopers who had followed their commander Del Valle aboard the boat; but there were also men from the headquarters company, from the Third Battalion of infantry and from Roberto San Román's Heavy Gun Battalion. Thrown together by chance in the desperate moments of defeat, they were representative of the Brigade: they ranged in age from eighteen to forty-three; they were humble men, educated men and one of them had been an Ambassador. Only one had had experience with a sailboat.

That first night, Wednesday, April 19, they entered shallow water and ran aground close to the lighthouse of Cayo Guano, south of the Bay of Pigs. An argument broke out: some wanted to go to the lighthouse, kill the occupants and take what food there was; the others were opposed. Del Valle and Roberto San Román, as the principal leaders aboard, decided against an attack. The men jumped into the water and pushed until the boat was free, and they sailed on.

In the morning they examined the boat more closely: they found a small water tank about a quarter full and a storage bin filled with fish. The three or four on top were edible, but underneath the fish were rotten and had to be thrown overboard. With a cigarette lighter and the few pieces of charcoal on board, the fish were cooked, cut into small pieces and divided. They drank the water and ate the fish. It was the nearest thing to a meal they had while on the boat.

On the second day, Friday, they caught two small fish with a hook tied to a lighted flashlight as bait. José García Montes, thirty-seven years old, who had been Cuba's Ambassador to Japan, a thoughtful, quiet man whom everyone respected, was appointed to cut the fish. While they stood watching silently, he carefully cut the fish into twenty-two tiny pieces, and took the last piece himself. They ate the fish raw, including its intestines. That night a storm came up and the boat was tossed about so severely they were certain it was their last moment. All night long they bailed with small tin cans, fearing they were about to capsize. Roberto San Román was so convinced it was the end that he pulled a piece of shrapnel from his face "just to see how big it was. We were thinking it was the last day on earth." The boat weathered the storm and on Saturday they were greeted again by bright sunshine.

Their first two days served as a pattern for the others. They took turns at the rudder and keeping the single sail to the wind. And always they talked about the battle, about the hated Americans, about what fools they had been to let themselves get in such a trap. Del Valle and Roberto tried to steer the conversation away from the invasion—not out of loyalty to the Americans, but in an attempt to maintain morale.

There were quarrels about what they should do. Some, especially those with relatives in Cuba, wanted to go back and land on the western coast of Cuba in Pinar del Rio Province, but Del Valle and Roberto convinced them to go with the wind. By now the coast certainly would be heavily patrolled. So they sailed on.

The sun was a punishment. On the first day, someone had suggested they lean over the boat close to the water and let the waves refresh them. Soon, when they were not attending to the boat, everyone was leaning overboard, splashing water over their bodies. It became almost an obsession: some even tried to put water in their ears, in their nostrils, anywhere that it might possibly soak into their body and save them. They would use the tin cans to dip up the water and pour it over one another. When a man would drop his can and lose it, violent accusations would be made. Because of the size of the boat, they had to sleep in layers—a head on someone's stomach, feet on someone else.

When they lost sight of the destroyers they planned to sail due south toward Grand Cayman Island, a British possession. But after the storm on the second night the wind changed from south to southwest, and they knew it was going to be a long trip.

"The thing that mattered then was to get someplace," Roberto said, "because after the second day we knew that nobody was looking for us."

For four more days they sailed southwest. Occasionally, they would see ships far off, and occasionally planes, flying very high. Each time, no matter how far off or how high, everyone started yelling, climbing the mast and waving furiously. Those who still had shirts held them into the wind and waved them back and forth. Each time, when the ship or plane was out of sight, everyone slumped back into the boat and began cursing the United States again.

On the fourth full day, Raúl García Menocal, twenty-one years old, the scion of a family that had produced presidents of Cuba, said he remembered reading that if you placed a cork over a bottle of urine and dropped it in the ocean the salt water would filter through the cork and the urine would become sweet and purified after an hour. Many men urinated in bottles, put the corks on and dropped them into the sea, tied by a string. Before half an hour had gone by, Menocal could not wait. He pulled up his bottle and drank. The experiment had not worked. He was so angry that he threw the bottle down, and from that time on as soon as he urinated he drank.

Each day they had been dropping their line overboard with the flashlight, and on the fifth day a shark nearly as large as the boat itself grabbed the bait and was hooked. For more than an hour, Del Valle and Armando López-Estrada, one of his airborne officers, fought to land him. Three or four times they succeeded in bringing the shark alongside, only to have it rush off the line. At one point, Del Valle said he was going to jump overboard and kill the shark with a knife, and his men had to restrain him. When the shark was pulled close the last time, Del Valle hit it over the head with a paddle. The shark got loose, the paddle was broken and the flashlight was lost. For one long day that shark followed the boat.

On the crude chart they were making they traced their course: from south to southwest. Then a wind shift forced them to turn northwest and it became apparent they were not going to reach even Central America. Although morale was steadily getting lower, it was not until the sixth day that they received their first great shock.

Inocente R. García, a quiet man, called the "uncle" by everyone, at forty-three was the oldest man on the boat. He knew something about a fishing boat, and he had helped to distribute the men so their weight would be better balanced. Since the beginning he had been coughing and by the end of the fifth day had become worse. He was lying in the boat, half conscious, calling for water and talking incoherently—about his mother, his friends or the war. He turned almost yellow and, to their horror, the men saw green pus coming from his eyes. When they awoke in the morning he was dead.

Del Valle seemed even more shocked than the rest: García had been one of his men, he had trained him and led him. A bitter argument began over what to do with the body.

"He didn't want to bury that man in the ocean," Roberto said. "I told him that his corpse was destroying our morale. Del Valle said, 'Let's wait a few hours to see if we are rescued and we can deliver his body to his family.'"

The rest of the men were equally divided. In the end Del Valle agreed to the burial. Someone spoke a brief eulogy, they knelt and said the rosary and the body, heavily weighted, was thrown into the sea.

García's death was a heavy blow. As they became weaker, they began talking constantly about food—the food they had thrown away in Guatemala, the food they were going to eat when they got back—and always about water and juices. They began making resolutions: they were going to be better husbands and fathers; they were going to work hard and make their families proud of them. Del Valle, who was single, told Roberto, who was married and had children, that he was going to get married and go to New York with him and forget about the war.

After García died the boat ran into a dead calm. For twenty-five hours they drifted under the broiling sun with the sail hanging slack. The cursing increased. In the midst of the calm a ship passed—close enough, it seemed, to see them. Again men climbed wearily up the mast and waved their tattered clothes and shouted. While they tried to attract attention, the rest laboriously cut part of a spar in two with dull combat knives until they had two rough paddles. Then they took turns paddling toward the ship. Some of the men were so weak that they were unable even to lift the paddle when their turn came. The ship disappeared, but they continued paddling. Now they could see sharks gathering around them.

García Montes, bleeding from the mouth, and so weak he could hardly move, was told to rest. He replied, "No, as long as I'm alive I won't be a burden for you," and he took his turn. Most maddening of all during the calm was the sight of fishes beneath the boat; but there was no way to catch them. At night the wind came up, and they picked up speed under shortened sail.

In the afternoon of the next day one of the men went berserk. He began screaming and shouting curses, blaming all of them for what had happened. He collapsed in the bottom of the boat, still screaming, but staring wildly and fixedly ahead. From those terrible, staring eyes they saw green pus coming. He was placed beside Raúl Menocal, who was also delirious and showing the fatal sign of green pus. The men bathed their sick companions as well as they could, but late in the day Menocal died. A quarter of an hour later, as it was getting dark, the second man died. García Montes, a lawyer by profession, had also studied medicine, and was asked to certify the deaths. With great effort he crawled across the boat until he reached the two men. He held Menocal's wrist to check his pulse and then called back, "I'm sorry, but I'm not sure if he's dead or not."

He was not feeling well himself, he said, and would wait until the morning to verify the deaths. In the morning all three men were dead, with García Montes still holding Raúl Menocal's wrist.

This time the service was brief. It was a great effort to throw the three bodies overboard and the men were exhausted when it was done. Nothing was left to weight the bodies and for nearly twenty minutes they could see them, floating.

At some point—no one knows exactly when—they had passed through the Straits of Yucatán and entered the Gulf Stream. In the Gulf the water was wonderfully clear, and the sky a brilliant blue. Very deep below them they could see large schools of fish. To the tormented men it seemed as though the fish were taunting them; swimming close and then deliberately moving away. Men dived into the water trying to snatch them, but it was no use. They had been eight days without food or water. Each day they took turns cooling their bodies in the water, holding onto the rope they had cut in escaping from Girón.

Among the men were two brothers, Joaquín and Isias Rodríguez. Twice Isias had thrown himself into the sea, saying he was going to kill himself. Both times the others had pleaded with him to come back, and both times he had swum back. But on the third time he refused. His brother called out that their mother was waiting, but Isias said he wasn't going to die as the others had. On the boat they began discussing whether they should swim to bring him back. The life of another man had become of such little value by then that Roberto San Román said, "I will go if you reserve that place for me." (It was a special place in the front part of the boat, that only one man could occupy.) The men agreed and Roberto swam to Rodríguez and convinced him by saying they were already in the Gulf and soon would reach the coast. "Well, he came back. But after I got to the boat that place had been taken by somebody else, and they didn't give it to me." The others spoke harshly to Rodríguez and told him that the next time he jumped no one was coming for him.

Some already had lost forty or fifty pounds. Their hair was long and matted, their skin was burned and cracked and their bodies were covered with blisters and boils. On each fingernail and toenail there was a distinct white mark, showing the place where the nails had stopped growing. They all had continual violent stomach cramps. Some had taken to raking in seaweed and eating it. From the second day, when they had caught the small fishes, they had nothing to eat until the ninth day.

Roberto was dozing on the front part of the boat that day when a seagull landed on his leg. Holding his breath and trying not to move his body, he edged his hand slowly toward the bird—but it flew away and perched on the mast. With the infinite patience born of desperation he climbed up until he reached out and caught it.

"When I caught the bird I was the important man on the boat," Roberto said. "Everybody came to me. I was so weak that I made a little pressure on the bird's head to kill it, but it's funny, I was not in a hurry to eat it. After that I put the bird in the water and started cleaning it."

Slowly, feather by feather, he cleaned the bird and then held the prize for all to see before dividing it.

"Some of my friends took a leg, another the head. What I took was the chest and the heart."

That afternoon they again sighted ships on the horizon and again yelled and waved, and again fell back in despair. Each man reacted according to his personality—some with prayers, some with blasphemies, some with silence. No one showed the strain more than Del Valle.

With the death of the first man, Del Valle had changed. He was still the recognized leader of them all, the one everyone turned to for the final decision and the one who, more than anyone else, maintained discipline. Yet the death of García had unsettled him. Already weakened from fighting with the shark, he seemed to fail rapidly and became weaker and weaker. Whether he lost his spirit or his faith, no one can say—but he was obsessed with dying. After García's death, he told Roberto that if he ever died he didn't want to be thrown overboard, and he didn't want to be buried at sea. "You must hang me on the mast or do something to take me to land." Every day he asked Roberto to inspect his eyes and every day Roberto told him he was all right.

On the night of the tenth day Del Valle became delirious. He was lying next to the mast, with Roberto's head on his stomach, calling out messages to the American advisor of the paratroop battalion. With his hand on the mast, he tapped out imaginary telegraph messages. He shouted out the coordinates of their position at sea and told the Americans to come and rescue them. The messages had a certain horrible logic: "We are weak and sick and dying"; then he would pause for a few moments and act as if he were receiving a message. The last thing they heard him say that night was: "We are saved. They are coming in a ship." In the morning he was dead.

"When Alex died it shocked all of us," Roberto said, "because he was the leader. He wanted to do everything. I didn't work on the part of throwing him over because he was my very best friend and I didn't want to touch him or see him dead."

The twelfth day at sea began with five men dead and seventeen dying. That afternoon Jorge García Villalta died, with the familiar green pus coming from his eyes. He was thirty-three years old and they felt his death deeply, for he had led them from the beginning in saying the rosary five or six times a day. He had been the kind of man who thought of others and who tried to make them forget their situation with a kind word or a smile or an expression of faith. With his death following closely after Del Valle's, it seemed that all faith was a mockery, and to hope was futile. For the next day they sailed on in silence.

Then, when there was no hope, the skies darkened and the night of the thirteenth day it began to rain. Momentarily they forgot their weaknesses and jumped up. There were brief fights over who would hold the two or three remaining cans to catch the water, and whether to drink it or save it. Some men opened their mouths as the rain beat down. They drank as much as they could catch. But in the morning they felt worse than before: the taste of the water had tantalized them and made them crave more. Their throats were swollen and they felt as if they had no air in their lungs. To make it worse, they had found another man dead when they woke up. Marcos Tulio, a very strong man, was the seventh to die.

That fourteenth day, the day after the rain, was hot and clear without a cloud in the skies. Suddenly, in the middle of the morning, they saw a sail coming closer. It was a two- or three-masted sailboat, and they could see people walking the deck. The boat spotted them and circled around them three or four times.

They put down their sail, beat on their tin cans, waved their clothing, shouted and tried to climb the mast once more. But the ship did not come closer. They waited and then someone said, "We must be close to land. That is why they don't pick us up." They raised the sail again and continued on. For some minutes the ship followed them; then it turned away and the Cubans moved on, straining to see the land they were sure must be ahead. The day passed and in the night one man called out, "Land!" He saw the lights of a village. They tried to alter their direction and sail toward the lights, until they realized they were the lights from a ship far in the distance.

Thursday, May 4, the fifteenth day at sea, dawned bright and clear. The fifteen men lay in the boat, barely able to move or talk.

"I remember that morning," Roberto said, "I was getting a little out of my mind. It is very difficult to explain. I don't know if I was crazy or not. It's like being dizzy. I remember I caught some seaweed and showed it to the men and said it had water inside it and I ate it."

In the middle of the afternoon he dived out of the boat and went as deep as he could into the water to try to get cool. When he came up he began drinking salt water—as much as he could hold. About 4:00 he lay down beside three others who were covering their eyes with canvas. López-Estrada joined them. Roberto pulled out his combat knife, handed it to López-Estrada and said, "Kill me. I don't want to die as the others." López-Estrada refused.

About 5:30 in the afternoon, when the sun was beginning to set and the water was very dark and the horizon very bright, Cuélla went to the mast and tended to the sail. He said the sail looked like the gown of the Virgin. He knelt down before it and began praying to the Virgin de la Caridad del Cobre, the patron saint of Cuba, who guards over men in distress at sea.

Joaquín Rodríguez, who was steering the boat, shouted across to him, "Don't pray to the Virgin any more. We have been praying for days. Only Satan can save us." And he began summoning the devil in a loud voice.

At that moment someone shouted, "A ship! A ship!" and the next thing they remember they were in the water, swimming toward a black ship.

Jane Kramer is the *New Yorker*'s European correspondent. She is the author of eight books, winner of an American Book Award and a National Magazine Award, and the first American, and first woman, to receive the Prix Européen de l'Essai. Dated August 1982, this profile was published in *Europeans* (Farrar, Straus and Giroux, 1988).

Joséphine Guezou

My friend Joséphine Guezou cannot forgive the Germans. Joséphine is a Breton villager of sixty-four, with a sick husband and a dipsy uncle around the house, five children, eleven grandchildren, and (at the moment) forty-one rabbits to worry about, and normally she does not have time for old antagonisms. I spent a few weeks in her village this summer—it is a gray stone village on a little estuary of the English Channel—and I know that one reason I felt at home there was that Joséphine worried about me, too. She looks after her villagers the way Mme Gonçalves, my concierge, looks after our Paris street, except that Mme Gonçalves is a professional and tends to regard local life as a challenge in housekeeping, whereas Joséphine is an amateur, a natural backwater busybody, who makes herself useful because she can't resist her neighbors' domesticity. Joséphine makes the rounds of the village and the nearby farms in a bright-blue Deux Chevaux, pinning up messages. She lets the vet know that one of the cows is sick at Crec'h Le Coz. She puts the artichoke farmer on the road to the market town in touch with the mason who wants to borrow the farmer's truck to haul some firewood to his grandfather's cottage. She writes on the back of used brown wrapping paper, which she gets from her cousin at the *quincaillerie*, starting small and shaping her letters carefully but always letting loose at the end with an enormous and enthusiastic JOSÉPHINE. There is satisfaction in that signature. It graces barn doors and village mailboxes like a royal seal, conferring a kind of confidence in the day's arrangements. Joséphine began writing messages for the village in 1942, when she was a ruddy young woman of twenty-four and her husband—the husband who is sick now, with a bad heart and failing eyesight—was underground with the Resistance, coming out in the dark to blow up German trucks or set flares for the Free French soldiers who would parachute into the artichoke farmer's fields at night, carrying cyanide pills and radio batteries and instructions straight from Charles de Gaulle, across the Channel. Joséphine offered herself to the Resistance with a stubborn and good-natured curiosity, just as she offers herself to the village now. She bought a grammar book and practiced writing. Soon no one in the commune moved against the Germans unless his orders were signed with her enormous JOSÉPHINE. The mayor and the policeman and the butcher who spied for them were bewildered, but they never stopped to consider why Joséphine—she had a bicycle then—was always pedalling across the countryside at odd hours. They knew that Joséphine was incorrigibly useful, that she liked bursting into other people's houses. They knew that anyway she had to deliver the oysters she dredged at low tide to trade for eggs and bread for her little boys. Certainly they never imagined that Joséphine was JOSÉPHINE. The Germans had a meeting, and brought in experts to break the JOSÉPHINE code, but the only code in Joséphine's messages was the fact that they were all written with her little boys' red crayon and by the time the Germans thought to search for a red crayon Joséphine had given it to the goat and the goat had eaten it.

Joséphine still writes her messages in red. (She has switched from crayons to red felt-tip pens, which she buys at a stall in town at the Friday market.) And she is still writing about Germans, though most of the Germans who concern her now were not alive forty years ago, and Joséphine—out of politeness, she says—has learned to spell "*Guten Morgen*," "*Guten Abend*," and "*Auf wiedersehen*." They are couples, mainly, and sometimes families. They come in the summer in groups of six and eight, and even ten, and they rent the new white cement house that Joséphine has built for her only daughter, Marianne, with the savings of a lifetime, and that Marianne and her husband are slowly furnishing with food processors and fitted sheets and electric lettuce dryers for their old age and their dying. Joséphine has always known where she was going to die. She wanted her daughter to have that same important information, in order to give her life its proper quality and her work its proper conclusion in her own village, her own *pays*, among her own people, and so Joséphine built the house. She sometimes says that the reason her interest in the sea stops at the oyster beds she dredged in wartime is that the treacherous North Breton currents kill so many of her neighbors before their time and rob them of the death they planned. In Joséphine's day, people left the sea and farmed if they had the good luck to get hold of some land of their own. They had to plant their cabbage and their artichokes in sandy coastal soil and graze their milk cows in fogs so thick that the only way to gather them in, most winter days, was by sniffing, but they could still get by if they worked hard. Now there is not much profit in farming the little peasant freeholds along the estuary. The oldest of Joséphine's four sons gave up his few acres and joined a merchant fleet, and comes home to his family only four or five times a year. Her second son is a kind of sea sweeper, working a rig that skims the oil slick from the Channel waters. Her last two sons are fishermen. But Marianne married a village boy to Joséphine's liking, and the two of them moved to Rennes and went right to work in a cheese factory—and Joséphine knows that one day they are coming home to their own house, with its clumps of pink and blue hortensia by the front wall, because Joséphine has thought to provide her daughter with the dowry of a peaceful dotage. While they are in Rennes—making money, raising children, *Gastarbeiter* in their own province—Joséphine pays their mortgage with the rent she collects from Germans on holiday.

Joséphine is not in business, like the old cartwright across the road, who moved his family into a shack and put their fine stone house on the market as a summer cottage. She watched the cartwright's boy grow up and go off to the big *lycée* in town and then to the university in Rennes, and, of course, she voted for him when he ran for town councillor, even though he lived far away in Limoges by then and showed up in the village only to campaign. She assumed that the councillor was coming home eventually. He had worked so hard to buy back the family house, she says, and his curly-headed Paris wife had even sent out Christmas pictures of all the neighbors standing in front of the saplings he planted in the back yard. That was ten years ago. Nine years ago, the councillor started renting his house to Parisians and bought himself a little villa in the South of France. Joséphine says that the house has lost its heart with its family—by which she means that it is getting sad and shabby, that the saplings are storm-bent and stunted, that the dish towels are frayed and losing their loops because no one is around on winter nights to mend them, that the upstairs bed is broken and resting on a log and the stuffing is falling out of the couch near the fireplace and the kitchen curtains are torn, and that there is no more wood in the woodpile. *Voilà*, Joséphine always says when she points it out to her Germans, there is a house without a family. It is part of Joséphine's little ritual of welcome. She greets the Germans at the village bar-and-grocery store, and then she asks them home for pound cake and a glass of wine, pointing out the councillor's house on the way. The councillor's house makes a proper contrast to her daughter's house, which has a neat mowed lawn and rows of dahlias and zinnias and pansies that confront the street like an audience. She likes to make the Germans smell her daughter's sheets, fresh from the clothesline, and feel the thick quilted pads on every bed and count the plates in the lacquered armoire in the dining room and try the cupboard underneath the kitchen sink in order to admire the new aluminum garbage pail from a Prisunic in Rennes, which pops open automatically whenever the cupboard door opens. She says, carefully, "*Tochterhaus*," so they will understand. She wants them to know that this is a house for coming home to. She hopes they will not break the glasses and burn the enamel pots, the way the Germans who came for the last two weeks of July in 1979 did, or adopt a tomcat that sprays all over the sitting-room upholstery, like the Germans that August.

Joséphine is still a little afraid of Germans, so she tries never to talk about the war or the German soldiers who moved into the village in '44, after the Allies landed, and ground out their cigarettes on the pine floors and used for firewood whatever furniture they didn't need. Now that she has built her daughter a house, Joséphine tends to think of those soldiers as demented vacationers—as tourists run amok in other people's lives and houses. It gives a kind of home truth to her war memories and, in a way, explains her experience. Early this spring, she confessed to the rental agent in town that she was sometimes uneasy having Germans in her daughter's house. The agent, a pretty young woman with a sideline in Common Market contraband involving the smuggling of local smoked salmon across the Channel to be sold as discount Scotch salmon, offered to find Joséphine British tenants—respectable salmon dealers from London—but Joséphine thought it over and said no, she would make do with the Germans she had. July's Germans came and went, and then August's Germans arrived—three hearty couples from Dortmund, who drove into the village with windsurfing boards strapped to the roofs of their little Audis and immediately put on rubber wet-suits and disappeared over the rocks in the direction of the Channel. Joséphine liked them. She looked after them as if they were outsize children. She gave them leeks from her kitchen garden and told them stories and left them notes whenever she felt a storm blowing up, so they would not drown in their toy sailboats or leave her daughter's best towels on the clothesline. Then, one night, the Germans had a party. They drank a lot and decided to race their Audis around Joséphine's daughter's garden. They rutted the lawn and flattened the dahlias. Cleaning up, they broke the aluminum garbage pail, and left it swinging from the cupboard door like a hanged partisan. The next morning, Joséphine drove to town and bought a red crayon. She left her message on the mailbox for everyone to see: "Attention, Allemands! La maison de ma fille n'est pas un bordel. Mon pays n'est pas un bordel. Vous n'êtes pas gentils. C'est moi qui vous le dit. JOSÉPHINE."

August 1982

Robert Donovan, formerly with the *New York Herald Tribune* and the *Los Angeles Times*, has written about the presidencies of Harry Truman, Dwight Eisenhower, and John F. Kennedy. This essay appears in his latest book, *Boxing the Kangaroo: A Reporter's Memoir* (University of Missouri Press, June 2000).

Twentieth-Century Odyssey

In Dwight Eisenhower's years in office, two changes drastically altered the presidency. One was the advent of television, which revolutionized American politics. The other change was the coming of the jet passenger plane. President Roosevelt had the Sacred Cow and Truman the Independence, but both were propeller planes. Long trips in either of them would be slow in comparison with a jet. In his first year in office, Eisenhower had a propeller plane, the Columbine II. Then in the summer of 1959, new scope was added to the presidency when he received a four-engine Boeing 707 jet. It was designated Air Force One, as have been all presidential jets ever since. The jet enabled Eisenhower and his successors to project themselves and their influence into countries around the globe. Theretofore, practical considerations limited how far a president could travel abroad and how long he could stay away. With the jet, no place was more than hours from Washington in case of emergency. When Eisenhower received Air Force One in 1959, he had invitations from heads of state in India and several Asian countries. He was delighted with the prospect of a historical international tour, and he and his party departed Washington on December 3, 1959. Reporters assigned to cover him traveled in a chartered commercial jet plane.

As an indication of his spirits, Eisenhower gave an unusual cocktail party the night before in the State Dining Room in the White House for those of us reporters and officials who would accompany him. The itinerary called for him to travel 22,370 miles to visit eleven nations on three continents. No president of the United States had ever before seen, or been seen, by such masses of people. When he was finally near the end of his journey in Morocco, more large crowds gathered to get a look at the American "sultan." Some of the scenes en route in India and Asia evidently conveyed the image of a ruler of an empire, although nothing like it was intended by the traveler.

Rome was the first stop, and the day was spoiled by ceaseless heavy rain. Eisenhower was welcomed at the airport by Giovanni Gronchi, the president of Italy.

"The ride in was fabulous on the old Appian Way," Eisenhower's confidential secretary, Ann Whitman, noted in her diary. "The road was lined with what I guess were tombs of Caesar's soldiers. . . . Later I saw parts of the old

Roman wall. . . . What beats me is how they have adjusted the modern age to the antiquities about them—traffic weaving beneath the old Roman wall, for instance."

The weather squelched the prospect of large crowds, but small groups dotted the route and the president heard for the first time on the trip what would be, dare I say, millions chanting "Viva Ike" or its equivalent in other languages.

Eisenhower was the guest at the four-hundred-year-old stately Quirinal Palace, which stands on one of the seven hills of Rome and is the official residence of Italy's presidents. The ceiling of his bedroom was painted with religious imagery.

The next day he had a private audience with Pope John XXII, which made him only the second American president to have had such an engagement. The "Star-Spangled Banner" was heard in a Vatican courtyard for the first time since January 4, 1919, when President Woodrow Wilson was received by Pope Benedict XV. Before his talk with President Eisenhower, however, John XXII decided to meet with the traveling reporters. I was fascinated, never having seen a pope. I hope no reader will be offended if I recall that when he entered, I whispered to a colleague, "My God, he looks like Mayor LaGuardia." The mayor, it will be recalled, was of Italian descent. The two men seemed to me to have similar builds.

In a short talk, the pope bade us never to betray the truth. "Truth," he said, "is the most precious thing of all." He ventured that if St. Paul, one of the early Christians, were alive in 1959, he would be a journalist. If so, Paul might be amazed at what reporters go through writing and filing copy on the run during 22,370 miles of often feverish travel with a president in a jet plane.

The spectacle that rain had prevented in Rome burst forth the next day in Ankara, Turkey. Ankara, we were told, had been built since the First World War and had a population of more than 500,000. Every single one in this capital of Turkey appeared to have turned out to acclaim the president of the United States.

"Turks Are Your Real Friends, Ike," read a large banner. On entering the city, his car was stopped while a folk dance of welcome was performed by a group of men called Zeybecks, who were dressed in peasant costumes and wore bandannas.

The presidential motorcade rolled through three miles of streets behind mounted lancers. Along the way were respected janissary bands. Janissaries, it was explained to us, were guards of the Sultans in the days of the Ottoman Empire. Thousands of people danced in the streets, wearing bright costumes, cheering, waving flags and shouting, "Yasha" ("Long Life"). On occasion after his car had passed, spectators ran after him. Wasn't it unusual for people to run after a foreign visitor? What did it signify? What did they know about a president that would arouse them? Were the crowds sophisticated enough to view Eisenhower as the man perhaps most likely to preserve peace? Whatever the reason, he was a magnet to crowds in every country he visited. One spectator in Ankara brandished a sign reading, "Welcome Aix." This was hardly up to "Ike," but still better than "Ick." Ankara University did best with a color portrait of Eisenhower painted by students and hanging six stories tall on one of the university's buildings.

At dusk, he drove out for a wreath-laying at what was considered the most sacred spot in Turkey, the tomb of Kemal Ataturk, the founder of modern Turkey, who died in 1938. The vast, sand-colored marble edifice with large columns crowned a hill overlooking Ankara. By the time we got there it was dark and cold. Wind blew through the columns. The lighting was dim. I could not remember a bleaker scene.

That night in Ankara, Eisenhower was honored at a dinner in the presidential residence. The menu was Turkish caviar, American soup, sea bass sautéed with shrimp sauce, roast beef, salad, Turkish pastry with cream, fruit and coffee. The wines were Cankaya, Yildiz Danlafi 1952 and champagne, which should have been enough to brace President Eisenhower for a very strenuous visit to Karachi, Pakistan, the next day, December 8.

All along the way in Asia we glimpsed the contrast between a certain splendor and prevalent squalor. It was in Karachi where, against the glitter of Eisenhower's triumphant procession, I could see scores of human eyes peering out through openings in mud huts. Eisenhower unquestionably saw life-sized tableaux of problems in Asia that increasingly occupied the attention of government officials in Washington. In the outskirts of Karachi, the president passed through a marsh so malodorous it had been sprayed earlier to reduce the stench.

In addition to military aid, the United States was then spending about $250 million a year in various forms of economic assistance to Pakistan. It was probably in reference to that that these signs along Eisenhower's route read "Thank You America."

In speaking to a large crowd at a polo ground, he promised that the United States would continue to help Pakistan raise its standard of living. He offered hope that some day nuclear energy could be harnessed to benefit this underdeveloped part of the world.

That was for the future. The scenes of Eisenhower's visit were spectacular. Estimates of a turn-out of a million persons may well have been accurate. Crowds were so dense that at one point, I could hear a band playing nearby, yet could not see it. The president first rode in an automobile, then changed to a horse-drawn coach behind a squadron of red-clad lancers. No "Viva Ike." The Pakistanis cried "Zinabad Ike." "Zinabad" means "long life" in Urdu.

The most common dress for men and women seemed to be loose-fitting white pajamas with rather long coats. In the 85 degree temperature most people wore sandals, although the obviously poor were barefoot. Some women wore veils with only a narrow aperture at the eyes. Others wore beautiful silk saris of lemon color or lavender or pink. Some were dressed in "dopattas," an open-face veil that hung all the way to the feet. Some men wore fezzes or Punjabi headdress or a kind of turban familiar to people of the region of the Khyber Pass. Stores along the way were strung with electric lights.

Then, of course, there were the snake charmers in turbans. At one square Eisenhower passed, he was feted by a man playing a flute-like instrument called in Ankara a "bansri," to which an undulating cobra was doing what was immediately dubbed in the press bus the latest Pakistani "rock 'n roll."

Russ Baker was certainly not a boaster, yet we all seemed to know that he had been a great high hurdler in high school. Before that day in Karachi passed, none of us doubted it. While he was walking along a sidewalk, a man sidled up to him peddling his wares in a large burlap bag. When a glimpse revealed that the merchandise was a mass of writhing snakes, Baker crossed a main thoroughfare in about six bounds.

That day President Eisenhower laid a wreath on the tomb of Mohammed Ali Jinnah, founder of Pakistan. Custom required that anyone who approached the tomb must either remove his shoes or cover them. Eisenhower covered his shoes with white canvas boots.

Flying next from Pakistan to Afghanistan brought us so deeply into Central Asia that it was puzzling at first why an American president would choose to visit Afghanistan. Still, Afghanistan bordered on the Soviet Union, and signs of Soviet influence would attract our attention. In fact, Soviet-built MiG fighters with Afghan pilots escorted Air Force One on the approach to Bagram Airport, built by Soviets. From there it was almost an hour's drive to Kabul, the capital. Stepping off the plane, I had never felt so isolated, and I wondered if the president had any such feeling. Glancing around, it looked as if time had been turned back a thousand years. The airport stood in a vast hollow surrounded by the distant, towering, snow-covered Hindu Kush mountains. The weather was cold. The road to Kabul thirty-eight miles to the north was narrow. It would have been sensible, if not acceptable, for the reporters to refuse to board the press bus of Soviet manufacture. The ride ahead was terrifying.

We could tell from the start that the bus was a very loose-steering vehicle. It had to be an instinct for survival that caused the driver to turn the wheel at the last possible moment to keep from going over embankments. Most horrifying were his spurts through numerous villages. On either side, the houses and other buildings came down almost to the edge of the narrow road. In every village, crowds had squeezed out to watch the Eisenhower motorcade pass. Each time, as it became obvious that the driver was not going to slow down, we covered our eyes for fear of seeing men, women and children mangled. Brakes were never used when coming into villages. Salvation was the horn.

In the isolated city of Kabul, the president's only appointment was with the khaki-clad King Mohammed Zahir Shah at the nearby Chilistoon Palace. Meanwhile, several of us reporters descended on White House Press Secretary James C. Hagerty and pressed him to get us another driver for the return to the airport. To good effect, he did.

Now we took off for the flight over the renowned Khyber Pass and on to India, always the goal of Eisenhower's odyssey. He arrived at Palam Airport in New Delhi after dark on December 10, 1959. A glimpse of the waiting multitude, it was said, made it seem as though the morning rush-hour crowd at Fifth Avenue and Forty-Second Street in New York ran into the evening rush-hour crowd just as the St. Patrick's Day Parade was passing through. Nevertheless, it was not the size of the crowd that counted, but its dynamic. It wrote the lead of my story to the *New York Herald Tribune*: "India exploded in a welcome to President Eisenhower tonight."

He was the first American president to visit India, and the scene quickly became frightening. As we tried to get into the press bus, teenage Indians struggled to push their way in with us. When we kept them out, they attempted to climb in through the windows only to find them barred. Then, what really seemed dangerous, especially in the warm weather, they scrambled up on the roof of the bus. How many could the roof hold without caving in, leaving a stifled mass of youths and reporters with no way for anyone to reach a door?

The motorcade was engulfed in a mass of yelling, shoving men, a serious problem for the Secret Service, which was responsible for a president's safety. In fact, Indian Prime Minister Jawaharlal Nehru jumped out of the car in which he was seated with Eisenhower and strove without success to flail the mob away. The car in which Ann Whitman and Colonel Andrew J. Goodpaster were riding was almost overflowing with tossed flowers. In spite of the darkness, both of them put on sunglasses to protect their eyes from cascades of marigolds. Eventually, the police were able to detach the president's car from the motorcade and rush him to the Rashtrapati Bahavan, an official residence. Once refreshed in his suite, he glowed over his reception, according to Mrs. Whitman. He invited his staff for drinks and dinner on that same day that they had breakfast in Pakistan and lunch in Afghanistan. The next morning they were awakened by a band playing in a courtyard.

During the week, Eisenhower addressed Parliament and later joined Nehru in addressing a huge outdoor gathering. The two leaders had met earlier in Washington. The president then remarked to Ann Whitman that Nehru "was wholly unaware of our general trend of thinking, just as we may be unaware of their thinking."

The president's visit to India would end the following Sunday in Agra where he would take a long-desired look at the white marble Taj Mahal. The *New York Times* bureau in New Delhi had a car, and Russ Baker managed to borrow it and its native driver so that he and I could go on ahead and glimpse the Indian landscape and then view the Taj Mahal at night. The ride was pleasant and the Taj Mahal a sight of ceaseless beauty rising out of a walled garden. We had rooms in a hotel in Agra and finished the night in a barn-like barroom downstairs.

We knew we would have to check out early the next morning because it was imperative for us to rejoin the Eisenhower entourage in downtown Agra. In the crowds that the president was sure to draw we could never make it to the airport ourselves in the car. We had to board the press bus in Agra. With our driver, we rolled away from the hotel for a couple of blocks. After that, we found ourselves in a massive traffic jam. In all directions, carts drawn by bullocks lumbered about. Old automobiles, hundreds of bicycles, farm wagons, pedestrians by the hundred were all creeping toward the Taj Mahal. Then came a ghastly interlude. I was sitting in the back seat of the car. Baker was in the front next to the driver. Suddenly emerging from a crowd, a wild-looking man in a turban and flapping clothes pushed straight to the right side of our car where the front window was down.

High in his left hand he held the throat of a huge snake, a python, I supposed. His right hand dragged the body of the reptile, the long tail of which disappeared in the crowd. What was the wild man up to? Was he just bringing a prize to show us? Could he have imagined that we would buy it? "Close the window!" I hollered. Baker spun it up just in time against the big face of the snake. If the window had not been closed as fast as it was, the wild man might have been able to shove the whole snake inside the car on top of Baker, the driver and me. It is much pleasanter to recall that even as we escaped this fright, we caught sight of our press bus, and our driver let us off as near as he could get to it.

President Eisenhower's principal visits were now behind him, but the road back to Washington was still a long one. After taking off from New Delhi following the visit to the Taj Mahal, he made it all the way to Athens by nightfall, with a stop en route in Tehran to call on Shah Mohammad Reza Pahlavi. Along the road from Mehrabad Airport to the royal palace, we were greeted by a succession of bands, practically all of them playing "The Colonel Bogie March," which had recently been popularized in the movie "The Bridge on the River Kwai." Of all the welcoming symbols we had seen since the beginning of our tour in Rome, nothing exceeded Tehran's. For at least a mile on the thoroughfare leading to the Shah's palace from the airport, the road was covered with Persian rugs. When I glanced down from an open window and watched the wheels of the heavy bus rolling over them, I wondered if we were guilty of vandalism. At a luncheon in the palace, Ann Whitman was told the buses were good for the carpets.

In Athens, we had time enough to visit the magnificent scene of the Parthenon.

From Athens, the president visited Tunisia and then France. In Paris, he had talks with Western leaders British Prime Minister Harold MacMillan, General Charles de Gaulle and the West German Chancellor Konrad Adenauer. On December 22, the last day of the trip, the president had breakfast in the Prado Palace in Madrid with Generalissimo Francisco Franco. After that he flew to Casablanca to talk with King Mohammad V of Morocco. It was a rifle-bearing Berber tribesman who said he had come to see the "sultan of America."

On the pre-Christmas return to the United States, no memorable pronouncements were made unless it was the statement of the speechwriter, Kevin McCann, who said: "I don't know how many friends we made . . . for the United States; in fact, we may have lost a few. But, by God, we kept the schedule!"

I felt that Eisenhower's odyssey was worthwhile. It was obvious that his visits aroused good will, but were of passing significance. He broached no new programs, no change in policy. In essence, Eisenhower's trip was one of self-fulfillment, a worthy statesman's dream. Already, December 1959 was late in his second term. In several months, the Democratic and Republican national conventions would meet and nominate John Kennedy and Richard Nixon, respectively, one of whom—Kennedy—would succeed Eisenhower. Nixon would enter the White House later. Thereupon, he topped Eisenhower a bit by taking a presidential trip completely around the world. I covered it for the *Los Angeles Times*, but the Nixon odyssey was no match for the spectacle of Eisenhower's, except for Mrs. Pat Nixon's charming press secretary.

Don Oberdorfer was a journalist for thirty-eight years, including twenty-five on the *Washington Post*. He is currently journalist-in-residence at Johns Hopkins University's Nitze School of Advanced International Studies in Washington, D.C. As a war correspondent covering Vietnam, his favorite place was the old imperial city of Hue. This report was published in the *Washington Post* on March 30, 1975, as Hue was falling in the final days of South Vietnam.

A Farewell to Hue

The helicopter roared in fiercely just over the treetops, beating its giant rotors in the air and rolling crazily from side to side to make a well-aimed shot more difficult from the ground. First we could see the tall Catholic cathedral, the legacy of Ngo Dinh Diem's brother the archbishop, and on the other side of the river the battlements of the old walled citadel, once the home of the Vietnamese emperors. None of the famous Hue sampans could be seen on the Perfume River. Only a few dozen people were scurrying along the tree-lined streets.

It was a strangely barren and empty city where we landed last Sunday afternoon. The essence seemed to have departed, leaving a mere shell of the Hue I had come to know and love. The long-familiar places were there, re-kindling memories of a great city in her moments of repose, challenge and disaster. But the places without the people meant very little, for it is the Hue spirit—independent, self-confident to an almost maddening degree, proud of the past and disdainful of the present—which gave the place so much of its charm. Without them, the experience was a bit like walking through the streets of Pompeii after most of the people had left but before the eruption.

In theory, it was a news-gathering mission to a city under growing military pressure and likely soon to be abandoned to North Vietnamese divisions to the north, west and south. In fact, it was also a journey of sentiment and emotion—a last call on an old friend, a final gesture of affection and a chance to say goodbye. As it turned out, my friend Paul Vogle and I were probably the last Western journalists to see Hue this time—and quite likely the last in quite a long time.

We had flown north from Saigon Friday morning by Air Vietnam hoping to go to Hue, but in the early morning, the Hue airport was closed due to heavy shelling. It was never to reopen. We landed in Danang instead and ventured north up the road toward Hue to find it choked with thousands upon thousands of refugees pouring south from the old imperial capital. The near-universal determination to get out before the advancing North Vietnamese created a monumental jam of trucks, buses, motorbikes, tractors and ancient

29

cars along the sixty-mile route from Hue to Danang. It was taking eighteen to twenty hours for a trip that normally takes three hours or less. Late on Saturday the North Vietnamese blew a bridge and cut the road to stop the traffic—but by then, nearly all the civilians were out.

Now a correspondent for UPI, Vogle has lived in Vietnam close to two decades and speaks fluent Vietnamese with a Hue accent. The U.S. consul in Danang, Albert Francis, knew of our long familiarity with the city and granted us two valuable places on his helicopter.

THE helicopter landed in the little park across from the provincial headquarters on the riverfront boulevard south of the Perfume River. The chopper avoided the military airstrip and helicopter pad in the walled citadel north of the river, where South Vietnamese army headquarters was located, because rockets were hitting there with regularity. Until the afternoon we arrived, North Vietnamese gunners had refrained from firing south of the river, where most of the remaining civilians were centered, in an effort to minimize popular antipathy.

A few dozen people gathered to watch our helicopter set down, and Paul and I hired two young men on motorbikes to transport us during our two hours or so in the city.

We set off down the boulevard going east. On our left was Quoc Hoc High School, the alma mater of quite a few men who have figured prominently in the history of this country: Ho Chi Minh, Ngo Dinh Diem, Pham Van Dong, and Vo Nguyen Giap, among others. That fact alone is a pretty good index of the influence of Hue.

First stop was the university, where Paul once worked and where I had many friends. I remembered long conversations with several of the rectors, all cultivated and astute observers. I thought of a student with whom I had spent an afternoon in talk nearly ten years ago when Hue was still untouched by the war and many young people—like him—had a semblance of hope as well as a strong desire simply to be left out of this conflict of the great powers. I wondered what had become of him. Probably long since into the army and, given the odds, quite possibly dead.

The university offices were shuttered and locked, but we found a few people living around the back and a single chicken strutting in the yard. He may have been a driver or caretaker but in true bureaucratic fashion one of them insisted on seeing our press cards. "No, nobody is left. They have all gone to Saigon or someplace."

Just then we heard the strange whistle of an incoming rocket and an explosion not far away, and saw people on motorbikes and bicycles racing past us at maximum speed from the direction from which we'd come. "These rockets are hitting in town; these people are fleeing!" shouted Paul, who had run out to the boulevard to take a closer look. We didn't tarry.

Next stop was Tu Dam Pagoda, where Paul and I had sat in privileged fascination with the then powerful and charismatic monk, Tri Quang, through the climactic days of the 1966 Buddhist crisis. He refused to see most other reporters and turned away the U.S. diplomats with a few curt words but he liked us and invited us to call morning, afternoon and sometimes at night. Finally General (and Prime Minister) Nguyen Cao Ky crushed the Buddhist movement with U.S. help, and Tri Quang departed for Saigon, long hunger strikes and self-imposed oblivion.

Now we walked into the familiar courtyard, where so often we had heard the resonant gong of the Buddhist bells and the singsong chant of the gray-robed monks, nuns and novices. Everything was locked and seemingly deserted. I spotted someone moving behind the administrative outbuilding. There we found a few refugees—all women and children—in a basement room. The last monk had left by motorbike that morning, they said.

On we rode up deserted lanes, past shuttered houses and shops, with only a few people in sight. There was a cluster of refugees—perhaps two hundred or more—under the vaulting and sturdy roof of the Phu Cam Cathedral.

During the Communist occupation of the city during the 1968 Tet offensive, more than four hundred men and boys had been summoned out of the cathedral by the occupying forces and marched away into an area of dense double-canopy jungle ten miles south where they were shot or battered with blunt instruments. Their bones were found nineteen months later. They were among some 2,800 people—many of them local leaders or government functionaries—executed in Hue during the twenty-five-day Communist occupation. Hundreds of other civilians—perhaps many hundreds—were killed in the murderous crossfire between the North Vietnamese-Vietcong forces and the U.S. Marines and ARVN troops. Small wonder that most people in Hue poured out of the city this time to escape the Communist occupation, the battle or both.

War and bloodshed, cruelty and disaster make up so much a part of the history of Hue that its sophistication, urbanity and charm seem almost miraculous. It is not an "ancient capital," as the newswires so often report, but was founded in relatively recent times, at least in an Asian perspective.

The Nguyen warlords who ruled South Vietnam established their capital at Hue in 1687 and built two great walls between the mountains and the sea, near the present-day "Demilitarized Zone," to protect themselves from the Trinh warlords who ruled in the north. The country was unified under the leader of a third group which vanquished them both, but ultimately the Nguyens triumphed anew around 1800 with the help of French weapons and advisers. The victorious Emperor Gia Long executed the surviving members of the previous royal family. The hands and feet of the fallen emperor were bound to four elephants and his body torn apart as the beasts were driven in different directions.

French advisers helped Gia Long build his fortress city, the walled citadel, on the model of the Imperial City at Peking—to which the Vietnamese had long paid tribute. Gia Long's successor expelled the French—but the French bombarded the place with warships and took control of the court about 1883. Bao Dai, the last of the Nguyen emperors, abdicated the Chinese red throne in the citadel's Palace of Perfect Peace in 1945 in favor of the Vietminh revolutionaries. But the French came back, and at the end of the first Indochina war in 1954 the north-south dividing line was drawn north of Hue near the ancient Nguyen-Trinh walls, and Hue became a part of what became known as South Vietnam.

Ngo Dinh Diem, the first president of the south, was the son of the grand chamberlain of the former Emperor Thanh Thai and of course a son of Hue. The Buddhist uprising against Diem (who was a Catholic) began in Hue in 1963 and ultimately led to Diem's downfall. The Saigon government crushed the Buddhist political movement by sending troops to Danang and Hue in May, 1966. The battle for Hue in the 1968 Tet offensive was perhaps the bloodiest event of the entire war. The destruction was massive—but somehow the city was rebuilt.

HUE was never much interested in the war, holding itself to be superior to money-grubbing Saigon and power-hungry Hanoi as well as to the rich and ignorant Americans. In its best days, before the modern devastation hit, Hue embodied the traditions and values of its Mandarin past as well as a disdainful, sometimes indolent European view of the present.

The spirit of the city was sadly affected by its modern calamities, particularly the 1968 battle and occupation, but in recent months it was said to be enjoying something of a renaissance. About six thousand students were registered at the university, which was booming, and groups of tourists were arriving by plane from Saigon to spend the day touring its sights. (Hue had nothing one could call a hotel in the accepted sense, so they rarely spent the night.)

Hue's population was listed as about two hundred thousand, but it gave an impression short of that. Though its history and culture were illustrious it seemed a pleasantly isolated small town. Now, with the place deserted—probably fewer than ten thousand civilians remained in town the day of our visit—it seemed smaller still.

The largest group we encountered were hundreds of refugees clustered close to the beach near the old river bridge, waiting for a boat to evacuate them upriver and the South China Sea to Danang. With the airport and main road closed, this was the only feasible way. Standing chest-deep in a well-built drainage ditch as protection against rocket rounds such as the one we'd heard, several of these people said they had come to Hue from surrounding areas when their own homes had been evacuated.

Just then another whistling projectile was heard, far louder than the ones which had been going overhead toward the citadel north of the river. Everyone scrambled down into the ditch and crouched low as the rocket hit not far away. A minute or two later another came in about the same place or a little closer. Our motorbike "taxi drivers" suggested we leave the area. We raced to the bikes and roared away past the old U.S. MACV compound, where a generation of U.S. advisers had reported on military progress or retrogression in the city and surrounding countryside.

We didn't understand the shelling at the time, but it turned out the North Vietnamese were trying to hit the bridges over the Perfume River, to isolate the walled city north of the river from the supplies and potential reinforcements from the south. No doubt the gunners were sitting in the nearby mountains looking down on us all, and their aim was good. These were probably Soviet-made 122 mm. rockets. One landed in the water near the newest bridge, and another on the approach to the bridge. I saw one body sprawled on the bridge approach. Paul saw two bodies. Later we were told that at least five had been killed there. This became a bit more personal when we met a fifteen-year-old boy weeping profusely. His father, a local soldier, was one of those killed by the rockets that day. His mother had already fled to refuge in Danang, and he was bereft and scared. (Later making sure he was too young for the army and thus not a deserter, U.S. counsel Francis found a scarce helicopter seat for the boy, out to Danang.)

In a small market area we found women squatting in a lane selling vegetables and passing the time in gossip and chatter. Prices which previously had soared now were coming down to the bargain level as the future closed in. Everyone was selling everything possible at almost any price to pay for a way out, or to finance food and shelter after getting out. An old man in a faded cotton Mandarin-style tunic was sitting atop a little table in the market lane, weeping quietly and steadily. With his thin, cultivated face and wispy white beard he looked to be the personification of old Hue. We didn't ask why he was weeping, but it wasn't hard to guess.

The rocket rounds in the city had convinced most of the few remaining people to hurry their exit. They began loading a few possessions onto their bicycles, into makeshift packs, onto the long poles with baskets at either end which women usually carry. One woman was shouldering a pole with two babies in the basket at one end. I wondered what the lives of these babies would be like.

In Saigon before we left for Hue the rumor had been strong that government military forces had agreed to hold defense lines around the former imperial capital until dusk of Saturday, March 22—and then would leave the city to its fate. Now it was Sunday afternoon, the 23rd. Some fighting south of town had been reported the day before but there was no indication of an imminent military pullout or collapse. Provincial soldiers we met in a market area said their orders were "to defend Hue and Thua Thien (province) to the end." They said they would do whatever their commanders ordered. Another young trooper said he was ready and willing to fight, and glad most of the civilians were out of the way.

While the Danang road was still open we had seen a curious sight: army troops loaded in trucks with their gear coming away from Hue in the direction of Danang, and marine troops in trucks with their gear inching up the road in the opposite way, toward the old city. There were reports of disagreement in the high command of whether to make a fight for the city, which is symbolically important but militarily difficult to defend.

President Thieu reportedly told intimates that his decision as a military commander was clear—to pull out—but that his role as a political leader led him to the opposite conclusion—to stay and make a fight. As a result, Thieu evidently changed his mind after partial withdrawals. In the end, his half-measures did not work. His troops did not get credit for a major fight, and yet two of his best divisions were dispersed, disorganized and separated from much of their equipment.

At the Hue railroad station, where Paul and I used to drink in a pleasant little bar overlooking the town and the river, a few people had gathered in the nearly empty square. Suddenly a heavy, gray-haired man stumbled uneasily into the clearing, yelling and muttering. He spotted us across the way and drunkenly moved in our direction. "Chopchop, number one," he yelled in GI English. "You want chopchop (food), man? Plenty beer, whiskey." Moving closer, he added "Cheap girl-girl, too." He must have thought us to be the vanguard of U.S. Marines, who retook the city at such bloody cost seven years before, instead of two of the last Americans to visit the city before the final Saigon government withdrawal.

OUR TIME in Hue was almost ended, and we rode down the deserted riverside boulevard to the state guest house (the former French governor delegate's palace), the appointed meeting place for the helicopter back to Danang. In the caretakers' shed outside were a soldier and several civilians, including two pretty, young girls with long black hair and slim figures. I first knew Hue in the springtime, when flowers were blooming in the park next door and the sampans were floating lazily on the river. One of the loveliest sights of all Vietnam in those days were the swallow-flights of schoolgirls—very much like these caretakers' children who remained—riding their bicycles down this boulevard to school, their long black hair and white ao-dai billowing behind them in the breeze. Now we could hear the boom of artillery again and the whistle of rockets, and it all seemed so long ago and far away.

The helicopter roared in and we clambered aboard eagerly, glad to be leaving this dangerous, nearly deserted place before the big fight began and the roof fell in. We could see the orange-and-red South Vietnamese flag flying from the pole atop the fortress gate of the citadel across the river. That triggered the memory, from the 1968 battle in the city, of the yellow-starred Vietcong flag fluttering from the same standard.

As the rotors beat the wind and the helicopters lifted off, I wondered what the future might bring. What would Hue be like under the permanent rule of the North Vietnamese? Would Premier Pham Van Dong and Defense Minister Vo Nguyen Giap remember the old ways and their school tie, or would that be far too bourgeois and sentimental? What would happen to the Hue people? One can guess that many of them eventually will drift back, whatever the dominant political system.

Government defenses were struck a sharp blow, from which they never recovered, a few hours after our afternoon visit. On Wednesday, at 6:00 A.M.— according to a "Liberation Radio" announcement—the Provisional Revolutionary Government flag was raised on the gate of Emperor Gia Long's walled citadel. There it or its successor flag will fly for a long time, maybe forever.

Leslie Cockburn is a contributing editor for *Vanity Fair*. She has produced and directed two dozen documentaries covering wars for CBS and ABC News, and was a correspondent for PBS's *Frontline*. She has won numerous awards for her journalism, including a George Polk Award and a National Press Club Award. This is an excerpt from her book, *Looking for Trouble* (Doubleday Anchor Books, 1998).

Looking for Trouble

It was a perfect Sunday. We had joined Eduardo the film-maker, with his face out of a Goya canvas, at Cali Viejo, an old hacienda that served spicy *ajiaco* soup and *aguadiente* with absinthe. Eduardo stroked his black beard and convinced us to pay a casual, unannounced call on the chief of production of the Cali cartel. We would drop by his home. It was not far.

The impregnable fortress walls told us we had arrived. Eduardo was in a jocular mood. He told us to wait in our car while he went in to announce us. We could hear children and men kicking a soccer ball inside the compound. Our first inkling that something was dreadfully wrong was the odd behavior of our driver. He had covered his head with a cloth. He seemed reluctant to move from a cringing position as he slowly sank in the front seat. His sweat was seeping through the cloth. Four angry-looking gunmen had emerged from the gate. They stood sentry, without moving for several minutes, before Eduardo emerged from chatting with his school chum.

Eduardo, the bon vivant, had lost all color in his face. He looked gray and appeared to be in a state of shock. Our driver was still under the tea cloth.

"Bad news." Eduardo gulped for breath like an asthmatic. "He's going to kill you if you don't leave town in twenty-four hours." More gulping. "He's also going to kill me for bringing you here."

Andrew directed the hooded driver to step on it, and, watched by the killers at the gate, we all thought hard about this nasty turn of events. The chief of production was known to be a man of his word. We drove to a deserted café and ordered espresso. We smoked. We apologized to Eduardo, who had lost his ability to speak, for invading his town and causing so much trouble. We had put him in such an awkward position. His fate was suddenly tied to ours, mere acquaintances, foreigners, strangers. We had all been sentenced to death. We ordered more coffee. In a wilted state, we retreated to the Intercontinental.

The prospect of being shot the following afternoon made me feel physically ill and then giddy. I reached into my past for the answer to this mess. What would Emily Post, the arbiter of manners, do under threat of execution? She would write a letter, I decided. A self-effacing letter displaying the best etiquette. I would extend my most profound regrets at having disturbed the family gathering and would plead graciously that Eduardo should not be blamed. It was all my fault. And as a token of our esteem, I would send along cassettes of one or two of our documentary films.

I wrote the letter, packed up the cassettes, and sent the peace offering by messenger. We waited. There was one faint hope, which was that the cartel's chief of production wanted to direct. He longed to direct feature films. His hacienda was equipped with the finest home studio cartel profits could buy. If he liked our films, which were beautifully shot and cut, he might give us a reprieve.

Night was falling. We had to plan our next move. Both Andrew and I agreed that if we fled Cali, our film project would be finished. Our fear of death was replaced with fear of failure, which seemed marginally worse. Our mood was black.

Before midnight, we received a message. The chief of production wished to retract his death threat. He extended an invitation to visit his studio on our next trip to Cali. (I had told him we hoped to return to film in December.) "You are," he added with the gallantry that Colombian men fire like a quick mortar round, "always welcome at my house."

Before making contact with the chief of production's reclusive superiors, we would have to wait until December. By then, circumstances had changed dramatically. Cali's sworn enemy, El Mexicano, had launched an offensive so reckless that in spite of generous gifts to generals and politicians, he had to be stopped. Cali crouched in the shadows while the arc lights were turned on the man with the passion for mariachis. That December, he ordered half a ton of dynamite delivered to the headquarters of the Colombian secret police. The explosion at morning rush hour tore a city block in half. Sixty-three people died. Two hundred were wounded.

It was the first time I had seen an office block with its face ripped off. General Miguel Maza, the chief of the Departamento Administrativo de Seguridad, known as DAS, invited us in to film the damage. On the upper floors of the nine-story building we wandered at will through the rooms without walls. The wind was whipping through the corridors, past staircases hanging in midair, blowing stacks of top secret documents like confetti into the street below. I stood on the edge, dodging glass shards sailing into space, looking down at the convulsion of twisted metal and churned-up concrete that had been morning traffic. Only later did I realize that the pillars supporting the floor I was standing on had been pulverized.

General Maza, with his wide Andean face and parched lips, had been the drug lord's target. The general had a reputation as the only man in Colombia who could not be bribed. He had been probing the insalubrious relationship between Rodríguez Gacha, El Mexicano and the Colombian Army. In the last assassination attempt, the army had provided details of his motorcade route. Maza was ambushed and survived.

He told us in his slow, thoughtful voice that in his office the blast felt like a small atomic bomb. The bulletproof plate-glass window behind his chair was torn out of its frame and landed on his desk. He had been inches away from being instantly crushed. Two weeks later, the general's men hunted down and killed Rodríguez Gacha, his bodyguards, and his son Freddy. They left a scene of raw carnage. The general found Gacha's bank records, detailing multimillion-dollar payoffs to whole brigades of the Colombian Army.

Cali erupted in celebration. As Colombian television ran pictures of the languid fingers of the corpses being rolled in ink and fingerprinted, the Cali cartel, having emerged as the clear victor in the drug war, rejoiced. The Cali men had not been sitting on the sidelines waiting for General Maza. The cartel's intelligence was better than the secret police. We were told that a go-between called the Navigator shared intelligence with the general.

We received a call from the Rodríguez Orejuela brothers, now the undisputed capos of the cocaine business, welcoming us back to Cali. They guaranteed our security and extended an invitation.

That night, we were collected from the Intercontinental and driven at top speed to a leafy neighborhood of Cali. Our escorts tried to shove a gun in my purse. I had to forcefully object, explaining that journalists don't carry guns. Once armed, you are more likely to be shot. I was determined to behave as though I was a guest at a dinner party like any other. The butler opened the door of the white house with soaring ceilings and a gold Salvador Dali sculpture in the sunken living room. Our little party was escorted through the Japanese garden to the gazebo. There were a half dozen other guests, all watching a portable TV set with rapt attention. One of the Colombian soccer teams was playing that night in Tokyo.

The guests sipping their Scotches were men you did not want to cross. I flashed smiles at everyone, not knowing which one was my host. The wives wore emeralds. The rustic and expensive gazebo had small figurines scattered around, like children's toys. On closer inspection, I realized that they were rare Inca artifacts.

Suddenly, the air crackled with cherry bombs, let off by soccer fans somewhere beyond the tall hedge. Everyone jumped, including a well-armed knot of gunmen hiding behind the bonsai trees.

Our host was disarmingly young and soft-spoken. The others spoke deferentially. The host called them by their cartel *noms de guerre*, "the Hindu," "the Black." Our elegant hostess chatted and fussed. She had a turkey flown in from Miami for the occasion, the occasion being the death of Rodríguez Gacha.

A delicate little girl appeared with her nanny and demanded her television set back. Her parents gave in, and moved the party inside, up a spiral staircase to a cozy alcove with another set. We were in a tasteful bedroom with a massive four-poster bed carved from solid white marble. There were shouts and catcalls as the Colombian team lost the match. Andrew and I expressed our condolences. The gentlemen of Cali laughed. They were delighted with the outcome. They had made a lot of money. The team was owned by the Medellín cartel and was therefore, like the corpse with its fingertips smudged with ink, their enemy.

We were asked repeatedly if we wanted to "take a break." It was slang for a snort of coke. We declined. The cartel men did not, as rule, indulge in their own product. They drank heavily, partly because the butler materialized whenever a glass was half-full, snatching the glass and pouring fresh whiskey into it. This peculiar way of freshening a drink may have been due to the inexperience of the butler, only recently promoted from hit man.

Dinner was served at half past one in the morning. There were rowdy toasts with Lalique glasses raised to commemorate the dead. The guests told "Freddy" jokes, for the son of the deceased drug lord had been pudgy and slow.

Our host reminisced about his last trip to the United States when he had served time for trafficking. He talked thoughtfully about the business, as though we were discussing Exxon or AT&T. He concluded, watching us intently, that the cartel's biggest problem was finding "good middle management." It was difficult to teach employees handling millions in cash not to be foolish, buying Mercedeses and New Jersey mansions. We wondered whether he was making a job offer.

In the days that followed, there was a cartel barbecue, a cartel symphony concert and benefit for factory employees, traditional Caleño food at a jammed cartel restaurant, and salsa till dawn at a cartel disco. When we announced we planned to spend an evening in the Amazon and needed to charter a plane, our cartel host offered to find us something. It was only at the airport that we realized we were staring at the handsome pilot and sleek personal jet of the Rodríguez Orejuela brothers.

We had arrived late, thinking that our rented plane would be waiting. There was confusion. The dispatcher explained that the plane had another passenger to collect in Bogotá. We protested that this was our charter. We were paying for it. The pilot realized that we did not fully appreciate that this was a cartel jet. He kindly ushered us to a hangar next door where there was a plane, run by a legitimate commercial outfit, for hire.

While we were socializing with Colombia's most dangerous men, they were ostensibly on the run. The entire Colombian Army was looking for them. Some of their Cali villas had been occupied by troops and stripped of their contents, including the paintings. The general in charge of this operation, famed for his ruthless campaigns against the guerrillas in the mountains of Cauca, was an art connoisseur. General Manuel José Bonnet melted at the sight of a Van Gogh. For him, the cartel manhunt, having yielded so many good pictures, was a great assignment. The general, making his inventory, telephoned Senator Alcantara, the Unión Patriótica painter, and teased him about being so "well represented" in the cartel collections.

One day we received an urgent message at the hotel. General Bonnet wanted to see us. We were alarmed. Did he know what company we had kept for the past weeks? Would we be interrogated? Expelled? At headquarters, there were thousands of soldiers in fatigues milling around, some just in from bloody skirmishes in the mountains. We were shown straight to the commander's suite. The general, with his lean, taut face and long aquiline features, looked like something from a frieze on an Inca temple. He shook our hands firmly and directed us to sit down. Before he could speak there was a blackout. The three of us stumbled around in the dark, looking for matches. The light illuminated his face like a death mask. "I have asked you here because I want to show you something." The generator was switched on and the general lost no time in producing a photograph. It was a handsome building in a town in the banana-growing region of Santa Marta. It was the town hall in the place where the general was born.

The general explained he had a dream. He wanted to found a great library, with thousands of books. He had used his military clout to force the mayor to vacate town hall. The first floor, he said softly, fingering the photograph, would be set aside for folkloric dancers. It was to be a tribute to his father, and the people of the town who had worked for the foreign banana company. When the company had pulled out, they left nothing. No clinic. No school. No books.

Would we be so kind, he asked, to send him some books? He wanted our own books, autographed, and anything else we might recommend. As we sat in the headquarters of the military commander for a vast swath of Colombia, in the middle of the drug wars and the search-and-destroy missions against the guerrillas, hearing about the general's dream of the great library, I thought of Gabriel García Márquez. In Colombia they say he is not a brilliant writer of fiction. He is just a good reporter.

Karl E. Meyer was a foreign correspondent and editorial writer for the *Washington Post*, and from 1979–98 a member of the *New York Times* editorial board. This essay, here excerpted, was published in *Pundits, Poets and Wits: An Omnibus of American Newspaper Columns*, which he edited (Oxford University Press, 1990).

The Forthright Estate: In Praise of the Newspaper Column

A newspaper is a court
Where every one is kindly and unfairly tried
By a squalor of honest men . . .
          Stephen Crane (1899)

Pick up a newspaper anywhere in the United States and you will be addressed by insistent strangers known generically as columnists because each occupies, more or less, a column of newsprint. The term also has an apt association with the I-shaped pillar from which the columnist can harangue the populace—as was literally the case with Simeon Stylites of Syria, who spent thirty years preaching from a column until his death in 459 A.D. He has come to be the patron of an unruly calling.

Some columnists are local institutions, a few so popular that they are said to "own" their city. Many more are syndicated, so that if you travel around the country their eyes seem to follow you from passport-style photographs used to relieve the grayness of Op-Ed pages. Judgments differ on how much influence senior figures wield. Marquis Childs, writing in 1975 when he himself was still a Washington columnist, guessed that his colleague James B. Reston of the *New York Times* had roughly the power of three United States Senators. Three seems a lot. Still, a columnist of rank like Reston enjoys an obvious advantage over a Senator. Members of Congress are elected, columnists are more like life peers in Britain's House of Lords. This helps explain the resentment on the part of successive Presidents over the need to placate these potentates; there is no two-term limit for a Scotty Reston.

Of modern Presidents, none was more transfixed by columnists than Lyndon Baines Johnson. He courted them incorrigibly with lavish flattery and shoulder-squeezing bonhomie. Once during a White House news session, he saw Walter Lippmann in the throng; rushing over and grasping him, the President all but shouted: "This man here is the greatest journalist in the world, and he's a friend of mine!" That was in early 1964, when a good many people would have agreed with Johnson. Lippmann had been sought out by nearly every President since Theodore Roosevelt; he was but twenty-six when he drafted Woodrow Wilson's famous Fourteen Points. In 1958, Nikita Khrushchev invited the columnist and his wife, Helen, to a hunting lodge in the Soviet Urals to discuss ways of thawing the cold war (the phrase was introduced by Lippmann). "Today and Tomorrow" appeared three times a week in more than two hundred newspapers, and by common consent Lippmann's lucid treatises were read and pondered by an influential elite that no President could ignore. In his years at the pinnacle, Lippmann was interviewed annually by CBS television, an eminence accorded to no other journalist, before or since. In his reckoning of columnists, Marquis Childs described Lippmann as Supreme Pontiff.

Alas, the honeymoon ended badly. That any journalist might differ with his policies purely on the merits was a notion that Johnson never seriously entertained. He had courted Lippmann's support ardently, attending the columnist's seventy-fifth birthday party and instructing his aides to show him drafts of forthcoming Presidential speeches. But Lippmann was a sphere-of-influence conservative who at first doubted then dissented from the Administration belief that vital United States interests were at risk in Vietnam. As "Today and Tomorrow" became increasingly critical, the President became testier, to the point of having his staff comb through old columns in quest of blunders by the Supreme Pontiff—these were then maliciously read aloud at White House dinner parties. By this time, the White House was scoffing that Lippmann had reverted to isolationism, prompting an impassioned reply, *ex cathedra*, that conveys something of Lippmann's grand manner:

> A mature great power will make measured and limited use of its power. It will eschew the theory of a global and universal duty which not only commits it to unending wars of intervention but intoxicates its thinking with the illusion that it is a crusader for righteousness, that each war is a war to end all war. Since in this generation we have become a great power, I am in favor of learning to behave like a great power; of getting rid of the globalism which would not only entangle us everywhere but is based on the totally vain notion that if we do not set the world in order, no matter what the price, we cannot live in the world safely. If we examine this idea thoroughly, we shall see that it is nothing but the old isolationism of our innocence in a new form. Then we thought we had to preserve our purity by withdrawal from the ugliness of great power politics. Now we sometimes talk as if we could preserve our purity only by policing the globe.

As such admonitions became more insistent, communications ceased between President and Pontiff, and soon senior officials boycotted social events at which Lippmann might be present. On May 25, 1967, Lippmann wrote his farewell column, explaining that after thirty-six years of "Today and Tomorrow" he no longer felt the need to find out "what the blood pressure is at the

White House, and who said what and who saw whom and who is listened to and who is not listened to." Two days later, the Lippmanns sailed for Europe, departing permanently from a capital that had grown too small for a columnist and President.

The point of the story is that it could have occurred in no other country. Where else does any chief of state care that much about the judgment of a journalist? And Walter Lippmann was scarcely an isolated case; there was also his longtime rival, Joseph Alsop.

The Indochina war that Lippmann opposed, Alsop supported, indeed even helped start by hectoring successive Administrations to take up France's burden after the fall of Dien Bien Phu in 1954. Lippmann and Alsop appeared on alternate days in the *Washington Post*, and their clash provided something like the ongoing duel between Government and Opposition benches in the House of Commons. But Alsop had an insider's advantage: he was the good friend and Georgetown neighbor of John F. Kennedy, on whom the columnist had a profound influence. A firm believer in global policing, Alsop became certain in the late 1950s that a deadly "missile gap" was widening, and that the United States was lagging perilously behind the Soviet Union in the production of Intercontinental Ballistic Missiles. Senator Kennedy seized on the issue, and brushed aside President Eisenhower's protestations that the "gap" was grievously overstated. When John Kennedy assumed office in 1961, he found that Ike was right. It made no difference. The new Administration proposed and won approval for the biggest peacetime increase in defense spending, thereby propelling an arms race that came to feed on itself without journalistic assistance. It is true that Alsop was not alone in pressing the missile issue on Kennedy, but the columnist knew better than others how to get under a politician's skin by turning a strategic argument into a test of manhood. Lyndon Johnson was once heard to murmur as he ordered fifty thousand more troops to Vietnam, "There, that should keep Joe Alsop quiet for a while."

Alsop's younger brother Stewart exerted a different kind of influence, less that of a public philosopher or needling debater than of a shrewd family lawyer dispensing good sense. Stewart initially teamed up with Joseph when the Alsops launched "Matter of Fact" in 1946, then parted a decade later and eventually began his own column in *Newsweek*, occupying the pulpit that had been created for Lippmann in 1962. In a turbulent era, Stewart Alsop had the knack of catching a mood and guessing what it meant with but-of-course reasoning. Thus he took correct measure of student antiwar demonstrations and forecast their demise when Richard Nixon reinstated student draft deferments. During Watergate, he came up with a sound explanation for the strange behavior of those embroiled in the scandal:

My theory derives from the peculiar relationship between two minority categories in the human race—the crazy-brave and the phony-tough. Most

43

people who have been in a war, and a lot of people who haven't, have come across specimens of both breeds. The crazy-brave, who are a lot rarer than the phony-tough, are always doing crazy things that ought to get them killed, or at least maimed, but nothing seems to happen to them. They also exercise a kind of hex or double whammy on the phony-tough, and they keep getting the phony-tough into terrible trouble.

The Watergate crazy-brave was G. Gordon Liddy, who offered to kill himself when the break-in misfired, and who threatened to kill a wide-eyed Jeb Stuart Magruder if his hand was not instantly taken from Liddy's shoulder. Thus, reasoned Stewart Alsop, the phony-toughs who dominated the Nixon White House were too smart to give an unambiguous green-light to the hare-brained idea of breaking into Democratic headquarters, but were too craven to stand up to the crazy-brave. Similarly, Lt. Col. Oliver North was the crazy-brave Marine years later who hexed his phony-tough White House superiors during the Iran-contra affair—or so theorized two professors who had clipped and saved the Alsop column and quoted its argument in a *Washington Post* Op-Ed article that began: "One of the enduring frustrations of journalism is the short half-life of the column, with the result that insights provided by the occasional exceptional column are eventually lost to future generations."

I understood their lament. My father, Ernest L. Meyer, wrote a column six days a week for fifteen years, first for the Madison, Wisconsin, *Capital Times*, then for the *New York Post*. In Wisconsin, my father was telegraph editor as well, and wrote his daily piece after locking up the final afternoon edition. He used a copy pencil for a longhand draft, then typed hunt-and-peck to exact space. He did something different every day, mixing commentary with light verse, parodies or recollections of his boyhood in Milwaukee, his first newspaper job (in Warden, Washington, for $4 a week plus board), his student years at the State University or whatever. Wherever he went, the column went along: on European trips, summers in Cape Cod, visits to Washington or Hollywood or with Frank Lloyd Wright at Taliesin. Like many other columnists, he delighted in exploiting his wife and progeny—my brother Leonard, sister Susan, and me—as walk-on extras whose continual prattling provided the ever-essential "peg."

After my father died in 1952, I came into possession of his scrapbooks, the potter's field of journalism. Some years later, having made my own way into the same business, I went carefully through these scrapbooks, better able to judge the skill and stamina that went into writing a fixed quota of literate prose every day, with no time allowed for indisposition. And it saddened me, not just on my father's account, to reflect how much first-rate work vanished into the common dustbin.

So I decided to attempt an anthology. My first surprise was the sheer number of columnists. By my reckoning, the feature syndicates and major newspapers distribute the offerings of 200 columnists, most of them writing two or three times a week. Then there are the local columnists—light essayists, gossip-mongers, specialized writers on chess or cooking, sports columnists, cracker-barrel wits, political pundits, or whatever—on 1,700 daily newspapers, 2,400 weeklies, 14,000 newsletters, 4,700 magazines, 3,000 specialized international publications, 900 ethnic and foreign-language periodicals, and nobody-knows-how-many student newspapers, daily and weekly. In America, it is fair to say, at least 15,000 columnists compose short signed articles at regular intervals—a truly vast garrulous army feeding on the depleting forests of Canada.

It is not only a ubiquitous calling, but is deemed reputable by exalted political figures. The two Presidential Roosevelts, Calvin Coolidge, Barry Goldwater and Ronald Reagan have this much in common with Eleanor Roosevelt, Jeane Kirkpatrick, Fiorello LaGuardia, Henry Wallace, Harold Ickes, and Fighting Bob LaFollette: each sought for a while to improve American minds through the medium of a newspaper or magazine column (in Mrs. Roosevelt's case, she did both simultaneously, writing for the Scripps-Howard newspapers and *Woman's Home Companion*).

Interestingly, the column continues to flourish, notwithstanding the decline of the print medium and the rise of electronic journalism. Television, if anything, has given syndicated columnists more influence plus a celebrity status useful in commanding vast speaking fees. During the reign of radio, Walter Winchell and Drew Pearson hawked their revelations on weekly broadcasts, and Franklin Pierce Adams enjoyed an autumnal renown as a panelist on "Information, Please," an early-day quiz program stressing wit more than prizes. But this only feebly adumbrated the star status of columnists who, beginning in the 1970s, became fixtures on current-affairs talk shows: George Will, Carl Rowan, Tom Wicker, William F. Buckley, Ellen Goodman, to name a few. Thus the shrinkage of a literate audience has been offset by the gain in the columnist's reach and influence.

Columnists, in short, have benefited the land of the free by contributing as Lippmann did to what President Bush has called "the vision thing." More commonly, they have been energetic advocates exerting influence through the quality of their arguments, and their independence from an electorate that has learned to put up with them. They have from time to time added sparkle and sense to the national discourse, disseminating phrases that quickly became commonplace (egghead, middle America, cold war, the Reagan Doctrine). And having been given a license to be rude, reckless, silly, and prejudiced, the columnist can in a single effusion entertain at breakfast and provide at dinner the stuff for post-prandial argument.

Roger Mudd, a former CBS, NBC, and PBS correspondent, is now the documentary host for the History Channel. These are some of his reflections on the media.

Code of Ethics

Given what the media have put the country through this past decade, it must come as a surprise to most Americans that the press has a code of ethics. It is one of the great secrets of American journalism. But the codes are obscure, they are voluntary, and they lack teeth.

Nonetheless, American journalists do have a generally agreed-upon set of standards: they do not make up stories; they do not fabricate quotations; they attribute information that is not self-evident; they seek out opposing views; they do not publish or broadcast offensive or grisly pictures; they do not use obscene words; and they acknowledge that each individual has a right to privacy.

But reporters and editors remain divided on how large that zone of privacy should be and to whom it should apply. Do they photograph without permission? It depends. Do they go through the garbage of public figures? It depends. Do they entrap? It depends. Do they lie about who they are in order to penetrate someone's privacy? It depends. And what it depends on, of course, is whether the story itself is worth the ethical compromise it requires and whether the competition is onto the story.

The Society of Professional Journalists, Sigma Delta Chi, first adopted its code of ethics in 1926 and revised it most recently in 1996. The code says, "The news media must guard against invading a person's right to privacy." But there is no definition of privacy, of "guarding against invading," of which persons have such a right and under what circumstances or whether invading a person's "right to privacy" differs from invading his plain privacy.

Most journalists now believe that a person's privacy zone gets smaller and smaller as the person becomes more and more powerful. In other words, the zone for the local county supervisor is almost as large as it is for the local businessman. But once the supervisor begins to ascend the ladder of political power or public celebrity, the zone begins shrinking. So that by the time he is sworn in as president of the United States, the zone is minute. In exchange for power, influence, command, and a place in history, a president gives up the bulk of his privacy. Most twentieth-century presidents have willingly surrendered that privacy when it suited their purposes. It is when the coverage was unfavorable or damaging that the White House accused the press of invading the zone.

It wasn't always that way. For decades, the journalistic norm had been that the private lives of public officials remained private unless that life impinged on public performance. During the 1930s, the press concealed President Roosevelt's infirmities from the public on grounds of patriotism and grounds that his paralysis was not affecting his presidency.

Drinking was generally protected by the zone. Back in the 1960s and 1970s, it was well known to the Washington press corps that a prominent senator from the Deep South had a serious drinking problem. But it went unreported because the press knew that even when inebriated the senator ran rings around 85 percent of his colleagues.

Sexual behavior was also generally considered off limits. Witness the white-out in the coverage of President Kennedy's extramarital escapades. In 1979, I was castigated for asking Senator Edward Kennedy on a CBS News documentary about the state of his marriage. It was an invasion of privacy, critics said and wrote. It was a voyeuristic intrusion for which there was no compelling public need, they said. My answer was then and is still that Senator Kennedy by campaigning for his party's presidential nomination had narrowed his zone of privacy; that his skillfully crafted public persona was that of a devoted husband, father, and Catholic; that his campaign played on that image; but that, in fact, his marriage was a shambles and existed only on select occasions or photo ops chosen to perpetuate the image; and that, under those circumstances, the question was entirely appropriate.

The ethics of editorial judgment, however, began to go through a sea change during the late 1970s and 1980s when the Carter and Reagan administrations deregulated the television industry. No longer did television license holders have to justify their performance every three years or even every year. Licenses could now be bought or sold every thirty days, like pork bellies on the Chicago hog market. Into television came a whole new breed of corporate owners, like Loew's Theaters (CBS) and General Electric (NBC). In came management teams and cost-cutters without institutional memory, without a decent respect for the tradition of a vigorously independent news division, without a belief in the old network operating maxim that news is a precious commodity and a public service to be subsidized by the enormous profits generated by the entertainment programs.

As electronic journalism came to be evaluated for its cost effectiveness, the network world began breaking up. No longer was it just ABC, CBS, and NBC but it was now PBS and C-Span and CNN and cable and VCRs and rental movies and Ted Turner this and Ted Turner that. The networks found themselves having to compete for an increasingly Balkanized audience.

The network upheaval also meant the dumping of programs that did not pay their own way. The first to go were the documentaries, their subject matter too serious, their cost too dear for the audience they drew. The second to go was the anchorman as journalist. He became a news actor. The old boys—

Walter Cronkite, Howard K. Smith, David Brinkley, and John Chancellor—were quirky and real and believable but they were also toast in the competition against Oprah and Larry and Sally and Geraldo and Maury. The third to go were the old guidelines. The news now had to win. It didn't necessarily have to be more perceptive or revealing or informative; it just had to win. And fourth, the upheaval meant the slow surrender to the tabloids—the tabloid press and the tabloid TV—and their falling standard of what constitutes news.

By 1987 sex had formally and journalistically lost its off-limits status when Paul Taylor of the *Washington Post* asked presidential candidate Gary Hart if he'd ever committed adultery. The American press has been struggling with the appropriateness of the Taylor question ever since. Two weeks after Hart's press conference, Congressman Barney Frank of Massachusetts announced he was gay. He said he felt vulnerable because of the media's "increasing interest in private lives." Within another two weeks, Governor Richard Celeste of Ohio withdrew from presidential consideration when the *Cleveland Plain-Dealer* published a front-page story, based on unidentified sources and citing an unidentified woman, alleging that Celeste had had three extramarital affairs.

That same month in 1987, the George Bush campaign was frozen in place by the rumor that the vice-president had had an affair with a woman on his staff. Although the story never surfaced publicly and the Bush rumor temporarily receded, others quickly filled the vacuum. In 1989, the Senate, for the first time, rejected a cabinet appointee of the incoming president when it turned down John Tower to be secretary of defense because of his private indiscretions. Then in January, 1992, came the *Star* tabloid story about Gennifer Flowers and President Clinton, followed in August by the *New York Post*'s resurrection of the George Bush rumor, which culminated in the vice-president being asked on live television the "Big A" question.

Since then, we have been through the abject end of Senators Brock Adams and Bob Packwood, the Vincent Foster suicide, Whitewater, Madison Savings and Loan, Paula Jones and the Arkansas State Troopergate, Monica Lewinsky, and, finally, the impeachment of the president.

So was it any wonder that William Cohen of Maine wrote as he left the Senate in 1997 that "there has been a breakdown in civil debate and discourse. . . . And increasingly public officials face the hair-trigger presumption of guilt pulled at the slightest whisper hint of impropriety." Or that Bill Bradley, upon his retirement from the Senate, wrote in his memoir that "reporters have begun to treat politics as though it were a sporting event. What's the score? Just how do you win this game? How do you feel about where you are in the standings?"

So how are we to explain this sorry state of affairs? Much of what Mr. Cohen calls the "hair-trigger of guilt" is a legacy from the official government lying during the Vietnam War, during Watergate, during Irangate, during Whitewatergate, during Travelgate, and during Bimbogate.

Journalists, who are skeptical to begin with, simply do not like to be lied to or made fools of. They don't mind being flattered or pandered or coddled or stroked but they can't stand to be duped because it goes directly to their credibility, which is most precious to a journalist. So once they learn not to trust the government or its politicians or its spokesmen, they give nobody in public life the benefit of the doubt. The relationship between press and politician—protected by the Constitution and designed to be happily adversarial—becomes sour, raw, and confrontational. The written tone and the spoken tone change and the reporters' disbelief in the veracity of the government spreads to the readers and the viewers.

Where to begin to break this cycle for which both press and politician are responsible? Michael Gartner, former editor of the *Louisville Courier-Journal* and former president of NBC News, once advised political candidates who feared gumshoeing reporters were hunting them down: "If you don't want it in the paper, then don't do it."

But the time has come for journalists to acknowledge that a zone of privacy does exist. That being quietly adulterous should be protected but that if the politician's private conduct, sexual or otherwise, is carried on without discretion, with callous disregard for contemporary mores, in defiance of community standards, with demonstrable effect on his public performance, then the zone of privacy evaporates.

Similarly, running a congressional hearing with a hangover is protected conduct; canceling a hearing because of a hangover is not. No matter what name we give it or how we judge it, a candidate's character is central to political reporting because it is central to a citizen's decision in voting. The media, therefore, have a major obligation—nay, a burden—to report on the character of our presidential candidates.

In the aftermath of the Gary Hart affair, Doris Kearns Goodwin, the Roosevelt biographer, put forward a checklist of questions to help the political reporter with character coverage of the candidates. The list has circulated through the Washington press corps ever since. It is not a bad list for the voter, either.

How much physical energy does the candidate display? Does he keep humming, or does he run out of gas?

How is he with people? Does he reach out and touch, or seem to shrink from physical and personal contact?

How does he react to the experience of campaigning? What does he say he's learned from being out there?

How does he deal with, and relate to, his staff? Is he a disciplinarian, a delegator? Does he play them off against each other?

What does the standard stump speech—or the changes and evolutions in it—tell us about the candidate?

Does he evoke emotion in his crowds? A leader is always in a relationship with his constituency. What relationship does he seek? What does he achieve?

Does he have interests beyond politics? When he's not campaigning, can he talk about anything else?

Does he have a sense of humor? Or irony? Or detachment? Is his humor always aimed at others, or can he kid himself?

What kind of relationship does he have with his political peers? How open is he with them? How candid can they be with him?

How does he deal with setbacks, aggravations, frustrations? Can he bounce back? Does he scapegoat, shift blame? Is he overwhelmed with guilt?

How truthful is his picture of reality? When recounting stories, is he accurate, or does he embroider or shade reality?

And I would add one more. In the company of his wife, where does he walk? With her, or in front of her?

Such questions might help the press delineate the character of our candidates without having to resort to the "Big A" question in all its forms.

But that's not all we could do to help break the cycle.

Could we not stop commissioning all those instant public opinion polls—ABC and the *Washington Post*; NBC and the *Wall Street Journal*; CBS and the *New York Times*? Because those polls aren't cheap, there is always front-office pressure to use them, to amortize their cost, even though they generally tell us what we already know, even though they oversimplify politics and turn it into a game of who's on first.

Could we not stop predicting what's going to happen tomorrow and concentrate on the meaning of what happened today? Could we not let the story play out by itself? Besides, our predictions are consistently wrong half the time. I'll cite just one example. February 9, 1988: "I would say, Robin," said the pundit, "the fact that Dukakis finished a weak third in Iowa . . . would raise the question whether, indeed, he is a national candidate."

You know who said that? I said that.

There was a recent study of the McLaughlin Group's predictions over the last several years. More than a thousand predictions by the group. They were right an average of 52 percent of the time. The highest score was Fred Barnes—56 percent.

I like the solution put forth by the late John Chancellor. Instead of a prediction of who is winning and who is gaining, why not just end the piece with, "And tomorrow the candidate flies to Cleveland."

Paul Taylor spent twenty-six years as a newspaper reporter, most of them covering politics. From 1992–95, he served as the *Washington Post's* bureau chief in South Africa. Since 1996, he has been active as a political reformer. Here are excerpts of his portrait of Nelson Mandela, which appeared in the *Washington Post* on February 13, 1994.

Father of His Country

EMPANGENI, SOUTH AFRICA

His head hasn't touched a pillow in thirty-nine hours, and the world's last hero is looking a bit decrepit.

His gait is a shuffle. His speech is lumbering. His face is drooping. His hearing aid is missing. Every time someone at this evening's campaign forum asks him a question, he has to have an aide repeat it directly into his ear. Not a pretty procedure.

Yet even in his diminished condition, Nelson Rolihlahla Mandela, 75, manages to radiate the regal self-assurance drilled into him six decades ago by tribal elders who groomed him for chieftaincy and by British missionaries who schooled him for modernity. Without a trace of self-consciousness, he begs pardon for having left his hearing device back in the hotel room. Then he parries questions from a skeptical audience for an hour and a half, all the while battling the fatigue brought on by a nonstop negotiating session he endured the night before to finish writing South Africa's first post-apartheid constitution. Very much to his specifications.

His aides had pleaded with him to blow off this campaign event, his fourth of a day that would enfeeble a candidate half his age. It's a People's Forum meeting geared for the minority (that is, white) community of a medium-size farm town; the room is half empty and there probably aren't a dozen votes for him here. The unscheduled all-nighter would have provided a perfect excuse, but Mandela wouldn't hear of it. "It is my duty," he told his handlers, in the mannered pattern of speech that has always been a trademark, "to honor commitments."

As soon as Mandela completes some brief opening remarks, Johan Davel, head of the Afrikaner Chamber of Commerce in Empangeni, rises from his front-row seat. "Forgive me, Mr. Mandela, but you are not a young man," Davel says, posing the unvarnished question that must be on the minds of millions of his countrymen, white and black. "You may die. . . . Once you are gone, who will be able to suppress the young Turks, the underdeveloped ones?"

In other words, without the indispensable Nelson Mandela, what will keep South Africa from flying apart?

Nelson Mandela labored a lifetime to bring this election campaign about; he seems to relish everything about it, even this kind of disagreeable moment. And why not? After having been kept voiceless and voteless for 342 years, South Africa's blacks will cast their first ballots in a national election April 26 through 28, and Mandela—the symbol of their struggle, the architect of their liberation—is on his way to a landslide win that will make him this country's first black president. It will also close the books on apartheid, a four-decade-old political system that amounted to a kind of legalized plundering of a black majority by a white minority.

"It's as though he spent twenty-seven years in prison getting wound up like some sort of mechanical toy, and now he's letting all the energy loose," says Tom Lodge, one of South Africa's leading political scientists.

So the Old Man, as he's known, pushes himself through punishing days on the campaign trail, and still bounces up at 5:00 the next morning, in time for calisthenics and a turn on the treadmill. His predawn exercise routine is sometimes attributed to the regimen of prison life; actually it dates to his youth as an amateur boxer, when he did his roadwork at 4:00 A.M. Mandela now says he can't believe he ever boxed: "I must have been mad," he insists. But it's clear that the competitive furies that drove him then drive him still. All that's changed is the arena.

When he emerged from prison four years ago this month, the world marveled at Mandela's lack of bitterness, his even temperament, his disarming wit, his genteel manners, his ready smile. Lovely as they are, these soft virtues don't go especially far in accounting for what he has achieved since then. At an age when most people are slowing down, Mandela the man had to measure up to Mandela the myth. Hundreds of millions of people all over the world had been shouting "Free Mandela" for a quarter-century. Now Mandela was free. The responsibility was daunting.

It troubled him in prison that his legend had grown so immense. "No one who is flesh and bones wants to be thought of as a saint," he says now, unless the definition of a saint is the only one he accepts—"a sinner who keeps on trying." But Mandela's successes have mostly been the product of his unsaintly qualities. He can be iron-willed, bullheaded, arrogant, autocratic, exacting, contemptuous—and, perhaps, a bit more bitter than he lets on. He doesn't advertise any of these traits—which only makes them more potent. Especially when he wields them in combination with the weapon he earned breaking rocks and collecting seaweed for more than two decades on a windswept prison island. A martyr's halo.

Consider Mandela's record since 1990. He had to transform the "world's oldest liberation movement," as the African National Congress still likes to call itself, from an underground, exiled imprisoned organization into a government-in-waiting. He had to unlearn the shibboleths of socialism that had been discarded by most of the rest of the world while he was out of circulation. He had to engender a culture of trust in a society that had spent more than four decades codifying its racial fears and hates into a grotesque body of law. He had to teach blacks not to wallow in bitterness, and whites not to fear retribution. He had to persuade a generation of supporters younger and angrier and more traumatized by apartheid than he was—a generation spoiling for war— that the negotiating table was every bit as legitimate a theater of struggle as the battlefield. And he had to manage all this while his wife was entangled in a soap opera of criminal, financial and sexual scandal that destroyed their marriage.

Mandela has triumphed by making all his adversaries feel the steel beneath his velvet. He has shamelessly bullied (but purposely not broken) his indispensable negotiating partner and Nobel Peace Prize co-laureate, President Frederik W. de Klerk. He has marginalized, often even ridiculed, the notoriously prickly leader who had the temerity to imagine he was a major rival of Mandela's within the black community, KwaZulu Chief Minister Mangosuthu Buthelezi. He and his ANC negotiators have outsmarted, outlasted and overmatched their National Party counterparts during two years of constitutional talks.

This last achievement is especially notable. De Klerk's ruling National Party government released Mandela from prison assuming it would be able to maneuver him into a constitutional deal that would effectively perpetuate white minority rule, but by some means other than apartheid. What the Nats didn't foresee is that as the talks dragged on, the power equilibrium between the negotiating partners would shift so dramatically. Once the April election had been scheduled, the bargaining was no longer between an incumbent government and a liberation movement; it was between a lame-duck regime and a government-in-waiting.

De Klerk made his final and most important concession two nights before Mandela's visit to Empangeni, when the two leaders and their top negotiators met face to face to resolve the contentious issue that had been left for the end—would the cabinet of the first government of national unity make decisions by a simple majority vote, or by a two-thirds vote? De Klerk had been holding out for the latter; Mandela had insisted on a normal majority. "Mandela simply would not budge," says ANC negotiator Joe Slovo, "and in the end, de Klerk didn't put up much of a fight. By then, he realized that the only option for him and for whites was going to be to trust the ANC."

So, after forty-five years in power—first creating apartheid, then trying to dismantle it on their own terms—the Nats became one more example of history's half-hearted-reformers swallowed by the forces they set loose. In another sense, though, the National Party's miscalculation may well have been unique. This is a sitting government that wound up negotiating its own abdication, despite never having faced a credible military threat. What's more, it now stands poised to submit to the rule of the very people it systematically oppressed for nearly half a century.

Obviously, Nelson Mandela didn't do all this by himself. The inherent madness of apartheid helped, for it generated a powerful internal and external resistance movement that turned South Africa into a pariah state, and gradually stripped its defenders of the will to defend. Nor has Mandela done it flawlessly. By far the bloodiest period of the four-decade anti-apartheid struggle has been the four years since his release, during which nearly 15,000 people have been killed, mostly in factional fights between supporters of Mandela's ANC and Buthelezi's Zulu-based Inkatha Freedom Party. The roots of that struggle—part political, part economic, part ethnic—go back long before Mandela's release, but Mandela has not been able to find a peace. Nor has he managed to draw the militants among the Afrikaners (white descendants of mostly Dutch settlers who arrived in the seventeenth century) into the election process.

What Mandela has done is isolate the hard-liners and place himself ever more firmly in command of what amounts to a "negotiated revolution." Although he won't take office until after the April election, he has been operating as a kind of shadow president for nearly a year. No major government decisions are made without his clearance. After the assassination last April of popular Communist Party and ANC leader Chris Hani, it was Mandela—not de Klerk—who gave the presidential-style address on state television appealing for calm. At that moment, one could see the old order giving way to the new.

Mandela's genius these past four years has been to understand the possibilities inherent in being Mandela. He knows he can approach every political transaction from the moral high ground. This can be an unfair advantage for any partisan, and Mandela sometimes pushes beyond the limit. For instance, he is forever accusing de Klerk of "conniving" in the black political violence in order to keep blacks too frightened to vote. This is a charge unsupported by facts or common sense. Worse, it probably fuels the mayhem in the black townships. By further eroding the already battered legitimacy of the government's security forces, it strengthens the vigilante culture in black townships that really *is* at the heart of the killings. Yes, there is evidence that rogue security forces were involved in fomenting some of the violence in black townships at least through the early 1990s. But de Klerk himself has never been linked to such schemes, and he (belatedly) cleaned house of suspect security force generals in late 1992.

The rule in the rest of Africa in this half-century of decolonization has been that when blacks take over, whites take off. South Africa is likely to be the exception. Its white population is by far the biggest on the subcontinent, numbering more than five million. Whites have been here for more than three centuries— as settlers, not colonists. They have nowhere to go home to; this is home. For all the infamous degradation they inflicted on blacks, they have built an economy that has a sophisticated First World infrastructure of mining conglomerates, stock markets, telecommunications and skyscrapers. All of this superimposed on a Third World economy of typhoid outbreaks, squatter communities, 50 percent joblessness. Most blacks won't be able to make the leap from one world to another, at least in the first generation. Apartheid has left them too unskilled. There's still not a single full-fledged black stockbroker in South Africa, and just a few dozen black accountants.

But if the white economy is beyond the reach of the masses, it is also their potential salvation. If it can be made more productive (and most of South Africa's productivity problems of the past two decades have to do with labor market distortions created by apartheid), then it can be the engine of growth that fuels the ANC's social reconstruction program. Thus the irony: South Africa is about to become the richest and most powerful black-run country in the world, but it will need whites to run things for the foreseeable future. If it wants to help its poor blacks, it has to keep its rich whites.

And so Nelson Mandela travels the country speaking to groups such as this one in Empangeni. His overtures clearly have made headway. A recent survey of one hundred top businessmen showed that sixty-eight favored him to be the country's next president. This reflects a healthy accommodation to reality by economic elites. It is not shared by most ordinary whites, however, to whom Mandela stands for the ills of the rest of black Africa come to wreck their comfortable lives. Some right-wing fundamentalists consider him the antichrist. Others, like Empangeni Chamber of Commerce head Johan Davel, are simply confused. When it comes to the ANC, he says, he likes the jockey but not the horse—a point he makes with unusual bluntness.

When he asks the question about the future of South Africa without Mandela, Davel probably doesn't mean to be as offensive as he sounds—he will later explain that by "the underdeveloped ones" he meant victims of apartheid, rather than genetic freaks. It's not clear Mandela hears the phrase anyway. He is not especially sharp in his response. He points out that young people are rowdy no matter what their race and background. "The ANC stands for peace and harmony . . . but whites think of us as public enemy number one. That's because we were banned for thirty years, we were voiceless. The only things you heard about us were from our enemies."

Davel is unimpressed. "My question wasn't based on what I'd heard about the ANC," he will say afterward. "It is based on what I can see going on right now—what we can all see—the war between the ANC and Inkatha." Still, he says he finds Mandela "a great man."

Mandela rallies a bit later in the meeting, when the leader of a small contingent of Inkatha supporters asks some questions. The mere presence of a dozen or so Inkatha members at an ANC event here in Natal Province is remarkable.

This is a place of political territoriality and intolerance; people of one political persuasion don't tend to show up at rival political gatherings. It isn't good for longevity. Nonetheless, Inkatha's Francis Gumede asks a series of pointed questions that go to the heart of the rivalry between the ANC and Inkatha. Mandela gives a rambling response in which he pays formal respects to Buthelezi and insults him in the same breath. He concludes with a sly twinkle, noting that the ANC is eager to recruit all capable people, and suggests Gumede would be a perfect candidate for conversion. This gets a delighted response from Gumede and his mates, who whoop it up and raise their fists in delight.

Given how little real dialogue there is across the ANC-Inkatha fence, it's a magic moment. But afterward, one ANC campaign official wonders aloud how much of a favor Mandela has done Gumede: "When word gets out what happened here," he asks, "how long do you think Gumede will survive?"

Nelson Mandela's ability to reach across barriers of race and ethnicity stems from his natural air of authority. He grew up in Qunu, a village of the Xhosa tribe in the Transkei "reserve," where his father measured his status in wives (five) and his wealth in sheep and cattle. His father died when Mandela was twelve, and the young boy was sent to become the ward of his cousin, the paramount chief of the region. Rolihlahla, his Xhosa name, means "someone who brings trouble on himself." He was suspended from Fort Hare University for political activism, and fled his village to avoid an arranged marriage with a girl he considered unattractive. In 1941, he moved to Johannesburg where he became an activist lawyer and a founder of the ANC's Youth League. In response to escalating state repression, he later helped organize the ANC's outlaw guerrilla army. For seventeen months in the early 1960s, he eluded police, disguising himself, most often as a chauffeur or garden boy, as he organized underground. It was then that the Mandela legend began to build, and he came to be known as the Black Pimpernel. He won international notice as the eloquent lead defendant in the Rivonia Trial, in which a group of ANC leaders were accused of plotting acts of sabotage against the government. Mandela turned the defendant's stand into an orator's stage. He never denied the charges; he simply spent hours explaining why he felt that justice compelled him to carry out such acts. "I have fought against white domination, and I have fought against black domination," he concluded on the stand. "I have cherished the ideal of a democratic and free society in which all persons live together in harmony and equal opportunities. It is an ideal which I hope to live for and to achieve. But if needs be, it is an ideal for which I am prepared to die." Mandela and seven codefendants got life sentences.

He was imprisoned from age forty-four to seventy-one, forced to spend the prime of any political figure's life doing menial labor. But he also studied, read, taught himself Afrikaans and conducted a kind of running seminar in liberation strategy. Much of the cream of South Africa's anti-apartheid movement was imprisoned with him on Robben Island. The ANC, the South African Communist Party, the Pan Africanist Congress and other organizations maintained their structures within the walls of the prison, as they debated Marxism, black consciousness and military tactics. The ANC was the dominant group, and Mandela the dominant personality. He had an especially strong influence over the younger generation of anti-apartheid activists imprisoned in the 1970s and 1980s—so much so that Robben Island came to be known in the movement as "Mandela U." "We all thought we were going to take power the Cuban way," says Tokyo Sexwale, "but by the time we came off the island, we knew we were going to do it Mandela's way. He taught us to confront the regime where it was weakest—at the bargaining table—rather than where it was strongest, on the battlefield."

"He was a mammoth of a man," says Eddie Daniels, who shared a cellblock with Mandela for fifteen years. "Whenever there was a political discussion, whenever there was some issue involving prison regulations, he was the leader." Daniels was the only inmate on the island affiliated with the tiny African Resistance Movement. Mandela would frequently give briefings to different groups of inmates on his negotiations over various prison-life issues with the authorities. "He would always brief me separately, as an organization of one. I finally told him 'Look, I'm a nonentity. You can just include me in the ANC briefing.' But he insisted on maintaining protocol."

Daniels, a retired schoolteacher, remembers once falling sick with a virus. He couldn't get out of bed for several days. "Mandela would come in and empty my chamber pot. He could have had someone else do it. But he did it himself. I will never forget that." He also recalls the stoicism with which Mandela accepted the two cruelest blows of his prison years—news of the death of his oldest son in a car crash, and the death of his mother. "On both occasions, he didn't say a word to anybody. He just went to his cell and lay down. Finally Walter [Sisulu, Mandela's lifelong friend and ANC comrade] went in and talked to him, and told the rest of us what had happened. But Nelson was a hard man to console, because he was always the one consoling you. Whenever you got down, became demoralized, hit rock bottom, Nelson was always there for you."

Since his release, Mandela has made some oblique references to food-for-favors scandals involving guards, but he generally hasn't dwelt on the harshness of prison life. Rather, he likes to recount how he became friendly with a few of the Afrikaner warders, and how they made him realize that negotiations might be possible even with the "hardest" part of the white community. "You had the warders arguing among themselves. Some said that when we left the island, we should be so completely crushed that we would never think in terms of taking up the armed struggle. Others said, no, they should treat the inmates decently, because we might win our struggle, and we should not think in terms of retribution."

Listening in on those debates, Mandela says, he decided to learn Afrikaans, the oppressors' language so hated by blacks that it sparked rioting when the apartheid regime tried to make it the medium of instruction in black schools in 1976. "If you talk to a man in a language he understands, that goes to his head," Mandela explains. "If you talk to him in his language, that goes to his heart."

Stuart S. Taylor Jr. is an opinion columnist for *National Journal* and a
contributing editor to *Newsweek*. He was legal affairs reporter from 1980–85
and Supreme Court reporter from 1985–88 in the Washington Bureau of
the *New York Times*. These pieces appeared in *National Journal* on May 1 and
June 5, 1999.

Workplace Discrimination

It was 2002, and the big law firm's profits were down. So when nine
senior associates came up for promotion to partnership, only Jane made the
cut. During the next few months, the eight others—Tom, Bill, Harry, Kirk,
George, Sally, Peggy, and Mary—sued the firm, one by one. All of them complained of job discrimination. And each of them belonged to a group enjoying
special protection under the ever-more-encompassing federal civil rights laws.

Tom sued under the Clinton-sponsored 1999 law protecting parents
against workplace discrimination. He claimed that the firm's partners had
criticized him for billing "only" 2,000 hours that year and for seeking to avoid
weekend and travel assignments to make time for things such as coaching his
daughter's soccer team.

Bill sued under another new law: the one barring discrimination based on
sexual orientation. Among his complaints was that the firm's partners had
excluded him and his live-in companion from networking get-togethers with
their families, and had pressed him harder to work weekends than they had
pressed co-workers with children (like Tom).

Harry, a 45-year-old former schoolteacher who had made a mid-career
switch to law, sued for age discrimination. Kirk accused the almost all white
partnership of racial discrimination. George, who had recently lost his eyesight, sued for discrimination against the disabled. Sally sued for pregnancy
discrimination: She received only dead-end assignments after her second ma-
ternity leave. Peggy sued for discrimination based on her religion (fundamentalist Christian), saying she had been treated like a member of a strange cult.

And Mary, a single parent, sued for gender discrimination, along with anti-
parent discrimination—not to mention her sexual harassment claim. She said
that the firm disfavored women (but not men) with small children, and had
made Jane a partner only because she was childless and single.

This is, of course, a reductio ad absurdum: Not everybody who could cook
up a lawsuit does. But it's not a stretch to imagine that each of the employees
in such a situation might be able to make a superficially plausible discrimination complaint—touching off years of litigation—even if the employer had a
strong basis for defending its decisions as merit-based.

Anti-discrimination laws have already proliferated to the point where the vast majority of workers are members of one or more protected minorities. Are we creating a formula for discrimination against the shrinking minority of people who are not (yet) protected minorities—childless young white males, for example? Have we already gone so far down this road that we might as well proceed? Is there any logical stopping point short of giving every employee a right to sue whenever he or she thinks some co-worker got a better deal?

Or should we, perhaps, stop creating new incentives for unhappy employees to take their grievances to federal courts, where they will incur the costs and inefficiencies of judges and juries second-guessing inherently subjective employment decisions, while much of the money that changes hands sticks to the lawyers?

The proposal to protect parents from job discrimination, which is currently being developed by the White House and Senator Christopher J. Dodd, D-Conn., is a poll-tested effort to court both working mothers and the pro-family vote. It's also fine by plaintiffs' lawyers, who give lots of money to Democrats.

As the father of two girls, I should, perhaps, be grateful that the President wants to give special protection to a group of which I am a member. But this proposal seems especially unwarranted—where is any real evidence of a big discrimination problem out there that needs solving? It also seems likely to foster costly litigation by parents whose discrimination complaints may in many cases arise from a sense that they are entitled to special accommodations. Such lawsuits would put pressure on employers to avoid liability by treating parents preferentially—which would often amount to (legal) discrimination against childless employees.

In contrast to the original impetus for job-discrimination laws, we obviously have no history of bigotry or animus against parents. Quite the contrary: In almost every line of work, for hundreds of years, most of the people who rise to the top—and who become bosses—have been parents.

Indeed, advocates for childless workers plausibly complain that these are the people who suffer from widespread discrimination: Family-friendly corporate policies, such as subsidized health care and day care for children, may deplete the pot of money available for fringe benefits for childless employees; flexible scheduling practices for parents can sometimes put pressure on childless workers to pick up the slack by working longer or less-convenient hours.

The only White House effort so far to demonstrate a pervasive problem of anti-parent discrimination has involved pointing to eight "case examples" culled from court reports. On inspection, they reveal nothing more than that a handful of people have claimed (not proved) that employers disfavored them because of perceived conflicts between their responsibilities at home and at work. In a nation of 130 million workers, that proves nothing.

But let's stipulate what common sense suggests: Many employers need people who are willing and able to work very long hours (including nights and weekends), or to be on call at all times, or to travel a lot. Many parents are less willing or able to do those things—and to that extent are less productive—than they were before having children; and some employers put parents (especially mothers) on slower career tracks.

Is this discrimination? Not when the parents have been slow-tracked because they have chosen (wisely, in my view) to give priority to the needs of their children at times when they could have been working. That is a choice the parent has made to be a bit less—or, in the case of those who go part time, a lot less—productive. In some cases the result is lower pay, missed promotions, or even lost jobs.

An employer discriminates against parents only when it acts on the incorrect assumption that particular employees will (as many do) spend less time working in order to make time for their children. Some employers—stupid ones—probably do discriminate in this way. But all employers have strong business incentives not to mistreat productive employees who happen to be parents. And it is already illegal gender discrimination to treat working mothers worse than equally (or less) productive working fathers.

A brief description of the Dodd proposal, issued by the Senator's office, is a bit confused (as Timothy Noah has noted in the online magazine *Slate*). Is the proposal's goal merely to bar real discrimination against working parents, or, in addition, to mandate special accommodations for them? It asserts that the problem is that employers "often falsely assume that employees with parental responsibilities are not capable of performing as well." But three sentences later, it implies that parents may need special accommodations: "Parents, balancing responsibilities at home and at work, should be valued, not discriminated against."

Even if the actual bill, which has not yet been made public, avoids overtly mandating special breaks for working parents, employers would still have an incentive to give them in order to avoid having to prove in court that they do not discriminate.

Federal law—especially the Family and Medical Leave Act of 1993—already pressures employers to make some limited accommodations for parents, and many employers are glad to do so. This is probably a good thing to the extent that parents can be accommodated without shifting substantial burdens onto their co-workers. But it would be going too far—and it would be unfair to childless workers—to create a financial incentive for unhappy working parents to jump into the litigation lottery.

In the event that this idea nonetheless catches the political wind, we should at least try to avoid the unintended consequence of putting new burdens on one group of mostly childless employees—those who are gay, and who have experienced far more discrimination than parents. I have a modest proposal that addresses this: Amend the parent-protection bill by adding a ban on discrimination against gay people. Call it the Family and Gay Job Protection Act of 1999. And see how *that* polls.

Harassment by Kids: Are More Lawsuits the Answer?

Such episodes as a North Carolina grammar school's much-mocked suspension of a six-year-old boy for kissing a six-year-old girl on the cheek, in 1996, may become more commonplace thanks to a well-intentioned but ill-conceived 1999 Supreme Court decision.

Of course, that was not what Justice Sandra Day O'Connor intended when she wrote the 5–4 decision holding that schools (and universities) that receive federal money can be sued for damages for "deliberate indifference" to the need to protect their students from serious harassment.

But sexual harassment lawsuits have proved to be a juggernaut of unforeseen destructive power—helping some victims, but taking a heavy toll on privacy, freedom of expression, and normal human relationships—since the Court authorized them in the workplace thirteen years ago.

Justice Anthony M. Kennedy may have exaggerated in writing for the four dissenters that the decision, *Davis vs. Monroe County Board of Education*, would produce a "flood of liability," potentially "crushing" school districts. But even if the liability does not reach flood stage, the ruling could do far more harm than good.

Granted, it will do *some* good—most immediately by providing a satisfying, if largely symbolic, victory for a young plaintiff whose claims of sexual harassment at school cry out for redress. LaShonda Davis and her mother, Aurelia, claim that while LaShonda was enrolled in the fifth grade at a Georgia elementary school, she was subjected to some eight incidents of sexual harassment over five months. A classmate, they say, grabbed at her breasts and genital area, said things like "I want to touch your boobs," and placed a doorstop in his pants in a sexually suggestive manner. Her teachers and principal allegedly spurned repeated requests to discipline the boy, refusing for three months even to let LaShonda move her assigned classroom seat away from his. Meanwhile, LaShonda had trouble focusing on her studies, and her grades dropped. (She also wrote a suicide note; it's unclear why.)

If all that is true, as was presumed in the early stages of the case, then LaShonda was a victim of harassment, and the teachers and principal were at fault. But a lawsuit is at best a crude remedy. In Davis' case, it was too late to stop the harassment, which ended six years ago, when the boy was charged with sexual battery in juvenile court. (He pleaded guilty.) A lawsuit cannot cure whatever psychological harm was done. It can only bring an award of money. And the money—LaShonda claims $500,000 in damages plus her attorneys' fees, which could take the total above $1 million—would come not from the teachers or the principal, but from the local taxpayers, who did nothing wrong.

Where is the justice in soaking the taxpayers? The answer is that the primary rationale for imposing liability in such cases is not to punish, or even to compensate, but to regulate. The hope is that if schools are threatened with liability, administrators will have an extra incentive to push principals, teachers, and others to be even more vigilant against harassment than they would be otherwise.

Experience suggests that many employers whose workplaces were pervaded by sexism needed a legal incentive to make them do the right thing. But is the same true of teachers and school officials, many of whom are women? They already have powerful incentives to protect their students from sexual harassment and other abuses by other students. These include the need to keep order and pressures from parents whose children complain of mistreatment.

Nobody suggests that we need federal lawsuits to induce schools to prevent schoolyard bullies from beating up *smaller* kids. What's so different about harassing girls? Are school administrators as a group so blinded by sexism that they need a judicial kick in the pants to alert them to the dangers of that particular form of bullying? Are teachers and principals—who deal firsthand with the boys and girls involved—less qualified than federal judges and juries to decide when routine flirtations, spats, teasing, and cruelties of student life cross the line into serious harassment?

Justice O'Connor strained mightily to minimize the risk of unwarranted lawsuits. She stressed that a school would be liable only for "deliberate indifference to known acts of harassment in its programs or activities," and then only if the harassment is "so severe, pervasive, and objectively offensive that it effectively bars the victim's access to an educational opportunity or benefit."

Such limitations on liability would be more reassuring if all judges and jurors were as reasonable as O'Connor. But that's not the case, and the Kennedy dissent is plausible (if hyperbolic) in warning that "the fence the Court has built is made of little sticks, and it cannot contain the avalanche of liability now set in motion."

As he noted, the O'Connor opinion seems to leave room for a girl to get her lawsuit to a jury trial by pleading little more than "that a boy called her offensive names, that she told a teacher, that the teacher's response was unreasonable, and that her school performance suffered as a result." In today's world of runaway damage awards, the prospect of a jury trial is terrifying to almost all prospective defendants.

And allegations of harassment are far from rare. According to a 1993 survey by the American Association of University Women, 80 percent of students said that they had been targets of "some form of sexual harassment" during their school lives. While this figure seems wildly inflated, it at least suggests what schools will be up against if even a tiny fraction of the girls who could complain do complain.

Many school officials are likely to assume that the safest course is to err on the side of discipline, even when the facts of an alleged instance of harassment are disputed, and even when the alleged conduct would strike many of us parents of teenage girls as normal (or, at least, tolerable) adolescent behavior: boys chasing girls at recess, bra-snapping in hallways, blowing kisses, saying "you look nice" in a certain way, and the like.

Ironically, the worst harassers may be the hardest to discipline, because their aberrant conduct can be blamed on the kinds of behavioral disorders that qualify them (under *another* federal law) as disabled—and entitle them to special protections against school discipline. Whipsawed by clashing legal obligations to those who say they've been harassed and the alleged harassers, schools may become more responsive to those parents who seem most likely to sue. Such fear of litigation is unlikely to produce better decisions than would simply relying on the best instincts—and experience—of teachers and principals.

Meanwhile, at the university level, the Court's decision seems a good bet to energize campus censors. Many administrators, students, and others have already been seeking to establish anti-harassment codes to punish not only sexually inappropriate conduct but also the expression in hallways, classrooms, campus newspapers, and elsewhere of political views deemed offensive by feminists, racial minorities, gays, and some federal education and civil rights bureaucrats. Now the push for censorship will be augmented by the threat of federal lawsuits.

Admittedly, my cost-benefit calculus is subjective, and reasonable people disagree with it. Such disagreements used to be worked out in Congress before potentially vast new liabilities were imposed on local and state governments as a condition of receiving federal funds (as almost all do). But Congress has never voted explicitly (or even implicitly) to unleash lawsuits for student-on-student sexual harassment.

Nobody dreamed that Congress was doing *that* when it enacted Title IX of the Education Amendments of 1972, the law on which the Court rested its decision in *Davis*. The statute provides that "no person in the United States shall, on the basis of sex, be excluded from participation in, be denied the benefits of, or be subjected to discrimination under any education program or activity receiving federal financial assistance." The main purpose was to protect people from sex discrimination in admissions, employment, and use of federally funded academic and athletic programs. Title IX did not explicitly authorize damage lawsuits at all, let alone lawsuits for sexual harassment—a concept that was, in 1972, unknown to the law.

To be sure, in previous decisions the Justices have unanimously found Title IX's language broad enough to authorize damage lawsuits against schools that are guilty of deliberate indifference to sexual harassment of students by teachers. But imposing liability for failing to stop student-on-student harassment is a bigger stretch by far.

The Justices' cure of choice—more lawsuits—is quintessentially American. But in this case, it may be worse than the disease.

Larry L. King's thirteenth book, *A Writer's Life in Letters*, was published in 1999 by Texas Christian University Press. This piece is drawn from *True Facts, Tall Tales and Pure Fiction* (University of Texas Press, 1997).

Driver's Education

I have a terrible confession to make, though it's not something I can blurt out in the daylight, so you've got to let me sidle up to it in my fashion. The shame is too old, the scars too deep, and laughter mocks me still. I almost would prefer admitting to a particularly horrid sex crime involving little boys, or that I have sold my country's military secrets for personal gain, than to utter the dark truth that perverse editors have bribed me to reveal.

I, er, ah, did not aaaaahhhh, that is to say—cough cough—er, ah learntodriveacaruntilIwastwentysixyearsold.

Being a non-driver was the bane of my teenage years. Teenagers, you may recall, have more pride than congressmen even if no more legitimate reasons for harboring it. To wander around Texas afoot—*absolutely incapable of driving a car*—in a state where the car succeeded the cowboy's horse and equals gonads, in a state that built a network of super roads eons before it provided marginally decent facilities for its orphans, aged, and mentally ill—was to be regarded as a social misfit on a par with chronic bed wetters. Had the word "nerd" then been in popular currency, I would have epitomized nerdhood simply by being unable to drive. For a long time I failed to admit my mechanical idiocy, saying that driving bored me or that I walked everywhere to keep in shape for football. Then came an incident that exposed me for the non-driving ninny I truly was . . . .

But look: I can't go on with this unless I'm allowed at this point to put on my defense. It is a story to touch the flintiest heart. A little fiddle music here, Maestro, of the hearts-and-flowers variety.

See, it was the fault of the damned Republicans. When I was born on January 1, 1929, all was right with the world. My father owned a goodly share of a prosperous farm and a blacksmith shop where the fires were seldom banked, thanks to a local oil boom in a time when dray horses and wagons were valued. He had just built a big new house with electric lights, running water, polished hardwood floors, and spiffy French doors. More, he had freshly purchased one of Mr. Ford's impressive "touring cars." The haughty, sleek sedan had racy snap-button window curtains, built-in cut-glass vases for flowers, and other luxurious amenities. Things looked so rosy that my father deserted the political party of his ancestors and voted for a Republican, one

Herbert Hoover. This would prove to be one of the worst ideas until pantyhose came along.

President Hoover almost immediately made the nation a gift of the Great Depression. My father, unable to collect ten thousand hard-money dollars due from hard-pressed debtors, lost his business. The family farm ledgers soon showed red ink due to depressed agriculture prices and a glut of produce that people had no money to buy. We shuttered the new house in Putnam to go on the road as itinerant cotton pickers. No doubt we made an incongruous sight: a tattered family going from field to field in a fancy touring car pulled by a team of mules because of no money for gasoline. During these cheerless peregrinations Herbert Hoover assured us that "prosperity is just around the corner." I guess we didn't make the proper turns.

My father sold the once-grand vehicle for junk prices when I was about four. For almost a decade the Kings traveled only by horse or mule-drawn wagons. I was thirteen years old in 1942 when my father bought a Model-T Ford coupe two years older than I was; it had the silhouette of a top hat and moved with all the grace of a staggering drunk, sputtering and coughing like a tubercular.

The old car had to be started by a hand crank that had the kick of a mule once the engine turned over; a wary fellow knew to release the crank handle the instant the motor caught. The first time I was given the responsibility of shifting the "spark" lever to encourage the motor during cranking, the crank handle kicked so fiercely it broke my old man's wrist. I don't know if it was my fault, God's, or Mr. Ford's, but Dad had little trouble deciding the issue: he hopped about howling and cursing, making it clear that in the future I was to keep my cotton-picking hands off the operable parts of his automobile.

Dad's decision would have long-range effects with respect to diminishing the value of my social coin. I already was considered mechanically retarded by my contemporaries, rural Texas kids driving tractors when eight or nine years old and graduating to cars as soon as their legs grew long enough to reach the gas pedal while permitting their fannies to remain on the front seat. We had no tractor on our hardscrabble acres. Though I became a hellacious mule driver, that talent somehow earned little or no respect.

In my fourteenth year, after we had moved from that wretched old farm to an oil town in the desert, my father bought a Model-A sedan only about a decade old. I announced that unless I was permitted to drive it, I would quit school, join the Foreign Legion, and raise funds to commemorate Herbert Hoover in marble statues.

Heated family debates were held around the kitchen table. One session revealed that the only time my mother had presumed to drive a car she ran over an immobile kiddie slide on the school grounds and that Dad himself once had driven his wrist-breaking old boxy Model-T off a wooden bridge smack into a swift-running creek. Mama believed it was something in the family genes. The consensus was that the public safety might be gravely endangered should yet another King be loosed upon the public roads. I scoffed, railed, and refused to take no for an answer.

Thus it was that one sunny Sunday morning I proudly climbed behind the wheel. My nervous father, in the front passenger seat, compulsively babbled instructions with the speed and intensity of a tobacco auctioneer. Sister Estelle and Mama perched tensely in the backseat, holding hands, their lips moving in silent prayer.

I still can't say what went wrong, exactly, though I suspect my first mistake was zooming out of the driveway at approximately 62 miles per hour. In reverse. Dad's loud and rather complex profanity competed with my sister's uninhibited screams and Mama's repeated shrill appeals to the Lord. During this cacophony I performed two complete circles and several neat figure-eights, all in reverse gear, before the car rather abruptly stopped of its own accord. This is because it had backed at a high rate of speed into one of only three trees in the town. Dad was rudely thrown out of the car, losing two teeth and cracking numerous ribs. Mama fainted. Sister vomited. You would be surprised how quickly a large crowd can gather in a small town, given the slightest bit of excitement. Gasoline had sprayed all over, somehow starting a few small fires, though I thought the local newspaper greatly exaggerated the damages overall.

I was so disgraced and shamed I didn't come out of the house for three weeks. Dad made it clear that when I did come out, by God, I would come out walking.

Not driving a car so severely handicapped my teenage love life that my high school counselor suggested I enter the priesthood, unusual for a Baptist. Most girls seemed prejudiced against walking dates or perching on my bicycle handlebars. When I asked Nellie Bess Cowan to be my date for the football banquet— intending to propose to her between the fruit cup and the chicken-fried steak—she curled her lip in an Eddie G. Robinson sneer and said, "My stars, Lawrence King, I wouldn't go with you to a dogfight! You can't even drive a car!" I shifted from foot to foot before saying suavely, "I bet I could if I wanted to." I soon learned not to depend solely on such sophisticated retorts. When baited about being a non-driver, I just reached for the largest available object and bashed my tormentor with it. Pretty soon folks quit teasing me.

One day I told Tommy Tabor that unless he permitted me to drive his Model-A coupe until I had mastered it, I would break both his legs. Tommy, small and timid, found mine a persuasive argument. I might have developed into another Mario Andretti had not Tommy overcoached me. As we approached a certain sandy lane Tommy said, "Uh, Big'Un, when you turn left up yonder just touch the brake and kinda slide around the corner." I touched the brake with such authority that we went into a revolving hundred-yard skid. Spectators, thinking they were witnessing a daring exhibition of trick driving, broke into applause—until the old tin lizzie flipped over. Ironically, Tommy Tabor broke a leg. He cut off my driving privileges despite my reasoned explanation that he was still a leg to the good compared to my original threat.

I had been in the United States Army almost a full week when a swaggering little Yankee sergeant sang out, "I need a volun-tahr who's a good drive-ah!" I quickly stepped forward screaming *Yo!* Happily thinking: *Here's my chance. I'll learn to drive at Uncle Sam's expense. Even if I have bad luck again, our hospitalization's free.* The smartass Yankee sergeant assigned me to drive a push-cart around the company area while filling it with soda cans, candy wrappers, cigarette butts, and other assorted litter. Most of my Army service was spent in New York, where the subway relieved me of further transportation embarrassments.

Working as a young newspaper reporter in small Texas towns, however, was a different matter. I solved my problem by bumming rides from politicians, policemen, football coaches, and others who wished a good press. Those who laughed on learning I could not drive got a bad press no matter how many miles they chauffeured me.

In that period I met possibly the only young woman in Texas who also could not drive a car. Figuring it might be my last chance for romance, I married her. I still wish the account of our nuptials in the local newspaper had not included the line, "Following a wedding breakfast at Mookie's cafeteria the happy couple left for a honeymoon to Fort Worth by Trailways bus."

I learned to drive of sheer necessity when I got a job with a Texas congressman and moved to a Virginia suburb a dozen miles from the Capitol dome.

The salesman who sold me that spanking-new pea-green 1956 Plymouth with back fins taller than the average Texas mountain could not believe it when, on closing the deal, I said, "Now drive me around the block so I can learn how this sumbidge operates." He did, all the while looking at me funny when I said things like "Stop on red and go on green, right?" and "Do the lights automatically go on when you start the motor or must I push one of them several doodads?"

No teenager has ever been prouder of a first car. I spent all waking hours polishing and shining that gleaming Plymouth, emptying its ashtrays after each cigarette, and refusing to permit anyone to ride in it unless they supplied written evidence of being freshly bathed and consented to take off their shoes. This admittedly irritated a picky few in the car pool.

After three or four months of weekend sojourns into the countryside to prepare for my solo trip to Texas upon the annual adjournment of Congress, I was eager to feel the wind in my hair and become king of the road. Unfortunately, my two small daughters—Alix, five, and Kerri, three—were inexperienced auto passengers and managed simultaneously to be overcome by motion sickness while I was backing out of the driveway. Thereafter they took turns upchucking about every five hundred yards, despite my pleas that they coordinate their seizures in the interest of efficiency. We made almost forty miles that first day out. Between Alexandria and Culpeper a fat man on crutches passed us six times.

I was then still married to the lady who did not drive. Neither did she ride exceedingly well. I have never heard a grown person so persistently scream, cry, and caterwaul over a few picayunish close calls and near misses. Somewhere in Tennessee I offered her the option of being bound and gagged or taking the bus. Her ticket cost me almost all my ready cash. All the next day the little girls cried for their mama. For once, so did I.

On the morning of the third day I instructed my precious children that what with one thing and another Daddy's nerves were a bit tattered and that the first little girl to open her yap while Daddy was attending his driving duties would get fed to a big old zoo booger. Some peaceful hours later, as we pulled away from a rustic roadside truck stop, little Kerri said "Daddy—"

"Hush," I sympathized.

"But *Daddy*, you—"

"Not another peep," I insisted. "Remember the big old zoo boogers, honey?"

Perhaps a dozen miles down the pike, touched by my little daughter's uncontrollable sobbing, I pulled over to spank her. "Why are you screaming and wailing and bellowing and carrying on?" I gently interrogated.

She said it was because she was lonesome and she wished I hadn't driven off from the truck stop without her sister.

I guess Alix would be about forty now, bless her heart. I seldom drive through Georgia without sort of looking for her, though I know it's probably a long shot.*

We were driving through one of those scrubby little Mississippi towns that makes you realize William Faulkner was more a reporter than a novelist when I accidentally ran a red light. A foot patrolman began trotting alongside my car, blowing a whistle and motioning me to the curb. I was not yet a licensed driver, see, having failed my driver's test in both Virginia and the District of Columbia because of this terrible prejudice they have up there against Texans, so I decided against honoring the policeman's gestures that I should tarry in his town. My escape route being blocked by mule teams and watermelon salesmen, I jumped the curb and took a shortcut across the courthouse lawn. Which tactic excited the foot patrolman to accelerate his whistle blowing and to change his gait from an easy canter to a headlong gallop.

Little Alix said, "Daddy, that policeman is waving at us."

---

* Just kidding. Alix is a useful, normal citizen of Albuquerque except for having this hang-up about truck stops.

"Be polite, honey," I said. "Wave back to him." My well-bred little girls gaily waved at the nice policeman until he faded from sight.

I am not a chronic scofflaw—only in emergencies—so upon reaching Texas I immediately reported to my hometown police station to volunteer for their driver's test. The police chief, an old friend, warmly introduced me to the testing officer and quite publicly wished me well.

I don't want to be too critical, but I don't think any officer as nervous as my tester ought to be put in charge of judging folks. All through my road exhibition he flinched a lot and kept making little whinnying sounds; when he filled out his written report I noticed his hands shook. Also, I thought he got a bit personal. Like when he said, "How, uh, well do you know the chief?" I said pretty well, since our mothers were identical twins. He asked if we were a close family. When I said, "Very close," he did that whinny bit again. He stared into space a long time and said, "Say you live Up North and don't git back home but 'bout once a year?"

"Right."

"You, uh, thinking about moving back anytime soon?"

"No."

He sweated, fidgeted, stared, and whinnied some more before muttering, "What the hail, I've came too far to blow my pension when I ain't but a year from retirement." Then he scrawled something on his report, thrust it toward me, said something that sounded like "God forgive me," and left like his shirt-tail was on fire.

Not until some months later did I notice that my new driver's license carried a prohibition that nobody has ever seen elsewhere or can satisfactorily explain: *After 1-1-57, Licensee is expressly forbidden to drive in the State of Florida.*

Irving Dilliard was an editorial writer for the *St. Louis Post-Dispatch* for thirty years. For nine of those years, he was editor of the editorial page. He is known for his studies of Supreme Court Justices and the preservation of civil liberties. During the Great Depression that preceded the Second World War, Dilliard wrote the preface to *Missouri: The WPA Guide to the 'Show Me' State*. The book was part of the now celebrated series of state books developed by the Works Projects Administration to provide employment for impoverished writers. Forth came the needy: Saul Bellow, John Cheever, Mari Sandoz, Studs Terkel, Richard Wright, Ralph Ellison, Kenneth Rexroth. The excerpts here from Dilliard's *Missouri* preface retain the ambience of the time, when travelers, stopping at filling stations, crossed the country on the surface. His catalogues of universally known Missourians included names that have since achieved obscurity, and omitted others whose fame would spread. He notes that Samuel Clay Hildreth and Ginger Rogers were born in Independence, and does not mention Harry S. Truman, who was Missouri's junior U.S. Senator at the time.

People and Character

The spare Ozark hillman, with his rabbit gun and dog, is a Missourian. So is the weathered open-country farmer; the prosperous cotton planter; the subsistence sharecropper with his stairsteps family; the drawling sawmill hand; the scientific orchardist reading his bulletins from the fruit experiment stations; the lead miner; the hustling small-town merchant; the Kansas City business man; the St. Louis industrialist with one eye on Jefferson City and the other on Washington; the smiling filling station attendant who talks to everyone crossing the continent; the silent riverman who lives in a shanty boat and sees almost nobody—all are Missourians. Most of them say "neether," some say "nuther," and a few in the fashionable residential sections affect the Atlantic seaboard's "nyther."

THE COUNTRYSIDE of Missouri is as varied as its people. It is the half-wild, rugged, valley-cut Ozark plateau, worn down from ancient mountain heights, where darkness drops quickly on cabin dooryards. It is the rich delta of the "boot heel," where great cypress trees are still coming down to make cotton acreage on the State's last agricultural frontier. It is blue-grass pasture and rolling orchard and the checkerboard of wheat and corn prairie. It is eroded bluff country which follows the waterways and the alluvial bottom land that fringes them. It is farspreading areas marked by towering remains of mining operations, vast mountains by day and ghostly shapes in the moonlight. It is mile on mile of municipal asphalt and two-family flats and apartment houses, of stores, and office buildings and warehouses.

MISSOURI'S eating is as good as it comes. Boone County ham steaks and red ham gravy, ham baked in milk, barbecued ribs and backbone, authentic country sausage and genuine fried chicken and baked chicken and chicken pie and dumplings and chicken soup, eggs from the henhouse and bacon from the smokehouse; sauerkraut with squabs, and turnips with spareribs, spring greens from the yard and roadside, and green beans with fat pork—bush beans as long as they last and then long pole beans until frost. Missouri tables are loaded with dish on dish of berries—strawberries, blackberries, raspberries, floating in cream; with Jonathans, Grimes Goldens, Winesaps, Black Twigs, Delicious; apple pie, apple cobbler, apple strudel, baked apples and fried apples; homegrown tomatoes and watermelons and horseradish grown in the country's horseradish center; an endless number of pickles, always including pickled peaches and "end-of-the-garden"; vast varieties of jellies and preserves; persimmons sweetened and whitened by frost; popovers, wheatcakes and honey, piping hot biscuits and melting butter and molasses; fruit shortcake always with biscuit dough; cornbread from yellow meal without so much as one grain of sugar.

THE PEOPLE of Missouri keep their heritage in play—party games, candy pullings, pie socials and box suppers and wiener roasts. They have barn dances with fiddlers sawing away by lamplight; auctions, carnivals, medicine shows, home-comings, old settler gatherings, and family reunions with cousins and uncles and aunts from far and near. They bring the products of their skill to county fairs, specimens from field and orchard and barnlot and housewife's kitchen. They fill cathedrals and fashionable churches and village meeting houses; they go to revivals and Sunday School picnics and prayer meetings. Now neon-lighted movies are everywhere, but showboats are still playing *Over the Hill to the Poorhouse*. Fourth of July at Edgar Springs finds a speaker extolling the virtues of democracy, and the crowd participating in the hog-calling contest, the horseshoe-pitching tournament, and the races. Scott County's annual Neighbor Day has a baby show, contests, and exhibitions. At the yearly singing convention at Cedar Gap folks come down from the hills with baskets of food to chant the hymns of their fathers through the whole of a June day. Masked revelers celebrate La Guignolée at Ste. Genevieve; German families at Washington eat herring salad on Christmas Eve so they "will never be in want."

Missouri's places remember people of many kinds of importance. In Franklin a youth named Kit Carson tired of work in a saddlery shop and ran away across the Santa Fe Trail. In Columbia thirty-one-year-old Abraham Lincoln wooed Mary Todd in 1840. Arrow Rock and its old tavern come down from covered wagon and ox-team days. Ed Howe drew the portrait of Bethany in his *Story of a Country Town*. In Springfield, where the streets are aisles of gold in autumn, Wild Bill Hickok served as a Union scout, and, in the Battle of Wilson Creek, General Nathaniel Lyon was killed. Boonville has Thespian Hall, oldest theater building west of the Alleghenies; and Washington its zither and corn-cob pipe factories. Independence had hardly recovered from the Mormon warfare when it was in the midst of the guerrilla raids of the Civil War. In Lexington, inscriptions on cemetery stones record migrations from the Atlantic seaboard and across the Atlantic. The grave of "Peg Leg" Shannon of the Lewis and Clark expedition is in Palmyra. St. Joseph saw William H. Russell start his colorful, if unsuccessful, Pony Express.

Mark Twain was born in a cabin in the hamlet of Florida; "Black Jack" Pershing on a farm near Laclede; George Washington Carver, Tuskegee's great research scientist, of slave parents near Diamond Grove; William Pope McArthur, hydrographer, first surveyor of the Pacific coast, in Ste. Genevieve; Tex Rickard and Courtney Ryley Cooper in Kansas City. Bishop Quayle was born of Manx parents in Parkville; Thomas Hart Benton, the artist, in Neosho; the Niebuhr brothers in Wright City. The list of native sons and daughters expands and became more varied, including Victor Clarence Vaughan, distinguished medical educator, conductor of the first American bacteriological laboratory, born at Mount Airy; Ginger Rogers, and the turfman, Samuel Clay Hildreth, born in Independence; Marion Talley, born in Nevada; Rupert Hughes, born in Lancaster; Glenn Frank, born in Queen City; James Cash Penney, chain-store magnate, born near Hamilton; F. W. Taussig, who ferried the Mississippi on the way to his chair in economics at Harvard; Bernarr Macfadden, born near Mill Springs; and Cole Younger and Robert Dalton and Jesse Woodson James.

Victor Navasky is publisher and editorial director for the *Nation* and Delacorte Professor of Journalism at Columbia University. This article appeared in the *Atlantic Monthly*, January 1998.

Saving *The Nation*

Arthur never called before 8:00 A.M. unless something was bothering him or he had some news. It was not quite 7:30, and I was lying in bed, waiting for the alarm to go off in my Cambridge sublet on Memorial Drive, when the phone rang. It was Arthur (Arthur Carter, my friend, boss, and sometimes bane), and this morning something was bothering him or he had some news, depending on how you look at it. How would I like to take over from him as owner of *The Nation*?

I was in Cambridge because after sixteen years as the editor of *The Nation*, America's oldest weekly magazine (it was founded in 1865 by a group of visionaries and malcontents in and around the abolitionist movement), I had persuaded Arthur that I could use a sabbatical. My plan had been to spend six months, starting in January of 1994, as a fellow at the Institute of Politics at Harvard University's Kennedy School of Government, where I would ruminate on the role of the journal of opinion in the post–Cold War world, and then spend the next six months writing. Arthur's call, five months into my year off, changed all that. This, I quickly figured out, was what is technically known as a wake-up call. Economics is not my strong point, but I did know two things: the magazine was losing $500,000 a year; and I didn't have $500,000 to lose—this year or any year. "There's no hurry," Arthur said. "Think it over and let me know by the end of the week."

Having done business with Arthur for the past half dozen years, I assumed that this was not an invitation to negotiate. It was more like a take-it-or-leave-it-and-if-you-don't-take-it-by Friday (you schmuck)-I-might-well-take-it-off-the-table.

So I took it. Or, rather, I consulted my brother-in-law the lawyer and gulped and took it. Here, as I learned after the lawyers got into the act, was the deal. Arthur wanted a million dollars for *The Nation* (which seemed to me a little steep, given its balance sheet), but he asked nothing down and proposed a payment schedule of $100,000 per annum at 6 percent interest. This, my brother-in-law the lawyer explained to me, was "cheap money." Furthermore, Arthur's idea was that I could continue my sabbatical until the end of the year—and although I would sign the papers instantly and take on legal responsibility immediately, he would continue as publisher and continue to cover the losses until I took over.

75

There was still the little matter of how I would explain to my wife, Anne, who lacked her brother the lawyer's understanding of higher mathematics, that buying a magazine that was losing $500,000 a year for $1 million that I didn't have was a deal worth grabbing by Friday. Especially since I knew that as a genre, journals of opinion almost never make money. Even that avatar of capitalism William F. Buckley Jr., when asked whether his own journal of opinion, *National Review*, might ever make a profit, had responded, "A profit? You don't expect the church to make a profit, do you?"

But I had an idea. Across the Charles River from the Kennedy School stood the world famous Harvard Business School, and on its faculty was my friend Samuel L. Hayes III, the Jacob Schiff Professor of Investment Banking. Well, he wasn't exactly my friend, but we had served on Swarthmore College's Board of Managers together, where Sam was one of the key managers of the college's investment portfolio, which that year was the No. 1 performer in the country. I told Sam that I might have the chance to acquire *The Nation*, and I explained my idea over baked scrod at the business school's faculty club. Suppose I opened *The Nation*'s books to a class of Harvard's brilliant young M.B.A. candidates. Was there a way that they could turn our little company into one of those famous case studies? The job would be simple but challenging: How to take a magazine that has lost money for 30-odd years and, without changing the magazine, turn around its economics.

Sam gently reminded me that although he didn't see *The Nation* regularly (or irregularly, for that matter), he suspected that his Republican politics were not exactly *Nation* politics. But he said he would think about it, and that I should send him my "financials." I signed with Arthur, and not long after, I sent Sam the numbers, along with a business plan I had worked up. He said he would let me know.

Although I had confidence in the modest projections I had developed with the help of an old friend, Jim Kobak, a leading consultant to the publishing industry (they showed us passing the breakeven point four years down the road, and they called for an investment of at least $3 million), I feared that Sam, who sat on the board of Tiffany's, might prefer more ambitious projections.

So when, some months later, Sam and I had our follow-up lunch, it was with surprise that I received his news that Harvard was going to help us become a capitalist success story.

Sam had "run" our numbers and was impressed that the actor Paul Newman had agreed to invest in our cause (I emphasize the "cause" here; the proprietor of Newman's Own salsa, spaghetti sauces, salad dressings, and lemonade knew more about business than I did, and he had few illusions about *The Nation* as a business proposition). Sam thought that *The Nation* might make a fascinating case study—not for the M.B.A. program but, rather, for a special course given for owners, presidents, and CEOs of companies with annual sales ranging from several million to several hundred million dollars. This is the Owner/President/Management Program (OPM), whose initials coincidentally also stand for "other people's money" (an apt acronym, it seemed to me, since the course—which is offered in three units of three weeks each over a three-year period, to accommodate the busy schedules of its students—cost an astronomical $12,000 a year).

Sam described the kinds of students (whom I immediately began to think of as unpaid consultants) that OPM tends to attract: self-made entrepreneurs who have had a successful business idea and now want to learn how to run the business; sons and daughters who went into the family business and now want to professionalize it; folks catapulted from middle management to the top of their companies; and foreign entrepreneurs who want to see how the Americans do it. The course is taught by the case-study, or "learning by analogy," method, and *The Nation* could be one of the cases. Sam explained that although the raw IQ scores of the M.B.A. candidates might be higher, the OPMers were livelier, cockier, and, because of their varied experience, in a unique position to make informed, creative, and perhaps even constructive suggestions. I would be invited on the day *The Nation* came up for discussion—not quite what I had had in mind, but not bad.

Sam proceeded to explain that OPM has three phases. Unit I deals with management skills, Unit II with profitability and growth, and Unit III with harvesting the wealth that OPMers have learned how to maximize in Unit II. He thought *The Nation* might fit nicely in Unit II. Then a diabolical smile crept over his face, and his eyes narrowed. "You know," he said, "we can do the case study, but whether or not we do it, you might want to take this course yourself." Only good breeding, one assumes, kept him from adding, "You don't know what you're doing."

There was, of course, no way I could or should take this course. My sabbatical had kept me away from the office for too long as it was. Although by the standards of our slice of the industry I had had some fundraising success, I had put together only a third of the capital I believed we would need. My essential fundraising strategy was to raise half the $3 million from a small group of large investors, and the other half from a large group of small investors (we were looking for a Circle of 100 to commit $5,000 a year for three years), and that would be labor-intensive work. Moreover, the magazine continued to lose around $50,000 a month. We were changing printers, redesigning, and computerizing all at the same time: a triple trauma. Our union contract had run out, and renegotiation time was upon us. The course tuition was unaffordable. And besides, even if I wanted to go, there was still the minor matter of admission: the deadline for application had passed. So, naturally, I applied.

As I was subsequently to learn, a balance sheet has two sides, and Sam, who served as a reference and used his pull to get the deadline extended, was right. Essentially I was an immigrant in the land of high finance. Here, at a minimum, was a chance to learn the language—how to read balance sheets, keep track of cash flow, talk to potential investors, find out what "good will" really meant, master such tools of business analysis as price-earnings and other ratios, become an effective manager, and all the rest. Besides, I had a daughter living in Cambridge, and maybe it was a good omen that I was looking to recruit a Circle of 100 and OPM that year had 101 students, not including me. Perhaps some of my self-made multimillionaire classmates would see the virtue of investing in a business with a mission (once I learned how to write a mission statement). Indeed, if I averaged only one new Circle member a year, I would cover my costs and then some.

On a windy Sunday in early March, along with fellow OPMers from eighteen countries, I arrived at George Baker Hall in time to be shown to my monastic dormitory room. (We had been told to leave our spouses behind, because this was to be a "total immersion" experience. A honeymooning classmate took this injunction so seriously that he left his bride in California.) It included a single bed, one window, a computer, a clock radio, a small bathroom, and no mini-bar but a narrow shelf fully stocked with case studies in five subject areas—financial management, general management, human aspects of business, accounting and control, marketing strategy—and an "HBS Executive Education" book bag in which to carry them.

I put on the name tag each of us was required to wear at all times and joined the welcoming cocktail party in the Baker Lounge, below, with only mild trepidation. It seemed to me auspicious that the first person I met— who was clad in a University of Florida basketball jacket—was Nathan S. Collier. When Nathan, who has an open, friendly smile and tousled blond hair, found out what I did, he told me that his granduncle had founded the late Collier's magazine, although he himself was in what he called the apartment-ownership-management business.

In fact, after the second—or was it the third?—vodka on the rocks, I concluded that a surprising number of my new classmates might see the business potential in America's oldest weekly magazine if they were only given a fair chance. Besides Nathan, there was Richard Elden, a Chicago-based investment manager who manages $2 billion. He told me that he had started out as an International News Service reporter, and that on the side he had recently helped to found a small company that hired investigative journalists to prepare in-depth reports on targeted industries and corporations.

And there was David Karam, the president of an Ohio company that owns and operates seventy-five Wendy's Old Fashioned Hamburger franchises. He told me his Lebanese father would be thrilled to know that his son had a classmate whose magazine, *The Nation*, had been the first to publish his personal hero, Ralph Nader, also of Lebanese extraction.

There were many more prospects, but here I'll mention only Maximiano A. (Max) Goncalves, the president and chief executive officer of Fenasoft, located in São Paulo, Brazil, which produces the largest computer show on the planet. He said he had a particular interest in U.S. journalists, and could we have dinner to talk about it?

Clearly, I had more in common with my fellow businessmen (I now for the first time began to think of myself as a businessman) than I had anticipated, and I could hardly wait for the next day's program to begin. As it turned out, I didn't have to wait long. I had set my clock radio for 6:30 A.M., so that I'd be up for my 7:00 continental buffet breakfast in the Baker Lounge and still have time to scan the papers that OPM provided gratis—the *Financial Times* and the *Wall Street Journal*—before the morning study group to which I had been assigned convened, at 7:45. Fortunately for my study habits the clock radio in the room next door sounded off at 5:30, as it would every day of the course, which gave me an extra hour to read and reread my cases.

Over our course of study we read and discussed something like 150 cases, so it doesn't surprise me that I don't remember which case it was that Professor Norman Berg, who headed up OPM, taught in his opening 9:00 A.M. class on general management. But I should have seen the handwriting on the wall, even if it was disguised as chalk marks on the electronically manipulated blackboard that he kept sending up and down like an elevator. Norm had asked the class to list the pros and cons confronting the company under consideration. A forest of hands went up, and we had our first con. The company had a union. What could be worse than that? Norm wrote "UNION" in big letters at the head of the con column, underlined it three times, and chalked in an exclamation point for good measure.

I got a big laugh and a lot of little snickers when I mentioned that unions can increase productivity. I should have realized then and there that I'd have to come to terms with a basic question: Did I want to spend my valuable classroom hours scoring political points against my (mostly) free-marketeer classmates; or did I want to concentrate my energies on learning how to bring *The Nation* to the break-even point?

Actually, it was a little more complicated than that. In my view, *The Nation*, with its pitifully small circulation (20,000 in 1978; 85,000 in 1994; now about 100,000), had survived all these years (while magazines with circulations in the millions—*Collier's*, *Look*, and all the rest —had gone under) because it was more a cause than a business. The only reason *The Nation* had not been organized as a nonprofit (which would entitle donors to all sorts of tax breaks and the magazine to lower mailing rates) is that nonprofits can't endorse candidates for political office or devote more than a small percentage of their resources to trying to influence legislation; and we didn't like the idea of leaving the tax status of our subversive weekly vulnerable to challenge by hostile Administrations.

Though I had signed on with OPM to learn to think like a businessman, I was not ready to abandon *The Nation's* tradition of dissent—its anti-business bias, if you will. (And, of course, it would have been bad for business.)

Case after case seemed to underline my dilemma. I remember the day OPM took up Wal-Mart. It was just after 3:00 P.M., and class was out, but the conversation flowed on. I was on the Harvard bridge, headed across the Charles to Cambridge. On my left Pedro Salles, who runs the fourth largest bank in Brazil, was zipping along in the electric wheelchair that took him from class to class. On my right was Tim Erdman, the chairman, president, and CEO of this country's oldest and largest designer-builder specializing in outpatient medical facilities. Tim, in his late forties, was on Rollerblades. I was in the center, huffing and puffing and not quite keeping up. Our destination was Cybersmith, a store that featured the latest in technology before it became generally available. But what really seemed to propel my fellow OPMers was the inspiring tale of Sam Walton, a J. C. Penney trainee who had had the idea of building discount department stores in small towns across the country which would all operate on small profit margins, and who converted this "niche marketing" concept, as they liked to call it, into one of the greatest business successes of all time. When he died, the *New York Times* put his family fortune at $23.5 billion, but the professor suggested that Walton was the kind of guy who would have cared more about the Wal-Mart cashier who had $262,000 in her retirement account after working for the company for twenty-four years.

I pondered whether to mention *The Nation* article, published the previous year, that had portrayed Sam Walton as the main threat to Main Street USA, the man responsible more than any other for the malling of America, for the destruction of community upon community. But before I could decide, we had arrived at Cybersmith, I was out of breath, and why spoil a good party?

By the time we considered the case of Cash America, however, I was less reticent. As it happened, that morning I was the leader (owing to daily rotation) of my 7:45 A.M. study group, and since I was up at 5:30, I had plenty of time to prepare. Cash America made its money from a chain of pawnshops, charging steep rates of interest. A prime purpose of the case was to assess the CEO's new strategy of attempting to destigmatize pawnbroking and simultaneously change what HBS likes to call "the value equation." Instead of lending as little as possible on collateral and selling it for as high a price as possible if it was forfeited, his revolutionary idea was to lend as much as possible and sell as inexpensively as he could, on the theory that he could make up in volume (from repeat customers, who were the most profitable) what he lost on the margins.

When I reported that according to a forthcoming *Nation* article (called "Cashing In on Poverty"), Cash America's typical loan rate hovered around 200 percent, I naively assumed that we would have an interesting dialogue on the morality of the pawnbroking business, especially given *The Nation* writer's assumption that it was immoral to exploit the poor merely to increase return on investment ("ROI," I had learned to call it) for the rich. Instead the study group immediately divided into those who believed that the poor were deadbeats who deserved what they got and those who felt that Cash America was providing the uncreditworthy poor a valuable service—let the market decide!

The bottom line of the HBS/OPM mentality—surprise, surprise—seemed to be that the bottom line is the bottom line. One morning in Professor Ben Shapiro's marketing strategy class we were discussing the marketing of a product subject to government regulation. Spotting David Karam's hand in the air, Ben made a beeline in his direction and asked whether he thought the regulation was appropriate. "It all depends on whether you believe Adam Smith or Karl Marx," David said. "Do you mean to tell me," the consternated professor shouted, "that this case has something to do with communism?" He then turned, looked at me across the room, and said with a sweet smile, "Sorry, Vic."

I didn't mind my status as class foil. And although we had our disagreements, my classmates and I gradually developed mutual respect. When Dan Roche absented himself from class during Unit II for all of two days and returned $36 million richer, having sold his software business, I enthusiastically joined in the applause despite my by now well-known antipathy toward corporate takeovers. When a small-town banker commiserated with another classmate, saying, "You're in a family business? I wouldn't wish that on anybody," my heart went out to both of them.

Note from my learning journal (we were instructed to make entries after each class about how the case applied to our own companies):

Everyone gets a great kick out of Sam Hayes's favorite trick—to dramatize the principle that financial leverage always involves risk, he spreads his arms like an acrobat attempting to keep his balance and then tiptoes out on what he calls "the debt limb." He explains that his financially conservative wife, Barbara, who disapproves of going into debt, "hugs the trunk," whereas he is generally inclined to go as far out on the limb as financial prudence permits. Today he is out "on the twigs." My problem is that every time Sam does his balancing number, it reminds me of my own delicate balancing act—the attempt to absorb HBS know-how without succumbing to HBS values. I am persuaded that if the HBS faculty ran the world, it would be a better place—that is, a more humane and efficient version of the status quo. But what attracted me to *The Nation* in the first place was its commitment to challenge the status quo. I'm not sure what this says about the idea that it is possible to apply the lessons of the typical HBS case to a company like *The Nation*.

I did my nightly homework and read all about MBO (Management by Objective), MBWA (Management by Walking Around), TQM (Total Quality Management), the New Intimacy (a catchphrase to describe the relationship between customers and vendors), the Price Performance Curve, the Value Chain, the Magic Matrix, the Order Cycle, Market Segmentation, and Market Share (said to be the management mantra of the 1980s—this decade it's the New Economics of Service). I kept in mind Professor Shapiro's maxim "There is only one reason to lose a good customer and that's death. His!" But I still had a lot of trouble analogizing case studies of Steinway pianos, Southwest Airlines, Mrs. Field's Cookies, and such to my venerable company.

This was partly because of *The Nation*'s status as a non-profit sheep in for-profit wolf's clothing, but also because my *Nation* self still tended to regard the profit motive as avaricious indifference to social consequences, while OPMers saw it as the key to business success. Not that my classmates were against doing good—they were all for it. Well, most of them were for it, but that had to do with the Service-Profit Chain (treat employees well and they will treat customers well). Even language compounded the problem. At OPM "downsizing" was a synonym for efficiency and savings, whereas at *The Nation* it signifies misery and unemployment. A word like "empowerment" in *The Nation*'s pages means granting the disenfranchised and the dispossessed more say over their destiny; at OPM it meant getting rid of middle management.

And then one day we took up the case of L. L. Bean, and I decided that maybe there was something to this learning by analogy after all. What impressed me about L. L. Bean, founded in 1912, was not the innovative systems that were the ostensible focus of the case but, rather, that the company's founder, against advice, had stuck to his idiosyncratic ways. And I said so.

To this day an L. L. Bean customer can return a product at any time, day or night, and get, at his or her option, a replacement, a refund, or a credit. If a customer returns a pair of boots after ten years, the company will replace them, no questions asked. This seemed to me a tribute to the maverick who started the business in his brother's basement, in Freeport, Maine (which is how it came to be open twenty-four hours a day). He sold his first hunting boots (based on rubbers his wife bought him, with leather tops stitched by a local cobbler) to friends and relatives (hence the no-questions-asked returns policy), and then refused to automate or adopt any of the efficiency measures advocated by his financially ambitious grandson.

When asked to put a value on the company, whose sales in 1965, the date of the case, were $3 million a year, classmates—especially the contingent from Latin America—expressed skepticism about the old man's unwillingness to move into the modern era. At this point Philip Adkins, a London-based investment banker who owns the J. Boag & Son brewery in Tasmania and who had arranged the financing for a Disney theme park in Japan, piped up. Philip said, "I agree with Vic. This image of Emersonian self-reliance adds untold value to the Bean brand name." Philip's estimate of the company's value was ten times as high as anyone else's. The professor ended the class by reporting on the current market value of L. L. Bean stock—more than a billion dollars.

At lunch I asked Philip whether he thought there was an analogy between the "brand recognition" of *The Nation*—which, after all, had a 135-year-old reputation for its nonconformist politics—and L. L. Bean. Yes, he said; in fact, as he thought about the worldwide possibilities for exploiting *The Nation's* "brand name" in the new electronic media, he decided that I was "sitting on a gold mine."

I generously offered to share with him my prospectus for the gold mine. He said he would review it with interest and asked me whether I knew that when Rupert Murdoch bought *The Times of London*, the first thing he did was to enter on its balance sheet a good-will item of as much as $50 million. When his solicitors said he couldn't do that, Murdoch asked, Why not? Why do you think I paid $27 million for it? For its printing plant? I'm shutting that down. For its staff? I'm getting rid of half of them. Talent is for hire. I bought it for its name. I own *The Times of London*.

Philip had all sorts of ideas about what I might do with *The Nation's* name, not to mention its balance sheet, pointing out that a good-will item of $10 million for the name (more than three times what I had listed) would impress potential investors. He said that he, at any rate, was impressed, and that I should consider him a potential investor. (True to his word, by the way, he's still a potential investor.) Of course, the big day for me was the last day of Unit II, when *The Nation* case was on the agenda.

Aside from my strategy of importing my wife, Anne, to sit by my side as a buffer against those classmates who tended to see visiting CEOs as an occasion for target practice, the class began like any other. "If you were the CFO of another magazine," Sam asked as his opening question, "what are the financial dimensions you would be looking for on a day-to-day basis?" He drew from the class the difference between *The Nation's* fixed costs and its variable costs. He had the class inventory our assets—intellectual as well as physical—and then diplomatically observed, "In terms of the balance sheet, this is not an asset-intensive business." I nudged Anne when Sam described the Carter note as "a very friendly arrangement." Perhaps I was not such a dummy after all.

But just a minute—there were not enough assets to cover obligations. How would the balance sheet handle that? As he referred the class to the good-will item on the balance sheet, Sam asked, "What is the kernel of value inside the husk?" Philip Adkins could have told him, but Philip had dropped out of Unit II for personal reasons. Sam called on Mitch Dong, who had been waving his hand for some time now, as was his wont. Mitch lived in Boston and embodied the entrepreneurial spirit that OPM did its best to cultivate. He had merged his environmental company with a publicly traded company, sold his interest a year later, and started a hedge fund that trades gold equities based on esoteric statistical models, all of which enables him and his family to alternate vacations between a boat in the Galapagos and a villa in Tuscany.

Mitch didn't have the answer to Sam's question, but he did, he said, have the solution to my problem. As he saw it, I had it made. *The Nation* had a $1 million sweetheart loan from its former publisher. It had a subscription list now approaching 100,000 names, worth $10 to $20 a name in the marketplace—maybe as much as $2 million. And it was bleeding $50,000 a month.

His solution: Kill *The Nation*. "That way," he happily explained, "you cut your losses to zero. You sell the subscription list to JFK Jr.— he's started a new political magazine, hasn't he? And with the two million dollars you get from the sale you buy long-term Treasury notes, which pay seven and a half percent interest [this was 1996, remember]. And you use the difference between the seven and a half percent you receive and the six percent you owe to settle your obligations, your severance payments, and your accounts payable. And on the difference you retire to the Galapagos, sipping piña coladas. If you get bored, Machu Picchu is right next door."

Lots of other ideas were generously offered. Carlos Adamo, an Argentine banker, said we should raise the subscription price: we had loyal customers and nothing to lose. Chris Bergen, who with his wife runs a pharmaceutical-testing company, thought we should consider going biweekly. Sam proposed that we find a way to segment the market, charging more for those willing to pay more. I liked Sam's idea, not least because it reminded me of a doctrine I had studied way back in a political-theory seminar at Swarthmore: "From each according to his abilities, to each according to his needs."

On March 21, 1997, Tom Potter, the managing director of Eagles Boys Dial-a-Pizza, in Queensland, Australia, who had never been to college, gave the graduation speech and got his Harvard diploma (so it was a certificate— big deal), along with the rest of us. As I sat there listening to Tom, I did a reckoning of my OPM experience.

The Nation has not yet passed the break-even point, and if I don't take up Mitch's proposal to kill the magazine, perhaps it will be a while before we turn a profit, but OPM was not a total loss. I failed to enlist any of my classmates as *Nation* shareholders, but . . . I went to Harvard thinking that ROE was Roe v. Wade. Now I know it is Return on Equity.

I went to Harvard thinking that the year was divided into seasons. Now I know it is divided into quarters. I went to Harvard not knowing the difference between the quick ratio and the acid-test ratio, and now I know they are the same thing (the sum of cash, current marketable securities, and receivables, divided by current liabilities—so there).

Finally, I went to Harvard believing that I was a buffalo and came back hoping I could become a goose. Let me explain. Prior to OPM I had assumed that in my new role as the company's leader my job would be to lead. Then, in Unit III, I read a book called *Flight of the Buffalo*, which summarized what I had already begun to gather from my more enlightened classmates—that a good business doesn't function like a herd of buffalo, with loyal followers doing what the lead buffalo wants them to do, going where the leader wants them to go. (That's how the early settlers were able to decimate the buffalo herds. They'd kill the lead buffalo. Then, while the rest of the herd stood around waiting for the leader, the settlers slaughtered them, too.) What a business really needs, the book said, is not buffalo but responsible independent workers, like a flock of geese who fly as a team in a V formation, the leadership changing all the time.

By the time we graduated, Nathan Collier, who was forty-five, and I had become good friends, and he shared with me his ambition. "It has three elements. I want to earn my first billion by the time I'm sixty. I want to have a helluva good time getting there. And if I can help mankind a little along the way, so much the better."

And indeed, I learned from the OPM bulletin board that between Unit I and Unit II, Nathan had made a $10 million bequest in the form of adjacent property to his alma mater, the University of Florida at Gainesville. He also took out a one-year subscription to *The Nation*.

I count David Karam among my new friends too, although his father's admiration for Ralph Nader was put in perspective on the last day of class, when David made a rousing speech denouncing unions to enthusiastic applause. I also discovered that David, who has a formidable intellect, is a member of the libertarian-conservative Cato Institute, and hopes down the road to run for high political office on what I suspect will be an anti-government, anti-union platform. Early on I crossed David off my list of potential *Nation* shareholders, but I was moved when one day he articulated his business philosophy: "To provide a high-quality product and service, to make a fair profit, and to improve the lives of our employees." If he does run for the Senate, I'll probably disagree with 90 percent of his platform and send him a campaign contribution.

When Richard Elden invited me to dinner, I thought at first that it might be the moment to make my subtle pitch. I would tell him about the good luck I was having rounding up my Circle of 100. But before I got to it, he told me about the good luck he had had rounding up a Circle of Four or Five for his investigative-reporting enterprise. We still get together when we are visiting each other's cities, and maybe if I ever make a financial success of *The Nation*, he will let me buy into his business with my profits.

Max Goncalves's interest in American journalists turned out to be an interest in recruiting five of them to serve as journalist judges for his high-tech expo in São Paulo. Happily for me, I turned out to be one of them, despite the fact that, as I made clear, I spoke neither Portuguese nor computerese. Our job was to give a "Max" Award to "the most innovative exhibit of Brazilian computer technology that has the best potential for export sales." As it turned out, my contribution was to add an additional criterion—social benefit. And I guess that if we ever put out a Portuguese edition, Max might want to subscribe.

Actually, I did come back with some Circle members from the Cambridge area—none of them OPMers, but more than enough to cover my tuition. And OPMers did account for twelve new *Nation* subscriptions. As an unexpected bonus, when Peter Norton, who created Norton Utilities and, with Paul Newman, is one of *The Nation's* principal shareholders, discovered that I had enrolled in OPM, he told me that he, too, had attended the program. He said, "I was in hog heaven. Until then I had never had a male bonding experience, and in terms of intellectual challenge it's one of the highlights of my life." By the time I graduated, Peter had significantly increased his *Nation* investment. Call it the old school tie.

On my return to the office our associate publisher asked me to give an example of what I had learned at Harvard, and I told her. Before OPM if a subscriber wrote in to cancel his or her subscription, the loss of the $48 never really bothered me. I agreed with the late *Nation* editor and owner, Oswald Garrison Villard, who said, "If I don't get my requisite share of cancellations every week, I fear my editorial hand must be slipping. But I did hate to lose an old friend, so I'd send a note asking, Are you sure you really want to do that?" About half of them were so thrilled to get a personal note from the editor that they would agree to stay on board.

Having been exposed to nine weeks of Ben Shapiro, who among other things introduced me to the concept of "the lifetime value of the customer," I now have a whole new calculus when I get a cancellation: Subscribers who have been with us four years or more renew at an average rate of 80 percent. The average age of our subscriber is 47.5 years. The average life expectancy of a 47.5-year-old is 31.6 years. So instead of saving the magazine $48 by preventing a cancellation, I am saving 80 percent of $48 times 31.6, and when one factors in the fact that 15 percent of our subscribers send gift subscriptions and extra money, and so forth, it's clear that the "value" of a *Nation* subscriber is well over $1,000 rather than a mere $48. You get the idea. When I explained all this to our associate publisher, she nodded and smiled and was obviously impressed, and then she asked, So what can we do about it? Well, I said, we can write a letter to anyone who tries to cancel and explain why he or she shouldn't. But you already do that, she pointed out. Yes, but as Sam implied at the outset, I didn't know what I was doing.

Richard Gilman is a professor emeritus of Yale. His latest book is
Chekhov's Plays: An Opening into Eternity (Yale University Press, 1996). The
following selection is excerpted from his book *Faith, Sex, Mystery*,
published by Simon and Schuster, 1986.

Faith, Sex, Mystery

At the age of nearly thirty an erstwhile militantly atheistic Jew, a boy
who had been brought up in a home where the letter of religion was observed
if not always the full spirit, an intermittently kosher household, depending on
whether his maternal grandparents were living there at particular times,
grandparents who spoke Yiddish much more easily and more often than they
did English and, particularly his grandmother, had gestures that included a
wide sighing shrug in reaction to what fate dealt them and a frequent clapping
(or klopping) of hand to forehead when destiny seemed especially bitter, and
who engaged from time to time in a mysterious and unpleasant ritual connected to death called "sitting shivah"; the boy who had been sent on roller
skates to Hebrew school three afternoons a week and had held the speed-
reading record there for some years (or until it was broken by a laser-eyed boy
whom, he was later told, everyone hated because he was fat and sweated a lot
and was so smart); had been bar mitzvahed with as much panoply as the
Depression years would allow, the gifts including the usual fountain pens and
a most unusual biography of Admiral Byrd, he of the South Pole; had eaten
gefilte fish, which he disliked, for the sake of the horseradish that went with
it; had been filled with nausea at the sight of his mother or grandmother
eviscerating a chicken, arm plunged to the elbow into the pale yellow creature's bowels, and could not eat that meat for years afterward; was familiar
with, even though he had an aversion to using, such words as "goyim" and
"shiksa" and even "Gentile"; had regarded as terrifying apparitions the nuns he
would occasionally see going in and out of—*scuttling* in and out of—the Catholic church a few blocks away from his home in the Flatbush section of
Brooklyn, a church from which an endless and similarly terrifying procession
of coffins seemed to emerge; who had been pleased that his parents had given
him the name Richard and not Seymour or Irwin or Myron and felt slightly
ashamed of that; who had thought of the names "Christ" and "Jesus" as suffused with death, verbal coffins; and who late into his twenties had thought of
himself as an exemplary product of a rational age, keen on art but on science
too, especially humanistic science—this person had become a Catholic, which
everyone will surely agree is considerably more problematic and consequential than becoming a fitness buff or subscribing dreamily to some Eastern cult.

87

There had been a preamble, something being prepared, but at the time I couldn't have known it. So it all seemed to begin abruptly, without warning, on a very hot day in the summer of 1952. I was twenty-seven and didn't have a job at the time (my wife had a very small income, and since money went a long way in those days it was enough for us to live on) and so I spent my days mostly reading and going to the movies, art galleries and museums. I read eclectically and thought about things very much the same way. Without a specialty, professional or otherwise, or any organizing principle, I was like a child going helter-skelter through an encyclopedia.

On that particular summer day I spoke of at the beginning of this section I remember waking up to a sense of boredom; I didn't have any ideas about the day nor plans of even the smallest kind. I muddled through the morning, fiddling with some scraps of writing, paying some bills, and then toward noon went to the bookshelves for something to read. Nothing appealed to me. At the time, not having much money and before the paperback revolution would come to my rescue, I didn't have a large collection of books of my own and so was an active user of the public library. So after lunch I walked over to Lexington Avenue from our tiny apartment on Seventy-ninth Street off Park and took the bus down to Fiftieth Street, where the Cathedral branch of the library was at the time.

I had seen the windows of this branch from the street but had never gone in and knew nothing about it. I usually went to a branch on Ninety-sixth near Lexington or to the main library at Forty-second and Fifth, but for some reason on that hot day I decided to try this other branch.

Inside the library I wandered among the aisles and browsed, with nothing particular in mind and growing more and more uncomfortable in the muggy heat. After an hour or so I had finally picked out five or six books. The only one of them I remember was a volume of the letters of Hart Crane, whose opaque poetry I had been reading, although I think there may have been an early novel of Evelyn Waugh's, maybe *Decline and Fall*. Anyway, I put them all under my arm and started to walk toward the checkout counter.

I had taken the last book from a shelf perhaps twenty feet from the desk, and before I could get halfway there something came over me or took hold of me—this is the only way I can describe what happened—some impulse made me turn back, hesitate, and then walk over to a section of the library, an alcove on the far side of the checkout counter, where I hadn't been before.

It was quite separate from the main part of the library and could easily be overlooked. There were maybe a thousand books on its shelves and when I got there and began to glance over the titles I could see that the books were all concerned in one way or another with religion. They were divided into a general section and then into the various faiths, a section on Judaism, one on Islamism, another on Catholicism, and so on.

There's nothing here that could possibly interest me, I remember telling myself. I had an aversion to religious books and even to ones about religion, and so never read any. Yet as I write this I suddenly recall that there had been an exception to this informal taboo, the circumstances of which seem worth interrupting my narrative chronology to recount.

A year earlier my wife and I had gone to Europe for the first time. On the boat—a charming old French liner called the *DeGrasse*—we had become friendly with a French family, a couple in their thirties and their two daughters, who were about eight and nine. Their name was Weil, and when I asked if they were related to Simone Weil, about whom I had vaguely heard (she was just becoming known in America, some years after her death), the man, André, who I would later discover was a famous mathematician, told me, with an odd touch of reluctance or embarrassment, I thought, that he was her brother.

I became infatuated with the girls, Sylvie and Nicolette, and their pleased mother, Eveline, invited me to visit them when we got to Paris. I went to their rambling old apartment on the Rue August-Comte behind the Luxembourg Gardens, where Eveline showed me some of Simone's books and papers. Then I took the girls to the Gardens for the Punch-and-Judy show and other divertissements, after which I bought them ice cream, a ritual we repeated three or four times over the following weeks.

Back home that fall I found out as much as I could about Simone and read her book, *Waiting for God*, which had recently been translated. I remember having been greatly moved by the life and mind of this brilliant, unclassifiable young woman, politically radical, intellectually rigorous, who, a Jew, had hovered for so long at the door of the Catholic Church and had died, in an extraordinarily sacrificial way, without having become able to go in.

Yet I'd also been discomfited by the book and what I'd learned of her life, unable to accommodate the specifically spiritual elements, seeing her religious hunger as eccentric if not pathological. Only after my own movement into the Church did I go back to her, avidly reading her books as they posthumously appeared, being stirred all over again and coming to regard her as a precursor whose spirituality dwarfed my own yet offered me exemplary hints and a certain solace.

To return to that summer day in 1952. Turning around, I started to walk back to the checkout counter. But I'd taken only a few steps when once again something prevented me from going on, stopping me in mid-stride and making me go back to the alcove. Once more, this time very much against my will, I began to look over the books, which I did without at first really seeing any of them.

After a while, the eerie pressure continuing to rise, I took one or two off the shelves—I remember some such title as *A History of Islam*—with my state of mind changing from bafflement to growing irritation at what was happening. A second time I started to leave the alcove and a second time I was impelled back to it as though by an unseen hand pressing me gently but authoritatively between my shoulder blades.

This time I found myself standing in front of the section of books on Catholicism. My annoyance continuing to mount, feeling also a prickle of disgust, even a touch of nausea, I ran my eyes over the books. I've said it was hot and I remember now that the sweat was pouring from my forehead, so that with the pile of books I'd picked out before under one arm I had to wipe my brow with my other forearm. I stood there for a moment with my eyes closed, until I finally opened them and began really to look at the shelves. I noticed some lives of saints, a type of being about which I had very little knowledge and a great deal of distaste, and some books by Cardinal Newman, of whom I had heard but couldn't place.

Then, standing there and literally struggling in the grip of the same insistent force whose pressure I'd felt from the outset of this weird experience, wondering if the dozen or so other people in the library were noticing anything, since I knew that I was trembling and scraping my shoes on the floor in an effort to turn round and get away—a kind of clown act or demented dance movement it might have seemed to an onlooker—I finally found myself reaching for a book and taking it off the shelf.

The book I'd taken down was called *The Spirit of Medieval Philosophy* and was by someone I'd never heard of, a man named Etienne Gilson. When I looked at the jacket blurb pasted on the inside of the front cover, the way library books often have them, I learned that he was a French philosopher, an authority on Saint Thomas Aquinas who had been teaching at some university in Canada. (Later I was to note the similarity of his last name to mine, but not make anything of it.)

The book was a big one, a real tome, and as I reluctantly leafed through it, turning the pages with an effort and forcing myself to read a few lines here and there, it struck me as dry, technical, full of alien language and ideas . . . as much as I could make out of those. In any case it was nothing in which I could conceivably have any interest, I told myself.

So I put it back on the shelf, picked up the books I'd chosen before, turned around, found myself without any power to move, turned back again, took the Gilson book from the shelf once more, put it back, repeated the whole mad cycle three or four more times and then, besieged, light-headed as though I had a fever, nearly sick to my stomach, put the book with my others and, muttering to myself something to the effect of "if the only goddamned way I can get the hell out of this goddamned fucking place is to take out this fucking goddamned book, then I'll just have to do it," went over to the counter, checked out all the books and walked out of the library into the glaring sunlight.

I got into an uptown Lexington Avenue bus (the avenue was two ways at the time) and sat down near the back of the bus with the books in my lap. I put the Gilson book on the top of the pile and kept staring at the cover, which was a dull red color, as I remember, while my annoyance kept growing. It was stifling in the bus, so I reached to open a window. After fumbling with it for a while and finally getting it open I had a sudden, nearly irresistible wish to fling the Gilson book out into the street, and went so far as to pick the book up from the seat and hold my arm out the window with it barely held in my grasp. For nearly a minute I fought the urge to drop it, shaking with tension, until my practical sense took over with the realization that I could ill afford to pay for what was clearly an expensive volume. So I brought my arm back in and, feeling strangely ill and exhausted, sat back and rode on to my stop.

That afternoon I read one of the books I'd brought home, a short novel I think it was, leafed through the Hart Crane letters and then, toward supper-time, found myself (I can't emphasize too strongly how in everything I've been describing and in nearly all the events that are to follow I kept "finding" myself in certain places or situations or doing certain things, not deliberately or even consciously choosing to be there or to do them), I found myself, as I say, toying with the Gilson book once again. I kept picking it up and putting it down, turning to something else and then picking it up again. Once I put it on a high shelf so as to get it out of my immediate reach.

But then, after an hour or two of this nonsense, in obedience to the same sort of spooky dictate I had felt in the library, I began to page reluctantly through it. After a few minutes of this I became aware that I wasn't going to get away so easily and so, with a shrug of acceptance of what I certainly didn't think of at the time as any sort of supernatural influence but, I remember thinking before I started, some temporarily mysterious unconscious prompting that would eventually be wholly explicable, I settled down to read the book.

It was hard going at first, as I'd expected, but very soon the difficulties dwindled and then vanished. To find myself caught up in this unprepossessing book couldn't have been more astonishing to me, but that was how it was. Very quickly I forgot the strange circumstances that had brought the book to me, or me to it, so that it very soon seemed as if it were the most natural thing in the world for me to be reading it.

What was most astounding was the effortlessness with which I was carried along. I had had some minimal training in philosophy (and not a bit in theology), an introductory course or two at Wisconsin and one on the Greeks at the New School after the war, and I'd supplemented that with some scattered, disorganized reading in Plato, Schopenhauer, Nietzsche, and the like, for the most part philosophers whom I considered to be more "writers," artists, than abstract thinkers or builders of systems. And so I was far from having the schooled, supple background and cast of mind such a book as this would seem to have required.

Yet I found myself following with nearly complete ease Gilson's intricate arguments and explications, all of them laid out with much heavy technical diction and with many references to works and ideas and figures I'd known nothing about. It was as though I'd suddenly and unaccountably been gifted with a great clarity of mind and speed of understanding, a lucidity such as I never imagined I could possess and which, to be sure, I was never again to enjoy to anything like the same degree.

I read on through the evening and into the night in the silent apartment (my wife was out of town), having a bite of supper which I ate with the book propped up on the table in front of me, keeping myself going later with numerous cups of coffee, smoking furiously, taking numerous notes, marking passage after passage, finally toward dawn dropping down on the sofa in my clothes for a few hours of sleep. When I woke up I grabbed the book and started reading again. I read through breakfast, a thin lunch, a thinner supper and on into the evening. At last, about one or two in the morning, I think it was, exhausted, my head swimming yet with a point of hard clear light at the center of my consciousness, I turned the last page (of 400, 500, more?), made my final notation, put the book down and said, aloud, to myself and to the air, in a voice that didn't sound like mine at all, feeling a little self-conscious as I did it, something like this: "It's true, all of it, it's all true."

True. Not beautiful or exciting or comforting, which were in fact qualities I associated with the experience soon afterward but weren't what I was thinking when I finished the book. True. I find it nearly impossible to explain or even describe what I mean by this, but I owe it to you to try.

It was as if what I had read during that day and a half had established an intellectual or philosophical world as solid and factual as the physical universe, as if the claims and arguments Gilson had made weren't claims and arguments at all but statements of what was actually so. I imagine that mathematicians and physicists have this extraordinary sense, when they've completed a proof or a demonstration, that something new exists now, not just in their minds but in reality. What now existed for me against all previous likelihood, all plausibility, was the Catholic religion, the arguments for whose truth had been made irrefutable for me during this long stretch of reading. Irrefutable, the way a rock is or the ocean. What hadn't existed for me before I read the book now did.

I can remember almost nothing of what Gilson wrote; all I can recall was a voice, a tone, a sense of authority, and my physical condition at the time: feverish, sweating, my back aching more and more, my eyes half-ruined. And I can remember some vague details of the apartment's decor: its austerity, which derived as much from lack of wherewithal as from taste; the rough bookshelves, a pile of records in a corner.

But I knew that the book wasn't in any way directly aimed at conversions, mine or anybody else's. It wasn't remotely an evangelical tract but a complex, difficult work of logic and rationality. At the time it seemed to me the most extraordinary product of rational thinking I'd ever come upon; it was unassailable and not to be resisted.

Richard Stengel is a senior writer at *Time* magazine. These first two articles appeared in *Time* on November 11, 1996, and March 16, 1998. *Space Invaders* was originally published in the *New Yorker* on July 24, 1995.

My Own Vox Pop

Pollsters, forget your focus groups, consultants, toss away your tracking polls. Campaign managers, abandon your game strategies. I am in unique possession of absolutely foolproof information about the results of the election. I have access to an infallible campaign crystal ball that has been tried, tested and proved right over and over again. Ladies and gentlemen, meet my father, my own vox pop, Robert B. Stengel, 75, a man who has voted in every presidential election since 1944 and has never once voted for a losing candidate. Not once. Ever.

A child of the Depression, he first pulled the lever for F.D.R. Then, like the American electorate, he zigzagged between Democrat and Republican: Truman, then Ike, J.F.K. and L.B.J., before deciding that Nixon was the one. He returned to the Democratic fold with Jimmy Carter, voted twice for the Gipper, once for George Bush and then opted for Bill Clinton last time around.

In short, my old man is a one-man national sample without a margin for error, the ultimate swing voter who always veers in the popular direction. He's a die-hard Democrat, Main Street Republican, an ornery independent, a Reagan Democrat, a Rockefeller Republican. He is the one voter every pollster, every ad maker, every candidate seeks to speak to—John Q. Public.

As a result of this family asset, I sometimes get lazy and don't bother interviewing the man or woman in the street. If I want to know what Americans think, I ask my father. So, Dad, what do you make of all this fuss about campaign-spending abuses and Indonesian billionaires? "Ah, they both do that stuff," he says. "It's the system." And what about the attacks on Clinton's character? "You know, I don't like to hear about that kind of thing."

Bob, as everyone calls my father, was born in Brooklyn in 1921, was the first person in his family to attend college, served in World War II, went into the family business and is now semi-retired. He reads the papers, watches television news, goes to the movies occasionally, never looks at a book and wouldn't miss a weekend football game—unless, of course, he's playing golf. He balances his checkbook, pays his taxes on time and drives a fancy foreign-made car that is his only extravagance.

Envious pollsters who are forced to use a much larger sampling might say my father's streak is just luck or that he voted for the right candidate for the wrong reasons. But my father votes in the majority for the same reason the majority does: he likes the winner better. "I vote for the best man regardless of the party," says my old man. His method is not scientific. He may watch a debate—and zip around the dial during the lulls. He doesn't really vote his pocketbook, at least not in a what's-in-it-for-me way. "I want someone who I think is talking to me," he says.

So, here's the poll result you've been waiting for—and it's free, at least until we open Stengel & Son, Pollsters Inc. The survey was conducted by telephone on November 2 among one adult registered American voter age eighteen or older. The margin of error is plus or minus 0%. So, Bob Dole? "You know I like Bob Dole," my father says. "I think I like him better in the Senate than as a presidential candidate." Perot? "Too nutty." Clinton? "He's talking about education—that's the only way to make this country great." Dad, if the election were held Tuesday (which it is), whom would you vote for? "The President," he said, before turning back to the football game on the tube.

Stardom? They'd Rather Pass

I'm not a fan. I never root for one team over another because I generally don't care who wins. But I admit I do feel vindicated by the Princeton University basketball team's 26-and-1 record and its rank of No. 8 in the country. I confess I wouldn't be all that disappointed if the team wins a couple of games in the NCAA championships that start this week. But only because it might teach a lesson to the guys I play pickup basketball with on Tuesday nights.

I was a scrub, a sophomore backup guard, on the last great Princeton squad, the team that won the National Invitational Tournament in 1975. I can't take much credit for the victory, except that I did occasionally force the first team to work up a sweat in practice, and I did absorb my fair share of the coaches' abuse. But the real curse of a Princeton basketball education is that it renders you unfit for pickup games for the rest of your life. No one looks for the open man. No one sees you when you go backdoor. Guys hog the ball and force shots from thirty feet. My inner coach wants to bench all these Michael Jordan wannabes. But it's a lost cause. You see such play everywhere these days. Especially in the NBA.

The current Princeton team plays exactly the way my team did, with a few new wrinkles and some better athletes. My coach was the ornery philosopher Pete Carril. Princeton's current coach, Bill Carmody, apprenticed under Carril for fourteen years. Carril saw the 94-ft. by 54-ft. hard court as a moral playground where the cardinal virtue was unselfishness. The embodiment of unselfishness was the assist, the small act of grace of giving up the ball to a teammate who has a better shot. Check out the box score of a Princeton game:

the team gets two-thirds of its baskets off assists, a rarity in this era of run-and-gun shooters who have eyes only for the hoop.

For the past thirty years, Princeton players have been bullied and brainwashed into looking for the pass first and the shot second. When the leather of the roundball touches your hands, your first thought is, Who else is open? Not, How am I gonna get my shot? It's not easy to learn, and it goes against the grain of me-first American individualism and the lure of million-dollar sneaker contracts. The highest skill of a Princeton basketball player is not to run, jump or shoot but to see. And it is still the rarest basketball skill of all.

Princeton is an anomaly not just because it starts five anonymous white guys in what has become a game of bigger-than-life black stars, but because in basketball today, individualism pays. Fans buy tickets to see darting one-on-one moves, awesome dunks and thirty-point games by players with multi-million-dollar endorsement deals, not pinpoint bounce passes and pretty pick-and-rolls by a bunch of unknowns whose leading scorer is averaging under fifteen points a game.

The real genius of the Princeton offense is not its moral idealism but its real-world practicality. At every moment you have a set of binary options that anticipates each possible move of your opponent—and gives you a way to overcome it. Is your man overplaying you? Cut backdoor. Is he sloughing off? Come out for the pass. If your teammate dribbles toward you, either cut away or scoot round for a hand-off. As if you were playing judo with a ball, you always use the strength of your opponent against him.

It just so happens that the Princeton offense, with its patient, intricate passing, is suited to the type of player who goes to school there: mostly kids who score at least 1,100 on their SATs, whose parents have houses with two-car garages, and who think about business school, not the NBA, after they graduate. It's a system designed for white boys who can't jump, though this year's team—which has beaten Texas, North Carolina State and Wake Forest and lost by only eight points to No. 2-ranked North Carolina—has kids who can. Mitch Henderson, the senior co-captain with eyes in the back of his head, had another option when he was accepted by Princeton: to play baseball for the Yankees.

At the moment, the five Princeton starters not only have to carry a complicated offense around in their heads but must also bear the weight of being the moral dream team of out-of-shape editorial writers who see the Tigers as the antidote to all the greed and thuggery of bigtime sports. But it's unfair to these kids to label them warriors of virtue in a venal world. I promise you, all they are thinking about is winning games, not winning hearts and minds.

But after they graduate, when they're taking depositions, not jump shots, and trying to keep away the paunch by playing in pickup games on weekends and evenings, they are going to find that they're playing a different game from everyone else on the court. Basketball is more than just a metaphor for who we are; we show who we are when we play it.

I've never bothered to try to explain to the guys I play with on Tuesday nights why I don't shoot more. Mainly, I'm just trying to get a workout and not get hurt, but I suppose on another level, I'm still looking for the open man.

Space Invaders

At my bank the other day, I was standing in a line snaking around some tired velvet ropes when a man in a sweat-suit started inching toward me in his eagerness to deposit his Social Security check. As he did so, I minutely advanced toward the woman reading the *Wall Street Journal* in front of me, who, in mild annoyance, began to sidle up to the man scribbling a check in front of her, who absent-mindedly shuffled toward the white-haired lady ahead of him, until we were all hugger-mugger against each other, the original lazy line having collapsed in on itself like a Slinky.

I estimate that my personal space extends eighteen inches in front of my face, one foot to each side, and about ten inches in back—though it is nearly impossible to measure exactly how far behind you someone is standing. The phrase "personal space" has a quaint, seventies ring to it ("You're invading my space, man"), but it is one of those gratifying expressions that are intuitively understood by all human beings. Like the twelve-mile limit around our national shores, personal space is our individual border beyond which no stranger can penetrate without making us uneasy.

Lately, I've found that my personal space is being violated more than ever before. In elevators, people are wedging themselves in just before the doors close; on the street, pedestrians are zigzagging through the human traffic, jostling others, refusing to give way; on the subway, riders are no longer taking pains to carve out little zones of space between themselves and fellow-passengers; in lines at airports, people are pressing forward like fidgety taxis at red lights.

At first, I attributed this tendency to the "population explosion" and the relentless Malthusian logic that if twice as many people inhabit the planet now as did twenty years ago, each of us has half as much space. Recently, I've wondered if it's the season: T-shirt weather can make proximity more alluring (or much, much less). Or perhaps the proliferation of coffee bars in Manhattan—the number seems to double every three months—is infusing so much caffeine into the already jangling locals that people can no longer keep to themselves.

Personal space is mostly a public matter; we allow all kinds of invasions of personal space in private. (Humanity wouldn't exist without them.) The logistics of it vary according to geography. People who live in Calcutta have less personal space than folks in Colorado. "Don't tread on me" could have been coined only by someone with a spread. I would wager that people in the Northern Hemisphere have roomier conceptions of personal space than those in the Southern. To an Englishman, a handshake can seem like trespassing, whereas to a Brazilian, anything less than a hug may come across as chilliness.

Like drivers who plow into your parked and empty car and don't leave a note, people no longer mutter "Excuse me" when they bump into you. The decline of manners has been widely lamented. Manners, it seems to me, are about giving people space, not stepping on toes, granting people their private domain.

I've also noticed an increase in the ranks of what I think of as space invaders, mini-territorial expansionists who seize public space with a sense of manifest destiny. In movie theatres these days, people are staking a claim to both armrests, annexing all the elbow room, while at coffee shops and on the Long Island Railroad, individuals routinely commandeer booths and sets of facing seats meant for foursomes.

Ultimately, personal space is psychological, not physical: it has less to do with the space outside us than with our inner space. I suspect that the shrinking of personal space is directly proportional to the expansion of self-absorption: people whose attention is inward do not bother to look outward. Even the focus of science these days is micro, not macro. The Human Genome Project is mapping the universe of the genetic code, while neuroscientists are using souped-up M.R.I. machines to chart the flight of neurons in our brains, taking snapshots of a human thought.

In the same way that the breeze from a butterfly's wings in Japan may eventually produce a tidal wave in California, I have decided to expand the contracting boundaries of personal space. In the line at my bank, I now refuse to move closer than three feet to the person in front of me, even if it means that the fellow behind me starts breathing down my neck.

Charlotte Grimes is head of the journalism program and Scripps
Howard Professor of Journalism at Hampton University. She was a reporter,
columnist and Washington correspondent for the *St. Louis Post-Dispatch* for
twenty years. She has been a visiting professor at the S. I. Newhouse School of
Public Communications at Syracuse University; a Fellow at Harvard University's
Shorenstein Center on the Press, Politics and Public Policy; and director of the
Scripps Howard Foundation's Semester in Washington program.

The following articles are from the *St. Louis Post-Dispatch*. The first article is
excerpted from an eight-page special section titled "Lives of Faith" for which
Grimes spent five months reconstructing the lives and deaths of five Catholic
missionaries killed in the civil war in Liberia. The second piece is excerpted from
a column during the 1992 Republican Convention in Houston.

The Country Is at Crisis Point

"When we were naked, they clothed us."
　　　　Jerry B. Mitchell, a neighbor of the sisters in Liberia

"Anyone could go there with their problems."
　　　　Daniel Kwabo, a friend of the sisters

A knock at the convent door. A woman and boy, standing on the porch,
offering a stalk of seventy bananas.

The woman's parents had died of cholera in Liberia's civil war. She had
taken in her four younger siblings to raise. Her sister also had been killed in
the war. She had taken in her nieces and nephews to raise. Eight children in
all in the household. The family was "very poor."

Sister Kathleen McGuire was home alone in the convent when the woman
and boy appeared at the door. A round-faced idealistic Irish-American Mid-
westerner, Kathleen had been in Liberia barely a month. Just long enough to
learn a bit about the local necessities of life:

How to chill the large bottle, called a "Greenie" for its color, of indigenous
Club Beer in a barrel of rainwater. How to use "small" in some of its many
meanings in the sing-song Liberian English patois, like "wait small" for "wait
a little while" and "small-small" for something close to "tiny" and "dress small"
for "squeeze together tightly," as in a crowded taxi. How to light a charcoal fire
for cooking when the coal "is damp, the paper is damp and the matches are
damp." And where in the convent to find the sisters' stockpile of household
goods, medicine, food and clothes.

The precious cache filled the room at the back of the convent, next to
Kathleen's bedroom. She rummaged through the stacks for a package with the

family's name on it. Then she found a pair of trousers for the boy; a skirt and blouse for the woman.

"She danced and laughed and hugged and kissed me. She made me so happy with her own joy," Kathleen wrote to a friend back in Illinois. Still, it was a humbling experience, to make someone so happy by doing so little. "Gave me a good healthy feeling," as Kathleen put it, "of being so 'small-small.'"

In the fourteen months that Sister Kathleen McGuire would have as a missionary in Liberia, the pattern became familiar. So many human needs. So easy to fulfill some of them; so nearly impossible to meet others.

The pattern was hard for Kathleen to settle into at first. The other four sisters—Shirley Kolmer, Barbara Muttra, Agnes Mueller and Joel Kolmer—returned that August of 1991 to find the country had changed. They had lost friends in the civil war, and they grieved for them. They found their work in tatters. The new Liberia was a painful disappointment. And for Kathleen, Liberia was a place in which, until very recently, she never thought she'd find herself:

"I have always expected some day to experience a call to Latin America—I keep studying Spanish to be ready for such a call. Shirley and Antoinette had often urged me to come to Liberia hut never before have l felt I was supposed to be there. Now I believe I am supposed to go."

McGuires have farmed in southeastern Illinois near Ridgway—"Popcorn Capital of the World," population around 1,100—for more than 125 years. They are very rooted there, especially in the community called Pond Settlement, outside of town. And Norma Katherine, called "Kay" by all her family, grew up in Pond Settlement in a childhood that, enshrined as it is in American folklore and now all-but extinct, could be exhibited in the Smithsonian: Learning in a one-room schoolhouse with a pot-bellied stove. Raising and showing a calf for 4-H Club (though Kay didn't care for it; her calf, Man O'War, was stubborn, and Kay was small and couldn't drag him where she wanted him to go). Walking with her family on Sundays to the neat country church.

In the church basement, a pair of Adorers of the Blood of Christ gave religion classes in the summer, and one day Kay walked home and announced: "I'm going to be a sister."

She was six years old.

As soon as she finished eighth grade in Ridgway, she was off to the boarding school that adjoined the Adorers' convent in Ruma. Over the next forty years, as Sister Kathleen, she grew into a teacher, a firebrand feminist, a passionate pacifist, a rebel with several causes.

After Vatican II, the new theology of social justice found a warm reception among many of the Adorers of the Blood of Christ.

Some joined anti-nuclear demonstrations, worked in inner city neighborhoods, marched in the civil rights movement. Sister Kathleen McGuire thrived in the church's new world order. She was one of the first in Ruma to shed the veil. Always spiritually moved by the communion celebration, she devised new private prayer services using symbolic bread and wine. Someone gave her a crystal goblet once, a wishful gift and only half-joke, for the day when Kathleen could celebrate Mass, as a priest.

In 1984, she became the coordinator for the Ruma province's "peace and justice" mission. With Kathleen cajoling and challenging, the Adorers became the only Catholic organization in the St. Louis area to defy the law and offer sanctuary to Central American refugees in protest of U.S. policy.

The work on behalf of the Central and Latin American people affected Kathleen deeply. She was drawn, intellectually and spiritually, to the region. On a trip to El Salvador in 1987, she made a pilgrimage to the graves of the five Maryknoll sisters murdered in civil war. By 1990, Kathleen was thinking of leaving the peace and justice post. The new leadership team at Ruma decided there was no reason for her to wait. Kathleen felt surprised and hurt.

She turned down a post in Texas. The way to Latin America as a missionary was not clear. Her friend and mentor, Shirley Kolmer, was trying frenetically to get herself and other missionaries back into Liberia. To the mystification of her family and friends, who knew her heart belonged in Latin America, Kathleen made her decision—Liberia.

In an unexpected, and later bittersweet, twist of timing, the fourteen months between August 1991 and October 1992 would turn out to be an uncommonly fruitful phase for the missionaries in the Gardnersville convent.

Within three days of her arrival, Kathleen was laid low by her special nemesis: Liberian insect life. Spiders as big as an adult's palm shared the sisters' house in Gardnersville. And the local version of the fire ant is a reddish-brown creature with a fierce bite. Liberians call them "mission ants," and the convent was acrawl with them. The ants seemed to single out Kathleen. "For awhile I felt like a prisoner in the house—I couldn't step outside without getting bitten," she wrote home. Liberians, when they take a seat, routinely stamp around the chair to squash any mission ants lying in wait. Kathleen went about armed with her can of Helltox insecticide. As the newcomer, Kathleen drew the chore of keeping the convent journal. In it and in her letters home, she painted vivid pictures of a lifestyle that to the veterans was no longer remarkable but to Kathleen was a combination of "a prolonged camping experience" and a trial.

Rats moved into the convent, and the sisters imported kittens to evict them. Electricity was erratic; most evenings were spent in candlelight or the glow of a kerosene lantern. "Bucket baths" were courtesy of the rain barrels.

As the months wore on, the missionaries settled into their routines. Joel

Kolmer managed St. Michael's elementary and high schools in the parish, and worked with the young Liberian women, the aspirants who came to live and study in half the convent. Agnes took on managing the Maria Clinic behind St. Anthony's. Barbara spent most of her time cruising Monrovia in her latest auto, a phosphorescent-orange Isuzu pickup, on daily rounds to collect supplies of rice, medicine and clothes. Once a week, she made the increasingly dangerous delivery run to Klay. At 7:30 most mornings, Shirley filled her leaky Thermos with coffee heavily laced with dried milk and set out on the five-mile drive into Monrovia and St. Patrick's School.

By the end of her first year, Kathleen had "come of age," with a clear-cut schedule: Monday and Tuesdays she worked at St. Michael's, teaching and managing. Thursdays and Fridays, she was at St. Patrick's with Shirley. "Wednesday, I keep the house and bake," she wrote home. "That's the day I really get tired."

In a morale booster for expatriates, the U.S. Embassy opened its canteen and bar twice a week. Friday night was "Happy Hour." Wednesdays were movies: "Uncle Buck" and Mel Gibson's "Hamlet" and Kevin Costner's "Robin Hood." The sisters were popular regulars. Once, when they couldn't come on Wednesday, the Embassy Marines gave them a private screening: "Star Trek: The Final Frontier."

In Latin America after Vatican II, Catholics had grown a grass-roots movement of intense community involvement. In small groups, they met to study scripture and figure out ways to apply religious teachings to daily life. The movement is controversial. "Love thy neighbor," when interpreted to mean "Do something about poverty, oppression and illiteracy," can be a threat to established political order. And the Catholic hierarchy is wary of individual interpretation of scripture. But the sisters saw it as "empowering" the people. For years, they had wanted to try it in Liberia. And finally, in St. Anthony's parish, they had their catalyst in the form of an enthusiastic young priest named Mike Moran.

At five feet six inches and 130 pounds, Moran might get overlooked in a crowd, if it weren't for the personality animating his spare, wiry frame. He has black hair, blue eyes and the kind of smile that involves his whole face. The laugh lines start at the corners of his eyes and run in deep curves down to his squared-off jaw. His voice is husky. He walks with a springy stride, and he preaches poised, eagerly, on the balls of his feet. When he's listening, he can be very still.

When the sisters heard that Moran was thinking of starting small community religious groups in St. Anthony's, they invited him to dinner at the convent and plied him with Club Beer, avocado dip, chicken and rice and fruit salad spiked with peach schnapps. Moran set about mapping St. Anthony's parish, dividing its five square miles and fifty thousand residents into fifteen neighborhoods. The sisters' convent was in Neighborhood No. 12.

The neighborhood identities caught on, as people bonded over scripture study in weekly meetings and in work on community projects. They cleaned up a dump. They made Christmas cards to raise money for the Chocolate City orphanage. They surveyed the parish, going home-to-home to find out who needed medical care, food, clothes. They coordinated delivering the emergency supplies. Liberians and the sisters together, white faces and black glistening with sweat, tromped through the swamps and over dusty trails to the farthest outlying homes.

Each neighborhood chose a chairperson. Seven elected women; eight elected men. The eighth man, a resident of the sisters' Neighborhood 12, announced that he and his wife would share the job because they were "equals." Sister Agnes Mueller's face "just glowed."

The neighborhood groups took root in Gardnersville's red sand. They continued to meet even as new warfare crept up on Liberia.

From the beginning of the missionaries return in the summer of 1991, the signs were there. Roving bands of "rogues" terrorized the neighborhoods. In September, friends pressed the sisters to raise their six-foot wall to ten feet. The sisters resisted. They didn't want to be cut off from the people. "Our present alternatives seem to be: (1) moving, but we are not sure we would find safer housing; (2) leaving the country or (3) raising the wall," Kathleen recorded in the journal. "So, we'll raise the wall." The wall of cinder blocks reached ten feet. Spikes of sharp glass topped two sides.

Through the months, Barbara was the barometer of the storm of violence brewing. On her weekly trips to Klay, she threaded through as many as fifteen rebel checkpoints; the twenty-minute drive often took two hours. She chatted up the soldiers, handed out spearmint gum. Sometimes they quizzed her, checked her papers, unloaded her truck and made her repack it. But she thought she was building rapport. By Christmas, she was in an auto-less funk, grounded in Gardnersville, and kept away from Klay by tension among the rebels for several weeks. She was determined to spend Christmas in Klay. On December 23, Kathleen wrote in the convent journal: "Barbara roused the Bishop from bed demanding a car! She got a truck and packed it and headed out. All we could do . . . was bless her and watch her go." Starting in February 1992, Barbara's trips measured a steady buildup of hostility. "There's tension behind the lines," Kathleen reported in the journal after Barbara spent her birthday driving supplies to Klay. In April, rebels held, interrogated and intimidated two Baptist missionaries for eleven days. The Baptists stopped by the convent to warn Barbara against more trips to Klay. She wouldn't listen. In August, rebels stopped Barbara, held her overnight, interrogated her and took her truck. Storming into the American Embassy, she fumed about her truck to Alex Leskaris, the consular officer. He and others with transportation enlisted in a conspiracy; no one would give Barbara a ride to Klay. They were too worried about her.

By the fall, all five sisters were living behind the convent's ten-foot wall. A new warring faction sprang up to fight Charles Taylor's rebels. "The country is at crisis point once again," Kathleen wrote in the journal in late August. "Sunday afternoon and evening over twenty thousand refugees crossed the Po River Bridge into Monrovia. . . . Just pray this gets resolved without an attack on Monrovia."

Many of the missionaries had great faith in the West African peacekeeping forces. They simply couldn't believe a full-scale war would come again. But to Sister Kathleen McGuire, the newcomer, things looked bleak. "Greetings from a suffering country," she wrote. She fretted about the graduating students. "No college, no jobs, no training possibilities. It must seem pretty pointless to them. . . ."

Sometimes she heard gunfire at night. Rebels slipped over the convent wall one night and seriously hurt two of the watchmen. "The long nights when you're afraid to fall asleep," she wrote, "seem to pass very slowly." The rogues seemed to be targeting places with cars and American money. The sisters knew that included them; they collected the fees from the schools and clinic. "We've pretty well relocated most of the cash so they won't get too much," Kathleen wrote to her family on September 17, 1992. It would be her next to last letter to them. "I just don't want them coming in."

Memo to Conservatives: Family Ties Are the Strongest Values of All

Democrats and Republicans alike have been repeatedly drawing portraits featuring wives with happy smiles, husbands with strong arms, strong backs and strong hearts and their stair-step children with fresh faces and bright eyes clustered around in a Christmas-card pose.

"Family Values," the caption reads in large bold letters. In definition, the subtext adds, Look like this; live like this; be like this; or you are not a family and you can't have values.

The religious right and conservatives, who are the loudest voices at this convention and who believe the portrait was drawn by the hand of God, often say so bluntly.

"Family values means the traditional family—a mother and father living together in marriage and raising their children together," one alternate delegate who described herself as a conservative explained over a barbecue lunch. She had a touch of exasperation in her voice because she was watching my face closely and no doubt it was showing that, by the time she'd finished, I was thinking of someone else.

Her name was Kate and she comes to mind especially vividly at times like that, and when the politicians are talking about family values.

Kate was the oldest of eight children who grew up, shortly after the turn of the century, in a hardworking farm family. The children all helped around the home, and Kate plowed the fields alongside her brothers with a mule. Kate's parents, like their community, were bedrock, church-going Christians whose values included a strict list: No drinking, no card playing on Sundays, no dancing.

The no-dancing rule was genuinely hard on Kate, who thought the sound of fiddles magic. In her late teens, she began to go about with her young man, who told her he loved her and promised they would get married, and in the way those things happen Kate soon was "in trouble." Her young man forgot about marriage, though Kate's father offered to remind him with a shotgun. Kate said no. She was beginning to find her own set of values. One of them was that you didn't need someone in your life who lies and breaks promises.

The doctor who attended Kate's delivery had some thoughts about young women like her, and Kate never forgot him standing over her, sweating and crying in labor, and telling her the pain was no more than she deserved and something she should remember. Kate had a daughter.

With only an eighth-grade education, Kate couldn't get much of a job to support herself and her baby. The child was pretty much taken over by Kate's mother, who thought Kate's behavior had been sinful and unclean. Often, as a child, the little girl could be found in the family's yard with a pail of water, washing herself, washing herself, over and over.

Eventually, Kate met another young man, married him, and her daughter came to live with them. The first time Kate found him with another woman, she forgave him. The second time, she picked up a glass ashtray, threw it across the room, hit him in the forehead and walked out. She never changed her value on deceit and broken promises. Over the next years, Kate worked hard to raise her daughter alone. She took a job in a defense plant to pay for her own divorce. She went to work as a fry cook, standing on aching feet and swollen legs and chopping onions, chopping onions, chopping onions for hours while her fingers burned and tears poured down her cheeks. Kate often hoped to never see another onion.

When her daughter was twelve, Kate finally asked to be called "Mother." She'd never felt she deserved it before. It must have been a defining moment for both of them, because both spoke sometimes about it, and for the rest of their lives the bond between them was so close, so strong that they were almost inseparable. They were a family. They shared each other's secrets, heartbreaks, joys and when her daughter married and also had a daughter,

Kate was never far away. Finally, Kate moved into her daughter's home and grew old there, a strong quiet presence in the heart of the household. Kate, in graceful old age, and her daughter, just finding the first gray hairs of midlife, died barely two years apart, almost as if the bond between them still drew them together.

I pieced together the story of Kate and her daughter over a number of years, as I was learning many other things from them. Kate taught me to fish, to be brave in thunderstorms, to think of myself as a worthwhile person and to value people who don't lie, who keep promises, and who give love like the unearned gift it is. Her daughter taught me to dance—as Kate had seen to it that she learned—and play poker, to read and write, to laugh from deep inside and to try to face life and death with grace and courage.

Kate was my grandmother, her daughter was my mother. And between them they taught me one, simple, clear family value: Who is in your family picture—pairs of parents, grandparents, children, cousins—doesn't matter as much as the bonds among them.

Barbara Crossette is a foreign correspondent for the *New York Times* and the author of four books on Asia. The following selection is excerpted from *So Close to Heaven: The Vanishing Buddhist Kingdoms of the Himalayas*, published by Knopf (1995).

All Sentient Beings

The monks at one of Bhutan's most venerated temples were having a spat with the security officer assigned by the district's civil administrator to guard the shrines and enforce new rules against littering and the harboring of stray dogs. On a winter morning when sunshine bathed the temple courtyard and glinted off the golden-brass butter lamps set out to dry after a scrubbing, the administrator had lined up the abbot and half a dozen monks like so many schoolboys for a dressing-down. The ineffectual security officer, standing a few feet away, head down almost to his chest, had reported that he was the victim of a monkish conspiracy. Nobody in holy robes obeyed him, he said, though at this temple they were wards of the state. Monks refused to tidy up their quarters. They gave leftovers to the pariah dogs. Worst of all, the care-taker-guard alleged, they threatened him.

The administrator was livid. Striding back and forth in front of the silent, expressionless monks in their maroon robes and assorted running shoes, he admonished them sternly, told them that their campaign of noncompliance was over and they would henceforth pick up their trash and stop feeding stray animals. He then turned sharply on his heel and strode out of the monastery yard. As he approached the gate of this sacred place, a tiny, velvety-brown puppy loped happily toward him out of curiosity, hunger, or a search for affection, as baby animals do. As their paths crossed, the administrator, without missing a step, kicked the little dog out of his way, sending it rolling and squealing in pain and fright across the stones.

"In this place, there will be no dogs and no pigs," the administrator later explained calmly. "They are filthy and spread disease."

Bhutan has a stray-dog crisis, and it goes to the heart of the conflict between piety and progress in a Buddhist universe, where sparing the life and sensibil-ities of an animal is supposed to be an act of faith. Not infrequently and in many realms of activity in Bhutan and elsewhere in the Himalayas, monks and lamas are running into conflict with an increasingly intrusive and scientific state. The argument may be over opposition to modern medicine or the growth of secular education outside the monasteries, the spread of tourism to holy sites, or the treatment of animals, domestic or wild. As Rigzin Dorji made clear time and again, some topics may be open to debate, but there is really no latitude on the issue of protecting nonhuman life. All of us, down to the smallest mouse or insignificant insect, are sentient beings and therefore sacred in Buddha's eyes.

"Today my mother may be human," Rigzin Dorji said. "But when I die, I may be reborn as a dog, and then my mother may be a bitch. So therefore, you have to think that all living beings are my parents. My parents are infinite. Let my parents not suffer."

Carried to extremes, the rule defies reason and overrides instincts of human kindness, leading to cruelties no less painful than outright abuse. On a path to Sherubtse College, a dog had collapsed and was obviously dying slowly and agonizingly, its hairless body riddled with open abscesses. Why not put it to death? I asked. Buddhism tells us not to take life, was the reply. I heard that again when I encountered along the road a horse turned out of a village because it had broken a leg and could not work. The bone-thin animal was hobbling clumsily along the bed of a stream beyond the farmers' fields, dragging a useless back leg as it hunted for anything green and succulent on which to graze. No one apparently wanted it, or could afford to feed it just for pity's sake. Yet no villager dared risk the karmic consequences of an act of euthanasia.

For the devout Buddhist, shouldering the burden of responsibility for animals can sometimes take tragicomic turns. In Nepal, where Hinduism and Buddhism coexist and sometimes overlap, Buddhists run from temple to temple in Kathmandu on certain Hindu festival days to pray for the souls of goats or other animals served up for ritual slaughter. In Bhutan, where Buddhists believe they can eat meat but not butcher animals, a farmer will bring fresh yak flesh to market but never admit to killing the yak. He will say that the yak, a surefooted, high-altitude animal, fell off a rock or met some other unlikely accident. Strips of meat are cured in the winter—sun-dried on the ground or air-dried on clotheslines—to make a delicacy appreciated everywhere in Bhutan. But I never saw a butcher shop. The only animal I saw butchered, in the privacy of someone's home, was a pig being cut up for the winter larder at the headquarters of a joint Bhutanese-European agriculture project. The pig, however, has very low status.

The annals of Bhutanese development economics are replete with tales of Buddhist intransigence in the face of new ideas that might affect the well-being of animals. Silk production will never reach the quantity or quality of neighboring countries, despairing officials say, because the Bhutanese will not throw cocoons with still-living silkworms into boiling water. In the town of Jakar, in Bumthang district, two young men from southern Bhutan, where Hinduism predominates, were tending a demonstration bee-keeping project when I dropped in one day. The royal government is urging farmers to produce honey for extra household income. Most Buddhist Bhutanese balk, saying that making honey kills bees. You can see them lying around on the grass, dead as can be, right in front of the hive, they insist. So many tiny souls at risk.

To the Bhutanese family living as high as thirteen thousand feet or more, all kinds of animals, wild and tame, are omnipresent and often essential in daily life. Domesticated beasts provide all the energy that can be harnessed in hamlets beyond the reach of roads, hydroelectricity, and kerosene-powered generators. Children come of age tending yaks or caring for horses, expanding their knowledge as they work. Father William Mackey, the Canadian Jesuit who has become a Bhutanese citizen and a high-ranking administrator in Bhutan's education department, said he learned decades ago when teaching math to village children that they instinctively understood numerical sets in a way a Western child did not. The knowledge came from tending animals.

"The little boy who takes the cows out, he knows he takes seven cows," the sprightly priest said as he passed around cakes during tea at his Thimphu home. "The foundation of sets, the mathematics of sets, that kid knows, because seven is not seven to him. There may be two cows up there on the hill, three down here in the field—where are the other two? Or four may be brown and three black. The concept of sets that kid knows before he comes to school. Or the little girl who lets out twelve chickens. She needs twelve back when she comes home, so she learns how to count them, six over here, five there, and so on. People on a farm have fantastic knowledge."

Beyond the farmyard, wild animals are omnipresent, blurring the lines that divide human habitation from the realm of other sentient beings, real or mythical, and the world of the spirits who share both spaces. Even in Thimphu, a capital city that is no more than a frontier outpost, bears and panthers prowl. Townspeople tell stories of big mountain cats that snack on chickens and pet dogs, disappearing afterward to sleep off the feast in the trackless surrounding forests. When terrorism began to empty hamlets in southern Bhutan after an ethnic Nepali insurgency took off in the early 1990s, loyal citizens who remained soon complained that wild beasts were returning from the tropical jungles to reclaim the abandoned fields and threaten the families who chose to stay behind. The south has a hot, dense landscape, where not only buffalo but also elephants, tigers, rhinoceros, and deer roam among the mixture of bamboo, chik grass, and temperate-zone trees.

Animals portrayed by dancers wearing huge lifelike masks are important components of religious festivals or, increasingly, classical dance performances. In the Stag Dance, which can be performed by monks or laymen or a combination of both, a hunter is brought before the Lord of Death to argue for the best afterlife possible based on his worldly deeds. Unfortunately, his life has included a lot of animal killing, and in the end he is doomed because the fruits of his vocation outweigh his many acts of Buddhist merit. The Lord of Death sentences him to be reincarnated as each of the animals whose life he has taken, and then to experience five hundred deaths in each of those beastly incarnations. In the dance that tells the story, performers wearing heavy stag heads leap and spin with extraordinary strength and vigor.

Animals and birds also play prominent roles in many moral tales, including the beloved fable of the Four Friends. In the Bhutanese version of this story, a bird, a rabbit, a monkey, and an elephant combine their talents to provide themselves a perennial supply of delicious fruit. The bird found and planted a seed, which was watered by the rabbit, fertilized by the monkey, and guarded by the elephant. When the tree grew and blossomed, the four again worked as a team to pick the fruit that soon appeared. The elephant stood by the trunk, and the rabbit, monkey, and bird climbed on its back to build a tower to the high branches where the best fruit grew. The Four Friends are painted frequently on the walls of temples as well as homes and shops.

At Simtokha Dzong, a seventeenth-century monastery and school, Sangay Wangchuck of the Central Monastic Secretariat paused before a large rendition of the familiar Four Friends parable and placed the tale in a theological perspective. A novice monk of about six or seven stood nearby, rapt (and runny-nosed) as the discourse progressed. As he watched us, his red robe slipped from his small shoulder, revealing a sweatshirt that said, in one of those grab-bag attempts at English so common to Asian bazaars, "High Casual Step It." It was oddly appropriate to the four creatures standing one atop another's back, all eyes on the ripening fruit.

"These are the four brothers, the four very, very good friends; best friends," Sangay Wangchuck was explaining. "So the bird is the Buddha, the rabbit is his closest attendant. He has two main disciples. The monkey is Shariputra, and the elephant is the Maudgalyayana." I nodded, convinced anew that I would never master the basics of a religion where Buddha always turns up where you least expect him, and in a new context. Shariputra, hailed for his wisdom, and Maudgalyayana, who had paranormal powers, were Buddha's chief disciples during his lifetime, I later learned from John Snelling's *Buddhist Handbook*. "Buddhists believe that if you have this one picture," Sangay Wangchuck went on, "then you pacify all the negatives and have better friendship." That part I understood.

I wonder: is it sheer coincidence that the Bremen Town Musicians of German folklore—the donkey, dog, cat, and rooster who scared away brigands—are also four animal friends, or, more precisely, three animals and a bird?

In Mongar, a mountain town of cascading bougainvillea, more beautiful than any overcrowded hill station in India, Dasho Lhakpa Dorji, the dzongda, told stories over dinner about local farmers' efforts to strike a balance among crops, animals, and religion. Several years ago, he said, farmers on the steep hillsides where every available bit of land that could be plowed had been planted found that they and their domesticated animals were vulnerable to wolves. Putting aside theology in the face of an economic crisis, the mountain people had begun killing any wolf identified as a predator. That is usually permissible in Bhutan if the culling takes place on one's own property.

"Well, then they found that with the number of wolves reduced, the wild boars were taking over," the dzongda said. "Wolves had been keeping the wild boar population down. Now we have to think about what can be done—to stop killing wolves, or limit the boars."

Killing boars isn't the answer here or anywhere else, advised Khenpo Phuntsok Tashi, a religious scribe, in an article in *Kuensel*. "In our belief, killing boars only causes them to multiply, assisted by local nature goddesses," he said. This path leads only to more destruction from a vengeful species, he warned. Better to protect the crops, the khenpo said. "If you want to protect your feet against thorns, you cannot cover the whole landscape with leather. It is easier and wiser to put a small piece of leather under your feet!"

It is that homeless dog population, however, that will truly test the limits of theology as Bhutan develops. Already, dogs take a lot of abuse, getting kicked and stoned regularly enough to make them wary of humans, Buddhism notwithstanding. But there is enough ambivalence on the issue of dog control to ensure a continuing supply of strays in the near future. Most wayfarers who inevitably arrive in Paro or Thimphu late in the day discover the dog problem unexpectedly in the middle of the night, just after drifting into a peaceful sleep in the pure mountain air.

Twilight does not linger in the high Himalayan valleys. The sun drops quickly behind the hills and peaks, taking the pleasant daytime temperature with it. As the thermometer's mercury plunges, life moves indoors and the kind of peace that dwarfs humanity in these gigantic natural settings descends on villages and towns. White and yellow pools of light from naked bulbs draw families around small stoves where rice is ready to be ladled into basket-plates, thick hot tea simmers, and children begin to doze. In Thimphu's central square, the busy jeep-taxis, parked backs to the wall, eager to spring out for a fare during daylight hours, collect the last of the marketgoers and vanish with the night. That's when the dogs take over.

Feral Tibetan apsos and former pets of foreign pedigree, local pyedogs of every size and hue, silken longhairs of unidentifiable breeds, and battle-scarred mutts from South Asia's infinite store of mangy mongrels—out of the shadows and rain gutters and construction sites they come; up from the Changlimithang archery field and royal basketball court, past the shuttered Yangchenma bookshop, down the hill through the labyrinth of lanes behind the Swiss Bakery. After sniffing their way around the square at a trot, they arrange themselves in ones and twos on the stoops of darkened shops and offices, nose to paws, and go to sleep. No longer on the lookout for stone-throwing citizens, they yawn and scratch and snuggle, looking like piles of fur left out to air. This is temporary.

Some time later, prompted by some secret, primordial signal, the half-wild dogs, as if uneasy in human civilization, begin to bark and howl. A piercing chorus of yaps and hoots shatters the heavy silence. In the distant, dark recesses of the narrow Thimphu Valley and from the driveways and byways of the nearer sheltering hills, dotted with houses, other dogs respond, rending the peace with fearsome announcements. And then it is over. But they have made their point. The square, the town, the valley, and the night belong to them.

Whether the dogs bark or howl, and where, is not without meaning.

"Bhutanese believe domestic animals can give us signs," Dasho Rinzin Gyetsen, the dzongda of Tashigang, told me in a conversation over tea one evening in the garden gazebo of a guesthouse overlooking his spectacularly situated dzong, more than twelve hundred feet above a narrow river valley. For reasons that would elude most people, the guesthouse management had contrived to block out the panoramic view afforded by the hexagonal pavilion by hanging cheap lace curtains on all the windows. "A horse that won't go forward can be a warning," the dasho said, as a respectful waiter hovered with a teapot. "And the dog howling in the night—see which way he points. If he points at a certain house, the devil has entered that house and claimed a soul. The person may not die right away, but his soul has been taken."

Some dzongdas, using their considerable powers over the lives of the districts they govern, have devised novel ways to curb the proliferation of dogs while stopping short of killing them and inflaming public opinion. It's a struggle, said Pem Dorji, the dzongda of Bumthang.

"Last year, I tried to get rid of the dogs, but the people were against everything I wanted to do," he said as we toured the countryside around Jakar. "Finally, I collected live dogs. People got a reward for bringing them in. I put three hundred dogs on trucks and took them over the mountains to Lingmithang." That's a distance of more than seventy-five miles, over two high passes—one of them, Thumsing La, at 12,465 feet, the highest road pass in Bhutan. The dzongda was bowled over by what happened next. "After two months, the dogs came back," he said incredulously. "They crossed the Thumsing La and they came back."

Not long ago in Shemgang, in south-central Bhutan, somebody decided on a drastic and probably misguided strategy. Pieces of meat were left around town laced with strychnine. More than one hundred dogs died, but in agony, according to a letter to the editor of *Kuensel* from a foreigner in town, who reported that some animals took up to five hours to die. "In this period, the dogs vomited, went into convulsions, got drowsy, and repeated the cycle." Cats also were poisoned, along with birds that pecked at the vomit of the doomed dogs. In all, it was a most un-Bhutanese event.

"If you are born among the animals, you don't have the chance to understand the truth, and you suffer," said Dasho Rigzin Dorji. But that does not give those in human form the right to use lethal measures when there is imbalance or disorder among speechless, uncomprehending beasts. "If you kill something, you are reborn among hell-beings," he said. "So therefore, breaking the vows as a Buddhist is a serious crime. Then for many eons, there is no chance of Buddhahood."

Ronald Steel, a biographer and commentator on political and social
issues, teaches international relations at the University of Southern California.
This article appeared in the *New York Times* on July 21, 1996.

When Worlds Collide

There is something both normal and frightening about our reaction to
the explosion that blew T.W.A. Flight 800 out of the air and killed 230 innocent people. Normal in that the unexplained destruction of any symbol of
American power and influence—a military base, a government building, a
corporate headquarters, an American-based airline—immediately leads us to
suspect terrorists. Frightening in that such acts lie beyond the customary rules
of innocence and guilt, cause and effect, by which we organize our lives. If this
should prove to be an accident rather than a crime, the best that we will be
able to say is that it was not terrorism this time.

Terrorism, the means by which the weak frighten and punish the strong,
has become part of our lives. We are no longer shocked by it. We have even
come to expect it. Sometimes, as in the case of the World Trade Center bombing, it comes bearing foreign accents and perplexing religious dogmas. Other
times, as in Oklahoma City, it takes the form of the strangers who are one of
us, with their familiar delusions of omnipotent enemies.

In truth they are one, the terrorists abroad and those at home: the ones we
do not know, and the ones we spawn. They are both products of a world
whose rules they do not understand and which they feel does not understand
them. They want to return to an earlier time in which they believe that they
would have an honored place. They are, to their minds, upholders of a true
faith—a faith that, whatever its tenets, will put them among the winners rather
than the losers, the respected rather than the ignored.

Although they are people whom, rightly or wrongly, time has passed by,
they are very much creatures of their time. They have taken the technology of
the strong and adapted it to their own ends. Technology may be a liberating
force, but what it unleashes resists and often defies those who create it. Chain
reactions, whether in nuclear furnaces or the cauldron of ideas, are constantly
in danger of going out of control. Just as a gun is a terrible leveler, erasing
status and privilege in an instant, so are the most awesome weapons of a state.
The United States may be able to intimidate any other state with the sheer
magnitude of its military power, but individual Americans are hopelessly vulnerable to those weapons in the hands of other individuals.

Terrorism eradicates the distinction, so essential in international relations,
between the state and the individual. States challenge one another or even go

to war. The wars may be terrible. But they are, for the most part, fought by certain clear rules. States rarely try to assassinate one another's leaders. Think how shocked we were by the C.I.A. schemes in the Kennedy Administration to kill Fidel Castro. They do not wantonly make civilians targets without some compelling military justification. Consider the continuing difficulty we have explaining to ourselves the destruction of Dresden and Hiroshima. Responsible states do not torture or kill their prisoners. When they do, we consider them guilty of war crimes.

States generally avoid such acts not because they operate under a higher moral code than do individuals, but because they fear retaliation in kind. Two can play the game of assassination and atrocity. Thus the "rules of war." But terrorists have no interest in such distinctions. They operate outside the contrived world of state-sanctioned violence. This is the source of their weakness, but also of their strength. They know that the kinds of retaliation that states use against one another—war, economic sanctions, embargoes—are useless against them. A few individuals may occasionally be caught—like the bombers at Riyadh, the World Trade Center and Oklahoma City—but the core group of true believers remains untouched.

Every modern state is highly vulnerable to such terrorism. Indeed, the more modern it is, the more technologically and sociologically complicated its structure, the more vulnerable it is. It takes only a power outage to shut down a great city, or an abandoned truck to instill fear among tens of thousands, as happened last week in Seattle. The U.S. is not alone in being a target or being vulnerable. Ordinary civilians, the more innocent the better, have been targets of I.R.A. and Algerian terrorists. Their objective is to neutralize power by assaulting it at its weakest link: public confidence.

Why the United States? Alas, the proper question is, why not the United States? Just as the American Government is the locus of power within this country (and thus the logical target for right-wing militia members who feel otherwise powerless), so the United States is the locus of power for a "new world order" that would render irrelevant traditional faiths and even whole societies. Americans pride themselves on being in the forefront of the modern, in being the world's leader. But not everyone finds that world as appealing, or even as inevitable, as we do. To many it is deeply threatening.

We proudly declare ourselves to be No. 1, the world's only remaining superpower. Naturally, the discontented of the world hold us responsible for their plight: their poverty, their ignorance, their weakness, their irrelevance. A nation cannot be No. 1 when it suits its convenience and be "Who, little me?" when it doesn't. In status begin responsibilities. We so much take for granted not only our status but our standards that it hardly occurs to us that others may look upon them with alarm. We extol such principles as democracy, individualism, consumerism and the marketplace of ideas as though they were uncontested virtues. We are sincerely puzzled when others find these notions threatening. We assume they must be either misinformed or obtuse. Like the Victorian traveler confronted by uncomprehending "natives," we start talking louder.

It was never the Soviet Union, but the United States itself that is the true revolutionary power. We believe that our institutions must confine all others to the "ash heap of history." We lead an economic system that has effectively buried every other form of production and distribution—leaving great wealth and sometimes great ruin in its wake. We purvey a culture based on mass entertainment and mass gratification: one that extols hedonism and accumulation even as it describes them as individualism and abundance. The cultural messages we transmit through Hollywood and McDonald's go out across the world to capture, and also to undermine, other societies.

Unlike more traditional conquerors, we are not content merely to subdue others: We insist that they be like us. And of course for their own good. We are the world's most relentless proselytizers. The world must be democratic. It must be capitalistic. It must be tied into the subversive messages of the World Wide Web. No wonder many feel threatened by what we represent. We are the apostles of globalization, the enemies of tradition and hierarchy. A chasm runs through the center of the globe. On one side are the modernizers, with their absolute belief in science, rationality, individualism and progress. On the other are the defenders of the faith and moral certainty.

The war between modernizers and traditionalists will continue for a long time to come. Two worlds are in collision, and all of us are in the front lines.

Isabel Wilkerson, a senior writer at the *New York Times*, won the Pulitzer Prize for feature writing in 1994. She is working on a book about the unfolding of the great migration. This article appeared in the *New York Times* on April 4, 1993.

First Born, Fast Grown: The Manful Life of Nicholas, 10

A fourth-grade classroom on a forbidding stretch on the South Side was in the middle of multiplication tables when a voice over the intercom ordered Nicholas Whitiker to the principal's office. Cory and Darnesha and Roy and Delron and the rest of the class fell silent and stared at Nicholas, sitting sober-faced in the back. "What did I do?" Nicholas thought as he gathered himself to leave. He raced up the hall and down the steps to find his little sister, Ishtar, stranded in the office, nearly swallowed by her purple coat and hat, and principal's aides wanting to know why no one had picked her up from kindergarten.

It was yet another time that the adult world called on Nicholas, a gentle, brooding ten-year- old, to be a man, to answer for the complicated universe he calls family. How could he begin to explain his reality—that his mother, a welfare recipient rearing five young children, was in college trying to become a nurse and so was not home during the day, that Ishtar's father was separated from his mother and in a drug-and-alcohol haze most of the time, that the grandmother he used to live with was at work, and that, besides, he could not possibly account for the man who was supposed to take his sister home—his mother's companion, the father of her youngest child. "My stepfather was supposed to pick her up," he said for simplicity's sake. "I don't know why he's not here."

Nicholas gave the school administrators the name and telephone numbers of his grandmother and an aunt, looked back at Ishtar with a big brother's reassuring half-smile and rushed back to class still worried about whether his sister would make it home O.K.

Of all the men in his family's life, Nicholas is perhaps the most dutiful. When the television picture goes out again, when the three-year-old scratches the four-year old, when their mother, Angela, needs ground beef from the store or the bathroom cleaned or can't find her switch to whip him or the other children, it is Nicholas's name that rings out to fix whatever is wrong. He is nanny, referee, housekeeper, handyman. Some nights he is up past midnight, mopping the floors, putting the children to bed and washing their school clothes in the bathtub. It is a nightly chore: the children have few clothes and wear the same thing every day.

He pays a price. He stays up late and goes to school tired. He brings home mostly mediocre grades. But if the report card is bad, he gets a beating. He is all boy—squirming in line, sliding down banisters, shirt-tail out, shoes untied, dreaming of becoming a fireman so he can save people—but his walk is the stiff slog of a worried father behind on the rent.

He lives with his four younger half-siblings, his mother and her companion, John Mason, on the second floor of a weathered three-family walkup in the perilous and virtually all black Englewood section of Chicago. It is a forlorn landscape of burned-out tenements and long-shuttered storefronts where drunk men hang out on the corner, where gang members command more respect than police officers and where every child can tell you where the crack houses are. The neighborhood is a thriving drug mart. Dealers provide curbside service and residents figure that any white visitor must be a patron or a distributor. Gunshots are as common as rainfall. Eighty people were murdered in the neighborhood last year, more than in Omaha and Pittsburgh combined. Living with fear is second nature. Asked why he liked McDonald's, Nicholas's brother Willie described the restaurant playground with violence as his yardstick. "There's a giant hamburger, and you can go inside of it," Willie said. "And it's made out of steel, so no bullets can't get through."

It is in the middle of all this that Angela Whitiker is rearing her children and knitting together a new life from a world of fast men and cruel drugs. She is a strong-willed, 26-year-old one-time waitress who has seen more than most 70-year olds ever will. A tenth-grade dropout, she was pregnant at 15, bore Nicholas at 16, had her second son at 17, was married at 20, separated at 21 and on crack at 22. In the depths of her addiction, she was a regular at nearby crack houses, doing drugs with gang members, businessmen and, she said, police detectives, sleeping on the floors some nights. In a case of mistaken identity, she once had a gun put to her head. Now she feels she was spared for a reason.

She has worked most of her life, picking okra and butterbeans and cleaning white people's houses as a teenager in Louisiana, bringing home big tips from businessmen when she waited tables at a restaurant in downtown Chicago, selling polish sausages from a food truck by the Dan Ryan Expressway and snow cones at street fairs. She is a survivor who has gone from desperation to redemption, from absent mother to nurturing one, and who now sees economic salvation in nursing. Nicholas sees brand-name gym shoes and maybe a second pair of school pants and toys once she gets a job.

She went through treatment and has stayed away from drugs for two years. Paperback manuals from Alcoholics and Narcotics Anonymous sit without apology on the family bookshelf. A black velvet headdress from church is on the window sill and the Bible is turned to Nehemiah—emblems of her new life as a regular at Faith Temple, a Coptic Christian church on a corner nearby.

For the last year, she has been studying a lot, talking about novels and polynomials and shutting herself in her cramped bedroom to study for something called midterms. That often makes Nicholas the de facto parent for the rest of the children. There is Willie, the eight-year-old with the full-moon face and wide grin who likes it when adults mistake him for Nicholas. There is Ishtar, the dainty five-year-old. There is Emmanuel, four, who worships Nicholas and runs crying to him whenever he gets hurt. And there is Johnathan, three, who is as bad as he is cute and whom everyone calls John-John.

That is just the beginning of the family. There are four fathers in all: Nicholas's father, a disabled laborer who comes around at his own rhythm to check on Nicholas, give him clothes and whip him when he gets bad grades. There is Willie's father, a construction worker whom the children like because he lets them ride in his truck. There is the man their mother married and left, a waiter at a soul food place. He is the father of Ishtar and Emmanuel and is remembered mostly for his beatings and drug abuse.

The man they live with now is Mr. Mason, a truck driver on the night shift, who met their mother at a crack house and bears on his neck the thick scars of a stabbing, a reminder of his former life on the streets. He gets Nicholas up at 3 A.M. to sweep the floor or take out the garbage and makes him hold on to a bench to be whipped when he disobeys.

Unemployment and drugs and violence mean that men may come and go, their mother tells them. "You have a father, true enough, but nothing is guaranteed," she says. "I tell them no man is promised to be in our life forever."

There is an extended family of aunts, an uncle, cousins and their maternal grandmother, Deloris Whitiker, the family lifeboat, whom the children moved in with when drugs took their mother away. To the children, life is not the neat, suburban script of sitcom mythology with father, mother, two kids and a golden retriever. But somehow what has to get done gets done.

When Nicholas brings home poor grades, sometimes three people will show up to talk to the teacher—his mother, his father and his mother's companion. When Nicholas practices his times tables, it might be his mother, his grandmother or Mr. Mason asking him what nine times eight is.

But there is a downside. The family does not believe in sparing the rod and when Nicholas disobeys, half a dozen people figure they are within their rights to whip or chastise him, and do. But he tries to focus on the positive. "It's a good family," he says. "They take care of you. If my mama needs a ride to church, they pick her up. If she needs them to baby-sit, they baby-sit."

It is a gray winter's morning, zero degrees outside, and school starts for everybody in less than half an hour. The children line up, all scarves and coats and legs. The boys bow their heads so their mother, late for class herself, can brush their hair one last time. There is a mad scramble for a lost mitten.

Then she sprays them. She shakes an aerosol can and sprays their heads, their tiny outstretched hands. She sprays them back and front to protect them as they go off to school, facing bullets and gang recruiters and a crazy, dangerous world. It is a special religious oil that smells like drugstore perfume, and the children shut their eyes tight, as she sprays them long and furious so they will come back to her, alive and safe, at day's end.

These are the rules for Angela Whitiker's children, recounted at the Formica-top dining-room table.

"Don't stop off playing," Willie said.

"When you hear shooting, don't stand around—run," Nicholas said.

"Why do I say run?" their mother asked.

"Because a bullet don't have no eyes," the two boys shouted.

"She pray for us every day," Willie said.

Each morning Nicholas and his mother go in separate directions. His mother takes the two little ones to day care on the bus and then heads to class at Kennedy-King College nearby, while Nicholas takes Willie and Ishtar to Banneker Elementary School. The children pass worn houses and denuded lots with junked cars to get to Banneker. Near an alley, unemployed men warm themselves by a trash-barrel fire under a plastic tent. There is a crack house across the street from school.

To Nicholas it is not enough to get Ishtar and Willie to school. He feels he must make sure they're in their seats. "Willie's teacher tell me, 'You don't have to come by here,'" Nicholas said. "I say, 'I'm just checking.'"

Mornings are so hectic that the children sometimes go to school hungry or arrive too late for the free school breakfast that Nicholas says isn't worth rushing for anyway. One bitter cold morning when they made it to breakfast, Nicholas played the daddy as usual, opening a milk carton for Ishtar, pouring it over her cereal, handing her the spoon and saying sternly, "Now eat your breakfast." He began picking over his own cardboard bowl of Corn Pops sitting in vaguely sour milk and remembered the time Willie found a cockroach in his cereal. It's been kind of hard to eat the school breakfast ever since.

Nicholas and Willie on brotherhood:

"He act like he stuck to me," Nicholas said of Willie. "Every time I move somewhere, he want to go. I can't even breathe."

"Well, what are brothers for?" Willie asked.

"To let them breathe and live a long life," Nicholas said. "Every time I get something they want it. I give them what they want after they give me a sad face."

"He saves me all the time" Willie said. "When I'm getting a whooping he says he did it."

"Then I get in trouble" Nicholas said.

"Then I say I did it, too, and we both get a whooping," Willie said. "I save you, too, don't I, Nicholas?"

"Willie's my friend," Nicholas said.

"I'm more than your friend," Willie shot back, a little hurt.

Once Willie almost got shot on the way home from school. He was trailing Nicholas as he usually does when some sixth-grade boys pulled out a gun and started shooting.

"They were right behind Willie," Nicholas said. "I kept calling him to go across the street. Then he heard the shots and ran."

Nicholas shook his head. "I be pulling on his hood but he be so slow," he said.

"Old slowpoke," Ishtar said, chiming in.

In this neighborhood, few parents let their children outside to play or visit a friend's house. It is too dangerous. "You don't have any friends," Nicholas's mother fells him. "You don't have no homey. I'm your homey."

So Nicholas and his siblings usually head straight home. They live in a large, barren apartment with chipped tile floors and hand-me-down furniture, a space their mother tries to spruce up with her children's artwork.

The children spend their free time with the only toy they have—a Nintendo game that their mother saved up for and got them for Christmas. The television isn't working right, though, leaving a picture so dark the children have to turn out all the lights and sit inches from the set to see the cartoon Nintendo figure flicker over walls to save the princess.

Dinner is what their mother has time to make between algebra and Faith Temple. Late for church one night, she pounded on the stove to make the burners flare up, set out five plastic blue plates and apportioned the canned spaghetti and pan-fried bologna. "Come and get your dinner before the roaches beat you to it!" she yelled with her own urban gallows humor.

Faith Temple is a tiny storefront church in what used to be a laundry. It is made up mostly of two or three clans, including Nicholas's, and practices a homegrown version of Ethiopian-derived Christianity. At the front of the spartan room with white walls and metal folding chairs, sits a phalanx of regal, black-robed women with foot-high, rhinestone-studded headdresses. They are called empresses, supreme empresses, and imperial empresses. They include Nicholas's mother, aunt and grandmother, and they sing and testify and help calm flushed parishioners, who sometimes stomp and wail with the holy spirit.

The pastor is Prophet Titus. During the week he is Albert Lee, a Chicago bus driver, but on Sundays he dispenses stern advice and $35 blessings to his congregation of mostly single mothers and their children. "Just bringing children to the face of the earth is not enough," Prophet Titus intones. "You owe them more."

Nicholas's job during church is to keep the younger children quiet, sometimes with a brother asleep on one thigh and a cousin on the other. Their mother keeps watch from her perch up front where she sings. When the little ones get too loud, their mother shoots them a threatening look from behind the microphone that says, "You know better."

On this weeknight, Nicholas and Willie are with cousins and other children listening to their grandmother's Bible lesson. She is a proud woman who worked for 22 years as a meat wrapper at a supermarket, reared five children of her own, has stepped in to help raise some of her grandchildren and packs a 38 in her purse in case some stranger tries to rob her again. On Sundays and during Bible class, she is not merely Nicholas's grandmother but Imperial Empress Magdala in her velvet-collared cape.

The children recite Bible verses ("I am black but beautiful," from Song of Solomon or "My skin is black," from Job), and then Mrs. Whitiker breaks into a free-form lecture that seems a mix of black pride and Dianetics. "Be dignified," she told the children. "Walk like a prince or princess. We're about obeying our parents and staying away from people who don't mean us any good."

The boys got home late that night, but their day was not done. "Your clothes are in the tub," their mother said, pointing to the bathroom, "and the kitchen awaits you."

"I know my baby's running out of hands," she said under her breath.

This is not the life Nicholas envisions for himself when he grows up. He has thought about this, and says he doesn't want any kids. Well, maybe a boy, one boy he can play ball with and show how to be a man. Definitely not a girl. "I don't want no girl who'll have four or five babies," he said. "I don't want no big family with 14, 20 people, all these people to take care of. When you broke they still ask you for money, and you have to say, 'I'm broke. I don't have no money.'"

Ishtar made it home safely the afternoon Nicholas was called to the principal's office. Mr. Mason was a couple of hours late picking her up, but he came through in the end. Nicholas worries anyway, the way big brothers do. He worried the morning his mother had an early test and he had to take the little ones to day care before going to school himself. John-John began to cry as Nicholas walked away. Nicholas bent down and hugged him and kissed him. Everything, Nicholas assured him, was going to be O.K.

Nancy Gibbs is a senior editor at *Time*. A longer version of this article appeared in *Time* on May 7, 1999.

Massacre at Columbine High School

High school is a haunted house in April, when seniors act up because the end is near. Even those who hate it sometimes cling to the devil they know. And for the kids who love it, the goodbyes are hard to think about. Two weeks ago, Sara Martin was chosen to be a graduation speaker for Columbine High, and she was struggling. She wanted to write about all the people she loved, in the choir and the Bible club and even the ones who turn left out of the right-hand lane in the parking lot.

"I have loved oysters at 7 in the morning in the teachers' lounge with Mme. Lutz and the halls that smelled like rotting Easter eggs," she wrote. "I have loved fire drills and Tai Chi on the lawn with Mr. Kritzer's philosophy class. I have loved you and our moments of folly together. . . ." And she wondered how to capture the spirit, "the humanity and integrity that walk the halls of our very own Columbine."

She was in the choir room last Tuesday when something very different was walking the halls. By the end of the day, by the time fifteen people had died, her friends among them, she had her yearbook of humanity and integrity signed in blood. As Dylan Klebold and Eric Harris prowled the school with their guns and bombs, this is what the children did: a boy draped himself over his sister and her friend, so that he would be the one shot. A boy with ten bullet wounds in his leg picked up an explosive that landed by him and hurled it away from the other wounded kids. Others didn't want to leave their dying teacher when the SWAT team finally came: Can't we carry him out on a folded-up table? A girl was asked by the gunman if she believed in God, knowing full well the safe answer. "There is a God," she said quietly, "and you need to follow along God's path." The shooter looked down at her. "There is no God," he said, and he shot her in the head.

Before we inventory the evil we cannot fathom, consider the reflexes at work among these happy, lucky kids, born to a generation that is thought to know nothing about sacrifice. They had no way of knowing what would be asked of them, what they were capable of. Among the kids who died and the ones who were prepared to die were the students who stayed behind to open a door, or save a friend, or build an escape route or barricade a closet or guide the descending SWAT teams into the darkness.

The story of the slaughter at Columbine High School opened a sad national conversation about what turned two boys' souls into poison. It promises to be a long, hard talk, in public and in private, about why smart, privileged kids rot inside. Do we blame the parents, blame the savage music they listened to, blame the ease of stockpiling an arsenal, blame the chemistry of cruelty and cliques that has always been a part of high school life but has never been so deadly? Among the many things that did not survive the week was the hymn all parents unconsciously sing as they send their children out in the morning, past the headlines, to their schools: It can't happen here Lord, no, it could never happen here. . . .

It was Free Cookie Day in the cafeteria, and there were hundreds of students draped around the tables and waiting in lines at the 11:30 lunch hour when the sounds of the firing erupted outside. Some kids thought it was the long-awaited senior prank; they had been expecting balloons filled with shaving cream. Surely those are firecrackers, they thought. Surely those guns are fake. Is the blood fake? Can a fake bomb make walls shake? Then they were screaming and running. One boy could feel the rush of a bullet past his head.

"Get down!" the janitor yelled. "Get under a table!" They dove for cover, then began crawling—under furniture, over backpacks, slithering toward the stairs. Then they ran as the shots came again. "We heard boom after boom," says sophomore Jody Clouse. "The floor was shaking from the explosions." Bullets clanged as they bounced off metal lockers. Some tried to run upstairs, to the safety of the library. But there was smoke everywhere, the fire alarms had gone off, and the sprinkler system was turning the school into a blinding, misty jungle.

Business teacher Dave Sanders was in the faculty lounge when he heard the trouble, raced toward the cafeteria and went to war. "He screamed for us to get down and shut up," says freshman Kathy Carlston. "We crawled on the floor and made it to the stairs." When the firing began again, they got up and started to run. Sanders, on the ground, propped himself on his elbows, directing kids to safety as the killers moved in.

Lexis Coffey-Berg, 16, saw Sanders running toward them, saw him shot twice in the back, with a jolt and spasm. "You could see the impact," she says. "You could see it go through his body. He was spitting up blood." He stumbled into a classroom, blood streaming from his chest, and collapsed over the desk, knocking out his teeth. A teacher got the paramedics on the phone, and the classroom turned into a trauma ward. Boys stripped off their shirts to make pillows for Sanders' head and bandages for the bloody holes in his torso. They found some emergency blankets stashed with the fire gear in that room and wrapped him up as his temperature started to fall. "I can't breathe," he murmured. "I've got to go." But they kept talking to him, pulled his wallet out of his pocket and held up the pictures of his daughters. Tell us about them, they said. They made a sign with the dry-erase board and held it up in the window for the rescuers to see: HELP, BLEEDING TO DEATH. But the time kept passing, and no one came. "I don't think I'm going to make it," Sanders said.

In the end, the killers did their deadliest work in the school's quiet place, the best place to find people in a school when finals are looming and everyone worries about getting term papers done on time.

The killers went round the library, asking people why they should let them live. Students heard one girl pleading for her life, then a shot, and quiet. They told wounded kids to quit crying, it will all be over soon, you'll all be dead. They approached another girl, cowering under a table, yelled "Peekaboo!" and shot her in the neck. Anyone who cried or moaned was shot again. Survivors said they treated it like a video game. "We've waited to do this a long time," they said. At one point one of the gunmen recognized a student and said, "Oh, I know you—you can go." And then, "We're out of ammo . . . gotta reload. We'll come back to get you three." Before they directed their last two shots into their own heads, the killers fired off an estimated nine hundred rounds, using two sawed-off shotguns, a 9-mm semiautomatic carbine and a TEC-DC 9 semiautomatic handgun.

The hardest thing about the search for an explanation was the growing fear there might not be one. There would be lots of talk about the venomous culture that these boys soaked in—but many kids drink those waters without turning into mass murderers. There would be talk of deep family dysfunction, something in their past or their present, but nothing in the first days of archaeology turned up anything tidy that explained something so massively wrong. The Klebolds were the kind of parents who came to all the Little League and soccer games. They even came to practices.

By the time the memorial services had been held and the flowers piled up in the soft spring snow in the parking lot, the recriminations were well under way. How could parents not know their garage was a bomb-making factory? How could a school not know the hatred in its halls was more than routine teenage alienation? Why had the SWAT team members been so cautious when people were trapped and bleeding to death? What if their kids had been inside?

In the meantime, the survivors were left with their fear and grief. The grocery stores ran out of cellophane cones of flowers. Prom pictures became obituary shots. A bunch of kids went out to dinner at Applebee's Thursday night. Everyone stared. "They knew we were kids from Columbine," says junior Scott Schulte. "No one said anything. Then a waitress dropped a booster chair. We all jumped."

Sara Martin has come to her own conclusions. The graduation speaker now hopes she won't have to speak at all. "When those guys walked into the hallways in their trench coats, with their guns and their bombs, they brought in fear and hate and pushed out everything else—every ounce of life." In its place, students planted crosses: four pink ones for the girls, nine blue ones for the boys—and two black ones, set apart, for the killers.

This article was reported from Colorado by Julie Grace, S. C. Gwynne, Maureen Harrington, David S. Jackson, Jeffrey Shapiro, and Richard Woodbury.

Deborah Tannen is university professor and professor of linguistics at Georgetown University in Washington, D.C. Her eighteen books include *You Just Don't Understand: Women and Men in Conversation*; *Talking from 9 to 5: Women and Men in the Workplace*; *The Argument Culture: Stopping America's War of Words*; and *I Only Say This Because I Love You*.

Gender in the Classroom

When my book You Just Don't Understand *was published, it surprised everyone, myself above all, by becoming a bestseller. That reader response forced me to think more deeply about the persuasive implications of gender-related patterns of communication. This essay, which appeared in the* Chronicle of Higher Education *under the headline "Teachers' Classroom Strategies," reflects some of that deeper thinking, as it applied to my own teaching.*

When I researched and wrote my latest book, *You Just Don't Understand: Women and Men in Conversation*, the furthest thing from my mind was reevaluating my teaching strategies. But that has been one of the direct benefits of having written the book.

The primary focus of my linguistic research always has been the language of everyday conversation. One facet of this is conversational style: how different regional, ethnic, and class backgrounds, as well as age and gender, result in different ways of using language to communicate. *You Just Don't Understand* is about the conversational styles of women and men. As I gained more insight into typically male and female ways of using language, I began to suspect some of the causes of the troubling facts that women who go to single-sex schools do better in later life, and that when young women sit next to young men in classrooms, the males talk more. This is not to say that all men talk in class, nor that no women do. It is simply that a greater percentage of discussion time is taken by men's voices.

The research of sociologists and anthropologists such as Janet Lever, Marjorie Harness Goodwin, and Donna Eder has shown that girls and boys learn to use language differently in their sex-separate peer groups. Typically, a girl has a best friend with whom she sits and talks, frequently telling secrets. It's the telling of secrets, the fact and the way that they talk to each other, that makes them best friends. For boys, activities are central: Their best friends are the ones they do things with. Boys also tend to play in larger groups that are hierarchical. High-status boys give orders and push low-status boys around. So boys are expected to use language to seize center stage: by exhibiting their skill, displaying their knowledge, and challenging and resisting challenges.

These patterns have stunning implications for classroom interaction. Most faculty members assume that participating in class discussion is a necessary part of successful performance. Yet speaking in a classroom is more congenial to boys' language experience than to girls', since it entails putting oneself forward in front of a large group of people, many of whom are strangers and at least one of whom is sure to judge speakers' knowledge and intelligence by their verbal display.

Another aspect of many classrooms that makes them more hospitable to most men than to most women is the use of debate-like formats as a learning tool. Our educational system, as Walter Ong argues persuasively in his book *Fighting for Life* (Cornell University Press, 1981), is fundamentally male in that the pursuit of knowledge is believed to be achieved by ritual opposition: public display followed by argument and challenge. Father Ong demonstrates that ritual opposition—what he calls "adversativeness" or "agonism"—is fundamental to the way most males approach almost any activity. (Consider, for example, the little boy who shows he likes a little girl by pulling her braids and shoving her.) But ritual opposition is antithetical to the way most females learn and like to interact. It is not that females don't fight, but that they don't fight for fun. They don't *ritualize* opposition.

Anthropologists working in widely disparate parts of the world have found contrasting verbal rituals for women and men. Women in completely unrelated cultures (for example, Greece and Bali) engage in ritual laments: spontaneously produced rhyming couplets that express their pain, for example, over the loss of loved ones. Men do not take part in laments. They have their own, very different verbal ritual: a contest, a war of words in which they vie with each other to devise clever insults.

When discussing these phenomena with a colleague, I commented that I see these two styles in American conversation: Many women bond by talking about troubles, and many men bond by exchanging playful insults and put-downs, and other sorts of verbal sparring. He exclaimed: "I never thought of this, but that's the way I teach: I have students read an article, and then I invite them to tear it apart. After we've torn it to shreds, we talk about how to build a better model."

This contrasts sharply with the way I teach: I open the discussion of readings by asking, "What did you find useful in this? What can we use in our own theory building and our own methods?" I note what I see as weaknesses in the author's approach, but I also point out that the writer's discipline and purposes might be different from ours. Finally, I offer personal anecdotes illustrating the phenomena under discussion and praise students' anecdotes as well as their critical acumen.

These different teaching styles must make our classrooms wildly different places and hospitable to different students. Male students are more likely to be comfortable attacking the readings and might find the inclusion of personal anecdotes irrelevant and "soft." Women are more likely to resist discussion they perceive as hostile, and, indeed, it is women in my classes who are most likely to offer personal anecdotes.

A colleague who read my book commented that he had always taken for granted that the best way to deal with students' comments is to challenge them: this, he felt it was self-evident, sharpens their minds and helps them develop debating skills. But he had noticed that women were relatively silent in his classes, so he decided to try beginning discussion with relatively open-ended questions and letting comments go unchallenged. He found, to his amazement and satisfaction, that more women began to speak up.

Though some of the women in his class clearly liked this better, perhaps some of the men liked it less. One young man in my class wrote in a question-naire about a history professor who gave students questions to think about and called on people to answer them: "He would then play devil's advocate . . . i.e., he debated us. . . . That class *really* sharpened me intellectually. . . . We as students do need to know how to defend ourselves." This young man valued the experience of being attacked and challenged publicly. Many, if not most, women would shrink from such a "challenge," experiencing it as a public humiliation.

A professor at Hamilton College told me of a young man who was upset because he felt his class presentation had been a failure. The professor was puzzled because he had observed that class members had listened attentively and agreed with the student's observations. It turned out that it was this very agreement that the student interpreted as failure: Since no one had engaged his ideas by arguing with him, he felt they had found them unworthy of attention.

So one reason men speak in class more than women is that many of them find the "public" classroom setting more conducive to speaking, whereas most women are more comfortable speaking in private to a small group of people they know well. A second reason is that men are more likely to be comfortable with the debate-like form that discussion may take. Yet another reason is the different attitudes toward speaking in class that typify women and men.

Students who speak frequently in class, many of whom are men, assume that it is their job to think of contributions and try to get the floor to express them. But many women monitor their participation not only to get the floor but to avoid getting it. Women students in my class tell me that if they have spoken up once or twice, they hold back for the rest of the class because they don't want to dominate. If they have spoken a lot one week, they will remain silent the next. These different ethics of participation are, of course, unstated, so those who speak freely assume that those who remain silent have nothing to say, and those who are reining themselves in assume that the big talkers are selfish and hoggish.

When I looked around my classes, I could see these differing ethics and habits at work. For example, my graduate class in analyzing conversation had twenty students, eleven women and nine men. Of the men, four were foreign students: two Japanese, one Chinese, and one Syrian. With the exception of the three Asian men, all the men spoke in class at least occasionally. The biggest talker in the class was a woman, but there were also five women who never spoke at all, only one of whom was Japanese. I decided to try something different.

I broke the class into small groups to discuss the issues raised in the readings and to analyze their own conversational transcripts. I devised three ways of dividing the students into groups: one by the degree program they were in, one by gender, and one by conversational style, as closely as I could guess it. This meant that when the class was grouped according to conversational style, I put Asian students together, fast talkers together, and quiet students together. The class split into groups six times during the semester, so they met in each grouping twice. I told students to regard the groups as examples of interactional data and to note the different ways in which they participated in the different groups. Toward the end of the term, I gave them a questionnaire asking about their class and group participation.

I could see plainly from my observation of the groups at work that women who never opened their mouths in class were talking away in the small groups. In fact, the Japanese woman commented that she found it particularly hard to contribute to the all-woman group she was in because "I was overwhelmed by how talkative the female students were in the female-only group." This is particularly revealing because it highlights that the same person who can be "oppressed" into silence in one context can become the talkative "oppressor" in another. No one's conversational style is absolute; everyone's style changes in response to the context and others' styles.

Some of the students (seven) said they preferred the same-gender groups; others preferred the same-style groups. In answer to the question "Would you have liked to speak in class more than you did?" six of the seven who said yes were women; the one man was Japanese. Most startlingly, this response did not come only from quiet women; it came from women who had indicated they had spoken in class never, rarely, sometimes and often. Of the eleven students who said the amount they had spoken was fine, seven were men. Of the four women who checked, "fine," two added qualifications indicating it wasn't completely fine: One wrote in "maybe more," and one wrote, "I have an urge to participate often but feel I should have something more interesting/relevant/wonderful/intelligent to say!"

I counted my experiment a success. Everyone in the class found the small groups interesting, and no one indicated he or she would have preferred that the class not break into groups. Perhaps most instructive, however, was the fact that the experience of breaking into groups, and of talking about partici-pation in class, raised everyone's awareness about classroom participation. After we had talked about it, some of the quietest women in the class made a few voluntary contributions, though sometimes I had to insure their participa-tion by interrupting the students who were exuberantly speaking out.

Americans are often proud that they discount the significance of cultural differences: "We're all individuals," many people boast. Ignoring such issues as gender and ethnicity becomes a source of pride: "I treat everyone the same." But treating people the same is not equal treatment if they are not the same.

The classroom is a different environment for those who feel comfortable putting themselves forward in a group than it is for those who find the pros-pect of doing so chastening, or even terrifying. When a professor asks, "Are there any questions?," students who can formulate statements the fastest have the greatest opportunity to respond. Those who need significant time to do so have not really been given a chance at all, since by the time they are ready to speak, someone else has taken the floor.

In a class where some students speak out without raising hands, those who feel they must raise their hands and wait to be recognized do not have equal opportunity to speak. Telling them to feel free to jump in will not make them feel free; one's sense of timing, of one's rights and obligations in a classroom, are automatic, learned over years of interaction. They may be changed over time, with motivation and effort, but they cannot be changed on the spot. And everyone assumes his or her own way is best. When I asked my students how the class could be changed to make it easier for them to speak more, the most talkative woman said she would prefer it if no one had to raise hands, and a foreign student said he wished people would raise their hands and wait to be recognized.

My experience in this class has convinced me that small-group interaction should be part of any class that is not a small seminar. I also am convinced that having the students become observers of their own interaction is a crucial part of their education. Talking about ways of talking in class makes students aware that their ways of talking affect other students, that the motivations they impute to others may not truly reflect others' motives, and that the behaviors they assume to be self-evidently right are not universal norms.

The goal of complete equal opportunity in class may not be attainable, but realizing that one monolithic classroom-participation structure is not equal opportunity is itself a powerful motivation to find more diverse methods to serve diverse students—and every classroom is diverse.

Jonathan Alter is a senior editor and columnist at *Newsweek*. These articles appeared in *Newsweek*.

Cop-Out on Class: Why Private Schools Are Today's Draft Deferments

(JULY 21, 1995)

I'm a part of the so-called "overclass"—and so are my bosses and many of my colleagues at *Newsweek* and elsewhere in the national media. There's no point in denying it. Whether by birth, effort, ability, luck or some combination, we are more successful and have more options than most Americans, and that inevitably pulls us away from the lives they lead. Neither eating pork rinds (George Bush) nor boasting of humble origins (Bill Clinton) can erase that fact for politicians any more than it can for the rest of the overprivileged. The object should be to achieve consciousness of class, then work hard to make the divisions it creates smaller instead of larger.

Until the 1970s, race was the rage in public debate. Class remained almost a secret—discussed in private and delineated by taste but subsumed in the assumption growing out of World War II that everyone except the very rich and the very poor was part of the great American Middle.

Exposing the existence of an overclass began in places like *The Washington Monthly*, a little political magazine. One day in 1970 the wife of the editor, Charlie Peters, was in a bookstore and overheard a hip-looking young man discussing the Vietnam draft. "Let those hillbillies go get shot," he said. When Beth Peters told her husband about the comment, Charlie turned the line into a cause: to convey to American elites the emergence of an unthinking and dangerous class bias in their ranks. Working-class Americans knew that Vietnam, unlike earlier wars in this century, had become a rich man's war and a poor boy's fight. But the people who ran the country hadn't yet faced up to the price of that division.

Five years later, a young *Washington Monthly* editor named James Fallows drove home the point by graphically describing his feelings of guilt after he starved himself at Harvard in order to flunk the physical for the draft. The widely reprinted article, entitled "What Did You Do in the Class War, Daddy?" angered many veterans, but it kicked off some serious soul-searching among baby boomers about their anti-military, anti-blue-collar bias.

Unfortunately, the chasm remained. I was too young for Vietnam (and never enlisted). But by the time I joined *The Washington Monthly* in 1981, my generation was beginning to face its own less bloody yet no less serious class issue: public education. To deny the existence of a class problem in the United States is to ignore the flight from public schools by perpetually anxious, upwardly mobile parents trying to cover their bets on their children's future.

I know the feeling, as my parents did before me. Starting in kindergarten, I attended the finest, most diverse private schools and have good memories of them. Yet the fact remains that private schools stand apart from society. They can compensate for that apartness with scholarships and good works but never fully bridge the gap from what America, in its Jeffersonian ideal, is supposed to be. I heard recently that at the tony St. Albans School in Washington, D.C.—alma mater of Vice President Gore—some teachers will tell a badly behaving student that if he doesn't shape up he may have to ship out to public school. They make it sound almost like going to Vietnam.

My wife and I have chosen public schools for our children in part because of the eagerness with which other parents we know are abandoning them. Instead of organizing to fix the public schools, they nearly bankrupt themselves escaping, often without even personal visits to see whether their assumptions might be wrong. Here's where race comes in. When they say "bad" they usually mean "black," even if they won't admit it. The result is often overclass children who aren't educated in a larger sense—who don't know their own community and country. They are what my wife calls "underdeprived" kids. They think the world owes them a nice vacation. I know. When I was 12, I was like that, too.

Does this mean our three children will never go to private school? No. Children should not have to sacrifice their education to their parents' principles. If the public schools in our area fail—either generally or for our particular children—we'll be gone. But in the meantime we should stay awhile and fight—for high standards, for choice and for accountability. (Beyond safety, a great advantage of private schools is that they can more easily fire bad teachers and administrators.) The single biggest reason for the decline of American public education is that so many capable and committed parents have opted out. That in itself is a bad lesson for their children.

Even if they don't send their kids to public schools, successful people should invest time there. Call it the case for Overclass Hypocrisy. "If you feel the public schools can't be changed in the time your kids are that age," says Charlie Peters, "you should take on an extra burden to make sure that the next parents coming along don't have that excuse." My own parents anticipated that point. After putting their children through private school, they now volunteer in Chicago's inner-city public schools.

To really break down class divisions, we need a draft that would require every young person to serve either in the military or in the community. John F. Kennedy went to private schools, but he shared a PT boat during World War II with a mechanic and a fisherman. That doesn't happen much today. While some overclass parents make a commendable effort to see that their children meet people from different backgrounds, this risks being just another resume entry. And many others actually believe that it is supremely important to introduce their children to more People Like Us—to create social shelters instead of real communities.

Ambition for yourself and for your kids is good; it's what makes the country go. But what really matters is how you view the rungs below, and how you use all of the extra choices you have for a purpose broader than getting into Princeton. The best answer to American elites is not to bash them or indulge in reverse snobbery. It's to pull them (us) into the great work of the country.

It's a Wonderful Legacy

(JULY 14, 1997)

Two of Jimmy Stewart's classic characters helped change how we view our politics—and ourselves.

When "Mr. Smith Goes to Washington" premiered in the capital, in 1939, about a third of the audience of dignitaries stormed out. "Not all senators are sons of bitches," fumed one senator. "It stinks," said another. Sen. George Norris, himself a Mr. Smith type, said of Jimmy Stewart's character: "I've been in Congress for 36 years, and I've never seen a member as dumb as that boy." In his memoirs, Frank Capra recalled how "hopping-mad Washington press correspondents belittled, berated, scorned, vilified and ripped me open from stem to stern" for having portrayed them as "too fond of the juice of the grape." Joseph P. Kennedy tried to keep the movie from being released in Europe. Bad for morale, he said.

When Capra first pitched Stewart on the role of George Bailey for "It's a Wonderful Life," the director was briefly seized by self-doubt: "This is the lousiest piece of cheese I ever heard of," he thought. Ticket sales in 1947 were so lackluster that Capra had to place his production company in bankruptcy. James Agee compared the movie to "A Christmas Carol," but many other critics savaged it. "A figment of pure Pollyanna platitudes," said the *New York Times*. The *New Republic* accused the film of trying "to convince audiences that American life is exactly like the *Saturday Evening Post* covers of Norman Rockwell."

A half-century later, these movies lie deep in the marrow of America. For all his acting brilliance in Hitchcock films and Westerns, Jimmy Stewart's most lasting contribution lies in two unforgettable roles. Sen. Jefferson Smith changed how we view our politics; George Bailey of Bedford Falls changed how we view ourselves.

"Mr. Smith" is now the premier allegory for idealism in Washington. That's good for inspiring integrity and resistance to special interests. Unfortunately, sanctimonious showboats pretending to be Mr. Smith now use the once rare filibuster as a parliamentary gimmick to defend pork at home. And the film's cartoonish qualities make it harder to see that complexity plays a larger role in politics than venality. Even so, Jeff Smith holds out the promise of using smarts (in the form of Jean Arthur) and shame to reclaim innocence. That's a powerful idea in a cynical world. By emblazoning those terms of debate on the consciousness of the American public, Capra and Stewart at least give virtue in politics a fighting chance.

"It's a Wonderful Life" is far darker than any Norman Rockwell picture and, with its dissection of the local power structure, far more socially conscious than most movies today. And it's not truly sentimental, a word that suggests a cheap, easy way into the heart. Like Jeff Smith, George Bailey is a much angrier man than the casual viewer may remember. "Will I ever get out of this crummy Bedford Falls?" he laments, as he sacrifices his ambitions for college and travel to fulfill responsibilities at home. He's prone to self-pity, not to mention the selfishness of suicide. But with the help of Clarence the angel, George comes to the central insights necessary for living happily in this country: a good man is a great man, friendship is the real wealth, no one is born a failure.

Most art challenges middle-class values. That is one if its important functions. But art can also illuminate and make precious what we take for granted. Jimmy Stewart managed to inhabit abstract ideas like democracy and community and make them real for millions. This didn't just tell us about ourselves; it made us try to be better, which is no small legacy for any man.

The Era of Bad Feeling

This article appeared in Newsweek *in December 1998, immediately following the vote in the House of Representatives to impeach President Clinton, and gives a flavor of the national mood at that time.*

And we are here as on a darkling plain
Swept with confused alarms of struggle and flight
Where ignorant armies clash by night
     Matthew Arnold, "Dover Beach," 1851

The history of the 1990s, so peaceful and prosperous for most Americans, will be of "ignorant armies" sounding "confused alarms" over nothing much at all. Bill Clinton is a sad and compelling human specimen who will be remembered as a cross between William McKinley (popular president in relatively placid times) and Andrew Johnson (railroaded by Radical Republicans). His impeachment was history as farce without the laughs. His foreign policy looked like a game of toy soldiers. His universe, at the end of the year, feels small, surreal and a bit scary.

Where was the grandeur? Where was the majesty? While most of America shopped for Christmas, Washington, D.C., on Saturday, December 19, 1998—a day that will live in inanity—felt like the set of a bad Peter Sellers movie. In the morning, Speaker-to-be Bob Livingston quit, a de facto admission that pornographer Larry Flynt was running the country. In early afternoon, the president of the United States was impeached for denying that he touched Monica Lewinsky "with the intent to sexually arouse" and for trying to get his secretary to clean up his mess. In late afternoon, Clinton and his fellow Democrats attempted, for the first time ever, to "spin" utter political humiliation—and it may even have worked. In the evening, the commander in chief committed the United States to a long-term, open-ended policy of occasionally irritating Saddam Hussein.

This year was the culmination of an American culture war that has been nasty, brutish and long. Leonard Garment, Richard Nixon's lawyer, was once asked why so many people hated Clinton with such intensity. "Because he represents the '60s," Garment said. The golfing Southern back-slapper with the cheatin' heart is actually a figure more out of the 1950s, but Garment had a point. As the *Wall Street Journal* editorial page inadvertently confirmed, Ken Starr was prosecuting not just Bill Clinton but "the generation that produced him." What makes Republicans especially frustrated about the events of 1998 is that the cultural war is over—and the '60s sexual revolution won. The biggest surprise of the whole year is that Clinton's approval rating has stayed high—well above Ronald Reagan's in his second term—for the duration. Puritanism, once the deepest impulse in the American character, is now a minor strain. We're not quite France yet, but we're getting there.

So having lost the war, the GOP stopped at nothing to win a big battle. Any potential defectors knew they risked losing their committee chairs and other perks. Members of the House were urged to vote their consciences—as long as their consciences didn't dictate censure, which would have won easily had it been an option. Rep. Tom Lantos, who escaped Hungary in 1947 after working in both the anti-Nazi and the anti-Communist underground, was practically shaking with rage when I saw him coming off the floor after an eloquent speech. "What distinguishes this House from the fake parliaments of police states is not voting—they all vote—but procedural fairness." To his GOP colleagues, he said: "I would defend their right to vote their conscience with my life if necessary. I find it unbelievable that they won't defend mine."

Beyond the sins of the president and Congress lie the media's many transgressions. In print, never have so many trees died to say so little. On TV, the air pollution was more toxic than ever this year. Clinton complains about "the politics of personal destruction," but he could just as easily focus on "personal distraction"—a major ailment in our celebrity-addled age. Of course, the press, which for years has enjoyed doing stories about politicians' private lives, is not solely responsible for today's sexual Armageddon. Politics and the law have been sexualized by politicians and lawyers; they are central to any disarmament, too.

The consequences of this era of bad feeling will be felt for years by the president, the Congress and the press. All have been demythologized in unhealthy ways. Clinton's squalid behavior helped strip his office of much of its grandeur. The Oval Office and the Lincoln Bedroom will never be viewed in quite the same light again. The House of Representatives has taken the solemn, even inspirational, bipartisan process of 1974 and turned it into just another blunt political instrument. All future attacks on future presidents will quickly descend into talk of impeachment, further debasing our currency of outrage. In fact, the I word is already losing its sting.

Meanwhile, in the real America, people are scratching their heads—and not just over why Henry Hyde and Bob Livingston seem to get all the girls. As Washington implodes, most people's lives are better reflected in the first line of Matthew Arnold's poem: "The sea is calm tonight." Even as real bombs fell on Iraq and rhetorical ones on Washington, 1998 was—by relative historical standards—tranquil. The cleavages are deeper in the Congress than in the country. Ideology is in decline. No matter what fate befalls Bill Clinton—no matter how loud our gauche Gotterdammerung—this will always be seen as a transitional era between the fall of the Berlin wall and whatever overarching global drama comes next. We are cursed to live in interesting and bitter times, but not deeply consequential ones.

Jim Hoagland is associate editor and senior foreign correspondent of the *Washington Post*. He was awarded Pulitzer Prizes for international reporting in 1971 and for commentary in 1991. These essays appeared in the *Washington Post*.

Two of a Kind

(APRIL 11, 1999)

The words can be the least important piece of interviewing a national leader. The music—the mists that emanate from the Great One, the body language, the evasions or unexpected silences—is more reliable. Essence lives on after The Chief's carefully groomed phrases drift off to the journalistic boneyard.

Fidel Castro remains vivid for me as a human fog machine. Moammar Gadhafi is the painting of evil Dorian Gray keeps hidden away. François Mitterrand was a feline, arched back and claws at the ready. Mikhail Gorbachev's angry flush when challenged on his imprisonment of a dissident outlives his buried presidential promises to fix communism and stay in Eastern Europe.

So it is with the two brutal despots bombed by the United States in separate air wars: the Serb Slobodan Milosevic and the Iraqi Saddam Hussein. U.S. rockets, and a mutual addiction to violence as the political tool of choice, unite them. Little else does, except for this: When I interviewed them fifteen years apart in their national capitals, one common characteristic sprang from each conversation that helps explain why Slobo and Saddam now wear bull's-eyes on their chests. Each man treated any mention of his opponents as an insult to his very presence. Each responded as if he were being accused of kicking at a snarling stray dog.

Without saying the word "subhuman," Milosevic in January 1990 made me understand that the Kosovars were in his view exactly that. They were not worthy of being in a question put to him.

His crude dismissal of the ethnic Albanians jerked me back to the segregationist American South of my childhood—except Milosevic's barbs outdid anything Strom Thurmond said in the 1950s. They were closer to what I heard in Baghdad when I asked Saddam about the rebellious Kurdish tribes of the Iraqi north in 1975. Saddam sat like a coiled boa constrictor of enormous size and violence behind the desk that separated us. He spoke as from a great distance, brazenly lying about what I had just seen in Kurdistan. We argued and parted, and I was not surprised when he launched a campaign of genocide and ethnic cleansing against the Kurds or when he brutally invaded Kuwait. Milosevic, more ferret than snake, circled each question anew, no matter how banal. He was the victim in this interview, squinting warily through a haze of cigarette smoke, a stoppered bottle of nitroglycerin about to tip over.

These two men have unleashed savagery from which the international community cannot avert its eyes. The reasons are more complex than the music of racism each played for me. In those reasons may lie a clue about the chances of bombing Milosevic into the submission Saddam defiantly resists. Slobo and Saddam are rulers whose countries, dreams and social systems were crashing down on their heads long before American bombs began to fall. They and their followers—the Serbs of ex-Yugoslavia, the Sunni Arabs who are a quarter of Iraq's population—are the "victims" of their countrymen and of history, which reaches out to oppress them anew.

"There is one type of fear more devastating in its impact than any other: the systemic fear that arises when a state begins to collapse," writes Michael Ignatieff in *Blood and Belonging*, his penetrating book on nationalism. "Ethnic hatred is the result of the terror that arises when legitimate authority disintegrates." Fear is cause and effect for both dictators. They inflict terror on others to calm the rising terror among their own—who must also submit to a reign of blood and steel for their own good. They fight to control the local police station more than the national parliament. "See? They hate you," Slobo or Saddam says to his populace as the bombs fall. "Only I can protect you from a world gone mad—or at least, get revenge for you." In the ruins of pan-Slavism and pan-Arabism, and of communism and Arab socialism, only atavistic tribal links remain.

A quarter-century of Saddam-watching convinces me that he goes to the extreme of his murderous logic. His people have failed him in wars against Kurds, Iranians, Kuwaitis and Americans. The Sunnis, unable to complete his great mission of rescuing them, deserve to perish, too. To expect Saddam to negotiate seriously because sanctions or bombing hurt his people is to misunderstand a man who does not trust or value negotiating skills. His is truly a kill-or-be-killed world. Is Milosevic different? The nations of NATO will find out only by pursuing their air campaign with a relentlessness and patience that shows Milosevic he cannot export his people's terror to others. If he persists, he will leave NATO no option but to take Kosovo from him by an allied ground offensive.

This cannot be done successfully without great awareness of how heavy a task bringing order to the Balkans will be. Consider these battlefront words from a cub reporter: "Nearly half a million refugees are in Macedonia now. How they are to be fed nobody knows, but in the next month all the Christian world will hear the cry: Come over into Macedonia and help us!" The dispatch was published in the *Toronto Daily Star*. The reporter was Ernest Hemingway. The date was October 20, 1922.

Truly a Nation . . .

(JULY 4, 1999)

A society reveals its values as well as its age through the choice of a national birthday. For many Americans it is simply The Fourth. Frenchmen have their Bastille Day. The phlegmatic of the world, such as the British, avoid revolutionary reminiscing altogether. They make the monarch's birthday or some other neutral event the center of their National Day celebrations. Some Third World countries go to the other extreme: They use independence day oratory to commemorate liberation struggles that occurred largely in myth. It is necessary to give crowds something to cheer other than a distantly remembered decision by a European government to haul its flag down and run up a new banner chosen by its local political allies.

Modern history's two most enduring political revolutions and the republics they created celebrate their national days in July. While Americans explode fireworks and char burgers on their Fourth, the French are laying in the wine and planning neighborhood dances for their Fourteenth. The perpetually illuminating contrast between these two revolutionary siblings is more than social. France commemorates a glorious, dramatic event: the destruction in 1789 of the king's prison and armory by mobs in search of arms and vengeance. America marks a different moment that enshrines its national identity: the signing thirteen years earlier of a document.

The United States is a nation "spoken into existence" and "fashioned out of ideas," historian Page Smith has written. The Fourth of July puts and keeps words at the core of the national American experience. We celebrate the declaration of a political promise, made by a landed gentry long since disappeared, to guarantee "life, liberty, and the pursuit of happiness" to those recognized as citizens.

The French and other Europeans are too experienced to take political promises that seriously. Promises commit only those who believe in them, not those who make them, one contemporary French politician has observed. Charles Pasqua did not intend that as a description of America's underlying political ethos and strength, but it serves nicely: Americans as a group continue to believe in life, liberty and the pursuit of happiness, if only to measure constantly and precisely how far their society falls short of delivering on them.

Continuing and renewing the belief is a purpose worthy of a national birthday party, especially on this final annual stocktaking of the twentieth century, which seems to find many Americans harboring contradictory moods and impressions about their country. A record-setting prosperity continues to lift balance sheets and swell bank accounts. The mountain of national debt that only a few years ago seemed poised to crush the republic's vitality is now projected to shrink to zero in a decade and a half. And yet public opinion polls show that a majority of the population thinks the country is "on the wrong track." Has America baked a sour apple pie for its birthday party? Too much can be made of such poll results. Taking statistical snapshots of a complex societal state of mind is tricky business. Connecting them to the impact of individual events or factors such as the Littleton shootings or presidential misconduct is guesswork.

The 223rd national birthday party is a time to take a longer and broader view. In his 1980 book, *The Shaping of America*, Page Smith suggested that there is a natural and constant tension in the American character shaped by the gap between the promise made by history and the reality of the present moment: "It was one thing to declare a nation; it was something vastly more complex to accomplish it. . . . It was primarily words that held the nation together. Having been defined by words, it had to be constantly redefined, articulated, spoken, explained."

Or explained away. The tension between the words of liberty and the fact of slavery had to be resolved through bloodshed before the United States truly became a nation. It was then reshaped by massive waves of immigration that brought forth a constantly self- examining, self-critical society that still believed in promises of larger equality for all.

The Fourth of July is a day for Americans to relax, enjoy and remind themselves of how much of the promise remains to be redeemed. It is as Yogi Berra said on meeting the Jewish mayor of Dublin: Only in America.

A Little Homer at the Beach

(JULY 26, 1998)

Ian McKellen's reading of *The Odyssey* on the car tape deck had reached a particularly engrossing moment when a police siren and a flashing blue light cut through Homer's intoxicating lyricism to remind me that I was on Highway 378 and not scudding along the wine-dark sea of the Greek islands.

Homecoming, Carolina style, would not feature the slaughtering of fatted heifers or other rituals that welcomed greathearted Odysseus back to Ithaca after his ten-year struggle to return. Looking in the rearview mirror, I knew I was a chicken about to be plucked for the greater good. Briefly, I thought of trying to good ole boy the tall young state trooper walking toward the car. After all, despite those Yankee-appearing license plates he was eyeing, I had grown up in South Carolina's red clay hill country, laughing with neighbors about York County's financial dependence on snaring New Yorkers or Washingtonians in rural speed traps such as the one I had just transgressed.

No sale, I quickly calculated. How about the truth—that I had been lost in this fine British actor's audiotape rendering of Menelaus's account of the siege of Troy and let my foot grow heavy on the pedal as I approached the hamlet of Manning on my way to the coast of my native state? It will never happen again, officer. In the passenger's seat Lee Hoagland, age twelve, laughed aloud at his father's half-mumbled notion. I probably would have more luck in interesting Homer in the story of this annual homecoming gone astray than in getting the advancing Johnny Bluelight to cut us some slack for driving under the influence of a blind Greek poet.

The damage came to $100. I could get on with my vacation by mailing a cashier's check within ten days in the self-addressed envelope the trooper handed over. Or I could come back to Manning and try out either the blind poet strategy or the good ole boy approach on the judge. I folded on the spot. The check would be in the mail. It was time to move on.

Except, I haven't. Here at this small beach community described by its residents as "arrogantly shabby," the accidental commingling of Greek myth and South Carolina highway reality has stirred one of those obvious realizations we usually are too busy and preoccupied to investigate—or even comprehend—but which are central to our lives.

Beach vacations permit such investigation. They in fact demand it. The unbidden thought comes galloping as waves softly batter you back into the sandy expanse of an endless Atlantic coastline or as you plunge deep into the cool waters of a Mediterranean cove or cranny. Wherever you are, the ethos of vacation is one you have created for yourself, possessing an enduring unity and logic that transcend shifts in locale and cast of characters. Look for it, and you will find a thread there that connects each quest for rest and renewal, however tenuously. The chance meeting of Johnny Bluelight and Homer illuminated such a thread for me: I realized that the summers of my adult life have been split almost equally between the Mediterranean (largely Greece, with a smattering of Italy, France and Spain) and the Atlantic shoreline of my native state. For me the eastern Mediterranean has been a way to be at home when I wasn't.

That feeling was explicit when I began visiting the Greek isles twenty-five years ago while living and working in prewar Beirut. On one island I found a village that duplicated the simplicity, solitude and starkness that prosperity has taken away from York County. I went back to Ano Mera every year for a decade to visit that solitude. Among the Greeks and the Arabs, I found much more than that one village to remind me of the American South. They are also to some extent peoples of lost civilizations and lost causes, reflecting on ancient glories that others cannot have experienced or even understood.

Absorbed in our myths, we speed along the roads of the world listening to our own fatalistic voices.

I am at home with the heritage of people who have endured through losing, at war and in other pursuits. Consider Israel as counterpoint: Israelis do not give the sense of being in love with lost causes. Any temptation in that direction would have been erased by Hitler, and by the once constant Arab threats to throw the Jews into the sea. For Israelis, losing is not tragic and romantic; it could be final.

Homecoming is a constant, unending voyage into a past we can never attain. Homer taught me that on this trip to the beach. I wish he had told me to let up on the pedal, too.

Lawrence Weschler, head of the New York Institute for the Humanities and winner of a 1998 Lannan Literary Award, has been a staff writer at the *New Yorker* since 1981. His books range from *A Miracle, A Universe: Settling Accounts with Torturers* and *Calamities of Exile,* to *Mr. Wilson's Cabinet of Wonder* and *Boggs: A Comedy of Value.* His book *Vermeer in Bosnia* is forthcoming. This piece appeared in the *New Yorker* on August 26, 1985.

Why I Can't Write Fiction

A young reporter we know writes:

Friends of mine sometimes ask me why I don't try my hand at writing a novel. They know that novels are just about all I read, or, at any rate, all I ever talk about, and they wonder why I don't try writing one myself. Fiction, they reason, should not be so difficult to compose if one already knows how to write nonfiction. It seems to me they ought to be right in that, and yet I can't *imagine* ever being able to write fiction. This complete absence of even the fantasy of my writing fiction used to trouble me. Or not trouble me, exactly—I used to wonder at it. But I gradually came to see it as one aspect of the constellation of capacities which makes it possible for me to write nonfiction. Or, rather, the other way around: the part of my sensibility which I demonstrate in nonfiction makes fiction an impossible mode for me. That's because for me the world is already filled to bursting with interconnections, interrelationships, consequences, and consequences of consequences. The world as it is overdetermined: the web of all those interrelationships is dense to the point of saturation. That's what my reporting becomes about: taking any single knot and worrying out the threads, tracing the interconnections, following the mesh through into the wider, outlying mesh, establishing the proper analogies, ferreting out the false strands. If I were somehow to be forced to write a fiction about, say, a make-believe Caribbean island, I wouldn't know where to put it, because the Caribbean as it is is already full—there's *no room* in it for any fictional islands. Dropping one in there would provoke a tidal wave, and all other places would be swept away. I wouldn't be able to invent a fictional New York housewife, because the city as it is is already overcrowded—there are *no apartments available*, there is no more room in the phone book. (If, by contrast, I were reporting on the life of an actual housewife, all the threads that make up her place in the city would become my subject, and I'd have no end of inspiration, no lack of room. Indeed, room—her specific space, the way the world makes room for her—would be my theme.)

It all reminds me of an exquisite notion advanced long ago by the Cabalists, the Jewish mystics, and particularly by those who subscribed to the teachings of Isaac Luria, the great, great visionary who was active in Palestine in the mid-sixteenth century. The Lurianic Cabalists were vexed by the question of how God could have created *anything*, since He was already everywhere and hence there could have been no room anywhere for His creation. In order to approach this mystery, they conceived the notion of *tsimtsum*, which means a sort of holding in of breath. Luria suggested that at the moment of creation God, in effect, breathed in—He absented Himself; or, rather, He hid Himself; or, rather, He entered into Himself—so as to make room for His creation. This *tsimtsum* has extraordinary implications in Lurianic and post-Lurianic teaching. In a certain sense, the *tsimtsum* helps account for the distance we feel from God in this fallen world. Indeed, in one version, at the moment of creation something went disastrously wrong, and the Fall was a fall for God as well as for man: God Himself is wounded; He can no longer put everything back together by Himself; He needs man. The process of salvation, of restitution— the *tikkun*, as Luria called it—is thus played out in the human sphere, becomes at least in part the work of men in this world. Hence, years and years later, we get Kafka's remarkable arid mysterious assertion that "the Messiah will come only when he is no longer needed; he will come only on the day after his arrival; he will come not on the last day but on the very last."

But I digress. For me, the point here is that the creativity of the fiction writer has always seemed to partake of the mysteries of the First Creation (I realize that this is an oft-broached analogy)—the novelist as creator, his characters as his creatures. (See, for example, Robert Coover's marvelous *The Universal Baseball Association, Inc., J. Henry Waugh, Prop.*, in which for "J. Henry Waugh" read "Jahweh.") The fictionalist has to be capable of *tsimtsum*, of breathing in, of allowing—paradoxically, of creating—an empty space in the world, an empty time, in which his characters will be able to play out their fates. This is, I suppose, the active form of the "suspension of disbelief." For some reason, I positively relish suspending my disbelief as long as someone else is casting the bridge across the abyss; I haven't a clue as to how to fashion, let alone cast, such a bridge myself.

All these thoughts have come to the fore for me just now on account of my recent summer reading. Larry McMurtry, one of my favorite novelists, has a big new novel out, the epic that all of us McMurtry fans have been hearing rumors about for years. It's called *Lonesome Dove*; it basically concerns a cattle drive from southernmost Texas all the way to the highlands of Montana back in the late 1870s, around the time Montana was beginning to be made safe for settling (or, actually, as the novel reveals, it was at precisely this time that brash exploits by characters such as these were going to make that north country safe for settling, although it sure as hell wasn't yet); and it's a wonderful book. McMurtry's ongoing capacity for fashioning fully living characters— filled with contradictions and teeming with fellow-feeling—is in full bloom here; he's created dozens of them, and he's managed to keep them all vividly distinct. Reading the book, one begins to think of the novelist himself as trail driver, guiding and prodding his characters along: some tarry, others bolt and, after a long, meandering chase, have to be herded back into the main herd; others fall out and stay behind; still others just die off. Why does he, I marvel—how can he—keep driving them along like that, from the lazy, languid Rio Grande cusp of Chapter 1 to the awesome Montana highlands past page 800? In many ways, McMurtry strikes me as not unlike his character Captain Call, the leader of the drive, who just does it, and keeps on doing it as, one by one, all conceivable motivations and rationales slip away. And yet, unlike Call, McMurtry seems overflowing with empathy for every one of his creatures—a lavishment of love which makes his ability, his negative capability, to then just let them go (after lavishing so much compassion in the fashioning of them), to just let them drift into ever more terrible demises—all the more remarkable.

I have so many questions I'd like to ask McMurtry about how he does it. But he wouldn't much cotton to my coming around and asking them. I know; I tried once. McMurtry lives part of the time in Washington, D.C., these days, where he runs a rare-book emporium in Georgetown. I remember, about five years ago, arriving by tram at Union Station and looking up the store's name in the phone book and calling the number from a pay phone and asking the answering male voice whether Mr. McMurtry was in and being told yes, it was he speaking. I said, "Great, don't move, I'll be right over." I hailed a taxi and was there in less than ten minutes. I started out pouring forth praise and appreciation and heartfelt readerly thanks, and then headed into my few questions. And all the while he stared back at me, completely indifferent. The sheer extent of his indifference was terrifying. I ended up stammering some sort of gaga apology and bolting.

A few weeks ago, two of McMurtry's more recent novels were reissued in paperback—timed, I suppose, to coincide with the hardcover publication of *Lonesome Dove*. They included new prefaces, and these prefaces helped me to appreciate the icy reluctance to talk about his own writing with which he'd greeted me that day. "I rarely think of my own books, once I finish them," he records in the preface to *Cadillac Jack*, "and don't welcome the opportunity, much less the necessity, of thinking about them. The moving finger writes, and keeps moving; thinking about them while I'm writing them is often hard enough." In the preface to *The Desert Rose* he plays a variation on this theme: "Once I finish a book, it vanishes from my mental picture as rapidly as the road runner in the cartoon. I don't expect to see it or think about it again for a decade or so, if ever." But those prefaces nevertheless suggest the contours of some answers to the sorts of questions I wanted to ask: questions about creators and creatures, free will and determinism—finally, I guess, about grace. At one point, he writes about the way one of his characters, Harmony, in *The Desert Rose*, "graced" his life during the time he was writing about her. (That's a good, an exact, word; I remember how she graced my life, too, as I read about her.) "In my own practice," he notes, "writing fiction has always seemed a semiconscious activity. I concentrate so hard on visualizing my characters that my actual surroundings blur. My characters seem to be speeding through their lives—I have to type unflaggingly in order to keep them in sight." Later, he records that he was "rather sorry," as he finished the book's composition, when Harmony "strolled out of hearing."

Characters stroll out of hearing all the time in *Lonesome Dove*, and strolling's not the half of it. They lurch, career, and smash out of hearing: they get snake-bitten, drowned, hanged, gangrened, struck by lightning, bow-and-arrowed. The untamed West of *Lonesome Dove* is a tremendously dangerous wilderness. McMurtry offers a luminous epigraph to his epic, some lines from T. K. Whipple's *Study Out the Land*: "All America lies at the end of the wilderness road, and our past is not a dead past, but still lives in us. Our forefathers had civilization inside themselves, the wild outside. We live in the civilization they created, but within us the wilderness still lingers. What they dreamed, we live, and what they lived, we dream." It occurs to me that as a reader I stand in somewhat the same relationship to McMurtry as that which Whipple suggests obtains between us and our forebears. Here McMurtry has gone and done it—created this tremendous epic massif. All the while, as he was doing it, he must have been envisioning us someday reading this epic; and now we, as we read it—or, anyway, I, as I read it—try to imagine what it was like for him doing it, making it, living through the writing of it. And the thing I keep wondering about, in my clumsy, gawky fashion, is this: Did he, too, feel the sorrow, the poignant melancholy, that he engenders in us as, one by one, he disposed of those, his beloved characters; or was he able merely to glory in the craft of it, the polish, the shine? Are they—his characters—more or less real for him than they are for us?

Blair Clark worked as a journalist in newspapers, broadcasting, and for the *Nation*, where he was editor from 1976–78. He was Eugene McCarthy's campaign manager in 1968. The following piece appeared in a commemorative issue of the *Harvard Advocate* published on the death of Robert Lowell.

On Robert Lowell

Where did his torrent of energy come from? His father, in his mid-forties when I first knew him, was sluggish and blocked. That astonishing drive's main source was certainly his mother, but the hysterical dynamo in her had no outlet and was therefore destructive of herself and of those around her—especially, of course, her husband and her son.

Somehow he survived those quite dreadful tensions and managed to invent himself. The being he created was a spring coiled by his own strong, fumbling hand. What he made of himself was a reaction to and against his parents. We are all, of course, formed in such ways, but he had special needs to slip from that parental vise and finally he found devices that made the escape possible. It was a tight one from the start, constraining his unruly nature in grotesque ways. His parents' attempt to control him could be called "conventional" except that their nagging campaign for proper dress, manners and attitude aimed beyond mere convention. It was an effort to control or subdue a phenomenon they feared, a spirit in revolt not just against them and their narrow world but against something more frightening, perhaps dangerous life itself, as they perceived it.

These dull parents fought hard to win the battle at 170 Marlborough Street. Charlotte Lowell's white gloves sheathed steely hands determined to wrest victory from her strange, rebellious only child. The fighting raged even when his childhood obsession was Napoleon (a bookshelf on Bonaparte in his bedroom, all read by the time he was fourteen), before his heroes became Homer, Dante, Shakespeare, Milton and then the rest.

At first his defensive weapon was humor, not of the sunny or winning sort but daring and aggressive, even grotesque. I remember Thanksgiving lunch, in 1932 or 1933, he and I freed for the day from St. Mark's cloisters, sitting at the mahogany dining-room table on Marlborough Street and giggling almost uncontrollably at obscure yarns he spun about friends of his parents. They were indirect attacks, of course (how could one dare to take on directly the friends of one's parents?). And so they were fantastic, full of invented episodes about cheeky servants and highly exaggerated misadventures of daily life in that proper world. The two of us almost choked on the turkey as we thus separated ourselves from these two parents trying to talk about the St. Mark's-

Groton football game and the details of life at a school of which his father's grandfather (or was it great-uncle?) had been the first headmaster.

Critics have praised him, and some have questioned his taste, for the lacerating accounts of himself and his parents in the "confessional" writing. My view, based on much observation of him and of them in those painful days, is that he spared them, and thus perhaps himself, in his accounts of their behavior. They could well have been dealt with much more harshly, and I have marveled at his rationalizations of what he went through at their hands. (I do have a letter from him calling them "pretty awful people," written in the 1950s.)

In those schooldays "loyalty" was the first principle of our friendship. Lowell was the unquestioned leader, whose dominance sometimes chafed, of a cabal of three classmates, alienated from the values of that school. The painter Frank Parker and I were the others and there was no effort to recruit more aspiring dissidents, nor did our classmates try to join our charmed, if scarcely visible, circle. Lowell deserved that leadership because Parker and I, having less reason than him to fight for survival against the parental enemy, were even more unformed. And he had a superior drive and commitment to the search for the "serious," an idea he embraced by the time we were sixteen.

He decreed that Parker would be painter and I a musician. He would be the poet (there was no talk of mere "writing"). His allocation of the arts among the three of us was based on the fact that Parker was already doing sketches and caricatures and the circumstance that I was in the choir (and what other art was left open?). Since Lowell was tone-deaf and since I had a mere trace of musical talent, he had to accept my dropping out of that niche in our pantheon. It remained a question of what to do with me in the arts. When I spent a summer with him in a cottage on Nantucket, in 1936, working hard on our nineteen-year-old intellects all the time, he made me read all the minor Elizabethan playwrights, and I still retain a tag or two from Dekker and Middleton. He assigned himself Shakespeare, Milton, Homer again, and the English lyric poets. It was not a fair or sensible division of labor, but I lacked the confidence to challenge him. One put up with his bullying. There were enough other rewards in the friendship, but they were tested when he chased me and knocked me down to force me to stop smoking (he who later smoked three or four packs a day).

If he invented himself in an unusually conscious and deliberate way, as I have suggested, that was as nothing compared to the way in which he created Robert Lowell the writer. He set about that task even before he had a notion of what it was to "write," or what there was for him to write about. Imagination needs material, experience, to grind, and that is famously just what is missing for the young artist. Two decades went by before Lowell could face, and deal creatively with, the matter that was closest at hand, his struggle with his family. So in the beginning the impulsion was abstract and purely moral: what is good and bad, bearable and unbearable, serious and unimportant, as one considers what to do with life? To find the answers, his answers, he went straight to literature, blindly and instinctively, I would say. He had little interest in philosophy or other sources of knowledge or wisdom. If in those early years at school he looked elsewhere than to the classics of literature for guidance (along with the scholarly commentaries on them, to learn how to read them), it was to painting in the volumes of reproductions in the Carnegie collection in a small room near the library.

Where did the nickname "Cal" come from? The scholars will bicker about that. I have never been sure whether Caliban or Caligula was the inspiration, so to speak, for his taunting classmates in the third or fourth forms. We were reading Roman history and *The Tempest* in the same year. So both names were handy for the smooth sons of Wall Street and State Street to hang on Lowell, the rough outsider with rumpled clothes and hair and untied shoelaces. I would say that Caliban was the main source—uncouthness rather than a mania that had not yet appeared. Physically the strongest boy in the class, he was looked on as odd, not crazy.

I know little about his two Harvard years, having fallen back a year because of illness and thus overlapping only one of them. My memory is that he was not much affected by *The Advocate*'s rejection of his candidacy—it was too much of a club and he knew he was not eminently clubbable. He encouraged me to concentrate in the Classics, which I did, and to join the *Crimson*, then somewhat less clubby than *The Advocate*. But we saw each other a great deal and I was heavily involved in his struggle to leave Harvard and all those family pressures that almost trapped him. I was of some use in this effort, presenting to his stubborn parents a conventional self and conventional careerist arguments for the move to Kenyon. But Dr. Merrill Moore, the transplanted Southern agrarian sonneteer and psychiatrist with a Harvard medical base and a Beacon Street practice, who knew Tate, Ransom, Warren et al., was, of course, much more influential with those parents. He certified Lowell's move as sane, and it helped that Lowell's mother ended up working as an aide in Moore's office; she had something to do at last beyond chivvying husband and son. Finally it got through to them that their difficult son might be better off away from them and that they might be spared, too, if he just went away.

Students of the life and work of Lowell have noted, but not sufficiently, I think, the way in which he systematically apprenticed himself to older writers. It began at school with Richard G. Eberhardt, then a young poet on the faculty whom we called "Cousin Ghormley," not out of disrespect but as a sort of joke. Then there was Ford Madox Ford, the only novelist in the list of mentors, whom he met in Boston in 1936 or 1937 and visited in Olivet, Michigan. Preeminently, there were Allen Tate and John Crowe Ransom, the latter moving from Vanderbilt to Kenyon, to which he attracted Randall Jarrell and Lowell, among other aspiring young poets. Later there were Pound, Eliot, William

Carlos Williams and Santayana, among others at whose feet he sat. He could learn from them not just the craft of poetry but something about how to think and live as a poet. It was done for enlightenment, not careerist calculation, though Lowell did not lack ambition for success.

Later, during the long period of manic-depressive "breakdowns," as he called them, which came at intervals of about eleven months, as I once figured, I often served as a way-station in the transit from abandoned home to hospital. In these episodes, some of them quite frightening, the point was to get him as soon as possible out of some wild entanglement and into the hospital. I did this several times in collaboration with his wife, the truly devoted Elizabeth Hardwick, and his psychiatrist, the remarkably impressive Dr. Viola Bernard. Once in the early 1960s I flew to Buenos Aires to persuade him to leave a clinic and his fantasies of that moment; after four days he agreed and we came back, an Argentinian doctor named Kelly accompanying us, his tranquilizing hypodermic at the ready, as required by Pan Am.

We were close friends for forty-five years, I think, though for most of that time our worlds overlapped more than coincided, and there were periods when circumstances prevented much contact. I was his best man at his first wedding, in 1940, while Allen Tate gave away the bride, Jean Stafford. At his marriage to Elizabeth Hardwick in 1948 I again handed him the ring after trying to dilute or turn aside the usual parental hostility. Mrs. Lowell asked me in that house in Beverly Farms, where the wedding was, whether I thought Elizabeth was "suitable" and would "take good care of Bobby," the same questions she had put to me about Jean, though the Lowells did not attend that unapproved service in New York. Had his mother been around for his third marriage, I would have had to give a different answer to that insistent question, which surely would have been posed once more. I was never able to conceal my doubts about that one, but they caused no trouble between us.

I remember once, a dozen years before he died, bringing him back to my house in New York in one of his crazed escapes from home. Watching him breathe in heavy gasps, asleep in the taxi, the tranquilizing drugs fighting the mania, I thought that there were then two dynamos within him, spinning in opposite directions and tearing him apart, and that these forces would kill him at last. No one, strong as he was, could stand that for long. And, finally, the opposing engines of creation and repression did kill him in a taxi in front of his own real home.

Alice Steinbach won a Pulitzer Prize for feature writing in 1985. Her most recent book is *Without Reservations: The Travels of an Independent Woman*, published by Random House. Steinbach's forthcoming book, *Universal Lessons*, will be published early in 2003. This essay is the title chapter of *The Miss Dennis School of Writing* (Bancroft Press, 1996).

The Miss Dennis School of Writing

"What kind of writing do you do?" asked the novelist sitting to my left at a writer's luncheon.

"I work for a newspaper in Baltimore," he was told.

"Oh, did you go to journalism school?"

"Well, yes."

"Columbia?" he asked, invoking the name of the most prestigious journalism school in the country.

"Actually, no," I heard myself telling him. "I'm one of the lucky ones. I am a graduate of the Miss Dennis School of Writing."

Unimpressed, the novelist turned away. Clearly it was a credential that did not measure up to his standards. But why should it? He was not one of the lucky ones. He had never met Miss Dennis, my ninth-grade creative writing teacher, or had the good fortune to be her student. Which meant he had never experienced the sight of Miss Dennis chasing Dorothy Singer around the classroom, threatening her with a yardstick because Dorothy hadn't paid attention and her writing showed it.

"You want to be a writer?" Miss Dennis would yell, out of breath from all the running and yardstick-brandishing. "Then pay attention to what's going on around you. Connect! You are not Switzerland—neutral, aloof, uninvolved. Think Italy!"

Miss Dennis said things like this. If you had any sense, you wrote them down.

"I can't teach you how to write, but I can tell you how to look at things, how to pay attention," she would bark out at us, like a drill sergeant confronting a group of undisciplined, wet-behind-the-ears Marine recruits. To drive home her point, she had us take turns writing a description of what we saw on the way to school in the morning. Of course, you never knew which morning would be your turn so—just to be on the safe side—you got into the habit of looking things over carefully every morning and making notes: "Saw a pot of red geraniums sitting in the sunlight on a white stucco porch; an orange-striped cat curled like a comma beneath a black van; a dark gray cloud scudding across a silver morning sky."

It's a lesson that I have returned to again and again throughout my writing career. To this day, I think of Miss Dennis whenever I write a certain kind of sentence. Or to be more precise, whenever I write a sentence that actually creates in words the picture I want readers to see.

Take, for instance, this sentence: Miss Dennis was a small, compact woman, about albatross height—or so it seemed to her students—with short, straight hair the color of apricots and huge eyeglasses that were always slipping down her nose.

Or this one: Miss Dennis always wore a variation of one outfit—a dark-colored, flared woolen skirt, a tailored white blouse and a cardigan sweater, usually black, thrown over her shoulders and held together by a little pearl chain.

Can you see her? I can. And the image of her makes me smile. Still.

But it was not Miss Dennis' appearance or her unusual teaching method—which had a lot in common with an out-of-control terrier—that made her so special. What set her apart was her deep commitment to liberating the individual writer in each student.

"What lies at the heart of good writing," she told us over and over again, "is the writer's ability to find his own unique voice. And then to use it to tell an interesting story." Somehow she made it clear that we were interesting people with interesting stories to tell. Most of us, of course, had never even known we had a story to tell, much less an interesting one. But soon the stories just started bubbling up from some inner wellspring.

Finding the material, however, was one thing; finding the individual voice was another.

Take me, for instance. I arrived in Miss Dennis' class trailing all sorts of literary baggage. My usual routine was to write like Colette on Monday, one of the Bronte sisters on Wednesday, and Mark Twain on Friday.

Right away, Miss Dennis knocked me off my high horse.

"Why are you telling other people's stories?" she challenged me, peering up into my face. (At fourteen I was already four inches taller than Miss Dennis.) "You have your own stories to tell."

I was tremendously relieved to hear this and immediately proceeded to write like my idol, E. B. White. Miss Dennis, however, wasn't buying.

"How will you ever find out what you have to say if you keep trying to say what other people have already said?" was the way she dispensed with my E. B. White impersonation. By the third week of class, Miss Dennis knew my secret. She knew I was afraid—afraid to pay attention to my own inner voice for fear that when I finally heard it, it would have nothing to say.

What Miss Dennis told me—and I have carefully preserved these words because they were then, and are now, so very important to me—was this: "Don't be afraid to discover what you're saying in the act of saying it." Then, in her inimitably breezy and endearing way, she added: "Trust me on this one."

From the beginning, she made it clear to us that it was not "right" or "wrong" answers she was after. It was thinking.

"Don't be afraid to go out on a limb," she'd tell some poor kid struggling to reason his way through an essay on friendship or courage. And eventually— once we stopped being afraid that we'd be chopped off out there on that limb—we needed no encouragement to say what we thought. In fact, after the first month, I can't remember ever feeling afraid of failing in her class. Passing or failing didn't seem to be the point of what she was teaching.

Miss Dennis spent as much time, maybe more, pointing out what was right with your work as she did pointing out what was wrong. I can still hear her critiquing my best friend's incredibly florid essay on nature. "You are a very good observer of nature," she told the budding writer. "And if you just write what you see without thinking so much about adjectives and comparisons, we will see it through your attentive eyes."

By Thanksgiving vacation I think we were all a little infatuated with Miss Dennis. And beyond that, infatuated with the way she made us feel about ourselves—that we were interesting people worth listening to.

I, of course, fancied I had a special relationship with her. It was certainly special to me. And, to tell the truth, I knew she felt the same way.

The first time we acknowledged this was one day after class when I stayed behind to talk to her. I often did that and it seemed we talked about every-thing—from the latest films to the last issue of the *New Yorker*. The one thing we did not talk about was the sadness I felt about my father's death. He had died a few years before and, although I did not know it then, I was still grieving his absence. Without knowing the details, Miss Dennis somehow picked up on my sadness. Maybe it was there in my writing. Looking back I see now that, without my writing about it directly, my father's death hovered at the edges of all my stories.

But on this particular day I found myself talking not about the movies or about writing but instead pouring out my feelings about the loss of my father. I shall never forget that late fall afternoon: the sound of the vanilla-colored blinds flap, flap, flapping in the still classroom; sun falling in shafts through the windows, each ray illuminating tiny galaxies of chalk dust in the air; the smell of wet blackboards; the teacher, small with apricot-colored hair, listen-ing intently to a young girl blurting out her grief. These memories are stored like vintage photographs.

The words that passed between the young girl and the attentive teacher are harder to recall. With this exception. "One day," Miss Dennis told me, "you will write about this. Maybe not directly. But you will write about it. And you will find that all this has made you a better writer and a stronger person."

After that day, it was as if Miss Dennis and I shared something. We never talked again about my father but spent most of our time discussing our mutual interests. We both loved poetry and discovered one afternoon that each of us regarded Emily Dickinson with something approaching idolatry. Right then and there, Miss Dennis gave me a crash course in why Emily Dickinson's poems worked. I can still hear her talking about the "spare, slanted beauty" in Dickinson's unique choice of words. She also told me about the rather cloistered life led by this New England spinster, noting that nonetheless Emily Dickinson knew the world as few others did. "She found her world within the word," is the way I remember Miss Dennis putting it. Of course, I could be making that part up.

That night, propped up in bed reading Emily Dickinson's poetry, I wondered if Miss Dennis, a spinster herself, identified in some way with the woman who wrote:

> Wild nights—Wild nights!
> Were I with thee
> Wild Nights should be
> Our luxury!

It seems strange, I know, but I never really knew anything about Miss Dennis' life outside of the classroom. Oh, once she confided in me that the initial "M" in her name stood for Mildred. And I was surprised when I passed by the teachers' lounge one day and saw her smoking a cigarette, one placed in a long, silver cigarette holder. It seemed an exceedingly sophisticated thing to do and it struck me then that she might be more worldly than I had previously thought.

But I didn't know how she spent her time or what she wanted from life or anything like that. And I never really wondered about it. Once I remember talking to some friends about her age. We guessed somewhere around fifty—which seemed really old to us. In reality, Miss Dennis was around forty.

It was Miss Dennis, by the way, who encouraged me to enter some writing contests. To my surprise, I took first place in a couple of them. Of course, taking first place is easy. What's hard is being rejected. But Miss Dennis helped me with that, too, citing all the examples of famous writers who'd been rejected time and time again. "Do you know what they told George Orwell when they rejected *Animal Farm*?" she would ask me. Then without waiting for a reply, she'd answer her own question: "The publisher told him, 'It is impossible to sell animal stories in the U.S.A.'"

When I left her class at the end of the year, Miss Dennis gave me a present: a book of poems by Emily Dickinson. I have it still. The spine is cracked and the front cover almost gone, but the inscription remains. On the inside flyleaf, in her perfect Palmer Method handwriting, she had written: "Say what you see. Yours in Emily Dickinson, Miss Dennis."

She had also placed little checks next to two or three poems. I took this to mean she thought they contained a special message for me. One of those checked began this way:

Hope is the thing with feathers
That perches in the soul . . .

I can remember carefully copying out these lines onto a sheet of paper, one which I carried around in my handbag for almost a year. But time passed, the handbag fell apart and who knows what happened to the yellowing piece of paper with the words about hope.

The years went by. Other schools and other teachers came and went. But one thing remained constant: My struggle to pay attention to my own inner life; to hear a voice that I would recognize finally as my own. Not only in my writing but in my life.

Only recently, I learned that Miss Dennis had died at the age of fifty. When I heard this, it occurred to me that her life was close to being over when I met her. Neither of us knew this, of course. Or at least I didn't. But lately I've wondered if she knew something that day we talked about sadness and my father's death. "Write about it," she said. "It will help you."

And now, reading over these few observations, I think of Miss Dennis. But not with sadness. Actually, thinking of Miss Dennis makes me smile. I think of her and see, with marked clarity, a small, compact woman with apricot-colored hair. She is with a young girl and she is saying something.

She is saying: "Pay attention."

Milton Viorst, who lives in Washington, specializes in Middle Eastern affairs. This account of his meeting Maguib Mahfouz is drawn from his book *Sandcastles: The Arabs in Search of the Modern World* (Knopf, 1994).

Meeting Mahfouz

Crossing Tahrir Square each morning to meet Naguib Mahfouz, the Nobel laureate in literature, was not easy. The hub of modern Cairo, Tahrir—Arabic for "liberation"—is a few steps from the east bank of the Nile. Along its periphery are the city's principal hotels, the offices of the major government ministries, the Egyptian Museum and the airline offices. The busiest shopping streets radiate from it in a half-circle. At its southern end stands a sprawling thirteen-story eyesore called the Mugamma, central workplace of the state bureaucracy, where, Cairenes like to say, more bodies are at rest than in all the tombs of ancient Egypt. Just to the west is the now rehabilitated headquarters of the Arab League, vacant between Egypt's expulsion for talking peace with Israel in 1977 until the Egyptians' restoration to their fellow Arabs' good graces a dozen years later.

Egypt had been the preeminent member of the Arab League since its founding in 1945. Indeed, throughout the modern era, Egypt has been the standard-bearer among the Arabs. Its population, currently nearly sixty million, makes it the largest of the Arab states, but that is not the only measure. It was Egyptians, the first Arabs seriously exposed to the West, who led in aspiring to European-style nationhood. Egyptian thinkers broke new ground in attempting to reconcile traditional Islam with the values of the contemporary West. Egyptian universities produced a stream of well-trained professionals and artists who fanned out to serve the Middle East region. Egypt offered the first Arab challenge to colonialism. An Egyptian friend recalls his grandfather solemnly reminiscing that when Japan defeated Russia in the war of 1905 and took its place among the modern nations, he and his friends believed that Egypt would be the next in line. It had, however, stumbled along the way. And, not surprisingly, the other Arab peoples were no more successful. When Egypt was expelled from the Arab League, an official predicted boldly to me that it would soon be back, since the Arabs needed Egypt. The League's return to Cairo vindicated his boast.

When I first saw Tahrir Square in 1973, the smiling face of Anwar Sadat, recently triumphant in the October war, beamed down from a huge painted panel upon the hordes of passersby. Eventually, his appeal faded, and in 1981 he was gunned down by Islamic terrorists. I found it hard not to think of Sadat whenever I saw Tahrir, and I was relieved to see that he had not been forgotten: the Tahrir station of Cairo's new subway bears his name. His successor, Hosni Mubarak, is a more prosaic figure. Without the flamboyance of Sadat, much less of Gamal Abdel Nasser, he is said to be like the typical protagonist of a Mahfouz novel: bumbling, a bit smaller than life. The Egypt over which he rules has reined in the nervous energy of the Nasser and Sadat eras and subordinated its taste for glory to a search for equanimity. Yet to cross Tahrir belied that equanimity. It was a task no less frenzied than I remembered it from my first encounter.

Leaving my hotel each morning, I made my way loftily past hucksters of Pharaonic-style papyruses, exotic native perfumes and guided tours of the pyramids. I navigated through an open-air terminal, where hordes of half-shaven men, whose street-length *galibiyas* proclaimed their rural origins, descended from battered buses to begin their morning's work at God-knows-what menial jobs. I cast an eye at the journals on the newsstand, with their headlines in loose, looping Arabic script, and I took in the pleasant odors of newly baked bread, meat and rice, and grayish hot cereals, offered for sale by elderly women, some of them tattooed, sitting cross-legged on the pavement. Finally, I reached the heavily trafficked boulevards that ring Tahrir, over which, I remembered, a Y-shaped iron footbridge, never painted and rarely swept, once crossed; no doubt it was removed to drive pedestrians into the network of underground passages that make up the subway, but the effort has been only partially successful. Cairenes clearly enjoyed defying oncoming traffic, some of it powered by horses or donkeys but most approaching at remarkably high speeds. Under the indifferent gaze of shabbily uniformed policemen, pedestrians even leaped the picket fences erected to keep them on the sidewalk. I was faced with a decision and, the first few mornings, I followed the underground route, but the psychology of the crowds won me over. On subsequent days I joined them in dashing mindlessly across the thoroughfares.

As I approached the Ali Baba Cafe, I would see Mahfouz sitting next to the upstairs window. On arriving in Cairo a few weeks before, I had turned to intermediaries for an introduction, and the word came back that Mahfouz had been used up by the hordes of journalists who descended after he was awarded the Nobel Prize. So I decided to approach him directly and learned that each Thursday evening he met with young writers at the Kasr-el-Nil, a heavily patronized cafe overlooking the Nile on the upper-income island of Zamalek. Sure enough, that was where I found him, in a downstairs room, surrounded by disciples who looked at me with some suspicion while I engaged the master in talk.

After hearing me out, Mahfouz agreed to meet with me, expressing some regret that he would have to put off a little longer getting back to the rigorous writing routine that for so many decades had dominated his life. He has written a few short stories, he told me, but the only regular writing he did now was a weekly column, usually on politics, for *Al-Ahram*, the Arab world's most celebrated newspaper. "The prize disturbed my life," he said to me, and no doubt he missed the tranquillity he had put to such creative use. Yet, when I knew him better, it was clear to me that this warm and sociable man, so long unknown outside the Arabic-speaking world, enjoyed the attention he was receiving from all points of the compass and that he was ambivalent about getting back to the lonely discipline of composing novels. That evening at the Kasr-el-Nil, Mahfouz invited me to join him the next day at the Ali Baba, where each morning he took his coffee.

In contrast to the neon-lit Kasr-el-Nil, the Ali Baba is a dark recess among the shops that face the square. It is one of a handful of cafes in Cairo and, in the summer months, in Alexandria where writers gather. Though he had forgotten, I had met Mahfouz at one of them before, in 1982, shortly after I was introduced to his work. I was researching an article which, I thought, needed a literary source, and I decided to approach Tewfik al-Hakim, who was then Egypt's first-ranking man of letters. I was told I would find him drinking coffee on the seaside in Alexandria, a four hour drive from Cairo across the lush Nile Delta, which for five or six thousand years has been the source of Egypt's riches.

With some difficulty, I found the Champs-Elysées, a small, weathered hotel on the boulevard that ran along the sea. Across from it was the beach, crowded with vacationing Egyptians, the men strutting about in dark suntans, the women seated passively, fully dressed, beneath umbrellas. Inside was a shabby cafe furnished with worn wooden tables and chairs. It was the haunt in the summer season of a group of writers known for their democratic and secularist views. Hakim was their leader. A blue-eyed octogenarian with a white walrus mustache, he spoke elegant French and habitually wore a beret, a vestige of his days as a student at the Sorbonne. The scene over which he presided made me think of a bistro painting by Cézanne, and from midmorning to early afternoon, he graciously orchestrated an exchange between me and the half-dozen men seated around him.

As the hour for the midday meal approached, some of the men drifted off, and when the circle finally broke up, I witnessed what I suspected was a daily ritual, with each member insisting it was his turn to pay the check. In the disarray, I struck up a conversation with a man in dark glasses who had not said a word all morning; he introduced himself as Naguib Mahfouz and he offered me his phone number in Cairo. I still had the slip of paper on which it was written. Later, in recalling the encounter, I asked why he had been silent. After a moment, he replied that he had always found it difficult to express himself around Hakim, who was his mentor, his professor and his literary idol.

For me, however, Mahfouz's work was more important than Hakim's. I was a beginner in the study of Egypt, and he offered me a clear look at the hidden dynamics of Egyptians' social and personal relations. Such relations, in any country, are usually impenetrable to a foreign observer. I found his view free of either apology or ideology. Though sympathetic to the characters he created on his pages, most of them everyday Egyptians, he was unrelenting in dissecting their flaws. He has frequently been called Egypt's conscience; his work, without heroes, made me wonder how Egyptians could read his stories without anguish.

Scholars of Middle East literature say that, as a stylist, Mahfouz writes with remarkable precision. Arabic, a florid language, requires most writers to choose between poetry and clarity; Mahfouz's choice makes his prose easy to translate. He is also a tireless experimenter in literary forms. Even his admirers often acknowledge that Mahfouz is not a great writer (Mahfouz, characteristically, says of himself that, judged on an international scale, he is third-rate), and is certainly not the peer in technique of a Dickens or a Balzac, to whom he has been compared. Yet few question that he deserved the Nobel Prize, in recognition of the unremitting honesty of his work, which sets a standard for other writers, in Egypt and throughout the Third World. For myself, I was grateful to him for bringing to me an Egypt that I could never have hoped to discover on my own.

Mahfouz's deference to Hakim in the Champs-Elysées revealed much about his perception of himself. Unlike the sophisticated Hakim, he was not educated abroad. Mahfouz was born in 1911, the last of seven children, in the rundown quarter of Gamaliya in the Islamic—that is, non-Western—part of Cairo. He attended Islamic elementary schools, earned a place in a secular high school, then attended Cairo University (called, in those days, King Fuad I University), where in 1934 he was awarded a degree in philosophy. To earn a living, he entered the civil service, and remained in the bureaucracy until 1971, when he retired. Only then did he become a full-time writer.

As a bachelor, Mahfouz, like most men of his generation, lived in his parents' home and only married when he was forty-three. He rarely traveled, and had never even seen Upper Egypt, the site of the great Pharaonic monuments, though the Pharaohs were ostensibly the subject of his early novels. (The real subject, lightly veiled in symbolism, was Egypt's struggle against colonialism.) "I didn't travel because I was poor," he told me. "If I had traveled like Hemingway, I'm sure my work would have been different. I understand that my work was shaped by my being so Egyptian." Since the 1930s, he has written almost exclusively about life in Cairo, with scenes occasionally set in Alexandria. In contrast to the Europeanized Hakim, he is considered a pure Egyptian and, since he has experienced little of life in the countryside, a quintessential Cairene.

Mahfouz declined to go to Stockholm to accept the Nobel Prize; his friends told me he was reluctant to travel so far and put on tails to be received by the Swedish king. "I'm very introverted," he said to me in one of our talks, "I don't enjoy leaving my milieu." His refusal created a dilemma in Egypt's literary

establishment until he gave in to his wife's urging to send his two daughters—
Um Kalthum, then thirty, and Fatma, twenty-seven—to represent him. To
chaperone them, he chose the playwright Mohamed Salmawi, one of his aco-
lytes. The two women, dressed in traditional Egyptian gowns, accepted the
award on their father's behalf and Salmawi delivered Mahfouz's Nobel lecture.
In it, Mahfouz said how proud he was to be the first to address the Nobel
assembly in Arabic, which he called "the real winner of the prize." Hakim was
now dead, and the prize ratified Mahfouz—though one or two others claimed
the title—as Egypt's first man of letters. It also made him Hakim's heir as the
leader of the democratic, secular circle in Cairo's literary cafes.

Each morning Mahfouz would wave when he noticed me on the sidewalk
outside the Ali Baba, and his smile would still be on his face when I reached
him. He rose in courtly fashion and extended his hand to greet me. He was
then seventy-eight years old and fragile. Thin, and with an unusually narrow
face, he wore glasses that appeared opaque. His hair was brushed straight back
from his high forehead. On most mornings he wore a leisure jacket of wool
over a turtleneck shirt. An untouched cup of coffee sat on the table next to
several newspapers, of which he said he read only the headlines because of his
poor eyesight. Mahfouz answered my questions freely, except on the subject
of his personal life. He was extremely private, I was told, even with longtime
friends—and he rejected, politely but firmly, all my efforts to visit him in his
home or to meet his family.

Mahfouz reached the Ali Baba on foot each morning, about two miles from
his apartment in the middle-class quarter called Agouza, on the west bank of
the Nile; it was an experience which contained hazards that went beyond the
racing traffic. For most of his life, he told me, one of his joys has been to roam
Cairo's streets. The habit has made him a familiar figure to many Cairenes who
would otherwise know him only from his books—or, more likely, from the
movies based on his books. It was also a habit which made him vulnerable
when the terrorist wing of Egypt's Muslim fundamentalists—the people who
assassinated Sadat—responded to his winning the Nobel Prize in the fall of
1988 by threatening to kill him.

Mahfouz's falling-out with orthodox Islam went back to 1959, when he
published the novel called in English *Children of Gebelawi*—Gebelawi being a
symbolic representation of a rather unpleasant God. A departure from his
normal preoccupations, which are worldly, the novel was a metaphysical allegory, scrutinizing the social codes practiced in the name of Judaism, Christianity and Islam; ultimately, it found them all profoundly wanting. That he
was evenhanded toward the three faiths brought him no indulgence in the
Islamic community, however. Serialized in *Al-Ahram* prior to publication, the
novel scandalized the orthodox, and before it appeared in book form it was
banned by the authorities of the Al-Azhar Mosque, which is Egypt's equivalent
of the official church. In 1967, a Beirut publisher began smuggling in a boot-

legged version, slightly expurgated, which was still available in a plain brown wrapper at a few downtown bookshops. I obtained a copy after spending an hour persuading a shop owner—who pretended at first never to have heard of such a thing—that I needed it for my research; most Cairo intellectuals also have their bootlegged copies. The fundamentalists feared that the Nobel award would become a pretext for Al-Azhar to lift *Gebelawi* from the proscribed list. But, more important, they had never forgiven Mahfouz for writing it, and they decried his receipt of the prize as an evil Western plot to discredit Islam.

The controversy took on another dimension a few weeks after the Nobel announcement, when Iran's Ayatollah Khomeini pronounced a death sentence on Salman Rushdie, an Anglo-Indian Muslim, for the allegedly sacrilegious content of his novel *The Satanic Verses*. The record shows that Mahfouz reacted promptly to defend Rushdie's right of expression, calling Khomeini a "terrorist." But, predictably, his position inflamed the fundamentalist *sheikhs*, who, in terms circumspect enough to stay within the law but fiery enough to permit the faithful to draw dangerous conclusions, denounced him in the mosques. The Islamic press added ominous warnings. In London, a writer in a Muslim newspaper that was much read in Cairo declared, "If only we had behaved in the proper Islamic manner with Naguib Mahfouz, we would not have been assailed by the appearance of Salman Rushdie. Had we killed Naguib Mahfouz, Salman Rushdie would not have appeared." Meanwhile, a high-ranking Egyptian cleric linked to Muslim terrorists told a Kuwaiti paper that, according to Islamic law, Mahfouz should have been killed when *Gebelawi* appeared, on the grounds that he had abandoned his religion. By the time the statement was picked up by the Cairo papers, the cleric had softened it with a proviso that execution could be waived if Mahfouz repented.

In fact, Mahfouz did repent—or, at least, he distanced himself from Rushdie. In a press conference at the Kasr-el-Nil cafe a few weeks after Khomeini's pronouncement, he rejected a comparison between *The Satanic Verses* and *Children of Gebelawi*, which he called "my illegitimate son," the product of a phase in his life that had ended thirty years before. He said that his early defense of Rushdie had been quoted out of context and, furthermore, had been made before he had read Rushdie's novel, which as a Muslim he found disgusting. A few weeks later, he gave an interview to one of Cairo's Islamic newspapers in which he said that while he might defend an author's prerogative to misinterpret Islam, he could not tolerate Rushdie's "insults and calumny against Islam and the Prophet."

During the course of our talks at the Ali Baba, which took place about six months later, Mahfouz said he considered himself a Muslim. But he declined to reply when I asked whether he prayed; it was the only question of mine that he flatly refused to answer. He acknowledged that after the death threats he shifted to what had become the standard position of Muslim "liberals" on the

Rushdie affair. It held that Islam has no immunity from criticism, and that Khomeini had no power to impose a death sentence, but it accepted the idea that Rushdie might appropriately be tried in a court of law for slandering Islam and the Prophet—much as any citizen would be tried for slandering a fellow Egyptian.

"I had to take the threats on my life seriously," Mahfouz said to me. "These people killed President Sadat and have tried to kill others. They could kill me." (In 1992, they assassinated a well-known secular Muslim writer, Faraj Foda.) Though the Egyptian government took no official position on Khomeini's pronouncement, the Mufti of the Republic—a high state bureaucrat, responsible for interpreting Islamic law—declared that any Muslim who sought to assassinate Mahfouz had to be insane. On a more practical level, Cairo's police offered bodyguards and asked Mahfouz to refrain from his long walks alone. They stationed guards outside his apartment and at that very moment, Mahfouz said, there might be guards standing in the crowd outside the Ali Baba.

"I could not change my routine," Mahfouz said to me. "When the police gave me the choice of staying home with my wife and daughters or facing the dangers of going to my cafes, I decided it would be less painful"—he smiled at what was meant as a male joke—"to take my chances in the outside world. I just try not to think about the danger."

I asked Mahfouz if he was disappointed that Al-Azhar, after his worldwide recognition, refused to lift its ban on *Children of Gebelawi*. He shrugged. Some had hoped that Egypt's politico-religious establishment, embarrassed at appearing medieval, would respond to the Nobel Prize by restoring Mahfouz's Islamic legitimacy. But the Rushdie fuss, if nothing else, made it impossible for the government and Al-Azhar to risk such an audacious action.

Richard Eder was a foreign correspondent and theater and film critic at the *New York Times* from 1962–82, before becoming a book critic with the *Los Angeles Times* and *Newsday*. He has been a book critic at the *New York Times* since March of 1999. This piece appeared on April 6, 1999.

Critic's Notebook

Annually for the last 83 years an editorial venture has sifted through several thousand published short stories to choose two dozen or so as America's most notable. "The Best American Short Stories of . . ." (filling in the year) has been the series title since 1915.

It approaches tautology. Whether the first editors were right to claim the short story as peculiarly American—John Updike suggests it has something to do with national restlessness and no second acts—"Best" reflects a characteristic if not exclusively "American" proclivity for thinking No. 1. (I daydream a Pulitzer Prize for Second-Best Poetry, for Second-Best American Short Stories. The choices might well shine brighter over time. Runners-up don't run faster, but—make of this what you will—they run longer.)

Houghton Mifflin, whose auspices span nearly all of the series' life, has arranged for Mr. Updike and Katrina Kenison, its general editor, to pick 55 stories from the 2,000 published over those 83 years. Selection goes way beyond that. Over the decades magazines had winnowed millions of manuscripts to print hundreds of thousands of stories that would be reduced to the 2,000 in the series and then squashed down by Ms. Kenison into the 300 mashed through Mr. Updike's 55-hole colander.

"A fathomless ocean of rejection and exclusion surrounds this brave little flotilla," writes Mr. Updike, who snores in epigrams. The result is "Best American Short Stories of the Century." "Century" is reasonable, even if the first 14 years and the last one are out of the game. "Best" is understandable, though it could use qualification.

To choose is to govern, and all government carries with it elements of misrule, secular decline and the shadow of revolt. Yet government is necessary. Choice is more than necessary; it is frail and admirable. Milovan Djilas, the Serb who wielded a power, now seemingly lost, to wrestle moral illumination out of history's chaos—how his absence aches today—praised what he called "the imperfect society." Imperfect choice is a humane value. It outguns canons.

Imperfection is gracefully acknowledged by Mr. Updike and by Ms. Kenison, who reads thousands of stories for each volume of the series and offers 120 to the novelist chosen to act as that year's editor. She has done it for nine years, an infant. Edward O'Brien, the series' inventor, was 25 years on the job when he visited wartime London, where a German bomb managed to accomplish upon him what never-selected authors like John O'Hara and Mary McCarthy no doubt wished to. Martha Foley, his successor, lasted 37 years, dying almost literally with reading glasses on.

Personally I felt faintly dizzy after three days and only these 55 stories. Short stories are sprints, and most of us need a breathing spell after every three or four. The reader should treat this centennial Best as an event of a season, not of an evening or two. The risk otherwise is esthetic shell shock. Whether vociferous or quiet, direct, distanced or revved-up absurdist, the form involves a detonation in a small space. Sometimes, in a number of the more recent stories, it is the detonation of what purposefully doesn't go off.

One of the discoveries in reading through the shifts of effect and intention by writers over the course of a near-century is an odd constancy. Throughout and with few exceptions, a short story remains a hole the author quite noticeably digs, whatever the camouflage, for the characters to fall into. The reader is pulled close enough (in the older ones) or shoved close enough (in the maneuvered ricochets of the newer ones) to be snagged as well. Almost always the holes are dark. Death or dying are not just ending but dramatic climax. (Classically, death was not tragedy but what followed tragedy.)

In Susan Glaspell's shiveringly affecting "A Jury of Her Peers" (1917), one of the collection's true resurrections, a farm wife kills her brutal husband. In Flannery O'Connor's "Greenleaf" (1957) a fading Southern aristocrat is gored by her caretaker's bull. Susan Sontag's perhaps too explicitly titled "The Way We Live Now" (1987) uses a dying AIDS patient as denunciatory charge against the trivial rivalries of a New York arts set maneuvering around the deathbed. In Annie Proulx's "Half-Skinned Steer" (1998) the hallucinatory end of a fierce old man in a blizzard is a near-biblical judgment.

If not death, the hole can be a desolating social circumstance: Bernard Malamud's "German Refugee" (1964); Carolyn Ferrell's black adolescent tormented by poverty, violence and his own gay loneliness in "Proper Library" (1994), or interior condition (too numerous to count, a number of them from the *New Yorker*'s chaste glory days).

Suburban wit and irony can light up the hole without diminishing it: "Gesturing" (1980), Mr. Updike's modest self-selection. Cheever's "Country Husband" (1955) brings in gods and dogs to give a friezelike mythic touch to more expensive suburbs than Mr. Updike's. Damnation hovers, nonetheless.

Early on, the writers' hole digging can be brittly obvious, as in remarkably similar stories by Ring Lardner and Dorothy Parker. With "City of Churches" (1973) by Donald Barthelme, pretty much the sole representative of the surreal absurd, the hole drops into a shape-changing fun house that is no fun at all except, itchily, for the reader. Only rarely is the hole uplifting. (Never mind the physics.) An anguished couple find reconciliation in a child's terrible death (Paul Horgan's "Peachstone," 1943). From Harold Brodkey: "Verona: A Young Woman Speaks" (1977), in which an adolescent on a ruinously lavish Italian holiday lives that brief moment when parents are gods of light. What more to make of this? Alfred Kazin is dead, Harold Bloom is busy, and I am not Elizabeth Hardwick. A couple of thoughts about the process.

There are so many ways to choose. The editors might have ignored the near-century span of the project and tried to pick, on quality and survivability alone, the finest 55 of the 2,000. But the result would have been less interesting. Instead, it was decided to represent each decade with anywhere from three to eight selections. Yes, there are some lumps—not too many—but it was the right decision.

Instead of a strictly contemporary judgment we have a running one: These were the stories that judges in the 1930's, 40's and 50's chose. We get a sense of how we and our writers have changed. And we avoid the deadly ahistorical numbness of ourselves talking to ourselves. A second decision, inevitable but with mixed consequences, was to get in the big and near-big names. Sometimes it works splendidly and usually creditably. But in a few cases, because of the rules of choice, the writers are not well represented.

The rules had it that only those stories selected for each year's volume could be considered. So, for example, Isaac Bashevis Singer, Eudora Welty, Katherine Anne Porter and Jean Stafford are displayed in stories that, though perfectly good, fail to convey their particular genius. Is this more damaging than the rules-governed failure to include a John O'Hara or Mary McCarthy because they were never chosen for the yearly volumes? Oddly enough, I believe so. Perhaps the jinx word "best" accommodates itself more easily to an omission than to our facing, in the reading rather than the missing, a "not really best."

What else? The easy and uninteresting mention of authors whom one would have included: Tobias Wolff, Christopher Tilghman, Mary Gaitskell. ("Eder, go edit your own book.") The subjective but perhaps more interesting mention of several venerably established stories to which my response was not, "Good to see you again, and of course you should be here." Instead it was, "I know you until I read you; and when I read you, it is as if I never knew you."

There is the perfect form of Hemingway's "Killers." The bottomless sorrow and beauty of Faulkner's "That Evening Sun Go Down." The joyful detail and stoic spaciousness of the Cheever. The unexpected (to me), rating of Philip Roth's early "Defender of the Faith" so high: the lyrical, unexplored energy of a knowingness that would later be so complexly explored. Here it is a new snowfall with only a single ski track.

Terrence Rafferty was a staff writer at the *New Yorker* for ten years and is now Critic-at-Large for *GQ*. He is the author of *The Thing Happens: Ten Years of Writing about the Movies* (Grove Press, 1993). This piece appeared in the *New Yorker*, November 5, 1990.

L'Atalante

Jean Vigo, who died in 1934 at the age of twenty-nine, was one of the greatest artists in the history of the movies, and probably the most tantalizing. His body of work consists of a pair of short documentaries, a forty-seven-minute fiction film (*Zero for Conduct*), and one full-length feature—all told, less than three hours of finished film. The feature, *L'Atalante*, was released in Paris in September 1934 (just three weeks before Vigo's death), in a version the filmmaker had never seen: the distributor had cut the movie by almost a third, added a mediocre popular song, and then, for good measure, retitled the picture *Le Chaland Qui Passe*, after the new tune. *L'Atalante* was largely restored in 1940, but it has retained over the years the aura of something fragile and patched up, and that quality of seeming slightly damaged is perhaps what has made it for many viewers an object of special devotion: it's a movie that people see again and again, and love in ways they find difficult to explain. Now *L'Atalante* has been given another major renovation. This version, prepared by Pierre Philippe and Jean-Louis Bompoint, adds about nine minutes of footage not included in the previous reconstruction, and the restorers discovered in the archives of the British Film Institute a pristine nitrate print of a cut of the movie which obviously preceded the distributor's intervention; *L'Atalante* now looks and sounds better than ever. (The prints that have been circulating for the last fifty years are uniformly atrocious.) Thanks to Philippe and Bompoint, we can see all the lucid beauties of Boris Kaufman's cinematography, rather than have to struggle to imagine them, and hear Maurice Jaubert's lovely score without distortion; we can even make out the dialogue, which in previous prints was often just a low rumble of undifferentiated sound. But the best thing about this shiny new *L'Atalante* is that for all the restorers' diligence, the film is still messy, imperfect, defiantly incomplete. Like everything Vigo did, like his frustratingly brief career, *L'Atalante* is an unfinished product, unsuitable for framing: even in its current spruced-up condition, it's essentially a collection of inspired fragments, the sketchbook of an artist whose imagination was, and will forever remain, gloriously immature.

This movie was, in part, Vigo's attempt to "grow up" as a filmmaker—to make a conventional commercial picture. His previous film, *Zero for Conduct*,

about a revolt in a boys' boarding school, was a celebration of the pure freedom of children's imaginations, a stirring expression of resistance to the forces
of authority and order—to anything that would impose discipline on the diverse, unruly energy of play. *Zero for Conduct* isn't constructed like an ordinary
movie; Vigo evidently considered the discipline of narrative a form of repression, too, and his indifference to it has a lot to do with why *Zero for Conduct*
still seems, fifty-seven years later, like one of the few truly subversive movies
ever made. And the French censors—as alert to insubordination as the dwarf
headmaster and the malevolent instructors who rule the world of Vigo's
schoolboys—banned the movie from public exhibition. For *L'Atalante*, Vigo
agreed to work within the constraints of a simple and apparently innocuous
story (from an original scenario by an undistinguished writer named Jean
Guinée). Jean (Jean Dasté), the captain of a river barge named *L'Atalante*,
marries Juliette (Dita Parlo), a girl from one of the villages on the barge's route.
As the newlyweds travel down the river, Juliette becomes increasingly restless
and disenchanted; she has escaped from her village, but all she's seeing of the
world is riverbanks, the inside of cramped cabins, and her husband and his
odd crew—a rambunctious old salt called Père Jules (Michel Simon) and a
quiet cabin boy (Louis Lefèvre). Bored and impatient, she sneaks off to see the
sights of Paris, but when she returns to the place where the barge was docked
she discovers that Jean has shoved off without her. She wanders on the shore,
he drifts downstream on the boat, and the separation makes them both miser-
able. Finally, they find each other again; life resumes its intended course.

The miracle of *L'Atalante* is that Vigo keeps breaking free of the story's
ordained course: he's incapable of simply riding that dull, even current and
making only the scheduled stops. He treats the story the way a jazz musician
treats a popular song, improvising on the melody by plunging into its carefully
sequenced chords and predictable rhythms and taking them apart to see what
they're made of. He hits notes that we had never dreamed were there but that
seem, once we've heard them, pure and essential, like pearls dredged from far
beneath the smooth, lulling flow of the song. In one of the film's most sublime
sequences, Jean, aching from the absence of Juliette, dives off the barge into
the river because his bride once told him that you see the face of the one you
love when you look under the surface of the water. Jean has tried the trick a
couple of times before, jokingly and unsuccessfully, but this time—now that
he is abandoned, mad with grief, reckless—he sees her luminous in her wedding dress, and laughing with an unforced, innocent joy that looks like the
sweetest of invitations, the promise of every kind of pleasure. The floating
images of Juliette superimposed on Jean's desperate, searching face are re-
minders of some of our earlier views of her, and especially of a ghostly image
of the bride in her white dress walking slowly along the top of the barge as it
glides down the river at twilight. In the underwater sequence, Jean seems, at
last, to be seeing his wife the way Vigo has seen her from the start—as an

ordinary woman who becomes radiant when she is looked at with desire. This sequence tells us most of what we need to know about Vigo's eroticized approach to the art of moviemaking: he forgets his orders, immerses himself in the ordinary beauties of the sensual world, and summons up visions that shine with the possibilities of earthly pleasure.

The other key to Vigo is his attraction to chaos, clutter, sheer profusion—a quality that is, in a sense, just another side of his eroticism. The toys and gadgets and bric-a-brac that fill his movies are played with and caressed by the camera with such loving attention that they seem like fetishes. And there are so *many* of them—so many objects to divert us from the implacable responsibilities of living, so many beautiful distractions. Père Jules' cabin, overrun by cats and jammed with bizarre mementos that are the residue of a full and gleefully disorderly life, is the image not only of its inhabitant but also of its creator. This museum of useless things—with which, in a long and brilliantly sustained sequence, the old sailor enchants Juliette—is Vigo's world in miniature, a place where something to tickle the imagination or to stir memories or simply to gaze at in wonder is always ready to hand. And the character itself, as it is conceived by Vigo and played by the magnificently peculiar Simon, is the presiding spirit of the movie: Père Jules is a comic metaphor for the diversity of the world's riches; he is, in his demented, random way, a living encyclopedia. At one point, he gets excited, and all sorts of strange stuff bubbles out of him, with startling alacrity: Indian war whoops, bullfighting moves, snippets of songs and dances from Russia, Africa, the Orient. (He takes us around the world in about eighty seconds.) His body is covered with crudely drawn tattoos, and in one of the most welcome of the newly restored shots he amuses Juliette by making a face tattooed on his belly appear to smoke by putting a cigarette in his navel. Père Jules is, of course, a child, both splendid and monstrous, and there is, too, something profoundly childlike about the way the character is conceived: only a very innocent eye could see this crazy old drifter as the epitome of worldly experience.

Vigo may have been trying, with some part of himself, to make a "normal" movie—one conventional enough, at least, to get past the censors and into the commercial cinemas—but L'Atalante shows how hopelessly, wonderfully unsuited he was to popular moviemaking. His storytelling is still casual, almost perfunctory: the narrative will slow to a languorous drift, then abruptly begin chugging forward, then stop to give us a long look at some unanticipated marvel off in the distance, then lurch irritably ahead again. And his approach to composition and editing is so personal that audiences expecting an ordinary movie might become disoriented: shots are taken from unexpected angles, are held longer than usual, are juxtaposed with other shots in unprecedented ways. Vigo was helplessly original; he seems at times to be speaking a different language from other filmmakers. (On seeing Vigo's work for the first time, James Agee wrote, "It is as if he had invented the wheel.") He is the most playful and the least rigid of the great film artists; he had the liveliest eye, and perhaps the freest imagination. Everything he shows us looks mysteriously new, full of possibilities, and so encourages us to linger on it, investigate it, dream it, have our way with it.

In a sense, the restorers' work on *L'Atalante* springs from impulses like those—from the feeling, evoked at virtually every moment in Vigo's films, that there's something more for us to discover. The latest version of *L'Atalante* is new only in the sense that this movie has always seemed new; it isn't changed in any fundamental way. The footage added by Philippe and Bompoint is just extra stuff, beautiful and inessential and thus fully in keeping with the movie's expansive spirit. They've given us a few more glittery things to hoard in our imagination and fondle in our memories when life gets a little dull. In Jean Vigo's movies, greater profusion only creates stronger desire: his images seduce us with the promise of a larger, richer world and unbounded freedom to roam in it—the promise, that is, of endless stimulation, inexhaustible sensations. There can be no definitive *L'Atalante*, because the world of Vigo's films subverts the very idea of definition. This extraordinary movie will always elude our attempts to grasp it and keep it in its place: we'll never see everything in Père Jules' cabin; the image of the woman in the water disperses when we try to embrace it, then forms itself again and leads us on.

Jeremy Bernstein, a former staff writer for the *New Yorker*, is a professor emeritus of the Stevens Institute of Technology. This piece appeared in the *Aspen Times Weekly*, December 19 and 20, 1998. It is a love story in two parts.

Annie of Corsica

PART I

It was the summer of 1960. I was giving lectures on theoretical physics, in a summer school in a Corsican village. The village was Cargese and at the time it had 852 inhabitants. There was one restaurant (the Cyrnos) and one hotel (the Thalassa) listed in the Michelin Guide. Both these names were Greek—Cyrnos, or Kyrnos, was the old Greek name for Corsica and Thalassa means the "sea" in Greek. The hotel was on a beach at the edge of the Mediterranean. (Because of its location the Michelin listing included a red rocking-chair—the symbol that indicates "isolated and tranquil.")

It was no accident that there were Greek names in Cargese. The Genoese, who had ruled the island since the late 13th century, had allowed 730 Greeks who had fled the Turks to settle there in 1676. The town was burned down some 50 years later by the native Corsicans whose families had been displaced by the Greeks; but when the French took over the island, in 1769, the Greeks were permitted to come back to re-establish their small village, a village of no special importance. I tell you all this to convince you that Cargese was the last place in the world you would have expected to find a summer school in theoretical physics.

The school had been started by a group of French physicists the year before I first taught there. They had discovered a half-finished white stucco summer house near the town. It had been abandoned and could be bought cheap. It had light fixtures but no lights, bathroom fixtures but no running water, and picture windows with no glass. But you could set up a blackboard and chairs in the living room. The students, who were not much younger than I was, lived in tents near a beach and the faculty lived in the Thalassa hotel, which was on another beach. The hotel was owned by a Corsican family of Greek descent. Their daughter Marie had recently married a young man from the village, Etienne, also of Greek descent. They got to know us pretty well and we got to like them a great deal.

I had come by car from Paris and had taken the ferry from Marseilles to Ajaccio, the capital of Corsica and, incidentally, the birthplace of Napoleon. I had no idea of what to expect once I got off the boat and still less of an idea of where Cargese was. With one thing or another, by the time I got there it was night and, not being able to find the hotel, I slept on the warm beach. This never failed to amuse Marie and Etienne who teased me about it often. After checking in, I was put in what was known as the Annex—sort of bungalows next to the actual hotel. The hotel and the Annex had only 11 rooms—just about enough to accommodate those of the faculty who did not want to camp out, as well as a handful of regular guests.

I soon developed a daily routine. My lectures were early in the morning when it was not so hot. I would drive over to the school, up the very steep dirt road that led from the hotel to the village, which was a little over a mile away and 240 feet up. The school was on the far side of the village. After giving my lecture, I would go to the Café au Bon Repos for coffee and a croissant and to read the *Nice-Matin*. The proprietor of the café, who usually had a cigarette dangling from his mouth had his copy of the paper so we could compare notes. ("Ça bouge"—"it moves"—was his usual comment on the news.) Then the students would begin to drift in; our students and students from the Continent who were on vacation. They would flirt and talk. One scraggly-bearded chap I remember had "HEGEL" painted on his shoes: "HE" on the left and "GEL" on the right. There were guitars, which often got lost in the chatter. And then there was Annie.

As I write this I can see Annie as I saw her for the first time. She had jet black hair and eyes as blue as a Mediterranean cove. She drove up to the café on a vintage Harley-Davidson motorcycle in her bare feet wearing blue jeans that had been cut short. She said almost nothing, but all the conversation seemed to be addressed to her. She had an infectious laugh. After a little while, a band of Corsicans—"mes cousins," she explained to the students in the café—rode up on their motorcycles and they all drove off together. I had no idea who she was, but I fell instantly in love with her. I thought that I had about as much chance of meeting her as dancing on the Moon. But a few days later there came a surprising turn of events.

A family from Paris appeared at the hotel. They too had a daughter, also very pretty and about Annie's age. The first night they were there they all came into the dining room for dinner. And there was Annie looking stunning in a blue summer dress, with two adults who were clearly her parents. Her mother looked as one thought Annie might look when she got older: very handsome. The hotel had a ping-pong table and after dinner there were often round-robin games in which we challenged each other. The Parisian man—whose name was Robert—seemed to be looking for a game so I challenged him. I was then invited to sit down with everyone. Robert asked me what I did. I said that I was an American physicist doing research in Paris. Much to my surprise his re-action was instantaneous and very hostile. I excused myself and left the group feeling both puzzled and hurt.

The next day I was on the beach when Robert spotted me. He came over to explain. Early in the war, he told me, the two families had joined the

Communist Party, which had people then engaged in the Resistance. They had seen enough of the German occupation to hate it and they all joined the Resistance. Annie's aunt, Danielle Casanova, was caught and executed by the Germans. There is a street named after her in Paris.

After the war, they all remained in the Party. The two girls even studied Russian and represented France in one of the youth festivals in Moscow. But then came the Hungarian uprising in 1956 and the Russian occupation. The two families split apart. Annie's family stayed in the Party. Her father was a very poorly paid Party functionary, which was one reason the family remained on Corsica, where the cost of living was a lot lower that it was on the Continent. Robert and his wife left the Party and the relationship between the senior members of the two families soured, although the girls remained the best of friends. This visit to Corsica was to be some sort of reconciliation. There was an understanding that they would not discuss politics. However, the fact that I was an American physicist and, for all they knew, working on nuclear weapons—which I was not—triggered a violent political dispute and I had been the inadvertent cause.

After that I spent a good deal of time with Robert and his family. I began going places with his daughter, whose name was Annick, and Annie. Then I began going places with Annie alone. We used to sit where we could look at the sea and talk. She told me something about her life. In the winters she studied in Paris at the Sorbonne. She knew most of the students who were vacationing in the village from the Latin Quarter. She didn't much like Paris. It was too far from nature. Later she showed me where she and her family lived. It was in an apartment above a café in Piana, a town on the coast about 20 kilometers north of Cargese. The town is on a cliff more than a thousand feet above the Mediterranean. From it, you can see what is one of the most beautiful natural wonders imaginable. Spires of red rock—cathedrals— cascade a thousand feet into the deep blue sea. At sunset and sunrise, the rocks catch fire. Perhaps if you lived in Piana you might get used to this. I never did and I don't think Annie did either.

Sometimes I had the fantasy that she might come with me back to America. I once asked her, but all she did was to point to the sunset.

PART II

I went back to Cargese for two more summers. Robert and his family were not there. No one knew why. I couldn't find Annie either. She seemed to have left the island. I never had the chance to tell her what an important part she had played in my life. When I came back to the United States after that first summer I took a job at the Brookhaven National Laboratory in Upton, Long Island. But I could not get Annie and Corsica out of my mind. I decided to try to write it all down—to write a letter to myself, which I called "Annie of Corsica." It was something like what is above . . . perhaps a more youthful version. Never having written anything professionally except physics, I didn't have in mind sending it anywhere. But some people at the lab read it and said that I should send it to the *New Yorker*. I knew no one at the magazine, so I simply addressed it "To The Editor" and went about my physics.

Months later, I was once again going back to Europe and was again planning to teach in the summer school in Cargese. I had heard nothing at all from the magazine so I decided to call them to see if my "letter" had ever gotten there. After some confusion I finally got to speak to a woman whose first words were, "Oh, you must be back from Corsica." Whoever she was, it was clear that she had somehow read my "letter." It had gotten there. Afterwards I learned that she was William Shawn's secretary and that Mr. Shawn, who called me a few days later, had accepted my "letter" for publication. It appeared in the issue of Nov. 11, 1961 under the rubric "Our Far-Flung Correspondents" and was sub-titled "Annie of Corsica."

I am retired from teaching now. I tell people that I take two vacations a year—each one lasting six months. For the last several years, during each of my six-month "vacations," I have taken a bicycle trip to some place I have always wanted to see—Bali, Crete, Portugal—places like that. If you do this sort of thing you will soon begin getting catalogs from tour companies all over the country. About a year ago I got one from a company in Arlington, Mass., named Ciclismo Classico. In it I found a tour called "Mediterranean Island Hopping, Cycling and Snorkeling on Sardinia and Corsica." It had a day-by-day description and this is what it said about the ninth day: "Today's ride [42 miles with 3 climbs] has an incredible variety of scenery. We start out with an uphill through a vast background of rugged mountains; then a fabulous descent through the Gulf of Liscia. For [the] next few miles we ride along a wonderful coastal road with white sandy beaches. After Sagone we start to climb gently towards Cargese, one of the most picturesque villages of the trip. Make sure to check out the Greek Orthodox church, not only for its wonderful mosaics but also its wonderful setting facing the bay and the town of Cargese. After lunch we begin a five mile hill (steep in [the] beginning then flattens out) across the saddle of lush rounded mountains. Have your camera ready and enough film for the next ten miles!" Those last 10 miles are the miles that go through Piana and down through the red-rock cathedrals into the seaside town of Porto.

Reading this was like reeling back a film of my life. It was 35 years since I was in Cargese. Was the Thalassa still there? And Etienne and Marie and, of course, Annie? I bought the latest Guide Michelin and looked under Cargese. The population of the town had now grown to 915. No restaurants are listed. But there are two hotels; the Spelunca and the Thalassa, still with its red rocking chair. Michelin did not say who owned it. I signed up for the trip.

My first sight of Cargese was a few miles from the town. When I was last in Corsica, it would never have occurred to me to ride these hilly and sometimes narrow and broken roads on a bicycle, but here I was. I could tell immediately that it was Cargese because of the two churches, Greek Orthodox and Roman Catholic, which face each other, and, out on a spit of land, the Genoese tower that, like many on the Corsican coast, guards the shoreline. On the outskirts of the town was a not particularly noticeable sign that read "Institut d'Études Scientifiques de Cargese." Our infant summer school has grown up. It has its own building with a restaurant and sleeping facilities for people who do not want to camp or stay in a hotel. I know this because you can read about all its programs on the Internet. You can even download a picture of the new building if you want to.

The town is a little farther along the road. It looked both familiar and strange. There were many more cafes and restaurants than I remembered. It was hard to get my bearings. I knew that the road down to the Thalassa was somewhere near the edge of the town, but I didn't recognize it. A group of local men were drinking Pernod on the terrace of one of the cafes, so I asked about the Thalassa. One of them said, "Oh, they closed for the season two days ago. You just missed them." I asked if Etienne and Marie still ran it and he said they did. He pointed out the road and told me that if I went down I might find Etienne and Marie.

I had not recognized the road because it was now paved, although still very steep. There were a number of houses along it that certainly weren't there 35 years ago. Then, there was nothing there but brush and trees. At the bottom of the hill—as far as you could go—was the hotel with its white columns, looking smaller than I remembered it. It also looked totally deserted. I went by the Annex, where I used to live and through the wooden gate that led to the beach. That at least seemed familiar. There was the sound of some sort of machine running in the hotel so someone had to be around. I knocked on all its doors with no response.

I tried the house next to the hotel. I went to the gate and a dog began to bark. A woman came out of the house. It was Marie, short and dark as I remembered her. I was wearing my biking clothes—helmet and all—so she didn't have the slightest idea who I was. I took off my helmet and immediately she recognized me. She was astonished to see me, but very pleased. She said that I must come inside and greet Etienne and her brother who were in the kitchen. Etienne looked just as I had remembered him but displaced in time— silver-gray hair and the same kind, wide face.

They said that they had never forgotten me and often asked physicists who came to stay a the hotel what had happened to me. I explained as best I could. But I must have lunch: Marie would make an omelette and we could catch up. First I asked about various students I had known. They now had students who had students—generations who now came to Cargese. Then I asked about

Robert. Why had they not come back? The family, they explained, had had a very bad time. Their daughter had a boyfriend during the Algerian war who was part of a guerrilla group fighting the French. He stored arms in Robert's apartment. The apartment was raided and the whole family was arrested. It was a disaster. They were ruined.

And finally, of course, I asked about Annie. I had no idea what to expect. After that first summer she too had disappeared. Perhaps she was now living in Piana so that I could at least say hello when I passed through. Had she married? Had she had children? Yes, they said, she had married a man who was somehow involved in diplomatic missions. A few years ago he had gone to Africa and had never returned. No one knew what happened to him. Not even his body was found. Perhaps it broke Annie's heart—they did not know. But a year or two later she died. She had had two daughters—*grandes filles*, Marie said. I said that I hoped they were as beautiful as Annie and that they rode around the island on motorcycles the way Annie used to do, careering through the narrow streets scattering man and animal. Etienne said he would put my bicycle on his camionette and drive me up the hill. When we parted he said, "I hope it does not take 35 more years for you to come back."

John Darnton is culture editor of the *New York Times* and author of
Neanderthal (Random House, 1996) and *The Experiment* (Dutton, 1999). This
article appeared in the *New York Times* on April 7, 1996.

Two Deaths—One Then, One Now:
On Losing a Father, a Newspaperman

Journalism is not just a job. Any reporter who is good at what he does
believes this on some level, no matter how he tries to wrap the sentiment in
cynicism. I don't know how others came to that conviction, but in my case it
was thrust upon me, accepted as part of family lore.

I was eleven months old when my father died in 1942, killed as a war
correspondent for the *New York Times* by friendly fire in the Pacific. I have
no memory of him; nor does my brother, Bob, who was two and a half years
older and who stood at the door and watched him walk away, a towering
figure in khaki uniform with a dashing moustache that stands out in all the
photographs.

The story of how he died was raised, in our tight little circle of three, to
the status of epic. A veteran of the Red Arrow A Division in World War I,
he was too old at 45 to fight in World War II but volunteered to go as a
correspondent.

In an advance landing craft, he was with a unit moving along the coast of
New Guinea. In a pocket-sized notebook, he scrawled sights and sounds along
the way, collecting color for his story (one bird had a cry that sounded as if it
were rebuking him for overwriting and "wasting cable tolls"). Then a plane
flew overhead, its markings unclear. "Jap or ours?" he scribbled. He continued
taking notes as the plane passed over. Then it returned and dropped a bomb.

It exploded some distance away, but shrapnel struck and killed the skipper,
Lieut. Bruce Fahnestock. My father grabbed the wheel. The plane circled,
returned and dropped a second bomb, which sent a piece of metal straight
into the back of his neck. Death, we were told at the time, was instantaneous.
No one else was hurt.

Our mother never remarried. From time to time my brother and I would
suggest a possible suitor, but she never followed up on our suggestions and I
suspect we would have been disappointed if she had. Often the discussions of
our father's death led to discussions of dictatorship and then of democracy
and the imperative to defend it, always.

Often the talks would move on to journalism. A family recovers from death
by giving it meaning, and in our family the article of faith was that he died as
a newspaperman, seeking out the truth and giving voice to people fighting for

their country half a world away. The talks were not always easy; even twenty-five years later, my mother would still cry while rereading a letter he wrote to his older brother Tom, in which he talked of the need to defeat Hitler and Hirohito to make the world fit for his two sons.

My brother tried newspapering after college, but gave it up for his first love, history. Family tradition had picked me for an engineer. But I suppose it was preordained that when I graduated from college and married, my thoughts would turn to a job on a paper. On my first day, I was scared, but I learned to hide the fear and watch other newspaper people to see how they went about what they did.

Over time, a strange thing happened—my father became not less, but more, of a presence. A handful at the *Times* remembered him, though often with a vagueness I found exasperating. A retired city editor told us he had filmed him on a home movie; my brother and I sat stiffly on a couch and watched as the back of his head passed for one second across a grainy screen. An elderly woman who said she knew him well called me to set up a meeting; my wife and I traveled to a Victorian house overlooking the Hudson, and as she opened the door, she stared into my eyes and gasped: "Yes, Barney Darnton's son." I retrieved his clips from the paper's morgue and read his coverage of an election in California and his war reporting. Once he dodged fire by jumping into a trench, where he landed his knee "in the back of a private from Brooklyn."

These episodes were like visitations. The most profound happened in 1976, eight years after my mother died, in the weeks before I went off to cover wars in Africa. A package arrived from the *Chicago Tribune*. It contained his note-book, taken off his body by a colleague who left it in a filing cabinet where it turned up 34 years later. In it I read of the birds and of Lieutenant Fahne-stock's death and saw the notation "Jap or ours?"—a foreshadowing of the confusion that led to his death, since the plane that attacked his vessel turned out to be American after all.

The visitations tapered off for awhile, but resumed recently with several letters from unknown men, veterans mostly. We realized they were writing because they had reached a certain age and were putting their affairs in order. Some of them wrote at length of the Pacific and the war, an outpouring of names and memories and descriptions that were surprisingly vivid. Some of the letters were very matter-of-fact, others sad in an almost wistful way. Some unburdened themselves of long-buried secrets. One man, contradicting what we had been told earlier about the circumstances of my father's death, recalled how brave our father had been as he was being rowed to shore, lying wounded for hours.

I thought of these things as I learned of the death of another *Times* corre-spondent, Nathaniel Nash, who died along with Secretary of Commerce Ron Brown and more than thirty others in a plane crash in Croatia—for Mr. Nash

was the first *Times* correspondent since World War II to be killed while working on a story. I thought of how, no matter what, Mr. Nash will be a presence
in the lives of his three children, who will hear of him for years to come from
his friends and colleagues.

And I was pleased to read that he had said, speaking of the challenge of
working at a newspaper, that "to thrive there you can't be cynical."

Geoffrey Wolff's tenth book and current enterprise is *The Art of Burning Bridges*, a biography of John O'Hara to be published by Knopf. He is fiction director of the MFA Program in Writing at the University of California, Irvine. This memoir was published in an anthology entitled *Family: American Writers Remember Their Own*, edited by Sharon Sloan Fiffer and Steve Fiffer (Pantheon, 1996).

Heavy Lifting

In the hot, breathless, soft, fragrant afternoon of my graduation from Princeton it seemed that everything good was not merely latent but unavoidable, folded and in the bag. I'd worked like a Turk those past years, and my labors had been rewarded and then some with fancy Latin on my fancy diploma, *summa* it said and summit I believed. Not one but two ex-girlfriends had come to the ceremony in front of lovely tree-shaded Nassau Hall, and so resolutely happy was I that it didn't even stain my pride to sweat through my shirt and gray worsted suit, to be capped like a monkey in tasseled mortarboard.

Each of my exes had brought me the same gift, a suitcase. It occurred to me that unarticulated longings were expressed by these mementos, and coming to them for visits wouldn't have answered their prayers. Sending me off solo on a long voyage would have been in the ballpark, Godspeed would have done their fantasies justice, *adios* was more like it.

And that too was as I wished it! All was jake, a-okay, on the come and coming! Admitted, I had no money, but a job was waiting nigh September, far, far away, teaching in Turkey, which was even farther from my father in California than I was now in the Garden State, and the farther the better. The last time I had intersected with him, two years before, he had swept through Princeton in a car sought for repossession, charging clothes and books and jazz records to my accounts. My stepmother, having just left him again and for good, gave me unwelcome word of him a year later; he was in Redondo Beach, in trouble.

For me, that June, what was trouble? A college friend with a different kind of daddy, the kind who owned a fifty-foot paid-for ketch, had invited me to spend the summer with him on that boat in Massachusetts Bay, Buzzards Bay, Nantucket Sound, Vineyard Sound, Narragansett Bay. It was our onus to sail that Sea Witch from snug harbor to snug harbor, cleaning and polishing and varnishing, making the boat ready for his parents' pleasure if they wanted to come aboard, which they wouldn't because they had better places to play that summer, as though there could be a better place to play than where we were to be fed and paid to play. I was warned that sunburn was lively danger, likewise hangovers from the free consumables at coming-out parties in Non-quitt and Nantucket, Newport and Edgartown. Dark and lonely work, but somebody had to do it.

Now, a few days after graduation, doing it, we were embarked. My suitcases and diploma were stored ashore with my passport and vaccination certificates and Greek tragedies in translation; we tugged at anchor off Cuttyhunk, drinking a rum drink to celebrate our third day at sea. There were four of us, two happy couples laughing and watching the sun fall, when my father got through on the radiotelephone. Writing about that conversation thirty-four years later I feel foggy dread, as though I've sailed on a cloudless day through deep clear water bang onto a reef. It's the nature of a radiotelephone conversation that everyone aboard can hear it, not to mention anyone else aboard any vessel within miles who wants to listen in.

This conversation mortified me. My dad stuttered flamboyantly. He did everything abundantly, elaborately, extravagantly, but his stuttering was grandiose. Moreover, he couldn't get the hang of the turn-and-turn-about of a radio conversation, in which one either speaks or listens. Listening was not my dad's thing, so I heard myself shouting at him, and worse, I heard myself stammering back, so that it must have seemed I was mocking the poor fellow, when in fact I was falling, as abruptly as a boat may fetch up on a shoal, into the speech defect I had inherited from him—nature or nurture, who cares?

While my friends, helplessly obliged to eavesdrop, pretended to have a conversation in the cockpit, I was below, where it was dark and close, as if the clean, salty air had been sucked from the cabin. I stretched the mike on its snaky cord as far from my friends as possible, but the loudspeaker stayed put, broadcasting his invitation:

My father wanted me to come to him for the summer, in La Jolla.

I said I wouldn't.

My father said he missed me.

I said nothing.

My father tried to tell me he had a j-j-j-job.

I said, really, how nice. (I thought, how novel, what a piquant notion, my dad working for a living.)

My father said congratulations on the degree.

I wondered how he'd guessed I had one.

He said congratulations on the job in Turkey, did I remember he'd lived there once upon a time?

I said I remembered.

He asked did I have a "popsie" aboard with me?

I reddened; it was quiet in the cockpit; I said I had to get off now, this was too expensive, far too complicated.

He said my brother was coming to La Jolla to visit from Washington state. Learned boy that I was, I didn't believe my father. I hadn't seen Toby for seven years.

My father said it again, Toby was right now on the road from Concrete, Washington, arriving in a couple of days.

I listened to static while gentle waves slapped the Sea Witch.

He said he'd send airfare.

I said sure. I thought fat chance.

I BORROWED ticket money from the yachtsman dad and hopped a hound (more accurately a Trailway—cheaper) in New York. This would be the place to detail the squalor of a cross-country summer bus journey from the noxious flats of Jersey to the uncompromising wasteland of Death Valley—you know the drill, you've ridden a bus, you've read about the Joads. Assume I was sad, hungry, and as funky as everyone else aboard our land yacht, our prairie schooner. The one constant in addition to the diesely whine while successive drivers went up through the gearbox—do-re-mi-fa-sol-la-ti-do—and down—do-ti-la-sol . . . —was the question I kept asking myself: *How had this happened to me? Why was I here?*

You might think—noticing the books I was conspicuously reading and annotating, and I'm afraid you were meant to notice them and me—that the question *why was I here?* was a Big Question and that I was questing for a vision from Sophocles, Erich Auerbach, Sartre, George Steiner. Boy oh boy, you think you know your aliens! I felt so apart from my fellow passengers that I believed I needed a visa to visit Earth. But at some point west of Gila Bend and east of El Centro, with the air-conditioning on the blink again, I commenced to reflect on the situation of La Jolla—seaside, wasn't it? Even a martyr had to take time off for a swim.

Hedonism, taking care of fun before taking care of business, was a legacy from my father. For this he had been thrown out of one boarding school after another, to the theatrical dismay of his mother and father, a Hartford, Connecticut, surgeon. For this he had also been thrown out of two colleges, neither of which, despite his testimony to the contrary, were fancy and ancient universities. For buying what he could not afford—sports cars and sports coats, Patek-Philippe wristwatches, dinners at Mike Romanoff's and 21, Leicas and Rolexes, Holland & Holland shotguns, whatever nice thing was around—he'd been fired from jobs. These jobs as an airplane designer (I know, I know: he was audacious) he had conned his way into with faked-up résumés. Getting fired would put him in a bad mood, so he'd buy more stuff; buying stuff intoxicated him, and so did booze. Drunk, he'd turn on his first wife, my mother and Toby's. After fourteen years of this, she told Dad to get lost, and I moved in with him. When I was seventeen, his second wife—her fortune and good mood seriously depressed by my old man—took a hike on him, and soon after that he took one on me. In the Wolff nuclear family, fission was all the rage.

Dad met me at the same bus station where he'd met Toby more than a week earlier. Visiting San Diego recently I was hard-pressed to find any site downtown as melodramatically seedy as my memory of that place, a garishly lit set dressed with tattoo parlors, bucket-of-blood bars, pawnshops, and, under the hard light of noon, my dad looking bewildered and lost. I had for many childhood years loved him recklessly, investing him with achievements and wisdom and powers beyond the reach of any mortal, and only a pinch less magnificent than the history and potential he had bestowed upon himself. Spare any father such impulsive love as I showered on that man. Later, when I became disillusioned, when I imagined that I understood Duke Wolff for what he really was—a deadbeat bullshit artist with a veneer of charm rubbed right through from negligent over-exercise—I hated him, and like the love before it, that hate too was indulgent, exorbitant.

This June afternoon outside the bus depot, examining my father blinking behind the thick lenses of owlish Goldwater specs, I was too wary to indulge contempt. The eyeglasses, out of register with Duke's formerly stylish presentations, were the least of it. Even at his lowest he'd enjoyed flamboyant temperamental resources: flash and spritz and nonchalance. Now he seemed timid, dulled, hungover. No: that wasn't it either; I was all too inured to his hangovers, which used to provoke in my dad a manic snap, as though he'd decided that if this was as bad as it got, bring it on, let's start another IV Mount Gay rum drip. What I was seeing lumbering toward me was a crummy linenish jacket. This wasn't what I'd have expected: seersucker, maybe, or the soiled white linen suit that Sydney Greenstreet might sport—tits-up in the tropics and all that—but not this, something on whose behalf a thousand polyesters had lost their lives, some rag that needed a cleaning the day it was sold, tarted up with cheapjack brass crested buttons. From Duke's good old bad old days of smart tailoring, what a fall was here! Halting toward me was a zombie. Dad Wolff looked as though he'd been shot smack in the heart with about 500 cc of Thorazine. Talk about taking the edge off! He looked like they'd sawed through his brain.

My brother, Toby, fifteen, was with him, hanging back gingerly, vigilant. I felt like someone to whom something bad would soon happen; Toby looked like someone to whom it had already happened. This was the more alarming because he looked so wakeful and sharp. He had a strong, bony face, with steady eyes and a jutting chin. He was tall and lean, handsome, like our mother. He didn't appear vulnerable; he gave an impression of competence, but after all, he was a kid.

I hadn't seen Toby during the past seven years, but we'd recently been in touch by telephone and letter, and I knew that he'd had a rocky time of it with his stepfather. Coming across the country to see my only sibling, I'd phoned from a roadside diner to tell Duke which bus to meet and I'd reached Toby. He didn't know where our father had disappeared to. No sooner had Toby arrived than Dad had taken off with a woman friend in a fancy Italian car. He had left his teenaged son with a hotel phone number and a vague assurance that he'd return to La Jolla in a few days.

Behind the wheel of the hubby-mummy rented Pontiac, driving to La Jolla, Duke was stiff and tentative. This was unlike him. I remembered him as a bold driver, fast and cocksure, every little journey to the grocery store a high-octane adventure in squealing tires and red-lined rpms. Now Dad held to the slow lane, glancing anxiously in the rearview. His face had once been imposing, Mussolini-monumental; now his nose was bulbous, stippled with burst blood vessels. The few times he spoke, I saw that his false teeth, what he used to call China clippers, were loose against his gums. I had questions: Where had he gone, leaving Toby alone? How could he take time off from his job? Asking this question I gave the impression, meant to give it, that I didn't believe he had a job. How soon could he give me cash (I came down hard on cash, to distinguish it from a check or an IOU) to repay my yachtsman classmate's yachtsman daddy? These questions immediately returned us to our fundamental relationship: I was the hectoring (and mind-dullingly dull) parent; Duke was the irresponsible (and charmingly fun-loving) kid. The exchange didn't leave much for Toby to do, except sit in the backseat and study his fingers, as though he might be looking hard at his hole cards.

Duke was miserly with basic information—what exactly he did for a living, where he had gone "in the desert" (as he put it) or why. But as we approached La Jolla he became effusive about his "lady friend." This conversation had the effect of making Toby visibly uncomfortable, inasmuch as it had been my father's stated ambition, made explicit to Toby, to re-up with our mom if everything this summer went swimmingly, as of course it had to. This nutty scheme had (no, wonders never do cease) a certain appeal to my mother, who has had a lifelong weakness for nutty schemes. Her marriage to her second husband, like her marriage to Duke before that, was a disaster, and Duke after all did live in southern California, and my mom, freezing up near the Canadian border, had always had, as she put it, "sand between my toes." But even this quixotic woman—who had decided a few years earlier that it was a sage idea to drive from Florida to Utah to explore for uranium without knowing what uranium was or why anyone wanted it—was on hold as far as a reenrollment in Dad's program was concerned, waiting to get a report card from Toby on Duke's attendance and comportment.

When we rolled up in front of a tiny bungalow east of Girard Avenue, my befuddlement increased. The woman who greeted us, as warily as Toby and I greeted her, was nothing like my father's type. He was drawn to palefaces, to blue eyes, to understated clothes. This woman was sun-burnt brown, her leathery skin set off with much jangly jewelry. She wore many, many rings of the turquoise family, accessorizing showy peasant duds from south of the border, busy with appliqué and bold stitching. She wore, for God's sake, cow-girl boots ornamented with horsehair.

We stood beside the car shaking her ringed hand and listening to her brace-lets ring like chimes; we admired her cactus garden; she got to listen to my father—and not, I suspected, for the first time—inflate my achievements at college and Toby's in high school; she didn't invite Toby or me inside. She didn't invite Dad inside either, but it was clear that inside was where he was going, and without his only children. He gave us rudimentary instructions to "my flat near the beach." Toby, manifestly eager to get away from where we were, assured me he knew the way. Duke said he'd be along soon, he'd bring home a nice supper. I asked how he'd get home from there, and he waved vaguely, mumbled "taxi." His lady friend seemed as unhappy as a person can be without flooding the earth with tears. Duke, by contrast, had abruptly come awake to joy; he was peppy, full of beans.

"Don't you two rascals go getting in t-t-t-trouble," he warned. "And if the manager badgers you about the rent, tell him to go f-f-f-f . . ."

"Go f-f-fish," I s-s-s-said.

DRIVING south through the attractive neighborhoods to our little second-floor studio apartment on Playa del Sur, fifty yards from the beach, I was mostly preoccupied with Toby, glad for the chance to be alone with him. He too relaxed, lit a Lucky Strike expertly with his lighter, inhaled intemperately, remarked that it had been an oddball visit so far. I asked him to steer while I lit a Camel expertly with my lighter, inhaled intemperately, and warned him that smoking was bad for his wind, especially if he planned to make a name for himself playing football at the Hill School back in Pennsylvania, where he was beginning on full scholarship in September.

My avuncular manner surprised me. I prided myself on being a laissez-faire kind of guy, I'll look out for me, you look out for you. Maybe I was practicing to become a teacher. Maybe I was out of my depth.

I unpacked my worldly goods—mostly books, a few jazz LPs (Bessie Smith, Bud Powell, the Miles Davis quintet, with Coltrane) I carried with me every-where—and Toby wanted to show me the beach. This generosity was all Wolff—sharing the good news, keeping alert to fun. By then it was late after-noon, and I worried that Dad might come home to an empty apartment, but Toby argued soberly that he didn't imagine Duke would be rushing home from his friend's house. I saw the wisdom in this hunch.

And so, dressed in long trousers and boat shoes and a white Lacoste tennis shirt, I accompanied Toby across Vista del Mar and Neptune Place to the Pump House, and down concrete steps to the beach. The first things I noticed were not the bitchin' sets of waves breaking way offshore, nor the surfers paddling way out there waiting to ride, nor the surfers with lots of white hair waxing their boards near the water's edge. I noticed, of course, the babes, and so did Toby.

"Hubba hubba," he said with reassuring irony, a family vice.

So we sat for a long time on a couple of hand towels, talking about the future, with our eyes cocked on the very here and now, avoiding the subject of our father. Toby was witty, resourceful, a hit parade of corny songs, which he was willing to sing out loud: "On the Wings of a Dove" and "Calendar Girl." He could do Chuck Berry's "Sweet Little Sixteen" and Hank Williams—"Hey, hey good-lookin', whatcha got cookin', howsabout cookin' something up with me?" He could do a Jimmy Rogers yodel in caricature of a locomotive whistle, and he knew the gospel classics, "The Old Rugged Cross." He did tenor lead, I did baritone. Even then, he remembered the words I'd forgot. The dynamite chicks stared frankly at us and our noise, with what I imagined that afternoon—but never imagined again—was interest.

It didn't get dark till nine or so. We waited. The landlord came asking for rent. He was kind, patient, pretended to believe that we didn't know where our old man could be found. He said it had gone on too long now, that Duke was months behind, that he had no choice . . .

"Do what you have to do," I said, thinking about a sailboat waiting for me back East.

"Such a shame," he said and sighed, "a man of his attainments, with his education!"

"Uh-huh," I said.

When the landlord left, Toby said, "Tell me something. Did Dad really go to Yale?"

"What do you think?"

"So that would pretty much rule out his graduate degree from the Sorbonne?"

We laughed together, bless us.

Sometime after midnight we quit talking, stopped listening to my jazz records and Dad's Django Reinhardt and Joe Venuti. We'd eaten a couple of cans of Dinty Moore stew, knocked back some Canadian Club we'd found on a high shelf of the mostly bare cupboard. We'd each asked aloud where the other thought Duke might be. We'd wondered aloud whether we should look for him, but I was sure he was drunk, and he had always been a mean drunk, and I didn't want to find him. I didn't trust myself to keep my hands to myself while he sat on the edge of his bed in his boxers, snarling about how ungrateful I was, how grievously I had kicked him in the ass when he was down: *You're a real piece of work, aren't you?* I'd heard it; I didn't think I could hear it again, especially if it came to be Toby's turn.

A couple of hours before dawn his lady friend phoned. She was hysterical, said she didn't know what to do, he wouldn't leave, wouldn't move, wouldn't speak. He'd rock back and forth weeping.

"You've got to get him out of here. I can't take this. What if my husband comes snooping around?"

So I phoned the police. By the time Toby and I got there, the police had called for an ambulance. Dad was breathing, but save for the technicality of being alive, he was gone from this world. His lady friend too said, as so many ex-bosses, ex-friends, ex-wives, creditors, teachers, doctors, parole officers before and after had said, *A man with his educational attainments, what a pity!*

They checked him into Scripps Memorial Hospital. The police had investigated his wallet and he had Blue Cross. Now this was a shock, because he had Blue Cross owing to the fact that he also had a job! Just as he'd said. He worked for General Dynamics Astronautics. By sunup I knew this, and knew as well that he was catatonic, and roughly what catatonia was. He would be removed that afternoon to a "more appropriate facility," and I could guess what that would be. As obdurately as my heart had hardened, I heard myself telling the doctor to tell Dad his sons were here for him, we were behind him all the way. Toby nodded.

"Well," the doctor said, "he has said a few words. He keeps asking for a woman who lives in town. Could you help out with this, maybe let her know he wants to see her?"

"No," I said.

That morning I worked out a deal with the landlord. On principle he wouldn't let us stay in the apartment on which so much rent was due, but he'd let me lease, in my name, an identical unit down the exterior hall, same monthly rent but this time he required an up-front security deposit, first and last month in cash or by cashier's check by the end of business tomorrow.

I borrowed it from a classmate, the roommate of the son of the yachtsman dad from whom I'd borrowed my bus fare. Tangled, wot? It took a boy of my educational attainments to keep all those debts straight, all the lines of credit, but a boy of my educational attainments also knew how to cash in on sympathy. My classmate friend cabled the money from New York that afternoon, and that night Toby and I moved our father's entirely unpaid-for worldly goods to our new residence.

Drunk on resourcefulness, I bought a car and found a job the very next day. The car caught my eye on the lot of Balboa Auto Sales. I'm confident of the name of the dealer because I still have a copy of my stiff reply from Istanbul to a bill collector in San Diego (Hi there, Mr. Ben D. Warren!) begging for the final $150 of the $300 purchase price on a '52 Ford convertible, cream, with torn red vinyl upholstery and bald whitewall tires and an appetite for oil that gave my jaunty wreck a range of about three miles between lube-stops, which made the drive to Tijuana, a popular excursion in the coming weeks, a hardship that only the señoritas of the rowdier cantinas could ameliorate. Ask Toby: he was in charge of oil changing, while I was in charge of drinking and whoring.

The job was easier to cop than the automobile. I simply went to Dad's employer, on the theory that they needed to replace him, and offered my services. A few weeks before in Princeton, getting my diploma, I'd suspected life was going to go smoothly for me, but this . . . *this* was silky! To build rockets during the age of the putative missile gap, the government had contracted with General Dynamics Astronautics to supply Atlas ICBMs at cost-plus. Now cost-plus, I don't have to tell you, is one sweet deal. The greater the cost, the greater the plus, so personnel basically threw money at me when I walked through its door with a bachelor's degree in English Literature. Every time I opened my mouth to mention courses I'd taken—history, American civilization, Spanish—they tossed in another jackpot, so that by day's end I was an engineering writer for more than eight hundred a month, with an advance from the credit union and a complete understanding of how my father had found a job with these cheerful jokers. Don't you miss the Cold War!

Dad was embalmed in an academy of laughter down in Chula Vista, not much of a detour from my weekend line of march to Tijuana. Toby and I were permitted to visit only on Saturdays, which suited my schedule fine, and when we visited he behaved like his old self, which, on the best day of his life, did not display a mastery of your everyday parenting skills. He seemed oblivious to any inconvenience he might have caused his sons, made no mention of the carnage of Toby's first week in La Jolla. Quotidian challenges were beneath his notice: whether he'd lost his job (he had), how much longer his insurance would support his treatment (not long enough), by what transport we'd conveyed ourselves to our audience with him (he did fret about a car "I had to desert in the desert," a play on words that amused him so exceedingly that he neglected the situation's starker implication, soon enough to weigh heavily on him).

We met a few of his new friends, men and women jollier than I would have expected, but their serenity might have been an outcome of the electric shock therapy Duke resolutely and justly resisted. He was busy with workshop therapy, making a leather portfolio into which he burned my initials. This was a difficult gift to receive, and to hold now.

Not least because it fell into a category of assets—personalized keepsakes—that opened a painful fissure between Toby and me. One thing, and it was a thing, was uppermost on my father's mind when my brother and I visited his asylum in Chula Vista. This was a silver cigarette lighter inscribed to him in London after the blitz by friends in the RAF when he was in England on behalf of North America to deliver P-51 Mustangs. He wanted that lighter; jeepers, did he desire that silver lighter; did we grasp that the lighter MATTERED to him? He decided that we had lost it during our move from one apartment to another. Oh, was he disappointed! His new friends would like to see that inscribed silver lighter, and he'd like to show it to them. Why didn't we just run back to La Jolla and find it, "chop-chop"?

It's amazing what kids—even kids as old as I was then, old enough to buy a car on the installment plan and to sign a lease—will accept as the way of the world. I don't mean merely that kids are subject to arbitrary tyrannies, though they are; I mean that until I had sons I never really understood how emotionally derelict my father was. I judged the cost of his selfishness on an empirical scale, by the measurable havoc he inflicted on me. It wasn't till I had sons that I began to understand that such lunatic solipsism as Duke's shook the rudiments of his sons' worlds, misaligned the paths connecting us, upset proportion, priority, ratio, reason itself.

How else explain us searching together the fifty-foot walkway connecting those two apartments, as well as the shrubs below that walkway, as well as our new apartment? What warped sense of duty provoked us to knock on the door of the new tenants' apartment during the dinner hour to persuade them that we needed to search every inch of their abode for a lost cigarette lighter? And failing to find it, to phone the car rental company, the very company that was seeking payment from our father, to ask if a silver cigarette lighter had been found in one of their Pontiacs?

I think now, considering my own dear sons, beginning at last to fathom how difficult it is to be anyone's son, that our father drove us insane that summer. I'll speak for myself: he pushed me to the edge and over it.

My LIFE with Toby seemed on the surface, subtracting weekend visits to the loony bin in Chula Vista and the brothels of Tijuana, workaday. After staring at my pencils and at my colleagues staring at their pencils for six of the eight hours I "worked" in a hangar, the Ford would stumble up the coast to La Jolla, trailing cloud banks of exhaust, a whole weather system. I drove with the torn top up to shelter myself from the black fog that swirled around me when I was stopped in traffic.

But there I go, looking at the dark side, getting gothic on you. At day's end there was home, simple but clean. And the beach. Ah, Windansea! Remember my first visit there, my eyes as big as plates, those surfer chicks, what Dad called popsies? Well, I hadn't completed my second walk from the Pump House south toward Big Rock Reef when a teen approached me.

"Hey!" she said. Her toenails were painted vivid red. Her hair was . . . guess what color. She was . . . (Did you guess pretty?)

I cradled my paperback. "Hey, yourself," I came back.

"You from around here?" she asked.

I chuckled. "No. No, not at all, just visiting on my way to Istanbul."

"Is that on the beach?" (No, of course she didn't ask that. There's no call to get snotty here, just because I was about to have my heart broken.) "Huh?" (That's what she said.)

"Are you from around here?" was my trenchant rejoinder.

She was, she said, she was. And her business with me was to invite me to a keg party that night down in Pacific Beach. She was glad I could make it. We'd have a lot of fun. Was I sure I had the address written down? She checked what I'd written on the title page of Camus's *The Stranger*.

"Thing is, me and my friends need some cash to front the keg."

Thing was, I didn't have any cash in my bathing suit. Could I bring it when I came? No? Okay, hang on, don't go anywhere, I'll just run home and get it, which I did. She was waiting by a VW van, pretty much holding her pretty hand out.

I don't have to tell you how the party went. What party, eh? What Surf Boulevard in Pacific Beach?

Seven years later, reading Tom Wolfe's title essay in *The Pump House Gang*, I felt a full flush of shame rise from my toes. The keg scam was a chestnut among the surfers and surfer-babes at Windansea. But that was the least of my mortification there. Frank laughter was the worst of it. Back home at the Jersey shore or on the beach at Watch Hill, blinking contemplatively behind my groundbreaking round, silver-framed glasses (so far ahead of the curve that the nickname "granny glasses" hadn't yet been invented), in my navy polo shirt to hide my chubby tits, in my Brooks Brothers madras bathing costume, by George I was a stud muffin! Here, carrying a Great Book past those hep longboarders in their nut-hugger nylon suits with competition stripes, I was a freaking joke!

So where, during these humiliating hours after work, was Toby? Safe inside, at his books, writing essays I assigned him. It took him a while to forgive me for practicing my apprentice teaching skills on him. To prepare him for the exactions of a classical education at the Hill School, I obliged him to do a day's work while I did a day's work, to read a book a day and write an essay every week: "Blindness and Insight in *King Lear* and the *Oedipus Tyrannus*"; "The Boundaries of Sea and River: Liberty and Bondage in *Moby Dick* and *Huckleberry Finn*." I guess what I knew best came in pairs. It was crazy the hoops I made my beleaguered, injured, perplexed little brother jump through. He wrote them; he was a better reader and writer for them. But I was a tin-pot despot, as arbitrary in my edicts as Duke sending us on a treasure hunt for his fire-stick. No wonder Toby stole from his father and lied to me.

Did you guess he'd had the sacred lighter all along? Used it to spark up that Lucky during our ride in the Pontiac from the leathery, jangly lady's bungalow to Dad's sea-near studio apartment.

He slept on a pull-out sofa bed in our one-roomer, and mid-August, when the alarm clock woke me for work, I saw the stupid, pretty thing on the floor beneath his blue jeans. In the sullen light of dawn, I made out an inscription engraved on it. My father's initials in elegant sans serif. No RAF boys, of course, but another name for sure, a new engraving, commissioned up on Girard Avenue, TOBY. I remembered the hours we'd spent together hunting for that costly goddamned thing, Toby's helpful suggestions where next to search: the beach, Dad's suit pockets, maybe it had fallen out of Dad's trouser pocket into one of the shoes in his closet?

That morning was awful, and I want to pull a curtain across it. Duke was coming "home" from Chula Vista that afternoon; I was meant to pick him up after work. I didn't know what we'd all do, where we'd live, how we'd sit together in a room, how we'd look at one another, what in the world we were supposed to do now. What I knew for sure: Toby hated us both, his father and his brother. I knew why he hated the one, but not the other. Now I think I know all I'll ever know about that aspect of that summer, and all I want to say to Toby is, Forgive me. Even though he has pardoned me, and himself, just this last time, Forgive me.

I fetched Duke; he raged at Toby. We sent my brother home to my mother on a bus. As bad as it was between my father and me, after Toby left it got worse. My father wasn't allowed to drink—all that medication—but of course he drank. How many days did the nightmare last? Few, I think. He tried to talk me into staying with him instead of going to Turkey. I managed not to laugh in his face. My work at Astro was a mercy, got me out of the apartment. My infamy on the beach was a joy, got me away from him. And I'd invited a couple of visitors, Princeton friends. One was coming up from Mexico in a Cadillac hearse, the other, from whom I'd borrowed the money to rent our apartment, was in the navy, coming to San Diego to join his aircraft carrier. I'd paid him back; breaking a Wolff family tradition, I'd repaid all my debts to friends that summer.

While my erstwhile classmate with the hearse was visiting, Duke was arrested in San Diego. For a wonder, he wasn't drunk and he wasn't up to mischief. He was buying breakfast food at a late-hours store and he'd made a U-turn in my Ford. He'd stuttered when the policeman stopped him. They took him downtown. It went hard on him. By the time my friend and I arrived in the hearse, they were ready to let him go. This was the old police station, gone now, surrendered to gentrification down near Seaport Village. Back then it had a holding tank, and my father was in it, stone terrified. Before they let him go they checked with Sacramento. They got back a complicated story. It went very hard on him, grand theft auto for the Abarth-Allemagne roadster in the desert, burned and sand-blasted by a desert storm. My father wanted me to go bail for him, but he wouldn't promise to show up in court, or even to stay in California.

I didn't go bail; I went to Istanbul.

Then was then. I try to explain to my wife, to my sons. They try to understand, and they've done a good job of it. The only way I know how to explain is on the page. It's a bitch getting the tone right. Now, writing this, I feel jumpy again after many years of feeling a warm embrace of resignation. That's okay. These shifts aren't spurious, I believe. Family stories are always fluid, and to be emotionally exact is to be inconsistent. Toby and I have talked a lot about this. We've talked a lot about a lot. We talk all the time, and as good as a friendship can get, that's how good I think ours is. When I told him I'd found the apartment where we spent the summer of '61, he seemed interested enough, but not too interested. When I told him I'd taken snapshots of the apartment, he didn't ask for copies.

He lifted a trinket that summer, my father lifted a car. Stealing: Jesus, Princeton had an honor code, it seemed like a really big deal, where could stealing lead? Where did it send my dad? That pal who loaned me money? The one I'd invited to visit just about the time my dad disappeared into the system and I fled to Asia Minor? He stole my dad's best shoes. He told me this in an expensive automobile driving to a fancy dinner party at a gentlemen's club on Society Hill in Philadelphia. We were purring along in his Mercedes, snug in our navy blue topcoats and leather gloves and cashmere scarves. It was snowing. I had mentioned a few hours earlier to my old chum that I'd been back in La Jolla after all these years, back to the apartment at Playa del Sur. He'd seemed uncomfortable to hear this, and I understood his discomfort to stem from the disgrace visited on my family name that summer.

"I've been in that apartment," my friend said.

"I don't think so," I said. "You were supposed to visit me there, but then Dad went to jail and I went to . . ."

". . . to Istanbul," my amigo finished. "No, I've been there."

"I don't believe . . ."

"Hush," he said. "Let me tell you."

We were purring along the Schuylkill River now, and the headlights from cars on the expressway dimly lit the black water. Big wet flakes flew at our windshield; the dash glowed greenly. The car was heavy and solid; we were heavy and solid. My friend had been successful in business, investing prudently but shrewdly the inheritances of people who trusted his judgment and honor. His voice was measured. He told me. He told me how he had got the landlord at Playa del Sur, who didn't yet know I'd run out on him just after running out on my father, to let him in. How he had waited there. How he had had a beer or two from the fridge, and then a glass or two or three of the Wild Turkey I was drinking back then. How he had listened to the record player. How he had stretched out and taken a nap. How he had wanted to walk down to the beach, but the landlord wouldn't give him a key. How he had waited and waited for me to come back from work. How he began to feel pissed off, put-upon. How he couldn't wait any longer; the Saratoga was cruising west; he was due aboard. How he had noticed my dad's shoes in the closet, really nice shoes, beautifully cared for, Church shoes, dark brown cap-toes. How something—boredom?—had urged him to try those shoes on his own feet. How they had fit as though they were made for him. How he had stolen them.

"And there was a jacket, too. Nice tweed job. I don't think it was your jacket. I didn't recognize it from college."

"What color?" I wanted to know.

"Greenish, heather, I guess you'd call it. Nubby but soft, a really nice tweed sport coat."

"It wouldn't have been mine," I said. "I didn't own a jacket that fits that description," I lied.

"How about that," my old friend said.

"What the hell," I said, "that was a long time ago."

You see, in Philadelphia, so far from Windansea that winter night, at last, I was finished with all this, who stole what from whom, who borrowed and who paid, who was owed what. I'm finally at the end of all that. This time I mean it. This time, again, I really mean it.

Christopher Wren, a reporter for the *New York Times*, was posted abroad for seventeen years as *Times* bureau chief in Moscow, Cairo, Beijing, Ottawa, and Johannesburg. He is the author of *The End of the Line, The Failure of Communism in the Soviet Union and China* (Simon & Schuster, 1990). This selection is from that book.

Lenin Peak

In the Soviet Union, I experienced the fatal insensitivity of the bureaucracy when I accompanied a team of American mountaineers on their first ascent of 23,400-foot-high Lenin Peak, the Soviet Union's third-tallest mountain.

I met Elvira Shatayeva in the Glade of the Edelweiss, an isolated alpine valley tucked high in the recesses of the Pamirs, a snow-covered range of mountains running north from the Himalayas along the Soviet-Chinese border. A striking blonde with high cheekbones and catlike blue eyes, she had come there to lead a team of the Soviet Union's best women climbers in an assault on Lenin Peak. That evening in camp, we chatted over strong tea in one of the mess tents, and I sensed a steel core beneath her lithe fashion-model exterior. Her husband, Vladimir Shatayev, told me later that Soviet mountaineers affectionately nicknamed her "the fairy of the mountains." Certainly, none of us had expected to encounter her beauty in so wild a place.

When I next saw Elvira Shatayeva, little more than a week later, she lay dead, a victim of one of the worst tragedies in modern mountaineering.

The Soviet press, when it finally acknowledged the disaster, blamed the deaths of Elvira and her seven teammates on hurricane-force winds and bitter cold that froze the women on the uppermost slopes of Lenin Peak. Everyone lamented the worst weather in the Pamirs in a quarter century. No one said anything about the obstinacy of the Soviet bureaucracy.

The Soviet Mountaineering Federation had invited mountaineers from ten Western countries to an international mountaineering camp at twelve thousand feet in the Glade of the Edelweiss. A wind-protected amphitheater not far from the unmarked frontier with China, it was populated seasonally by semi-wild camels, yaks, sheep, and Kirghiz herdsmen.

The foreign climbers were assigned by nationality to their respective rows of tents in one encampment, while the Russians had their own campsite across a small creek on the far side of the grassy meadow. Our hosts encouraged us to fraternize with each other but not with the Soviet mountaineers in the area. We sometimes met them on the trail as we transported our heavy gear up the glacier, and we stopped to compare equipment and chat. But it was always understood that we were climbing separately. On other high mountains, climbing parties tend to keep in contact by radio, but the Soviet Mountaineering Federation calibrated the emergency radio of each nationality to a different frequency, so our messages to each other, even high on Lenin Peak, had to be relayed through the Soviet base camp.

For our own communications, the American expedition had seven powerful Motorola radios, which arrived in Moscow a day after the climbers. Soviet customs officers, nervous about the range and sophistication of the radios, impounded them. We were lent Soviet-made radios of poorer quality in place of our own.

Despite its formidable height, Lenin Peak was considered more of an endurance slog than a technically difficult ascent. But our climbing seemed doomed almost from the outset. Seven of us Americans set out for a first ascent of a 22,500 foot satellite peak, from which we could traverse across to Lenin Peak, bagging both summits. A few inquiries disclosed that it had been called Moscow-Peking Peak back when Soviet-Chinese friendship was declared eternal. After relations soured, Soviet geographers unnamed the mountain.

To reach our target, we had to ferry our equipment and food over Krylenko Pass, a 19,000-foot snow-covered col linking Lenin Peak and 19th Party Congress Peak, so named after Stalin's last Party Congress in 1952. At 17,000 feet, we paused to rest under a tall serac of ice protruding from the steep face like a snag tooth. The silence was suddenly broken by two loud cracks. Snow, ton upon ton of it, slammed down on us. The avalanche roared as if a subway train were rolling over us. Crouched on hands and knees, I flailed to keep the flying snow from freezing around my face.

Fortunately, the full blast of the avalanche was taken by the serac, which saved our lives. We lost much of our gear but we salvaged what we could and retreated down the slippery slope, which had been scoured clean down to the glacial ice. Fresh falling snow touched off smaller powder avalanches and obscured our vision in the failing twilight.

Four teammates attempting the first ascent of the north face of 19th Party Congress Peak were not so lucky. Another massive avalanche hit them as they slept, killing Gary Ullin, a young airline pilot from Seattle. The three others lost most of their gear and one suffered snow-blindness because he was left without his goggles. They took shelter in a snow cave they dug with their hands.

The response of our Russian hosts at base camp was magnificent. Despite the appalling weather, they summoned a helicopter. Its burly bush pilot hovered dangerously close to the sheer face in high winds so that Peter Lev, an American climber, could drop new ice axes and sleeping bags to the survivors. The constraints against fraternization were ignored as Russians enlisted American, French, German, Swiss, and Dutch volunteers in two rescue parties that immediately set off up the mountain. Our comrades trapped on the north face retrieved the air-dropped gear, and after wrapping Gary in an American flag and burying him in the snow, they worked their way across to the northeast ridge in time to meet the ascending rescuers.

It was the kind of spontaneous international cooperation from which inspirational movies are fashioned. The Russians organized a memorial service for Gary, let us build a rock cairn in his memory, and lowered the camp's American flag to half-mast. But when the drama had passed, the Russians in the rescue effort were sent back to climbing with other Russians, leaving the foreigners to each other. We heard that yet another avalanche had swept a party of Estonian climbers off the east face of Lenin Peak, killing at least three of them—we were never told how many, though I was told later that two more died in the hospital. The mountaineering officials were reluctant even to concede to foreigners that the Estonians were missing. We only realized something was amiss when the best Russian climbers left abruptly.

When the weather seemed to brighten, I went back up the mountain with two American teammates, Allen Steck and Jock Glidden, to try Lenin Peak by its northeast ridge. On the first try, we ran into unstable snow that seemed ready to avalanche and backed down. On the second try by a less hazardous route, we reached nearly 22,000 feet before the big storm hit us.

A passing team of descending Siberian climbers had told us that Elvira Shatayeva's party was ahead of us and pushing for the summit. When we had signed out with the Soviet authorities, we were not told the Russian women were on the mountain. Since they included the Soviet Union's best female mountaineers, we assumed they were already descending by another ridge. We had our own problems as we dug in to ride out the storm. The screaming wind reached such intensity that our aluminum tent pole snapped, and we burrowed for warmth in our sleeping bags, wearing all our clothes and boots in case the tent blew apart. We kept trying to radio base camp, which lay two vertical miles below us, but the Soviet-made walkie-talkie was too weak.

We spent two restless nights before the storm passed over. We had cached our rope lower down to cut down on weight, so we moved independently, gasping in the thin air. Six Japanese climbers emerged on their own ascent from behind a rock outcrop, and we took turns breaking a trail through knee-deep snow. In a few hours, we reached the last snow slope, at 23,000 feet, leading to the summit.

Someone seemed to be lying asleep in the bright sunshine. An odd time for a nap, I thought. Despite the snow goggles, I recognized Elvira. She was frozen. We contacted base camp over the Sony radio lying next to her body. But when we got through, the Russian on the other end only asked if we had seen the other seven women.

We began finding them as we climbed up the summit snowfield. Three sprawled across a cloth tent lacerated by the storm. Another was doubled over a climbing rope. Two more lay as if they had fallen down the snowfield. We searched for the eighth around the 23,400-foot summit and assumed she was blown off the mountain, though Elvira's husband told me later she lay tucked under one of her comrades. Some of the women had lost their mittens and pulled socks over their hands in a futile attempt to keep warm. They still wore metal crampons on their frozen boots. Their ice axes were strewn about as if mislaid. The only sound was a stiff flutter of parkas and torn tents in the wind. We marked the bodies with willow wands in case another storm deposited more snow and, too exhausted to do more, started down.

We reached the base camp two days later to learn the details of the tragedy. The women had bivouacked at the summit before descending the mountain's northwest ridge. Rather than retreat when the storm came in, they made a miscalculation to wait until the visibility improved. I suspect that they did not want foreigners to think Russians were quitters.

Once the whirling snow and wind of the storm took away the visibility, it was too late to go down and the women began dying. During those final hours, they talked with base camp over their Japanese radio. The Soviet officials never told them that we might be just below them; not having heard from us, they feared that we too had perished. Elvira reported that they were weak and the snow had frozen too hard to dig a cave to escape the icy blasts. The girls were beginning to go, she said. Because our radio was not tuned to their frequency, we could not hear the dialogue little more than a thousand feet above us. But our expedition's climbing leader, Robert Craig, was at base camp and overheard Elvira's last words: "And now we will all die. We are very sorry. We tried but we could not. . . . Please forgive us. We love you. Goodbye."

The Soviet press did not report the deaths of the country's best women climbers until after I had returned to Moscow and revealed the disaster in the *New York Times*. A government inquiry subsequently concluded that the eight had died "not from mismanagement or mistakes, but from a natural disaster."

Vladimir Shatayev, a fine mountaineer, went up to locate and bury his wife. "Something dreadful must have happened because they were all dressed warmly, especially Elvira," he told me when I visited the Federation in Moscow to offer my testimony on the accident. "It took only eighteen hours for them to die. I was troubled that the tragedy happened so fast, because we have had cases where people fight for their lives three or four days.

"It is very difficult to imagine how the girls behaved when we were not there. I kept thinking what I could have done if I had been there."

I did not tell the grieving Shatayev I had the same thought. What if a common radio frequency had been given to all parties climbing a major peak in such unpredictable weather? What if Soviet customs had let us keep our powerful American radios, so that we could have known enough to mount a rescue? What if the women surrendering to the storm had been assured that a well-equipped American team was only a thousand feet below them? What if we had not been kept segregated from the Russian climbers in the first place?

The Soviet Mountaineering Federation awarded me a flashy enamel badge attesting to my ascent of Lenin Peak, then thereafter found excuses to keep me from climbing anymore in the Soviet Union. A few months after I returned from the Pamirs, I heard that an Estonian filmmaker who visited the international climbing camp was going to screen his documentary before an audience of Soviet climbers in Moscow. I walked in uninvited that evening, but the surprised officials did not ask me to leave because I took the precaution of wearing my Lenin Peak badge.

The color film delved at length into the death of Gary Ullin and the heroic efforts of the Russians to help rescue our surviving comrades. It talked about the intensity of the storm. But there was nothing about the Estonians swept off Lenin Peak's east face or the eight Russian women who died on its summit. I was not the only one stunned at this selectivity. When the film ended, the filmmaker walked out on stage to discuss his work. The first question called out from the audience drew a vigorous murmur of angry assent: "What about Elvira Shatayeva?"

Jonathan Weiner won a Pulizer Prize in 1995 for *The Beak of the Finch*. His most recent book, *Time, Love, Memory* (Knopf, 1999), from which this profile is drawn, won a National Book Critics Circle Award in 2000. He is Writer in Residence at Rockefeller University.

From So Simple a Beginning

The ancient precept, "Know thyself," and the modern precept, "Study nature," become at last one maxim.
Ralph Waldo Emerson, *The American Scholar*

The nearest gnat is an explanation.
Walt Whitman, *Song of Myself*

Seymour Benzer's laboratory runs along two corridors of Church Hall at the California Institute of Technology in Pasadena. His private workroom is at the corner where the corridors meet. Here he keeps his own tools and trophies, and an owl's hours. It is a windowless room lined with plastic bins that Benzer labeled decades ago in his spidery black script: *Lenses, Mirrors, Needles, Wires, Pencils, Switches, Toothpicks, Pipe Cleaners*, anything and everything he might need for an experiment in the middle of the night, including *Teeth (Human and Shark)*.

The benchtop is all test tubes and bottles: mostly standard-issue laboratory stock, but here and there a half-pint milk bottle with heavy scratched glass and antique advertising ("5 cents—Just a Little Better") stoppered with a foam-rubber cork. These tubes and bottles hold a sampling of the thousands of mutants that Benzer and his students, his students' students, and his competitors have engineered.

The mutants are fruit flies, and their mutations have changed their behavior. One of them is *timeless*, a clock mutant. In a windowless room like this one, the fly seems to wake and sleep at random intervals, as if it has broken its covenant with day and night, so that day and night will not come at their appointed time. Another is *dissatisfaction*, a female mutant that does not like males and keeps flicking them away with her wings. Then there is *pirouette*, which moves at first in big arcs, then in smaller and smaller arcs, like certain problems in science, turning at last on a single point, until it sometimes starves to death.

In the seventeenth century, the French philosopher Blaise Pascal looked up at the night sky and then looked down at a mite, picturing "legs with joints, veins in its legs, blood in the veins, humors in the blood, drops in the humors, vapors in the drops," and onward and downward to the atoms. "The eternal silence of these infinite spaces fills me with dread," he wrote. He meant two infinite spaces, which he called the two infinites of science, one above and around him, the other below and inside him. Of the two infinites, the space that frightened him more was the space that he could not begin to see, the stardust of atoms that made up his very thoughts and fears and moved the fingers around his pen. "Anyone who considers himself in this way will be terrified at himself."

The twentieth century was a long spiral inward on Pascal's path, beginning with a single mutant fly in a milk bottle in the century's first years, and reaching the atoms that Pascal dreaded to see near the century's close. If the spiral leads where it now promises or threatens to lead, this may be remembered as one of the most significant series of discoveries since science began, matching or surpassing the discoveries of twentieth- century physics. In the universe above and around us, physics opened new views of space and time; in the universe below and inside us, biology opened first glimpses of the foundation stones of experience: time, love, and memory.

What are the connections, the physical connections, between genes and behavior? What is the chain of reactions that leads from a single gene to a bark, or a laugh, or a song, or a thought, or a memory, or a glimpse of red, or a turn toward a light, or a raised hand, or a raised wing? The first scientists to look seriously at this question were the revolutionaries who figured out what genes are made of atom by atom—the founders of the science now known as molecular biology. Seymour Benzer was one of those revolutionaries, and he and his students took the enterprise farthest. Benzer's work on the problem was quiet, his students' work was quiet, and their story has never been told. But to a large extent the hard science of genes and behavior came out of their fly bottles. In this sense the fly bottle is one of the most significant legacies that the science of the twentieth century bequeaths to the twenty-first, a great gift and disturbance that human knowledge conveys to the night thoughts and day-to-day life of the third millennium. Pascal quoted Saint Augustine: "The way in which minds are attached to bodies is beyond our understanding, and yet this is what we are."

From a shelf in his workroom, Benzer takes down a dusty set of test tubes. They are bound together in such a way that he can slide one test tube mouth to mouth with another test tube, like one cup lidding another, to form a series of sealed glass tunnels. They look something like panpipes. The design is so simple that the first model he built back in the 1960s still works. Now the London Science Museum has a replica, and someone from the San Francisco Exploratorium wants to automate one so that it will cycle through its paces over and over inside a glass display case.

Benzer dusts off the test tubes and lays them down flat on the benchtop before him. Then he lays a dim fluorescent bulb of fifteen watts on the far side of the benchtop. When he switches off the overhead lights, the fluorescent bulb glints on the test tubes and gleams on his reading glasses. The rows of bottles and bins, the stacks of books and manuscripts drop halfway into shadow. The light just catches the outlines of an ammonite propped against the far wall, a fossil shell the shape of a coiled elephant's trunk; and a row of trilobites, stone fossils with bulbous eyes. In the far corner of the sanctum a human brain sits in the dark. Benzer keeps meaning to find a proper jar for the brain. He wants to put it on his desk as a *memento mori* or a *memento vivere* ("Remember to live"). The brain waits in a bucket of formaldehyde, and what is left of its spinal cord curls in the bottom of the bucket like the lifeline of an embryo.

Benzer got the idea for his panpipes one night in 1966, when he put two test tubes mouth to mouth to make one long tube with a single fruit fly trapped inside it. He turned out the light; he rapped the tubes on his benchtop to make the fly drop to the bottom; and he laid the tubes flat on the benchtop with the fly at one end of the tunnel and a small dim light at the other. Sitting in the shadows, he watched the fly in the tunnel move toward the light, just as he had expected it to do, because according to the textbooks a grown fruit fly in a dark place is attracted to light—so is a grown human being in a similar situation. The next fly also moved toward the light. But he was surprised to see that when he put a single fly through this simple trial a few times in a row, the fly did not always do the same thing. One fly raced to the light once, walked to it the next time, and then quit. Another fly ignored the light the first time and then raced for it at the next opportunity. Most flies did choose the light most of the time, but each trial seemed unpredictable.

In 1966 it was already clear that however else historians would remember the twentieth century, they would remember it for the discovery of the atomic theory of matter and the atomic theory of inheritance. Physicists and geneticists had developed both theories early in the century. At mid-century a small circle of young scientists, including Benzer and Francis Crick (both lapsed physicists) and James Watson (a lapsed ornithologist) had united the two theories. They discovered what genes are made of atom by atom—the double helix, the spiral staircase of DNA; they mapped the fine structure of the gene down to the level of its atoms; and they cracked the code in which the genetic messages are written. They now knew precisely what a gene is physically, although they did not know how to connect the details they were looking at, which were atomic, with the details of the living world that most interested them and interest all of us: hands, eyes, lips, thoughts, acts, behavior. Within ten years the physicists-turned-biologists had learned so much about genes that they had begun to look around and above the genes for new worlds to conquer. To the boldest, many worlds beckoned, innumerable lines of work radiated outward from the gene, including the problems of the origin of life; the growing embryo; consciousness; and behavior, a problem that Crick called "attractively mysterious, one of the last true secrets in biology."

Watson, Crick, Benzer, and their circle had arrived at the double helix by working with viruses and *E. coli* bacteria in petri dishes. But they knew that geneticists before them had worked out the atomic theory of inheritance using fruit flies in milk bottles. Benzer has a strong, somewhat sentimental sense of history, and it appealed to him to make the next great leap forward by going back. Fruit flies are bigger than bacteria, but they are still tiny. They are grains of sand with wings, small enough to crawl through the mesh of screen doors, almost as small as Pascal's mites, so small that Aristotle mistook them for gnats. Coming from physics and from *E. coli*, Benzer saw them as atoms of behavior, and he thought they might be the perfect creatures with which to found a new science, an atomic theory of behavior.

By chance, the very first published laboratory study of *Drosophila*, or fruit flies, a long-forgotten paper that he tracked down some time afterward, had been a report on the flies' behavior: their reactions to light, gravity, and mechanical stimulation. Even that first report, which appeared in 1905, had suggested that the flies' instinct for light is not simple. If their jar was sitting on the windowsill—a biologist at Harvard reported—most of the flies would come to rest on the sides of the jar with their heads pointed away from the sun. But turn the jar slightly, and nearly every fly instantly flew toward the window.

To Benzer, *Drosophila* looked like just the happy medium he was looking for. An *E. coli* bacterium is a single cell. In a sense, he could think of it as a nervous system with a single neuron. At birth, a human baby has about one hundred billion neurons, one for every star in the Milky Way. A fruit fly has about one hundred thousand neurons, so it is the geometric mean between the simplest and the most complicated nervous system we know. Likewise, the mass of a single *E. coli* bacterium is one ten-trillionth of a gram. The mass of a man is one hundred thousand grams. The fly is roughly the geometric mean, at two thousandths of a gram. And a bacterium has a generation time of a hundredth of a day, while a human being has a generation time of ten thousand days (ten thousand days, to pick a generous round number, before one human being produces another). A fly has a generation time of about ten days, again roughly a geometric mean between the two. Even the number of genes in the fly is a mean between bacteria and human beings. In very round numbers a bacterium has 4,000 genes, a human being has 70,000 genes, and a fly has 15,000 genes, which puts it once again between the simplest and the most complicated creatures we know on the planet.

Benzer modeled his test-tube experiment after a laboratory routine that he had learned from a chemist. The chemist used a simple trick to separate two compounds that were mixed together. One of his compounds would dissolve slightly more easily in oil and the other more easily in water. So the chemist put his mixture in oil and water and shook it up. He let the oil and water separate, oil above and water below. Then he transferred the top layer to a new tube and the bottom layer to another tube. He added fresh oil and water and shook them up again. When he had done this enough times, he found that he had separated the two compounds. The tube of oil now had an almost pure sample of the compound that liked oil, the tube of water an almost pure sample of the compound that liked water. Chemists call this the counter-current distribution method because in a sense it sets currents flowing in opposite directions: one compound flowing upward, the other flowing downward.

So Benzer decided to make his own countercurrent apparatus. He assumed that most of the flies in the world's fly bottles like the light somewhat more than the dark but that a few might like the dark somewhat more than the light. He wanted to let the flies sort themselves into two more or less pure sets of particles, the light-lovers and the dark-lovers. Then he would look for the genes that made the difference. After some trial and error he hit on the idea of the panpipes. By mounting a set of test tubes in such a way that they could slide against each other, he could carry out a series of simple sorting operations, just like the chemist's.

Sitting now in the half-dark of his sanctum, he uncorks one of his antique milk bottles ("Just a Little Better"), and he inserts a few dozen fruit flies into the tube on the far left of his countercurrent apparatus: Tube Zero. Then he raps the whole set of tubes on the benchtop a few times. In the quiet of his workroom in the middle of the night, the sound is like a pounding on the door. The raps knock the flies to the bottom of Tube Zero, and the flies swarm there a moment in the half-light, flailing as if in free fall. They are so small that they really do look like the Greek idea of atoms, points whirling in space, almost invisible and absolutely indivisible. (*Atomos* means "unsplittable.")

Benzer lays the countercurrent machine back down on the benchtop. The flies at the bottom of Tube Zero are now at one end of a glass tunnel. The only light they can see is the light at the far end of the tunnel, the fifteen-watt fluorescent tube. The flies can stay put in the bottom of Tube Zero, or they can move toward the light. As Pascal says, "There is enough light for those who desire only to see, and enough darkness for those of a contrary disposition." So the flies are facing a simple choice. If they do not move forward, they will remain in Tube Zero. If they do move forward, they will find themselves in the next test tube, Tube One.

Some of the flies walk, some of them run, some of them fly, and some of them meander. By the time fifteen seconds have passed, all but two of the flies have gone toward the light.

Benzer picks up the apparatus and slides the test tubes around. Now the flies that went toward the light—almost all of the winged atoms in the ma-chine—are in Tube One, while the two flies that did not go remain in Tube Zero.

"Everybody gets another chance," Benzer murmurs. Again he raps the appa-ratus on the benchtop. Again he lays it flat on the benchtop. Within fifteen seconds, most of the flies again go toward the light. But this time one of the flies in Tube Zero decides to go too, and a few of the flies that went the first time choose not to go.

"What are they doing now?" Benzer says. "They're wandering around." This is why he built the countercurrent machine in the first place. Facing the same choice point, the flies do not always make the same choice. As a swarm, as a mass, they are predictable, but as individuals they are unpredictable. Even fruit flies in a test tube do not always act the same way twice. Why not? Watching their decisions and revisions by the light of the fifteen-watt bulb back in 1966, Benzer got an inkling that flies might be more than atoms of behavior. He had thought they would be simple, regular, predictable, like the particles in the chemist's test tubes. Instead the flies act as if they are improvising from moment to moment, based on what each fly sees in front of it, what has happened in its past, and what can only be called the personality of that fly.

"Flip it over, switch it back." Now the flies that have chosen the light twice are in Tube Two. The flies that have chosen the light once are in Tube One. The fly that has never chosen the light is still in Tube Zero, moving erratically in the half-dark. To human eyes it looks like a troubled fly.

"Now we'll give them *another* chance." Benzer rocks and slides his gadget: the same operation, the same fifteen-second wait. Then again and again: *knock, knock, knock.* Each time, most of the flies move toward the light.

"OK, there we are," Benzer says at last, switching on the overhead lights. He can read the results at a glance. Tube Six contains flies that moved to the light six out of six times. Most of them are in there. Tube Five contains flies that moved five out of six times. And so on, all the way down to Tube Zero, the home of the troubled fly, which may be damaged goods.

To prove that he is really testing what he thinks he is testing, Benzer dumps all of the flies back into Tube Zero and sets the apparatus on the benchtop again. This time he sets it down with the flies next to the light. Now the flies face the opposite choice. They are near the light. They can choose to stay where they are, or they can move away. When Benzer runs the experiment this way, most of the flies stay put in the bottom of Tube Zero. They do not hurry into the darkness the way they hurried into the light. Running the experiment backward this way is Benzer's control. It proves that in the first rounds the flies were not indifferent to the light; they were not advancing through the tubes just for the sake of advancing through the tubes. He is looking at what he thinks he is looking at. The light is the key.

John Noble Wilford, a senior science writer for the *New York Times*, is the author or co-author of eight books. He was awarded a Pulitzer Prize in national reporting and is a fellow of the American Academy of Arts and Sciences. The first of these pieces was published in the *New York Times* on April 26, 1983; the second appeared in the *Times* on January 1, 2000, alongside Malcolm Browne's article, which also follows in this volume.

Pioneer 10 Pushes Beyond Goals, Into the Unknown

Out there, far, far away where Earth is a mere pinpoint of light and the Sun is a pale disk of diminishing consequence, a hardy little spacecraft cruises on and on into the unexplored. No machine of human design has ever gone so far. Pioneer 10 has traveled to the reaches of Pluto, a distance it achieved yesterday, and is advancing toward the edge of the solar system.

From out there, now 2.7 billion miles away, Pioneer's eight-watt radio transmitter sends faint messages back to Earth every day, whispers of discovery. The transit time of these reports, traveling at the speed of light, is 4 hours and 16 minutes. And by the time the signals arrive at tracking antennas, they have all but vanished, their strength reduced to 20-billionths of a watt.

But scientists with the patience to extract the signals out of the background noise and to decipher their messages are learning for the first time what it is like in the outermost solar system. It is cold and dark and empty, as they knew it must be. A tenuous wind of solar particles, the million-mile-an-hour solar wind, still blows outward. Cosmic rays race inward. A virtual vacuum it may be, but nothingness, it seems, is a relative condition.

If the spacecraft survives long enough and the scientists are clever enough, more exciting discoveries could lie ahead for Pioneer 10. It might be able to detect gravity waves, which have been theorized but have never been observed. It might locate the source of the mysterious force tugging at Uranus and Neptune, a gravitational force suggesting the presence of some as yet unseen object—perhaps the long-sought Planet X or a dim companion star to the Sun. The spacecraft may also function long enough to report back the answer to the question, Where does the solar system end and interstellar space begin?

"We are constantly entering unexplored territory," says Dr. Aaron Barnes, an astrophysicist at the Ames Research Center in Mountain View, Calif., where the Pioneer mission is directed. "We really don't know what we'll learn."

Travel was never more broadening. When Pioneer 10 was launched March 3, 1972, from Cape Canaveral, Fla., no spacecraft had ventured farther than Mars. Pioneer made its way safely through the asteroid belt, a region littered with rocky debris between Mars and Jupiter. It flew within 81,000 miles of Jupiter's cloud tops on December 2, 1973, returning the first close-up images of the Sun's largest planet. The pictures revealed the cyclonic forces of the Great Red Spot roiling Jupiter's dense hydrogen and helium atmosphere. Pioneer made the first detailed observations of Jupiter's powerful radiation belts and discovered that the planet's sphere of magnetic influence extended to the orbit of Saturn, a distance of half a billion miles.

Pioneer had by then accomplished its mission and exceeded its designed 21-month lifetime. The 500-pound craft had been blasted by Jovian radiation and pelted with micrometeoroids. "No one dreamed then we'd still be hearing from Pioneer today," recalls Dr. James A. Van Allen of the University of Iowa, one of the mission's scientists.

Still Pioneer kept going, its nine-foot dish antenna always cocked in the direction of Earth. It dutifully kept sending home a travelogue on interplanetary space as it crossed the orbit of Saturn in 1976 and the orbit of Uranus in 1979.

Pioneer 10 had now made believers out of its creators, the engineers for the National Aeronautics and Space Administration and the spacecraft manufacturer, TRW Inc. Like the little engine that could, this was the little spacecraft that could probably push on to the frontier of interstellar space and still be living to tell the tale.

After more than eleven years in flight, according to Richard O. Fimmel, the project manager at NASA's Ames Research Center, all the craft's scientific instruments, except the magnetometer, are working normally. He estimates that deep-space antennas should maintain communications with Pioneer for eight more years, out to a distance of five billion miles. That is when the craft's radioisotopic power unit will no longer be generating enough electricity for operations.

Right now Pioneer is, in effect, leaving the realm of the known planets. At 5:00 P.M. yesterday the craft, traveling 30,613 miles an hour, sped farther out than Pluto. It was then almost 2.8 billion miles from the Sun; Earth is 93 million miles away from the Sun. At the time, however, Pluto was on the other side of the Sun.

On June 13, Pioneer's outbound trajectory will cross Neptune's orbit, 2.81 billion miles from the Sun. Normally Pluto is the outermost planet, but because its orbit is highly elliptical, unlike the roughly circular orbits of the other planets, Pluto is now nearer to the Sun than Neptune and will be for the next seventeen years.

Each day flight controllers at Ames typically send Pioneer a message when they arrive at work. By quitting time eight and a half hours later, which is the round-trip communications time, they receive Pioneer's reply.

They also receive about sixteen hours of scientific data each day from the spacecraft, mainly information defining the extent and behavior of the heliosphere, the Sun's extended atmosphere. Blowing away in all directions from the Sun is the solar wind, an electrically charged gas composed of protons (hydrogen nuclei) and electrons that stream out from the Sun's corona. The wind carries along with it the Sun's magnetic field.

It is as if the Sun is blowing a pressure bubble out into space, a tear-shaped magnetic bubble that acts as a barrier against intrusions by most particles from the interstellar medium. The bubble is streamlined by the motion of the solar system through this interstellar gas. At the solar system's leading edge, so to speak, the bubble is blunted. In the opposite direction, the bubble forms a long tail. Pioneer 10 is traveling down the tail of the heliosphere.

Before Pioneer, some scientists believed the boundary, the heliopause, might be just beyond Jupiter. But the spacecraft is six times that far out and has yet to encounter the boundary.

The spacecraft's instruments indicate the heliosphere "breathes" in and out once every 11-year solar cycle, as reported by Dr. John Simpson, a Pioneer experimenter from the University of Chicago. When the Sun is most turbulent, which last occurred in 1980, shock waves from its magnetic storms seem to persist throughout the heliosphere for as long as a year. The effect may be to change the bubble's shape.

Moreover, at the time of maximum solar activity, the bubble seems to be more impervious to cosmic rays from out in the galaxy. Pioneer's detectors found the cosmic-ray particles half as numerous then.

For the rest of Pioneer's working lifetime, scientists will be monitoring the data for signs of the boundary crossing. Scientists are not sure what to expect. Dr. Barnes says Pioneer would probably encounter changes in the outside temperatures and discernible turbulence as the solar wind was buffeted by the incoming interstellar gases. The speed of the solar wind should drop suddenly from supersonic to subsonic. Dr. Van Allen, however, doubts "anything dramatic" will be observed at the heliopause.

Other spacecraft, Voyager 1 and Pioneer 11, may find a sharper boundary. Though not as far from Earth as Pioneer 10, they are traveling in an opposite direction, toward the blunt edge of the bubble. Dr. Edward C. Stone of the California Institute of Technology, Voyager's chief scientist, believes the spacecraft should encounter a kind of bow shock caused by the solar wind slamming into the dominant and relatively stationary interstellar environment. It may even be possible to hear the boundary crossing. Energies produced by the interactions may give off whistling noises that Voyager will radio back to Earth.

Because of its great distance away, Pioneer 10 could give scientists their first evidence of the existence of gravity waves. According to Einstein's General Theory of Relativity, cataclysms in the universe, collapsing or exploding stars, should send waves of gravitational radiation across the galaxies. Dr. John Anderson of the Jet Propulsion Laboratory says that a painstaking analysis of radio transmissions from Pioneer to Earth might reveal the jiggling effects that a gravity wave would have on the craft or Earth itself.

Accordingly, Pioneer 10 may lead scientists to the discovery of some massive object toward the edge of the solar system. It may be, as some astronomers suspect, a "brown dwarf" star, a celestial object that was not quite massive enough for its thermonuclear furnace to ignite. Since most stars are paired, it is not unreasonable to assume that the Sun might have such a dim companion.

Or the force could be from a 10th planet, the long-sought Planet X. Evidence assembled in recent years has led several groups of astronomers to renew the search for a large planet out beyond Pluto and Neptune.

Someday, of course, even the durable Pioneer 10 will lose touch with those who sent it off on its long journey. The little radio that has already transmitted more than 126 billion bits of scientific data will go dead. Sensors will lose sight of the Sun.

Even then, silent and derelict, Pioneer 10 will cruise on and on, the first human artifact to leave the solar system. About once every million years, as nearly as anyone can calculate such things, the craft might expect to come close to another star system. It might then be found by other intelligent beings.

With that eventuality in mind, Pioneer's makers indulged in an act of infinite hubris. They attached a plaque engraved with images of a man and a woman, the location of Earth and some points of basic science—possibly the little spacecraft's ultimate message.

Get Set to Say Hi to the Neighbors

If there is life here on Earth, why not elsewhere?

The question has long inspired wonder and some fear, doomed a few to the heretic's stake and invigorated recent investigations of other planets in the solar system and of the stars beyond. If life is indeed the inevitable outcome of cosmic evolution, a "cosmic imperative," in the words of the Nobel Prize-winning chemist Christian de Duve, the first clear evidence of extraterrestrial life will most likely be discovered in the first century of this new millennium.

One reason for the optimism is as old as speculations by the ancient Greeks and Romans impressed by the vastness of the heavens. "Space contains such a huge supply of atoms that all eternity would not be enough time to count them and the force which drives the atoms into various places just as they have been driven together in this world," wrote the Roman philosopher Lucretius in the first century B.C. "So we must realize that there are other worlds in other parts of the universe, with races of different men and different animals."

The modern variation of this reasoning stems from astronomy's recent estimates of upward of 100 billion galaxies, each with tens of billions of stars. So many opportunities for life to have emerged, as it did on one planet of one star, the Sun. And everything scientists learn shows that the physical forces nearby apply everywhere; there is no reason to think that the solar system or its Milky Way galaxy are unique.

Biological studies on Earth suggest that, if anything, scientists have been underestimating the potential for life and its resilience in seemingly adverse environments. Drilling deep into Earth's crust, geochemists have encountered bacteria living there, without sunlight and probably on a diet of chemicals. Similarly, oceanographers have been surprised to find undersea vents disgorging mineral-rich hot water that supports a teeming community of exotic life, also existing without sunlight.

"The question may not be the probability of the origin of life," Dr. Norman R. Pace, a University of California biologist, has said, "but rather the probability that life, having arisen, survives and comes to dominate a planet."

Seekers of extraterrestrial life, at least in its humblest forms, were encouraged by discoveries in the 1990's. The Galileo spacecraft found strong evidence of a global ocean of water, where simple life just may exist, under the ice of Europa, a moon of Jupiter; Europa will be a target of life-seeking exploration in coming years. A report that a meteorite from Mars contained circumstantial evidence for microbial life created a stir; though the findings were suspect, they galvanized a renewed drive to explore Mars for fossil or extant life.

Of surpassing significance, the recent discovery of planets around other stars is fixing for scientists the places to look for extraterrestrial life. Knowing where to search, the National Aeronautics and Space Administration is developing instruments for spacecraft to be launched over the next two decades. These instruments will be capable of finding Earth-sized Planets and detecting there the chemical signatures associated with life: oxygen, water and carbon dioxide. The absolute clincher, scientists say, would be to find oxygen and methane together.

Current efforts to detect radio signals from other intelligent beings, begun in the 1960's, are a long shot. But for the first time in human history the technology exists to search other planetary systems for worlds harboring life in some form. The results could be the most reverberating scientific discovery of the new century.

Malcolm W. Browne is a Pulitzer Prize winner and a senior science writer at the *New York Times*. The first article appeared in the *New York Times* on January 1, 2000, with John Noble Wilford's piece about extraterrestrial life. The others were published on June 9, 1981, August 12, 1980, and March 11, 1980.

Left the Light On, But Nobody Came

In 1939, the physicist Enrico Fermi posed his famous paradox: If life is common in our galaxy, why have we never seen extraterrestrial visitors on Earth?

Since then, and particularly since 1960, scientists have searched the cosmic radio spectrum for signals of intelligence, landed robotic laboratories on Mars to look for hints of biological activity, probed meteorite fragments for chemical or geological evidence of life and tried to invent chemical pathways analogous to those from which life arises.

So far, all efforts have failed to show the existence of life anywhere except on Earth.

To find just one extraterrestrial microorganism (or better, a bug-eyed Martian humanoid) would be sensational. But I think the human race must reconcile itself to the strong possibility that it is alone in the galaxy—perhaps even in the universe. I would bet that the 21st century will pass without anyone finding conclusive evidence of extraterrestrial life, intelligent or not.

There have been many false alarms in the past, like the discovery of "canals" on Mars, which proved to be illusions imagined by the American astronomer Percival Lowell. There will be many more. And many investigators will take comfort from the Copernican Principle, the assumption that no particular place or time is likely to be special and that inhabited planets like Earth must therefore be common.

But one of the faults of statistical estimates of extraterrestrial life is that it is impossible to extrapolate anything from a single data point. And that's all we have: Earth.

The environmental conditions favoring the creation of life may not be nearly as common as was postulated in 1961 by Frank Drake, one of the main instigators of SETI, the search for extraterrestrial intelligence. The Drake Equation, as it came to be known, incorporated estimates of the rate at which stars are born in the galaxy, the fraction of stars with planets, the fraction of those planets on which life originates and so forth. By that calculation, there should be about 10,000 civilizations in our galaxy capable of interstellar communication.

But in the 39 years since radio telescopes began searching, nothing has turned up.

Certainly, sending signals across tens, hundreds or thousands of light years poses staggering difficulties. But a more fundamental reason for our failure to find extraterrestrial life could be that we are, indeed, alone.

Many astronomers have suggested that the conditions for life can exist only on a rocky planet with lots of liquid water and other possibly rare assets like a reliable sun producing steady radiation over a long period; a Jupiter-size planet in the outer solar system to sweep up asteroids and other objects that would otherwise continuously bombard an Earthlike planet; and an exceptionally large moon like ours, to cushion the disruptive gravitational influences of other planets. These and other conditions may be so unlikely as to rule out all life except that inhabiting a unique fluke—Earth.

We have already searched for signals from nearby stars like Alpha Centauri and found nothing.

Lots of reasons can be adduced to explain these failures, but the simplest explanation—and so the one favored by Occam's razor—is that there is nothing out there to find. In any case, I'm not holding my breath.

The Invisible Flying Cat

The late Paul Gallico, a distinguished sports journalist and writer of short stories, believed in the vital importance of something he called "The Feel." To acquire "The Feel" of one aspect of prizefighting, for instance, Gallico once went into the ring with Jack Dempsey and got knocked flat. As a result, he wrote, "I knew all that there was to know about being hit." The season for valedictory pronouncements is at hand and a few parting thoughts about science come to mind. The main one has to do with Gallico's "Feel."

Getting a kick out of science does not necessarily require the feel of the practicing researcher (although it helps). Because science touches every aspect of human existence from sewer mains to symphonic composition, it offers something for everyone.

Even those with no real interest in its techniques and insights may take comfort from the fact that science can lengthen life, improve health, defend us against enemies and make existence more comfortable.

For others, the outlandish curiosities science turns up—cloned mice, black holes, pigeons psychologically reinforced to play Ping-Pong, and so on—offer the same class of amusement as circus freak shows. The discovery and identification of dinosaur fossils during the last century touched off a furious race to unearth more of the old monsters, and for a time the scientific investigation of paleontology was shouldered aside by the likes of P. T. Barnum.

But for some lucky people, science is fun for its own sake. For them, watching a good television program about some aspect of science can be at least as absorbing as a Saturday football game or a Shakespeare play. They find deep satisfaction in reading of discoveries about our genetic codes, about the exotic atmospheres of outer planets, about our complex relations with the parasites living within us, and all the other things science examines.

But there is an even more satisfying stratum of science to be mined, and it has to do with the feel. A cook who has experimented with a recipe by changing the amount of some ingredient and comparing the result with the original knows something about scientific feel. The gardener who sets up controlled experiments with seed varieties, soil conditions and hybrids encounters the feel.

It's hard for most of us to capture the feel of today's frontiers of science. Contemporary experimental science generally requires paraphernalia costing tens of millions of dollars and big teams of researchers.

Nevertheless, the personal act of reaffirming a known scientific principle can impart a warm glow in itself. There is a pleasurable feel in retracing Archimedes' steps, as one discovers how to estimate the gold content of a wedding ring with a weighing balance, a glass of water and some thread. Jupiter's moons glitter through ordinary binoculars, and even household chemicals can reveal the heart of nature.

There are good books about the feel derived from home experiments, one of the best of which is *The Flying Circus of Physics*, by Jearl Walker.

But many of the world's greatest scientists have foregone laboratory research completely, relying instead on what Einstein called "thought experiments." And anyone can profit from thought experiments.

In simplest terms, a thought experiment examines the logical consequences of some hypothetical action or assumption, comparing them with observed reality. A thought experiment comparing the timekeeping of a clock hurtling through space with an identical clock resting on Earth helped lead Einstein to his special theory of relativity.

The reasoning techniques of thought experiments are not necessarily difficult. To test the statement that the world is infested by invisible flying cats which invariably avoid human beings, we would consider the consequences of such a situation. It would seem, for instance, that invisible flying cats would have such advantages as predators that they must quickly bring about the extinction of sparrows. But since we continue to see lots of sparrows, the invisible flying cat hypothesis becomes improbable.

In a world enveloped by the cant of the propagandist—commercial, political, ideological and religious—the scientific feel for shooting down invisible flying cats becomes an attribute of survival.

Like Gallico after a blow from Dempsey's glove, the amateur may go down under the impact of an encounter with molecular biology or quantum mechanics. But the mind needs to jump in the ring sometimes, even against the most impenetrable ideas of science. The Feel alone makes it worth the bruises.

MALCOLM W. BROWNE

At Least the Monsters Survive

Science has opened our minds to bright vistas of understanding and has given us a civilization which, with all its faults, is more comfortable than hunting and gathering. But we have to live with the fact that science can sometimes be an awful wet blanket. It roots out and destroys something precious within the core of our primal nature: the sense of mystery.

A few years ago, Jacques Cousteau, the marine naturalist, trundled two miniature submarines up the Andes mountains to explore Lake Titicaca, the 12,000-foot-high lake separating Bolivia and Peru. The fascinated Aymara and Quechua peoples of the region gathered by the thousands, huddling in blankets against the bitter weather as they watched the operations.

According to Indian tradition, the cold, black depths of Titicaca are bottomless and magic. On its shores, legend has it, some of their sixteenth-century Inca ancestors made a last stand against Pizarro, finally flinging their greatest cultural treasures into the lake to save them from the Spanish despoilers.

Cousteau's submarines, armed with the latest in sonar, photographic equipment and sample-collecting devices, plumbed the entire lake, and the Indians waited expectantly through the passing days and nights to see what he would find. Finally the expedition was finished. The lake was not bottomless, it was only a few hundred meters deep; and there were no Inca artifacts, not so much as a pottery shard. What Cousteau did discover was a hitherto unknown species of bottom-dwelling frog, several specimens of which were brought up and exhibited in buckets.

The Indians were shattered and several actually wept. "The Frenchman has found some frogs, but he has killed our past," one remarked.

Science often inflicts lesser wounds on the rest of us.

When Viking landed on Mars, the wonderful monsters who inhabited that planet up to then were destroyed forever. Even if Viking had discovered real Martian dragons, they would be commonplace by now—interesting, but scarcely more mysterious than the platypus at the Bronx Zoo.

So far, the Loch Ness monster and the Himalayan yeti have been spared, despite the earnest efforts of science to stuff them in collecting jars. Science has not quite been able to disprove their existence absolutely, nor has it found the monsters. The mystery is shaken but intact.

Meanwhile, we content ourselves shriveling lesser mysteries. The relics of Tutankamen, once supposed to have carried a lethal curse for all beholders, were taken on a world tour and the millions of viewers who lined up to see them contracted little more than athlete's foot. Preparations are being made to lower cameras to the wreck of the Titanic, if it is found, exchanging what little mystery the ship may retain for, perhaps, some dry new insights into the ecology of barnacles.

Everest has been climbed (often), the Marianas Trench has been plumbed and the misty demons of Tibet's Lhasa have fled before the march of housing developments and burgeoning industry.

In *The Hound of the Baskervilles*, we realize with regret that the phantom hellhound and sinister shadows of Baskerville Hall are doomed forever, not so much by Sherlock Holmes' investigation as by Sir Henry Baskerville's announcement that he will install the latest Swan and Edison electric lights around the grounds.

We take grizzly delight in the skewering of vampires on wooden stakes, but some among us wince at seeing vampires exposed to something far more lethal—the shadowless light of science.

Babies love peek-a-boo games and advertisers know that products sell better when concealed by tantalizing packages. In *The Little Prince*, Saint-Exupery is asked by the hero to draw a sheep he can take home to his asteroid to keep the local vegetation under control. The author fails to satisfy the Little Prince with explicit pictures of sheep until in despair he draws a picture of a box, explaining that the desired sheep was inside.

One of the few sad things about science is that it destroys those boxes. Keats, a physician and friend of science as well as a poet, put it this way (in the poem *Lamia*):

> . . . Do not all charms fly
> At the mere touch of cold philosophy?
> . . . Philosophy will clip an Angel's wings,
> Conquer all mysteries by rule and line,
> Empty the haunted air, the gnomed mine—
> Unweave a rainbow, as it erewhile made
> The tender-person'd Lamia melt into a shade.

Beauty, as Scientists Behold It

There's something in a song, a rushing mountain creek, the night sky, the human form and a thousand other things that touches all of us occasionally, piercing the core of our primal feelings and making existence seem inexplicably good. We call it beauty.

Unfortunately, most of us can't spare much time to ponder that mysterious quality. Beauty is fine, but it doesn't do the laundry, buy groceries, cure measles, fill gas tanks or keep our enemies at bay.

Science, on the other hand, which can help do all those things, seems at times as practical and ugly as a toilet plunger.

And yet, when scientists shed their dirty lab coats and don blue jeans for an evening of beer and pretzels, they talk about beauty as if it were the central driving force of their work and lives. The beauty they have in mind manifests itself as equations scribbled on blackboards rather than as poetry, concerts or *Playboy* centerfolds, but it is as real to them as a Bach fugue, something felt with the heart as well as the mind.

They say something startling: Beautiful solutions are better than merely practical solutions because they are more likely to reveal profound scientific truth.

Can a mass of numbers and Greek letters joined by squiggly lines really be a thing of beauty?

One of the world's leading authorities on how stars evolve, Subrahmanyan Chandrasekar of the University of Chicago, says he feels the same "thrill" beholding a beautiful mathematical relationship as he does a Michelangelo sculpture.

Disdaining sloppy thinking, scientists demand the right nut for the right bolt, but they don't think of themselves as mechanics. They like to quote Jules Henri Poincaré, the great French physicist and mathematician:

"The Scientist does not study nature because it is useful to do so. He studies it because he takes pleasure in it, and he takes pleasure in it because it is beautiful. If nature were not beautiful, it would not be worth knowing and life would not be worth living."

Scientists tinker with machines that cost taxpayers hundreds of millions of dollars. To justify their work, they must sometimes go before committees of laymen to explain how their work may harness fusion energy, keep us ahead in the arms race or bring cancer under control.

Though such goals may be important, they are less important to the scientists themselves than their quest for some difficult but compellingly beautiful abstraction, such as the field equations of James Clerk Maxwell and Einstein's General Relativity. Among themselves, they speak of such things in the same awed tones as those of an architect describing a Gothic cathedral.

The ancient Greeks were elated to discover that a rectangle whose proportions are three to five is more beautiful than a simple square. Today's scientists say they sense the same artistic exhilaration from some far-reaching new discoveries about the behavior of sub-nuclear particles.

Until recently, traditional scientific thinking held that, ultimately, everything in the universe has a symmetrically equal and opposite counterpart, and that the Asian notion of yin and yang is literally true. But a beautiful theory has led to the finding that universal symmetry (or parity) in the behavior of nuclear particles is sometimes slightly violated, and scientists believe they have come upon a truth even more beautiful than the simple perfection of symmetry.

The discovery seems to them a marvelous example of how an instinctive perception of beauty can penetrate truth more deeply than conventional logic.

When physicists think about such mysteries as gravitation and black holes, they are increasingly drawn to a class of mathematical tools called "gauge theories," which attempt to bind together two or more different kinds of relationships.

To people versed in mathematics, gauge theories often seem superbly beautiful, but they are extremely difficult to prove by scientific observation. They also sometimes seem to fly in the face of accepted wisdom. But as experimentalists grope to test some of these beautiful ideas, there is growing concrete evidence that gauge theories really do point the way to ultimate understanding of reality—to the Grand Unified Theory of which science has long dreamed.

As the evidence mounts, the theorists smile and quote Keats: "Beauty is truth, truth beauty."

James Gleick is the author of, most recently, *Faster: The Acceleration of Just About Everything*. He contributes two articles around a common theme, "the hidden costs of coping with the technology we love." They are from the *New York Times Magazine*, April 8, 1996, and July 13, 1997.

Manual Labor

Good morning—Daylight Savings Time has begun, and you have work to do. Maybe you have already reset your wristwatch and bedside clock, but the odds are that you have neglected one or more of the following time-keeping devices: VCR. Automatic coffeemaker. Telephone answering machine. Camera. Digital thermostat. Television set. Microwave oven. Stereo. Personal computer. Car.

Of course, these appliances have other functions, but they generally contain clocks, and, as a citizen of a technological age, you may feel a responsibility to keep your technologies in order. Or you may not—your household may contain more than a few LCD's permanently lit with that flashing **12:00:00**. Either way, you're well aware that the days when you could set a clock by pushing the minute hand with your forefinger or turning a simple knob are long gone. In fact, for some of these machines, you are going to have to find—and at this point a shudder is understandable—the instructions.

Few tasks so perfectly crystallize the problem of inhuman design—design for engineers instead of for users—than the simple business of setting a clock. There are rental cars all across America that will never see the right time on their dashboard clock radios, because too many tiny unlabeled buttons are serving too many simultaneous functions. There are answering machines that tag phone messages with the correct time only from October to April; from April to October, their owners resignedly live with a one-hour error.

Too many functions—not enough buttons. Or too many buttons: a typical VCR can no longer be controlled without the remote control, and the remote control has 41 buttons, two rocker switches, four cursor-control keys, a "TV-VTR" toggle, and a big, complicated "REW-FF" adjustable-speed knob. Even so, none of those controls has anything to do with setting the clock. That function is relegated to a computer-style menu that the user navigates by scrolling and "executing." No wonder the instruction manual (have you found yours yet?) devotes two of its 64 pages—14 numbered instructions, 12 illustrations, and 4 extra small-type Notes—to explaining the use of the "Auto Clock Set feature." And be patient: as one Note instructs: *If nothing happens even after you wait about 30 minutes, set the clock manually.*

The craft and business of technical writing have bloomed in recent years. The world's novelists are vastly outnumbered by writers whose mission is, pure and simple, *how to*. There are fast-growing university programs, academic journals, consulting firms and professional societies—the Society for Technical Communication alone has more than 20,000 members.

Still, as you wander from appliance to appliance, manuals in hand, you may just occasionally feel that there is room for further progress. You may sometimes sense that, while each individual word is English, you are gaining fresh insight into the syntax and tonality of a foreign, probably Asian, language. You may marvel at the mingling of the obvious and the obscure . . .

Here's how to pick up your handheld vacuum:
Remove the DUSTBUSTER from the charging bracket by gripping middle of handle and gently pulling unit from bracket (Figure 6).

What to do with it when you're finished vacuuming:
The DUSTBUSTER will automatically turn off when your thumb is removed from the button.

Here is the dryer. Start with the "interior light":
The light inside the dryer drum comes on automatically when the door is opened. When the door is closed, the light turns off.

Easy! But they're just softening you up for the body blow of the "wrinkle-rid/cycle signal":
This knob controls the volume of the audible cycle signal for both the wrinkle-rid feature and the regular end of cycle signal. . . . It should always be turned to an on position when using the wrinkle-rid feature which is built into the Knits/Perm Press Auto Cycle.

And this is old technology. New technology has silicon, and silicon seems to engender instructions along the lines of (for a cellular phone) this:
There are three ways to select a memory location. You can select a specific location number; you can choose to autoload which will store the information in the next sequentially available location; or you can arrange the location into blocks.

Authors of manuals also find that, like it or not, they have company attorneys as writing partners. This is why a typical manual may contain three boxes headed "Caution: Product Damage," four "Warning: Electrical Shock Hazard," two "Warning: Personal Injury Hazard" and one "Caution: Floor Damage," each with an oversized exclamation mark inside a bold triangle. It is an American phenomenon, especially.

"European product-liability laws don't make it necessary to warn against abnormal use, like using a TV set to melt the snow in front of your house," says

Peter Ring, a Danish consultant. He says lawyer-driven manuals do manage to cut down on lawsuits, however: "Nobody can find out how to use the product. It is consequently put aside and causes no harm."

Or the instruction manual itself is put aside (and causes no harm). It is an article of faith in the consumer electronics business that, no matter how much companies invest in manuals, customers will not read them. It is the same in the software business, responsible for an equally numbing sort of linguistic fog. Before there was computer software, who could have predicted the appearance in the universe of human discourse of sentences like the following (recent winner of a worst-technical-writing-of-the-month contest run by COREComm, a Houston technical-writing company)?

Type the field name Name in the Field Name field.

A gem—words of one syllable. Like so many instruction manuals, it is mesmerizing. You find yourself staring at it, the way you would stare at one of those 3D stereograms, until a kind of meaning may start to flicker into focus. If only for an instant. It's almost poetry.

Maintenance Not Included

Forgive me, for I have recharged my cellular-phone battery before it was fully drained of power.

I have carried AA batteries loose in my pocket, where contact with keys and other metal objects might have caused them to short, leak or rupture. I have left worn-out batteries for months—yes, even years—in toys and cameras, risking corrosion and battery leakage.

I have mixed old and new batteries in my portable compact-disk player. I have stored batteries in damp places and at abnormal temperatures. I have neglected to ensure proper alignment of the positive and negative terminals of the batteries in my tape recorder, thus causing it to halt in the middle of an interview.

I have unwittingly subjected rechargeable batteries to the vile "memory effect." I have gone blurry on the difference between nickel cadmium and nickel metal hydride. I have forgotten, till it was too late, about the less visible members of the battery population: those empowering wristwatches, arming the handsets of cordless phones, and protecting the volatile memory of unpluggable appliances like VCR's. I have wasted batteries, mistreated batteries, and disregarded hundreds of pages of written instructions, in many languages, concerning batteries.

Citizens of the modern world—those, anyway, who have chosen to possess pocket telephones, camcorders, Diskmen, Gameboys or, worst of all, laptop computers—have taken on a new and complex management role. We may as well add it to our resumes: Strategic Coordinator of, and Footservant to, Batteries.

No one quite planned for this. Advancing technology always has hidden costs that sneak along with it into the future, and somehow this most mundane of objects has become a time swallower in the everyday lives of this consumers. During the generations we now realize were merely the dawn of electrical age, the nuisance was confined to leakage in flashlights and Batteries Not Included with toys. Now, in terms of care and feeding, rechargeable batteries have changed all that. They rival pets in their demand for attention. At least the average Rottweiler owner can get by without much knowledge of inorganic chemistry.

"Each of the different battery chemistries do require a different care," says Ken Hawk, a self-described "frustrated user" who has sensed a market and founded 1-800-Batteries, one of a small platoon of specialty companies— battery boutiques. "It's pretty foreign to most people, and if you don't take good care of them, you can kill them in a month and a half."

His company and others now offer thousands of words of instructional text online and offline—hints, tips, how-to's—to supplement the ponderous manuals you aren't reading anyway. These tips are cheery: "Burp Your Battery"; "Clean Your Contacts"; "Work 'Em Out" (that is, in case you have some free time: "to increase the life of your batteries, don't leave them dormant for extended periods").

Have you, meanwhile, absorbed and retained Motorola's eight or more pages of instructions for managing the cute pair of battleship-gray batteries that came with that cellular phone, along with their "two pocket automatic switching IntelliCharge II Rapid Charger"? Are you keeping your eye on the "multicolor lamp" in each pocket? Anyway, do you know the difference between "rapid charging" and "trickle charging"? Do you use the little tabs on the batteries to record their status? Once you put the batteries in the charger, do you remember to take them out within 24 hours?

Standardization came early to the world of consumer batteries, where the vast majority of the billions sold each year belong to the big five: AA, AAA, C, D, or the quaint-looking matchbox-size "9-volt." Double-A batteries alone account for about half of battery sales in the United States; you can buy black-market and gray-market versions with foreign-language packaging from street-hawkers, and if you ever actually computed your household's annual Double-A budget, you would be unamused. By contrast, designers of modern consumer electronics—laptop computers, especially—have thrown standardization to the winds. A given brand—the IBM ThinkPad, for example—can require a dozen or more different and incompatible batteries, depending on model number. Meanwhile, the laptop makers are also letting their power-hungry processors and display screens get ahead of battery capacity, forcing users to carry extra batteries on long flights. So 1–800-Batteries carries an astonishing assortment of 6,000 different types of battery—and these days, you're expected to buy a few for the road.

For many people, the most frustrating single fact of battery management is that most rechargeable batteries do need to be drained of power before they are charged again. A laptop-computer battery with half of its charge remaining is a particularly unwelcome object as you begin packing for your plane trip; you are supposed to use that charge before you fill it up again. Otherwise, particularly with nickel cadmium—the most common of the rechargeable-battery chemistries—the "memory effect" takes hold. Because of gas bubbles building up on the active cell plates, the battery actually remembers that it was used for only a half-hour before recharging—and becomes, henceforth, a battery with a half-hour useful life.

The more modern types, nickel metal hydride and the even more promising lithium ion, avoid the memory effect, though consumers are still expected to condition them by discharging them and recharging them several times. The next trend will be "smart" batteries, with embedded computers monitoring their status and, just maybe, taking over some of the management chores from consumers.

Still, the technologies for generating electricity in miniature packages have not leapt forward at the kind of pace associated with computers. Batteries remain the worst obstacle to progress in designing the next generation of portable computer or electric car. They have not obeyed Moore's Law—the observation that chips of a given size and price double in capacity every year and a half. If they had, our automobiles would be running quietly and fume-lessly for months on double A's. Instead . . . well, forgive me.

Gina Kolata is a science and medical reporter for the *New York Times*, and the author of four books. These articles appeared in the *New York Times* on June 24, 1993, and February 23, 1997.

At Last, Shout of "Eureka!" in Age-Old Math Mystery

More than 350 years ago, a French mathematician wrote a deceptively simple theorem in the margins of a book, adding that he had discovered a marvelous proof of it but lacked space to include it in the margin. He died without ever offering his proof, and mathematicians have been trying ever since to supply it. Now, after thousands of claims of success that proved untrue, mathematicians say the daunting challenge, perhaps the most famous of unsolved mathematical problems, has at last been surmounted.

The problem is Fermat's last theorem, and its apparent conqueror is Dr. Andrew Wiles, a forty-year-old English mathematician who works at Princeton University. Dr. Wiles announced the result yesterday at the last of three lectures given over three days at Cambridge University in England. Within a few minutes of the conclusion of his final lecture, computer mail messages were winging around the world as mathematicians alerted each other to the startling and almost wholly unexpected result. Dr. Leonard Adelman of the University of Southern California said he received a message about an hour after Dr. Wiles's announcement. The frenzy is justified, he said. "It's the most exciting thing that's happened in—geez—maybe ever, in mathematics." Mathematicians present at the lecture said they felt "an elation," said Dr. Kenneth Ribet of the University of California at Berkeley, in a telephone interview from Cambridge.

The theorem, an overarching statement about what solutions are possible for certain simple equations, was stated in 1637 by Pierre de Fermat, a seventeenth-century French mathematician and physicist. Many of the brightest minds in mathematics have struggled to find the proof ever since, and many have concluded that Fermat, contrary to his tantalizing claim, had probably failed to develop one despite his considerable mathematical ability.

With Dr. Wiles's result, Dr. Ribet said, "the mathematical landscape has changed." He explained: "You discover that things that seemed completely impossible are more of a reality. This changes the way you approach problems, what you think is possible."

Dr. Barry Mazur, a Harvard University mathematician, also reached by telephone in Cambridge, said: "A lot more is proved than Fermat's last theorem. One could envision a proof of a problem, no matter how celebrated, that had no implications. But this is just the reverse. This is the emergence of a technique that is visibly powerful. It's going to prove a lot more."

Fermat's last theorem has to do with equations of the form $x^n + y^n = z^n$. The case where $n = 2$ is familiar as the Pythagorean theorem, which says that the squares of the lengths of two sides of a right-angled triangle equal the square of the length of the hypotenuse. One such equation is $3^2 + 4^2 = 5^2$, since $9 + 16 = 25$.

Fermat's last theorem states that there are no solutions to such equations when n is a whole number greater than 2. This means, for instance, that it would be impossible to find any whole numbers x, y and z such that $x^3 + y^3 = z^3$. Thus $3^3 + 4^3 (27 + 64) = 91$, which is not the cube of any whole number.

Mathematicians in the United States said that the stature of Dr. Wiles and the imprimatur of the experts who heard his lectures, especially Dr. Ribet and Dr. Mazur, convinced them that the new proof was very likely to be right. In addition, they said, the logic of the proof is persuasive because it is built on a carefully developed edifice of mathematics that goes back more than thirty years and is widely accepted.

Experts cautioned that Dr. Wiles could, of course, have made some subtle misstep. Dr. Harold M. Edwards, a mathematician at the Courant Institute of Mathematical Sciences in New York, said that until the proof was published in a mathematical journal, which could take a year, and until it is checked many times, there is always a chance it is wrong. The author of a book on Fermat's last theorem, Dr. Edwards noted that "even good mathematicians have had false proofs." But even he said that Dr. Wiles's proof sounded like the real thing and "has to be taken very seriously."

Despite the apparent simplicity of the theorem, proving it was so hard that in 1815 and again in 1860, the French Academy of Sciences offered a gold medal and 300 francs to anyone who could solve it. In 1908, the German Academy of Sciences offered a prize of 100,000 marks for a proof that the theorem was correct. The prize, which still stands but has been reduced to 7,500 marks, about $4,400, has attracted the world's "cranks," Dr. Edwards said. When the Germans said the proof had to be published, "the cranks began publishing their solutions in the vanity press," he said, yielding thousands of booklets. The Germans told him they would even award the prize for a proof that the theorem was not true, Dr. Edwards added, saying that they "would be so overjoyed that they wouldn't have to read through these submissions."

But it was not just amateurs whose imagination was captured by the enigma. Famous mathematicians, too, spent years on it. Others avoided it for fear of being sucked into a quagmire. One mathematical genius, David Hilbert, said in 1920 that he would not work on it because "before beginning I should put in three years of intensive study, and I haven't that much time to spend on a probable failure."

Mathematicians armed with computers have shown that Fermat's theorem holds true up to very high numbers. But that falls well short of a general proof.

Dr. Ribet said that twentieth-century work on the problem had begun to grow ever more divorced from Fermat's equations. "Over the last sixty years, people in number theory have forged an incredible number of tools to deal with simple problems like this," he said. Eventually, "people lost day-to-day contact with the old problems and were preoccupied with the objects they created," he said.

Scientist Reports First Cloning Ever of Adult Mammal

In a feat that may be the one bit of genetic engineering that has been anticipated and dreaded more than any other, researchers in Britain are reporting that they have cloned an adult mammal for the first time. The group, led by Dr. Ian Wilmut, a fifty-two-year-old embryologist at the Roslin Institute in Edinburgh, created a lamb using DNA from an adult sheep. The achievement shocked leading researchers who had said it could not be done. The researchers had assumed that the DNA of adult cells would not act like the DNA formed when a sperm's genes first mingle with those of an egg. In theory, researchers said, such techniques could be used to take a cell from an adult human and use the DNA to create a genetically identical human—a time-delayed twin. That prospect raises the thorniest of ethical and philosophical questions.

Dr. Wilmut's experiment was simple, in retrospect. He took a mammary cell from an adult sheep and prepared its DNA so it would be accepted by an egg from another sheep. He then removed the egg's own DNA, replacing it with the DNA from the adult sheep by fusing the egg with the adult cell. The fused cells, carrying the adult DNA, began to grow and divide, just like a perfectly normal fertilized egg, to form an embryo. Dr. Wilmut implanted the embryo into another ewe; in July, the ewe gave birth to a lamb, named Dolly. Though Dolly seems perfectly normal, DNA tests show that she is the clone of the adult ewe that supplied her DNA.

"What this will mostly be used for is to produce more health care products," Dr. Wilmut told the Press Association of Britain early today, the Reuters news agency reported. "It will enable us to study genetic diseases for which there is presently no cure and track down the mechanisms that are involved. The next step is to use the cells in culture in the lab and target genetic changes into that culture."

Simple though it may be, the experiment startled biologists and ethicists. Dr. Wilmut said in a telephone interview that he planned to breed Dolly to determine whether she was fertile. He said he was interested in the technique primarily as a tool in animal husbandry, but other scientists said it had opened doors to the unsettling prospect that humans could be cloned as well.

Dr. Lee Silver, a biology professor at Princeton University, said last week that the announcement had come just in time for him to revise his forthcoming book so the first chapter will no longer state that such cloning is impossible. "It's unbelievable," Dr. Silver said. "It basically means that there are no limits. It means all of science fiction is true. They said it could never be done and now here it is, done before the year 2000."

Walter Sullivan was a science writer for the *New York Times* and the author of many books. This piece is excerpted from *We Are Not Alone: The Continuing Search for Extraterrestrial Intelligence* (Plume Books, 1993).

What If We Succeed?

On the night of October 30, 1938, there were manifestations of panic in widely scattered parts of the United States. They began shortly after Orson Welles, the actor and producer, sat in front of a microphone in the New York studios of the Columbia Broadcasting System to introduce an adaptation of *The War of the Worlds*, written in 1898 by H. G. Wells. Orson Welles told his nationwide audience how, in recent years, people on earth had gone about their daily lives in complacence: "Yet across an immense ethereal gulf, minds that are to our minds as ours are to the beasts in the jungle, intellects vast, cool and unsympathetic regarded this earth with envious eyes and slowly and surely drew their plans against us. . . ."

The dramatization that followed, consisting of simulated news bulletins, interviews and sometimes fearful sound effects, was so realistic that thousands believed Martians had, in fact, landed in New Jersey—hideous creatures that slew all opposing them with a sinister "heat-ray." People rushed into the streets only partially clothed or struck out aimlessly across open country. Cars raced wildly through crowded cities.

Is this a hint of what might happen if we did, in fact, make contact with a superior civilization? Possibly so, according to a report submitted to the federal government in 1960. For so dramatic an effect, the encounter would presumably have to be physical, but even radio contact would lead to profound upheavals, the report said. The document was a by-product of the historic action taken by Congress on the heels of the first *Sputniks* in establishing an agency for the exploration of space. The National Aeronautics and Space Act of July 29, 1958, called for "long-range studies" of the benefits and problems to be expected from space activities.

Pursuant to this act, NASA set up a Committee on Long-Range Studies and awarded a study contract to the Brookings Institution. More than two hundred specialists were interviewed by a team led by Donald N. Michael, a social psychologist who later became director of the Peace Research Institute in Washington. Pertinent portions of the resulting report were reviewed by such figures as Lloyd V. Berkner, head of the Space Science Board, Caryl P. Haskins, president of the Carnegie Institution of Washington, James R. Killian, chairman of the Corporation of M.I.T., Oscar Schachter, director of the General Legal Division of the United Nations, and Margaret Mead, the anthropologist.

The document was submitted to NASA only a few months after Project Ozma's attempt to intercept signals from two nearby stars, and much in the minds of those who drafted it was the question of what would happen if we discovered another, far more advanced civilization. The report did not rule out the possibility of direct contact, such as the one so vividly dramatized by Orson Welles, and it suggested that artifacts left by explorers from another world "might possibly be discovered through our space activities on the Moon, Mars, or Venus." Nevertheless, it said, if intelligent life is discovered beyond the earth during the next twenty years, it most probably will be in a distant solar system and manifest itself by radio. Such circumstances, it added, would not necessarily rule out revolutionary effects.

Anthropological files contain many examples of societies sure of their place in the universe, which have disintegrated when they have had to associate with previously unfamiliar societies espousing different ideas and different life ways; others that survived such an experience usually did so by paying the price of changes in values and attitudes and behavior.

Since intelligent life might be discovered at any time via the radio telescope research presently under way, and since the consequences of such a discovery are presently unpredictable because of our limited knowledge of behavior under even an approximation of such dramatic circumstances, two research areas can be recommended:

1. Continuing studies to determine emotional and intellectual understanding and attitudes—and successive alterations of them if any—regarding the possibility and consequences of discovering intelligent extraterrestrial life.

2. Historical and empirical studies of the behavior of peoples and their leaders when confronted with dramatic and unfamiliar events or social pressures.

Such studies, the report continued, should consider public reactions to past hoaxes, "flying saucer" episodes and incidents like the Martian invasion broadcast. They should explore how to release the news of an encounter to the public—or withhold it, if this is deemed advisable. The influence on international relations might be revolutionary, the report concluded, for the discovery of alien beings might lead to a greater unity of men on earth, based on the "oneness" of man or on the age-old assumption that any stranger is threatening.

Much would depend, of course, on the nature of the contact and the content of any message received. Man is so completely accustomed to regarding himself as supreme that to discover he is no more an intellectual match for beings elsewhere than our dogs are for us would be a shattering revelation. Carl Gustav Jung, the disciple of Freud, who later went his own psychological way, said of a direct confrontation with such creatures: "The reins would be torn from our hands and we would, as a tearful old medicine man once said to me, find ourselves 'without dreams,' that is, we would find our intellectual and spiritual aspirations so outmoded as to leave us completely paralyzed."

The Search for Extraterrestrial Intelligence (SETI) project has led to a debate on whether our new acquaintances would, in fact, be "nice people" or the monstrous villains depicted by Orson Welles. Much of the population has been conditioned by science-fiction tales of evil genius at work among the stars, of death rays and battles between galaxies. This may, in part, have accounted for the popular reaction to the Welles broadcast, and the fears of such scientists as Sir Martin Ryle. Some of those concerned with the search for life in other worlds have sought to counter this attitude.

Thus Philip Morrison, in one of his lectures, questioned whether any civilization with a superior technology would wish to do harm to one that has just entered the community of intelligence. If he were looking through a microscope, he said, and saw a group of bacteria spell out, like a college band, "Please do not put iodine on this plate. We want to talk to you," his first inclination, he said, would certainly not be to rush the bacteria into a sterilizer. He doubted that advanced societies "crush out any competitive form of intelligence, especially when there is clearly no danger."

Ronald Bracewell, in a 1962 lecture at the University of Sydney, asked whether beings in another world would covet our gold or other rare substances. Do they want us as cattle or as slaves? He replied by pointing out the literally astronomical cost of transport between solar systems. Any civilization able to cover interstellar distances would hardly need us for food or raw material, which they could far more easily synthesize at home. "The most interesting item to be transferred from star to star," he said, "is information, and this can be done by radio." In 1977, at the height of the Cold War, he concluded that, since technology on earth had been honed by warfare, with a premium placed on cunning and weaponry, much the same would prevail elsewhere. "That is not to say that some gentle Buddha could not have influenced whole populations to follow quite different, less competitive paths," he said. "But if our own history is any guide, such a population would have been overrun by those who value technical mastery of nature. Technological life, rather than merely intelligent life, is what will determine membership in the galactic communication network."

Bracewell cited a 1975 report prepared by the Library of Congress for the House Committee on Science and Technology which pointed out the danger of a hasty reply: "Since we have no knowledge of their nature," it said, "we may be aiding in our own doom. Although it is tempting to assume that any civilization advanced enough to travel over interstellar space would have overcome the petty differences that cause wars, they may not be sure if we have. They may have encountered other warlike peoples and learned . . . to arrive . . . ready for combat."

Bracewell said he himself found it hard to imagine much of any threat, particularly of a familiar kind. And there is, he said, no point in remaining silent if a probe has already reached the solar system and reported our presence.

Another among those who envisioned worlds corrupted by technology was Freeman Dyson, the imaginative physicist at the Institute for Advanced Study in Princeton. In a 1964 letter to *Scientific American*, he questioned whether one was justified in assuming that the distant creatures with whom we may converse are moral by our standards.

"Intelligence may indeed be a benign influence," he said, "creating isolated groups of philosopher-kings far apart in the heavens and enabling them to share at leisure their accumulated wisdom." On the other hand, he added, "intelligence may be a cancer of purposeless technological exploitation, sweeping across a galaxy as irresistibly as it has swept across our own planet." Assuming interstellar travel at moderate speeds, he said, "the technological cancer could spread over a whole galaxy in a few million years, a time very short compared with the life of a planet."

What our detectors will pick up is a technological civilization, he argued, but it will not necessarily be intelligent, in the pure sense of the word. In fact, he continued, it may more likely be "a technology run wild, insane or cancerously spreading than a technology firmly under control and supporting the rational needs of a superior intelligence." On the other hand, he said, there is also the possibility that a "truly intelligent" society might not feel the need, or be interested in, technology. "Our business, as scientists is to search the universe and find out what is there. What is there may conform to our moral sense or it may not. . . . It is just as unscientific to impute to remote intelligences wisdom and serenity as it is to impute to them irrational and murderous impulses. We must be prepared for either possibility and conduct our searches accordingly."

Nevertheless, it seems hard to believe that a race of villains or a civilization run amok would not have blown itself to smithereens long before it reached into other solar systems. An achievement of lasting peace and stability seems to be an important element in qualifying for membership in the interstellar community. While Dyson is understandably dismayed at what technology and population growth are doing to the face of our planet, a society that could not bring such trends under control would seem destined to disintegrate. The achievement of great stability and serenity would seem a prerequisite for a society willing to make the expensive and enormously prolonged effort required to contact another world.

What, indeed, do we know about the roots of evil—of greed, aggression and treachery? On earth they are clearly manifestations of a complex society that has not reached stability. Animals, as a rule, are aggressive only when necessary. The well-fed lion lies near the water hole while his traditional victims, sensing his satiety, quench their thirst in peace. Man's inherent aggression has made wars possible—though it does not necessarily initiate wars. But it would appear that, if man is to survive, this aspect of his personality will have to be controlled—an achievement that in the past few years has seemed increasingly possible.

There is, however, no agreement on whether or not we should reply. The advice of the Czech astronomer Zdenek Kopal is: "For God's sake, let us not answer." George Wald, professor of biochemistry at Harvard, winner of a Nobel prize and a firm believer that life has evolved beyond earth, has said: "I can conceive of no nightmare so terrifying as establishing such communication with a so-called superior (or, if you wish, advanced) technology in outer space." To be attached, "as by an umbilical cord," to a more advanced civilization would be a "degradation of the human spirit," Wald told a 1972 symposium at Boston University. The possibly devastating effects of such a contact were cited in the Brookings Institution study commissioned by NASA soon after it was formed. The fate of the American Indian would be a case in point.

Another analysis was made by Michael Michaud, a Foreign Service officer who, in addition to handling such problems as European Security, NATO and arms control, had developed a special interest in SETI. While on the State Department's Iran Desk in 1972 he published an article in the *Foreign Service Journal* titled "Interstellar Negotiation," in which he listed a variety of possible dangers following contact. He rejected the argument that interstellar travel is impractical: Distance does not guarantee security "any more than an advanced civilization guarantees peaceful intentions." Regrettably, he said, "the stereotype of the benevolent, super-intelligent alien may be as unrealistic as the stereotype of the bug-eyed monsters carrying off shapely human females. . . . A species which had experienced nothing but hostile contacts with others, perhaps resulting in military conflict, would be predisposed to be hostile and to make military preparations." A great galactic empire "might regard us as nothing more than a troublesome infestation to be circumscribed or eliminated."

One of the primary roles of government is to protect its people from external threats. The dangers from beyond the earth could take a number of forms, Michaud said. "In a standard science fiction scenario, the aliens might use super-weapons to blast us from orbiting vehicles. They might use chemical or biological fumigation. Or they might have the power to trigger an explosion in our sun, turning it into a nova which would fry the earth."

There was no certainty, he said in a later article, that the aliens would have any more concern for human beings than we do for whales and dolphins.

Since the aliens might have competing states, he wrote (showing his foreign affairs background), it would be important to learn whether the message came from only one of them. "An expansionist species might have colonized many planets, creating a far-flung empire or federation. We would need to know if we were communicating with a strong central authority, a weak one losing its grip, or a rebellious colony. We could unwittingly become involved in an interstellar civil war."

Our reaction to a signal, he said, could be either silence or a reassuring response that was prelude to "interstellar negotiation." "The latter," he said, would be "the most difficult diplomacy Earthmen have ever attempted. It could last centuries, it could risk human survival; or it could bring an incalculable richness of knowledge, physical instrumentalities, and cultural growth, and open a door to a Galactic society."

Arthur C. Clarke, one of the most knowledgeable of science-fiction writers, has pointed out, however, the difficulties of administering a galactic empire, be it benign or tyrannical, because the distances would make communication so slow. Radio messages to our nearest neighbors would take decades and those across the galaxy would require tens of thousands of years.

In a 1977–1978 journal of the American Institute of Aeronautics and Astronautics, Michaud warned that the first detection of an alien message might not be from a scientific search but by such a source as military surveillance, and might be kept secret. There would be a strong temptation, he said, "for individual nations or groups to conduct separate dialogues with the aliens to exploit contact for their own purposes." When contact became public knowledge, that "almost certainly would cause many more humans to attribute events on Earth to aliens; there would be an upsurge in witch-hunting and UFO sightings."

On the other hand, he said, "many of us would be excited by this outside stimulus, with its suggestion of a break with conventionality and of new prospects for the future; the world needs a shared adventure." He cited Philip Morrison's argument that contact with alien worlds could bring us a richer store of information than that inherited by medieval Europe from ancient Greece. It could lead to a new and greater Renaissance. What an enriching experience it would be to learn of the histories, political and economic organizations and cultural achievements of entirely different civilizations! It is sometimes argued that we might learn a cure for cancer or how best to harness the fusion reaction that powers the sun, but what we learn medically from beings that evolved via a different biochemical route might be meaningless and we might since have conquered the fusion reaction ourselves.

In time, said Michaud, communication with a civilization more advanced than ours could be "the beginning of the end of Man as we have known him." Our culture "might fade and vanish, becoming a quaint historical memory, as we merged with a superior culture."

In the early 1980s a committee of the International Academy of Astronautics began discussing what to do if signals were detected, and a number of papers on the subject were presented at subsequent annual congresses of the International Astronautical Federation. Allan F. Goodman of the School of Foreign Service at Georgetown University proposed a code of conduct at the federation's 1986 congress in Innsbruck, Austria. Finally a draft prepared by Michaud and two key SETI figures, John Billingham and Jill Tarter, was presented and approved at the federation's 1990 congress in Dresden, Germany. Titled "Principles for Activities Following the Detection of Extraterrestrial Intelligence," it has subsequently been approved by the Committee on Space Research (COSPAR), a surviving element of the International Geophysical Year of 1957–58, as well as by other international organizations. It has been put before the International Astronomical Union and is designed for ultimate endorsement by the United Nations, possibly after the first evidence of extraterrestrial intelligence is observed.

The parties to the declaration are "We, the institutions and the individuals participating in the search for extraterrestrial intelligence." One of its key principles is that no detection be announced until all parties to the declaration have been informed, so that they can try to confirm the observation. If the evidence is credible, the IAU's Central Bureau for Astronomical Telegrams in Cambridge, Massachusetts, is to be informed, as well as the secretary-general of the United Nations, as provided by the UN Outer Space Treaty. An intergovernmental treaty on the subject is not recommended at this stage.

"The discoverer should have the privilege of making the first public announcement," the declaration says, providing also that "No response to a signal or other evidence of extraterrestrial intelligence should be sent until appropriate international consultings have taken place," as specified in a separate declaration yet to come.

Possible provisions of the latter were discussed by John Billingham at the 1991 Russian-American conference in Santa Cruz. Any message, he said, should be on behalf of all humanity, speaking "with one voice." The decision to act should be by an appropriate, all-encompassing international body. Silence is to be maintained until it is finally decided whether or not to respond and what to say if we do.

Still mysterious is the nature of those we might be dealing with. Because we have information on only one form of intelligent, technical life, we tend to think of such life elsewhere as resembling ourselves far more closely than is justified. The creatures in which we are interested, besides having minds, must be able to move about and to build things. That is, they must have something comparable to hands and feet. They must have senses, such as sight, touch, and hearing, although the senses that evolve on any given planet will be determined by the environment. For example, it may be that, for various reasons, vision in the infrared part of the spectrum will be more useful than sight in the wavelengths visible to human eyes. Creatures fulfilling such requirements might bear little resemblance to man. As Philip Morrison has put it, they may be "blue spheres with twelve tentacles." They may be as big as a mountain or as small as a mouse, although the amount of food available would set a limit on largeness and fixed sizes of molecules must limit the extent to which the size of a complex brain can be compressed. Life spans in some worlds might be extremely great. The cells of our bodies (with a few exceptions, such as brain cells) are constantly replenishing themselves. It would seem that barring accident or disease this should continue indefinitely, but because of some subtle influence the replacement process is imperfect. This, the essence of aging, is now under intensive study. It is not inconceivable that it can be controlled. Progress in the transplantation of human organs and the manufacture of other body components (such as heart valves) has led some of the most sober medical men to believe we may ultimately be able to extend lifetimes considerably. Lives measured in many centuries instead of barely one would make the slowness of interstellar signaling (or travel) far more acceptable.

There is also the possibility that other civilizations will learn the secret of aging and completely neutralize it. On earth mortality is characteristic of multicelled, sexually reproducing creatures, but not of single-celled ones that reproduce by cell division. It is factored into the individual cells of our bodies. While a cell from an infant, when cultured in the laboratory, subdivides many times, it eventually dies. A cell from an older person subdivides many fewer times before doing so, as though there is a mortality factor hidden in its genetic material. The nature of this factor remains elusive. It may have evolved because it had survival value for a species. If a species lived only long enough to produce a viable new generation, then died to make way for its offspring, the species could evolve to meet a challenge far more rapidly than one in which there were long intervals between generations.

Among those who believe that most, if not all, inhabitants of other worlds are immortal is the SETI pioneer, Frank Drake. "I fear we have been making a dreadful mistake," he wrote during 1976 in *Technology Review*, "by not focusing all searches—including those to be accomplished by a system such as Cyclops [the proposed "orchard" of radio antennas]—on the detection of the signals of the immortals. For it is the immortals we will most likely discover. . . . It has been said that when we first discover other civilizations in space we will be the dumbest of them all. This is true, but more than that, we will probably be the only mortal civilization." Carl Sagan has discussed the possibility that the inhabitants of other worlds might not only have become immortal but lost all motivation for "interstellar gallivanting."

When one looks out among the stars and contemplates the possibility that the miracle of life may have occurred on only this one planet, the thought is frightening, for our stewardship has not been notable. In numerous ways we have transformed the earth and its atmosphere to suit us, but not the millions of other species. In 1992 the National Academy of Sciences issued a report saying that if current trends continue, a quarter of the world's species of plant and animal may have vanished within fifty years. In the past, evolution has not allowed one species to dominate the planet for long. There always emerged a predator, a disease, a competitor, or exhaustion of its sustenance that brought it in check or to extinction. So far the human race, through exercise of its "intelligence," has avoided this, but can it do so indefinitely? An awesome responsibility falls on our shoulders. Our heritage becomes cosmic, and measures to preserve the species and the environment cannot easily be dismissed as too costly. To meet the challenge is the supreme test of our intelligence.

Harrison E. Salisbury, a long-time *New York Times* correspondent, wrote extensively about Russia and China. The pages that follow are excerpts from *The 900 Days: The Siege of Leningrad* (Harper & Row, 1969).

Deus Conservat Omnia

Above the iron gates of the Sheremetyev Palace on the Fontanka embankment where Anna Akhmatova lived, the legend was inscribed on an old coat of arms: "Deus Conservat Omnia." From her window she looked out upon the palace courtyard, guarded by a great maple whose branches reached toward her, rustling nervously through the long winters and gently stirring during the soft daylight of the white nights. Now the maple's scarlet and golden leaves had fallen, spattering the pavement with pastels that gradually turned to mud in the autumn rains. Now it seemed to Anna Akhmatova that the naked black branches of the maple reached out to her more urgently, calling to her, telling her to stay, to stay in Petersburg.

Anna Akhmatova was the queen of Russian poetry. She was, perhaps, the queen of Leningrad. Surely no one had more of the city in her life, in her blood, in her experience—its fears, its hopes, its tragedies, its genius. She was not Petersburg-born. But her parents had brought her to the northern capital, to the gentle pleasure gardens of Tsarskoye Selo (Pushkin), when she was a child. Her first memories were of "the green damp magnificence of the parks, the meadows where my nurse used to take me for a walk, the hippodrome where little dappled horses galloped, the old railroad station." There she grew up, breathing the air of poets—of Pushkin, of Lermontov, of Derzhavin, of Nekrasov, of Shelley. The princess, the queen-to-be—none so mad, none so gay, so feminine, so passionate, so lyric, so romantic, so urgent, so madcap—so Russian.

Before she was five she spoke French. She went to a girls' school, studied law, studied literature, raced to Paris, fell in love with Modigliani (she didn't know he was a genius, but she knew he had "a head like Antonius and eyes that flashed gold"). She saw the Imperial Ballet of Diaghilev in its Paris triumph. She saw Venice, Rome, Florence. She married a poet, the love of her schoolgirl days in Tsarskoye, Nikolai Gumilev, a dark, brilliant, difficult man. With him she founded a new school of poetry, a neoclassical movement which they called Acmeism. Everything was possible, everything experienced. Her life was a poem of mirrored images, of galloping sleighs in white snows, of warm summer evenings in leafy parks, of boudoirs, of boulevards, of Paris, of golden stars. Of love. Of tragedy. These were, she later understood, the luminous lighthearted days, the hour before dawn. She did not know that shadows soon would pass at her window, terrifying, hiding behind lamp posts, changing the gold to drossy brass.

But tragedy's hand clutched early at her life. She saw it overhanging Petrograd in the war of the Kaiser and the Czar. She saw the "black cloud over mournful Russia." She saw her Petrograd transformed from a northern Venice to a "granite city of glory and misfortune." By the end of World War I Gumilev brought anguish and divorce to her. The tragedy deepened when he faced a Bolshevik firing squad in 1921 and was shot as a White Guard conspirator. The golden years of Tsarskoye Selo had ended. Now came the iron years of the Revolution's mills, grinding ever more harshly until the terror of Stalin's police closed in and swept away her son, Lev.

For seventeen months she stood with the other women in the prison lines of Leningrad, waiting for word of her son's fate, bringing him food, bringing him packages. Once a woman next in line, a woman whose lips were blue with cold or fear, asked her, "And this—can you write about it?"

"Yes," Anna Akhmatova replied, "I can."

The woman smiled a strange and secret smile.

Anna Akhmatova did, finally, write about those days:

> Would you like to see yourself now, you girl so full of laughter?
> The favorite of her friends,
> The gay sinner of Tsarskoye Selo?
> Would you like to see what's happened to your life?
> At the end of a queue of three hundred,
> You stand outside Kresty Prison,
> And your hot tears are burning holes in the New Year's ice.

By this time her son had been cast into exile, there to remain until Stalin's death in 1953.

In this September of 1941 Anna Akhmatova's life was taking another turn. She was leaving Petersburg, Petrograd, Leningrad. September was ending and she had to go, orders of the City Party. The plane—one of the few—was waiting. Already she had moved from the palace on the Fontanka to the building at No. 9 Griboyedov where so many writers had their home. Pavel Luknitsky dropped in to say good-bye. He found her ill and weak. She emerged from the dark little porter's house wearing a heavy coat and they talked together on a bench. Anna Akhmatova told how she had been sitting in a slit trench outside the Sheremetyev Palace during a raid. She was holding a youngster in her arms when she heard the "dragon's shriek" of falling bombs and then a "tremendous din, a crackle and a crunch." Three times the walls of the trench quivered and then grew quiet. How right it was, she said, that in their ancient myths the earth was always the mother, always indestructible. Only the earth could shrug at the terrors of bombardment. The first of the bombs fell next door in the former Catherine Institute, now a hospital. It did not explode. But two exploded in the Sheremetyev gardens, one at the corner of Zhukovsky and Liteiny and one in the house where the writer Nikolai Chukovsky lived. Fortunately he was at the front.

Anna Akhmatova confessed that the explosions left her crushed and feeble. A feeling of terror came over her as she looked at the women with their children wearily waiting in the bomb shelter during the raids—terror for what might happen to them, for what fate held.

The terror for the children of Leningrad did not leave her. From the desert oasis of Tashkent, to which she was evacuated in early October, she wrote in memory of Valya Smirnov, a little boy whom she might have held in her arms, a little boy who was killed by a German bomb:

> Knock on my door with your little fist and I'll open it. . . .
> I did not hear you moan.
> Bring me a little maple twig
> Or simply a handful of grass,
> As you brought last spring.
> And bring a handful of cold, pure Neva water
> And I'll wash away the traces of blood
> From your little golden head. . . .

Deus Conservat Omnia. . . .

Now ANOTHER of the Nazis' allies moved into Leningrad: cold . . . winter . . . snow. . . . The first flakes fell at eleven in the morning on the fourteenth of October. The thermometer dropped. It was below freezing. "Ski day," the day the snow cover reached ten centimeters (about four inches), came October 31—an unprecedentedly early date. Always in Leningrad the first snow marked a holiday. This was the winter capital, the capital of snow and ice, the sparkling city of frost. But now the cold and snow brought forbidding thoughts. What about the water pipes? There was hardly any heat in the buildings. Most people got only a ration of 2.5 liters of kerosene in September. Now there was none. Nor would there be any until February. It was cold in the great stone buildings along the Neva. And it was growing colder. Luknitsky noticed ice on the sidewalks in the morning.

Autumn had ended, such an autumn as Leningrad had never known. Winter was setting in. Perhaps, he thought, it would help Russia—as it had against Napoleon. He did not then know how right he was. Winter would help Russia. But it would come near to destroying Leningrad.

He noticed a change in himself. He was constantly on the move between Leningrad and the front, now in Leningrad for four or five days, then at the front for a week. At the front he lived on army rations. The troops still were fed fairly normally—800 grams of bread, almost two pounds, a day, 150 grams of meat, 140 of cereals, 500 of vegetables and potatoes. For a day or two after coming back from the front he did not feel hungry. Then hunger overwhelmed him. From morning until late night he wanted to eat. The evening dab of cereal or macaroni did not satisfy him. He went to bed hungry and woke up hungry after five or six hours.

All over the city this was happening.

People grew thinner while you looked at them. And they grew more like beasts. Yelena Skryabina had a friend, Irina Klyueva, a beautiful, elegant, quiet woman, who adored her husband. Now she fought and even beat him. Why? Because he wanted to eat. Always. Constantly. Nothing satisfied him. As soon as she prepared food he threw himself on it. And she was hungry herself. Before October ended Irina Klyueva's husband had died of hunger. She did not even pretend to grieve.

Each person tried to make the ration go further. Yelena Skryabina's mother divided each piece of bread into three portions. She ate one in the morning, one at noon, one at night. Madame Skryabina ate her whole portion in the morning with her coffee. That gave her strength to stand in food queues for hours or hunt about the city for food. In the afternoon she usually felt so weak she had to lie down. She worried about her husband. He had a military rear-area ration, but it was not much better than that of the civilians. He got a cup of cereal with butter in the morning. But he saved it for their son, Yuri. The food queues grew so long that it was almost impossible to get into a store before the small supply was exhausted. Finally, her husband got their ration cards registered with a military facility where the family received eight bowls of soup and four bowls of cereal every ten days. By this time speculators were getting 60 rubles for a small loaf of bread, 300 rubles for a sack of potatoes and 1,200 rubles for a kilo of meat.

Yevgeniya Vasyutina sat at home like a troglodyte. There was no heat. She wore her greatcoat and felt boots, removing the boots only when she slept. But not the coat. She covered herself with the mattress and pillows, but when she rose her body was stiff and sore. She heated her tea and food on a tiny grill set between two bricks. Thin shavings provided the fuel. There was no electricity. A *burzhuika*, a little potbellied stove (the name *burzhuika* had come from their use by the "former people" during the cold and famine of Petrograd's 1919 and 1920), was beyond her dreams. More than anything in the world she just wanted a simple tea—tea with sugar and a roll. But this was impossible. She divided her ration of bread into three pieces, each the size of a chocolate bar. She put a little butter or oil on each. One she ate for breakfast, one for lunch, and the third she hid in her lamp shade, the one with a little dancing girl on it. She liked to spin the shade so that the dancer twirled in a rosy whirl. Now the electricity didn't work. No one would think, she devoutly believed, of looking there for food.

Hunger and cold had begun their harsh regime. Bombs and shells rained down. On only two days between September 12 and November 30 did the

Nazis refrain from shelling Leningrad. The bombardment was continuous: in September 5,364 shells, 991 explosive bombs, 31,398 incendiaries; in October 7,590 shells, 801 explosive bombs, 59,926 incendiaries; in November 11,230 shells, 1,244 explosive bombs, 6,544 incendiaries; in December 5,970 shells, 259 bombs, 1,849 incendiaries. There were fires without number—more than 700 in October alone.

In these dreary fall months occurred 79 percent of the air raids which were to strike Leningrad during the whole of the war and 88 percent of the air-raid casualties.

BUT LIFE went on. Vera Ketlinskaya broadcast over Leningrad radio on October 19, marking the seventeenth week of war:

> I was teaching my little son his first uncertain steps when the radio brought into our lives that new all-engulfing word—war. Now seventeen weeks have passed. War has changed the lives of each of us, in big things and little. I have put aside the book I was writing about happiness in order to write about struggle, about bravery, about unyielding stubborn resistance. My son sleeps in a bomb shelter and knows the sound of the air-raid sirens as well as the words "to walk" and "to eat." . . . There is no good news. Not yet. But we will wait. We will fight . . .

The Philharmonic put on a concert in the big hall on October 25. Aleksandr Kamensky played Tchaikovsky. He did the Prater Waltz for an encore. The concert was given during the afternoon, and deep shadows filled the unheated hall. Spectators sat in their greatcoats. Many were military men.

Most of the famous old secondhand bookstores were still open. The painter Ilya Glazunov and his father visited their favorite, from time to time, at the corner of Bolshaya Sadovaya and Vvedensky streets. Not much had changed since the war. Old men in overcoats, with chapped hands and gold-rimmed spectacles huddled together and peered at calf-bound volumes. There were stacks of a new edition of Dickens' *Great Expectations*. It had come off the press just before the blockade. Now all the copies were penned up in Leningrad. On the cover there was a drawing of a little boy, his hand held by a middle-aged man, looking at a ship vanishing into the distance, far, far into the distance. It made a small boy dream.

The astronomer A. N. Deich undertook to rescue from the Pulkovo observatory whatever remained of the telescopic lenses, the scientific equipment, the valuable charts of the stars, the catalogues of the heavens, the remarkable library and archives. Battle had raged in and around the observatory buildings for weeks. The great dome of the main telescope site had been badly smashed, but Deich discovered that the central vaults in which most of the materials had been stored were still in Russian hands and apparently undamaged. He led an expedition to the observatory late in the night of October 13. The German lines were only a few hundred feet distant. Under cover of darkness the most valued observatory possessions, the incunabula among them, were removed. They had to be carried by hand for a quarter of a mile because the trucks could not mount the observatory hill.

Three nights later Professor N. N. Pavlov and a convoy of five trucks started for the observatory, also at night. They were spotted about a mile from the observatory and had to halt as the Germans brought them under fire. They took refuge in a ditch but finally were able to remove a full load of records and equipment. On their way out they again came under German fire.

One October night when the bombardment was particularly heavy Nikolai Tikhonov, the poet who was now a war correspondent, encountered a familiar figure in one of the lower corridors of Smolny—a stout little man without a hat, with hair like King Lear and a beard like Jove—Professor Iosif Orbeli, director of the Hermitage.

Orbeli greeted Tikhonov with enthusiasm.

"You haven't, of course, forgotten the Nizami anniversary?" Orbeli said eagerly. Nizami was the national poet of Azerbaijan. His eight hundredth anniversary was October 19. Long before the war the Hermitage had made plans to mark the occasion. As Orbeli talked, Tikhonov could hear the crash of bombs, the bark of guns.

"Dear Iosif Abramovich," Tikhonov said. "You hear what's going on all around us. In these circumstances a celebration might not be very triumphant."

Bombs or no bombs, war or no war, Orbeli was determined to stage his meeting. He persuaded Tikhonov to speak. He persuaded the military authorities to release "for one day only" half a dozen leading Orientologists, serving on the Pulkovo or Kolpino lines. He promised that they would be back in the trenches before dawn.

Precisely as scheduled, the meeting was held at 2:00 P.M. on October 19 in the Hermitage and completed a few minutes before the customary late-afternoon alert. It was, Tikhonov later discovered, the only celebration in all Russia of the great poet's anniversary. Neither in Moscow nor in Baku was the day marked.

"People of light"—that was what Tikhonov called the people of Leningrad in these times.

THE FIRST day or two or three were the worst. So Nikolai Chukovsky found. If a man had nothing but a slice of bread to eat, he suffered terrible hunger pangs the first day. And the second. But gradually the pain faded into quiet despondency, a gloom that had no ending, a weakness that advanced with frightening rapidity. What you did yesterday you could not do today. You found yourself surrounded by obstacles too difficult to overcome. The stairs were too steep to climb. The wood was too hard to chop, the shelf too high to reach, the toilet too difficult to clean. Each day the weakness grew. But awareness did not decline. You saw yourself from a distance. You knew what was happening, but you could not halt it. You saw your body changing, the legs wasting to toothpicks, the arms vanishing, the breasts turning into empty bags. Skirts slipped from the hips, trousers would not stay up. Strange bones appeared. Or the opposite—you puffed up. You could no longer wear your shoes. Your neighbor had to help you to your feet. Your cheeks looked as though they were bursting. Your neck was too thick for your collar. But it was nothing except wind and water. There was no strength in you. Some said it came from drinking too much. Half of Leningrad was wasting away, the other half was swelling from the water drunk to fill empty stomachs.

It was not true, Chukovsky felt, that you feared most your own death. What was most terrible was to see the people around you dying. What you feared was the inevitable process, the weakness that seized you, the terror of dying alone by degrees in darkness, in cold and in hunger.

As Maria Razina, a Party worker, noted: "Leningraders live so badly it is not possible to imagine anything worse—hunger, cold, and darkness in every house with the fall of night."

October had been hungry, and it was stormy after the fourteenth and snowy. The bombs and shells took their toll. In November the deaths began. Not only the deaths from hunger. The elderly slipped quietly away of many diseases. Younger people died of galloping consumption, of grippe. Any disease finished you quickly. An ulcer was fatal. Half the food you ate was inedible. People began to stuff their stomachs with substitutes. They tore the wallpaper from the walls and scraped off the paste, which was supposed to have been made with potato flour. Some ate the paper. It had some nourishment, they thought, because it was made from wood. Later they chewed the plaster—just to fill their stomachs. Vera Inber visited her friend, Marietta, a pharmacologist at the Erisman Hospital where her husband worked. She noticed that the cages for the guinea pigs and rabbits that lined the corridor were all empty now. Only the smell remained. Outside the bomb shelter she saw a watchdog, Dinka. The dog, like most of those in Leningrad, was trained to go to the shelter when the air-raid siren sounded. But already dogs were becoming rare in the besieged city. You noticed those that remained. You thought about them.

A whole new standard of values was arising. Women would trade a diamond ring for a few pounds of black bread so coarse it seemed to be baked of straw. When Luknitsky returned from the front, women waited outside the railroad station. They tugged at his shoulder, saying, "Soldier, wouldn't you like some wine?" They had a bottle or two of spirits to trade for bread, which was in better supply with the troops. Sometimes at the Writers' House there would be a bit of meat in the soup—horse meat.

Hunger brought other changes. Sex virtually disappeared. It was not only that physical sex traits vanished—menstruation halted, women's breasts shriveled, their faces sagged. The sex drive evaporated. Women made no effort to beautify themselves. Lipsticks were eaten as food in December and January. The grease was used for frying ersatz bread. Face powder was mixed into ersatz flour. The births dropped catastrophically in 1942 to only one-third the 1941 figure. In 1943 they dropped another 25 percent. The birth rate in 1940 was 25.1 per 1,000. In 1941 it was 18.3, in 1942 only 6.2.[1]

When rations began to increase, when starvation moderated, sex began to return to normal. The war gave rise to new forms of relations between men and women. "Front love" was what it was called in Leningrad—the love which sprang up between men and women, girls and boys, fighting in the lines together, serving in the AA crews, the love between the nurses and the men they cared for. Many of them had wives or husbands from whom they had long been separated. They did not know whether they would survive the war—or even the week. Chukovsky felt that "front love" commanded respect as a warm and necessary human relationship, one which was only natural in the unnatural conditions of the war and the siege.

[1] In December, 1943, for the first time since the start of the blockade the birth rate exceeded the death rate.

Jean Strouse is the author of *Alice James, A Biography* (1980), which won the Bancroft Prize in American History and Diplomacy, and of *Morgan, American Financier* (Random House, 1999). The publications in which her essays and reviews have appeared include the *New Yorker*, the *New York Times*, the *New York Review of Books*, *Newsweek*, *Vogue*, and *Slate*. The following piece is the introduction to her biography of J. Pierpont Morgan.

Introduction to *Morgan, American Financier*

When Pierpont Morgan died in 1913, at seventy-five, he was the most powerful banker in the world. He had organized giant railroad systems and corporate "trusts," presided over a massive transfer of wealth from Europe to the United States, and, at a time when America had no central bank, acted as monitor of its capital markets and lender of last resort. In the process, he helped transform a largely agrarian society into a modern industrial state— and entered into a struggle over the nature of the country's identity that dates back to Jefferson and Hamilton.

Anyone who occupied that contested ground would have drawn political fire, and it is not surprising that Morgan was exalted by the right as a hero of economic progress and vilified by the left as an icon of capitalist greed. Yet a hundred years later the terms of the argument have not appreciably changed.

The best of Morgan's biographers, Frederick Lewis Allen, suggested some of the reasons why: sparse information about a deeply reticent man, dry financial reporting, ambiguous facts, and passionately held opinions. "There were legends and anecdotes galore," Allen concluded in 1949, "but many of them were of uncertain veracity . . . [W]hat evidence had accumulated about Pierpont Morgan was strikingly divided between the one-sidedly laudatory and the one-sidedly derogatory."

On the laudatory side, a Yale professor conferring an honorary degree on Morgan in 1908 compared him to Alexander the Great, then invoked a higher power: "'Unto whomsoever much is given, of him shall much be required; and to whom men have committed much, of him they will ask more.'" Switching Testaments eight years later, B. C. Forbes, the founder of *Forbes* magazine, called Morgan "the financial Moses of the New World." Morgan's authorized biographer, his son-in-law Herbert Satterlee, gathered useful information but offered no analytic appraisal, left out large pieces of the public and private life, and got important facts wrong. Intent on answering Morgan's critics by emphasizing his patriotic spirit and jolly Christmas parties, Satterlee drained all vitality from the tale.

The critics drew sharper pictures. Wisconsin's Republican Senator Robert W. La Follette described Morgan in 1910 as "a beefy, red-faced, thick-necked financial bully, drunk with wealth and power, [who] bawls his orders to stock markets, Directors, courts, Governments, and Nations." In the 1930s, the banker appeared in John Dos Passos's novel *1919* as the "boss croupier of Wall Street," a "bullnecked irascible man with small black magpie's eyes," famous for "suddenly blowing up in a visitor's face and for that special gesture of the arm that meant, *What do I get out of it?*" Matthew Josephson, in his history *The Robber Barons* (1934), portrayed Morgan as "imperiously proud, rude and lonely, intensely undemocratic . . . equal to throwing articles of food or clothing at his servants when they nodded and forgot his wants." Half a century later, in E. L. Doctorow's *Ragtime*, Morgan figured as "a burly six-footer with a large head of sparse white hair, a white moustache and fierce intolerant eyes set just close enough to suggest the psychopathology of his will."

When I first considered writing about Morgan in the 1980s, at the urging of my editor, Jason Epstein, I thought the story would be worth trying to tell again if new evidence made it possible to see past the legends and anecdotes—and then I learned that the Pierpont Morgan Library in New York had vaults of uncatalogued biographical documents, including Morgan's childhood diaries and schoolbooks, his adult letters and cables, volumes of business correspondence, hundreds of photographs, and extensive files on his purchases of art. Only Satterlee had seen this material, and used it selectively; Allen saw some of it, but drew a well-crafted three-hundred-page sketch, not a full-scale portrait.

Over the next several years I found additional documents in private hands, at the Morgan Grenfell archives in London, and in other repositories on both sides of the Atlantic. Eventually I began to write, and got about halfway through a draft before I saw that it wasn't working. Months later I realized why. From the outset I had found Morgan's detractors more convincing than his champions: they were better writers, they reflected popular American assumptions (including my own) about the "robber baron" chapter of our history, and their bracing hostility gave the story force. The advocates, by comparison, seemed defensive and fawning. As a result, I had been looking for a modified, human-scale version of the "boss croupier" of Wall Street—the cynical tycoon who subjected the entire U.S. economy to the "psychopathology of his will"—and that was not what I had found. The evidence didn't support the picture I had preemptively drawn, and I hadn't been noticing what it did suggest.

For example: Matthew Josephson in *The Robber Barons* reported that after Morgan precipitated the "peculiarly atrocious and wanton" panic of 1901, which "ruined thousands of people" and "was felt in all the financial capitals of the world," he "swore at 'idiots' and 'rascals' who sought to interview him, and . . . threatened one reporter with 'murder.'" Asked if some statement was not due the public, the banker announced, "*I owe the public nothing.*" This story turns out to be largely fiction. Briefly: a group of Morgan's rivals tried to take over one of the railroads he controlled, the Northern Pacific, by secretly buying its stock while he was in France. When his partners in New York caught on, they cabled him for instructions, then began to buy up the remaining shares. They quickly acquired what they needed, which drove up the price of NP and incited speculators to "short" the market—to sell stock they didn't own, expecting to make a profit by buying shares for delivery as the price came down. But the price did not come down, because no one was selling. Instead the "shorts," desperate to buy stock they had to deliver, drove NP from $146 to $1,000 a share. To raise cash for these preposterous prices, they dumped their other stocks, the market crashed, and the panic of 1901 was on. Morgan, knowing that the crisis could ruin thousands of people and unhinge the U.S. economy, arranged by cable for his partners and the raiders to postpone receipt of stock they had bought, and to sell enough shares at $150 to allow the shorts to cover. He then went to London and stopped a nascent panic there by offering roughly the same terms—not the actions of a man who thinks he owes the public nothing.

Josephson cites as his source Lewis Corey's antagonistic biography, *The House of Morgan* (1930), and Corey cites Joseph Pulitzer's *World* for May 11, 1901. In fact on May 11 the *World*—competing with William Randolph Hearst's *Journal* for crowd-pleasing sensationalism, and noted for its antipathy to plutocrats—described Morgan arriving in Paris and working around the clock to stop the panic. One headline reads, MORGAN WINS IN NP FIGHT AND STOCKS REBOUND. The banker had declined at first to give an interview to the *World*'s correspondent, saying he did not yet know very much. Several hours later he told the press, "The situation looks a little better." On May 12, the *World* reported not that Morgan swore at "'idiots' and 'rascals' who sought to interview him," but that he denounced the men who had started the panic as idiots and rascals for "tangling themselves up in a situation which he had particularly warned them to avoid." He had, the paper went on, worked until 3:00 A.M. and risen at 7:00 to take a quiet drive in the Bois de Boulogne. As he sat alone on a bench, "lost in thought," the *World*'s correspondent asked again for an interview, "but the magnate threatened murder and reentered the carriage." He said, "I can't be interviewed now. I am leaving tomorrow morning for London." End of story. All these dispatches are datelined Paris. Then at the bottom of the column an odd second ending to the article appears, datelined London. In this version, a reporter (the writer who filed from Paris? a new one? an imaginary one?) approaches the banker saying "you told me yesterday to come again," and asks whether, since Morgan is being blamed for the panic, some statement is not due the public. It is in this dubious context that the *World* has him say, "I owe the public nothing"—yet historians since the 1930s have relied on Josephson's account.

Born into a wealthy family, Morgan had a patrician sense of noblesse oblige and unusual motivations: he could have made a lot more money than he did, if that had been his primary aim, and unlike many sons of rich men, he worked hard all his life. He spent half of his fortune on art. About his collecting, as about his financial career, the experts disagreed: the German-educated scholar William Valentiner called Morgan "the most important art collector I ever met," while the British critic and curator Roger Fry announced that "a crude historical imagination was the only flaw in his otherwise perfect insensibility [to art]."

Even Morgan's personal appearance gave rise to legend. He had a skin disease called rhinophyma that in his fifties turned his nose into a hideous purple bulb. One day the wife of his partner Dwight Morrow reportedly invited him to tea. She wanted her daughter Anne to meet the great man, and for weeks coached the girl about what would happen. Anne would come into the room and say good afternoon; she would not stare at Mr. Morgan's nose, she would not say anything about his nose, and she would leave. The appointed day arrived. Mrs. Morrow and Mr. Morgan sat on a sofa by the tea tray. Anne came in, said hello, did not look at Morgan's nose, did not say anything about his nose, and left the room. Sighing in relief, Mrs. Morrow asked, "Mr. Morgan, do you take one lump or two in your nose?"

The problem here is that Dwight Morrow did not join the firm until after Morgan died. Still, I checked with Anne Morrow Lindbergh. She wrote back: "This ridiculous story has not a grain of truth in it," but "is so funny I am sure it will continue."

As Morgan slowly came into focus in my imagination, I learned more about the staying power of the stories. Associates as well as biographers complained that he was difficult to know. His British partner Edward C. Grenfell reported in 1906 that "JPM" was "an impossible man to have any talk with. The nearest approach he makes is an occasional grunt." Brusque, publicity-shy, and neither introspective nor articulate, Morgan had no coherent philosophy and never explained his decisions. The high-stakes business of merchant banking required strict confidentiality, but he carried that ethos further than most. After a dinner in his honor in Chicago one night, the *Tribune* ran the headline MONEY TALKS BUT MORGAN DOESN'T. On the mantel in his private study, he kept a white enamel plaque that read, in blue Provençal script: *Pense moult, Parle peu, Écris rien* (Think a lot, Say little, Write nothing).

He is said to have observed, "A man always has two reasons for the things he does: a good reason—and the real reason," yet when it came to his own behavior he acknowledged not the slightest difference between "good" and "real" reasons. Asked why he had merged a group of railroads or bought a controlling interest in an insurance company he said, "I thought it was the thing to do"—at once shutting out inquisitors, displaying his Olympian self-assurance, and telling the partial (in both senses of the word) truth. He was, as Henry Adams said of Theodore Roosevelt, "pure act."

At times he seemed made of contradictions. Conservative by nature and reverential toward tradition, he had meritocratic instincts and an astute receptivity to new ways of doing things. Though physically robust—he outlived and outworked several younger partners—he worried constantly about his health. He was sociable and shy, deliberate and impulsive, ingenuous and shrewd, domineering and flexible, exuberant and depressive, extravagant and frugal, worldly and religious, inscrutably reserved and deeply sentimental.

He actually left many more records in his own voice than previous biographers have found, and a huge cast of characters supplies testimony as well—including U.S. presidents, European statesmen, art scholars, business associates, his father, rector, physicians, and son, his first and second wives, his favorite daughter and his rebel daughter, and his delightfully indiscreet librarian, Belle da Costa Greene.

A woman in her nineties, whose family knew him well, told me that when Morgan entered a room "you felt something electric. He wasn't a terribly large man but he had a simply tremendous *effect*—he was the king. He was *it*." William Lawrence, the Episcopal bishop of Massachusetts, noted that a visit from Morgan left him feeling "as if a gale had blown through the house." Belle Greene pronounced her "Big Chief" "the most *exhausting* person I know. He often tells me he 'likes my personality,' and yet when I leave him I feel utterly divested of it—as of a glove one draws off and gives to a friend because he likes it."

E. C. Grenfell, who had complained about Morgan's conversational skills in 1906, saw something else three years later. He wrote to a friend at the end of 1909: "[T]he popular idea of this man is very wide of the truth. He is neither hard nor cunning. Outwardly he is rough because he is very strong & yet very shy & has no command of words. . . . He has made big mistakes & even when his schemes are well conceived, he runs big risks of being tripped up or attacked in flank by meaner or smaller men. . . . His shortcomings are so patent that they almost add to his attraction."

Though cast as the high priest of modern capitalism, Morgan did not really believe in free markets. All his adult life he tried to stabilize the emerging U.S. economy, to discipline speculative profiteers and bring the market's destructive forces under control. With his eye on the lenders of capital (the United States was a net debtor until 1914), he took personal responsibility for maintaining the dollar's value and coaxing economic adversaries to the bargaining table—workers and managers as well as warring railroad and steel barons—while urging Washington to modernize the country's antebellum banking system. He privately subsidized social reformers who worked with the urban poor, and prominent labor leaders considered him singularly fair. Still, people suffered under policies he supported, especially farmers squeezed by falling crop prices and the rising cost of debt. And by 1900 much of the United States was horrified at the power of the trusts. Convinced that he was guiding the country toward a spectacularly prosperous future, Morgan made no distinction between his own interests and the national interest, although he was not an objective arbiter in the long-standing struggle over America's identity but an active partisan representing people who had billions invested in the outcome.

As Grenfell noted, Morgan made "big mistakes" and had "patent shortcomings." Had he been more concerned with the social costs of industrialization, he might seem more sympathetic now, and had he been able to explain himself, he would have been easier for me to write about—but biographers aren't supposed to speculate about what might have been.

Although the proponents of big business secured political ascendancy at the end of the nineteenth century, it was the opposition—populists, Progressives, and their intellectual heirs—who won the battle over how the story would be told. They depicted Morgan as a ruthless predator who robbed America's farmers and workers to line his own pockets. Offered that scenario, most of us would side with the farmers and workers, but it does the democratic tradition an injustice not to see other dimensions of the story now.

Many people have known a more complex version all along. Leading critics of big business during Morgan's lifetime, including Lincoln Steffens, Ida Tarbell, and Theodore Roosevelt, recognized that the demonization of capitalists had gone too far, but their revision did not trickle down (or up) into popular opinion. Steffens's disciple Walter Lippmann observed in 1914 that muckraking exposés had tapped into deep and legitimate dissatisfactions—otherwise, a "land notorious for its worship of success would not have turned so savagely upon those who had achieved it." Still, Lippmann mocked the "sense of conspiracy and secret scheming" in which "'Big Business,' and its ruthless tentacles, have become the material for the feverish fantasy" of people whose lives had been radically altered by economic change: "all the frictions of life are readily ascribed to a deliberate evil intelligence, and men like Morgan and Rockefeller take on attributes of omnipotence, that ten minutes of cold sanity would reduce to a barbarous myth."

Nearly a century later, as fresh evidence and historical distance make it possible to take a more realistic look at Morgan, the questions his life raises are once again at the center of national debate—only now the markets are global, the emerging economies are Asian, and the corporations under scrutiny are Microsoft and Intel rather than railroads and U.S. Steel. Can central bankers effectively "manage" the business cycle? In economic crises, which tottering governments or banks ought to be bailed out, and which allowed to fail? What is the best way to control inflation? Does industrial competition naturally lead to consolidation? Are big corporations inherently bad? How can affluent societies offset economic inequality? How and when should government intervene in commercial markets?

At the end of the twentieth century, responsibility for sorting out answers to those questions rests with the Treasury and Justice departments, the Federal Reserve, the SEC, the FTC, the Group of Seven, the IMF, and the World Bank. At the end of the nineteenth, with predictably mixed and controversial results, Morgan acted largely on his own.

Robert K. Massie is the recipient of a Pulitzer Prize in biography for *Peter the Great*. He also wrote *Nicholas and Alexandra* and *Dreadnought: Britain, Germany and the Coming of the Great War*. This passage is taken from his book *The Romanovs: The Final Chapter* (Random House, 1995), an account of the execution of the Romanov family in 1918 and the later discovery of their bones in a Siberian forest.

Down Twenty-Three Steps

At midnight, Yakov Yurovsky, the leader of the executioners, came up the stairs to awaken the family. In his pocket he had a Colt pistol with a cartridge clip containing seven bullets, and under his coat he carried a long-muzzled Mauser pistol with a wooden gun stock and a clip of ten bullets. A knock on the prisoners' door brought Dr. Eugene Botkin, the family physician, who had remained with the Romanovs for sixteen months of detention and imprisonment. Botkin was already awake; he had been writing what turned out to be a last letter to his own family.

Quietly, Yurovsky explained his intrusion. "Because of unrest in the town, it has become necessary to move the family downstairs," he said. "It would be dangerous to be in the upper rooms if there was shooting in the streets." Botkin understood; an anti-Bolshevik White Army bolstered by thousands of Czech former prisoners of war was approaching the Siberian town of Ekaterinburg, where the family had been held for seventy-eight days. Already, the captives had heard the rumble of artillery in the distance and the sound of revolver shots fired nearby on recent nights. Yurovsky asked that the family dress as soon as possible. Botkin went to awaken them.

They took forty minutes. Nicholas, fifty, the former emperor, and his thirteen-year-old son, Alexis, the former tsarevich and heir to the throne, dressed in simple military shirts, trousers, boots, and forage caps. Alexandra, forty-six, the former empress, and her daughters, Olga, twenty-two, Tatiana, twenty-one, Marie, nineteen, and Anastasia, seventeen, put on dresses without hats or outer wraps. Yurovsky met them outside their door and led them down the staircase into an inner courtyard. Nicholas followed, carrying his son, who could not walk. Alexis, crippled by hemophilia, was a thin, muscular adolescent weighing eighty pounds, but the tsar managed without stumbling. A man of medium height, Nicholas had a powerful body, full chest, and strong arms. The empress, taller than her husband, came next, walking with difficulty because of the sciatica which had kept her lying on a palace chaise longue for many years and in bed or a wheelchair during their imprisonment. Behind came their daughters, two of them carrying small pillows. The youngest and smallest daughter, Anastasia, held her pet King Charles spaniel, Jemmy. After the daughters came Dr. Botkin and three others who had remained to share the family's imprisonment: Trupp, Nicholas's valet; Demidova, Alexandra's maid; and Kharitonov, the cook. Demidova also clutched a pillow; inside, sewed deep in the feathers, was a box containing a collection of jewels; Demidova was charged with never letting it out of her sight.

Yurovsky detected no signs of hesitation or suspicion; "there were no tears, no sobs, no questions," he said later. From the bottom of the stairs, he led them across the courtyard to a small, semibasement room at the corner of the house. It was only eleven by thirteen feet and had a single window, barred by a heavy iron grille on the outer wall. All the furniture had been removed. Here, Yurovsky asked them to wait. Alexandra, seeing the room empty, immediately said, "What? No chairs? May we not sit?" Yurovsky, obliging, went out to order two chairs. One of his squad, dispatched on this mission, said to another, "The heir needs a chair . . . evidently he wants to die in a chair."

Two chairs were brought. Alexandra took one; Nicholas put Alexis in the other. The daughters placed one pillow behind their mother's back and a second behind their brother's. Yurovsky then began giving directions— "Please, you stand here, and you here . . . that's it, in a row"—spreading them out across the back wall. He explained that he needed a photograph because the people of Moscow were worried that they had escaped. When he was finished, the eleven prisoners were arranged in two rows: Nicholas stood by his son's chair in the middle of the front row, Alexandra sat in her chair near the wall, her daughters were arranged behind her, the others stood behind the tsar and tsarevich.

Satisfied with this arrangement, Yurovsky then called in not a photographer with a tripod camera and black cloth but eleven other men armed with revolvers. Five, like Yurovsky, were Russians; six were Latvians. Earlier, two Latvians had refused to shoot the young women and Yurovsky had replaced them with two others.

As the men crowded through the double doors behind him, Yurovsky stood in front of Nicholas, his right hand in his trouser pocket, his left holding a small piece of paper from which he began to read: "In view of the fact that your relatives are continuing their attack on Soviet Russia, the Ural Executive Committee has decided to execute you." Nicholas turned quickly to look at his family, then turned back to face Yurovsky and said, "What? What?" Yurovsky quickly repeated what he had said, then jerked the Colt out of his pocket and shot the tsar, point-blank.

At this, the entire squad began to fire. Each had been told beforehand whom he was to shoot and ordered to aim for the heart to avoid excessive quantities of blood and finish more quickly. Twelve men were now firing pistols, some over the shoulders of those in front, so close that many of the executioners suffered gunpowder burns and were partially deafened. The empress and her daughter Olga each tried to make the sign of the cross but did not have time. Alexandra died immediately, sitting in her chair. Olga was killed by a single bullet through her head. Botkin, Trupp, and Kharitonov also died quickly.

Alexis, the three younger sisters, and Demidova remained alive. Bullets fired at the daughters' chests seemed to bounce off, ricocheting around the room like hail. Mystified, then terrified and almost hysterical, the executioners continued firing. Barely visible through the smoke, Marie and Anastasia pressed against the wall, squatting, covering their heads with their arms until the bullets cut them down. Alexis, lying on the floor, moved his arm to shield himself, then tried to clutch his father's shirt. One of the executioners kicked the tsarevich in the head with his heavy boot. Alexis moaned. Yurovsky stepped up and fired two shots from his Mauser directly into the boy's ear.

Demidova survived the first fusillade. Rather than reload, the executioners took rifles from the next room and pursued her with bayonets. Screaming, running back and forth along the wall, she tried to fend them off with her armored pillow. The cushion fell, and she grabbed a bayonet with both hands, trying to hold it away from her chest. It was dull and at first would not penetrate. When she collapsed, the enraged murderers pierced her body more than thirty times.

The room, filled with smoke and the stench of gunpowder, became quiet. Blood was everywhere, in rivers and pools. Yurovsky, in a hurry, began turning the bodies over, checking their pulses. The truck, now waiting at the front door of the Ipatiev House, had to be well out of town before the arrival in a few hours of the July Siberian dawn. Sheets, collected from the beds of the four grand duchesses, were brought to carry the bodies and prevent blood dripping on the floors and in the courtyard. Nicholas's body went first. Then, suddenly, as one of the daughters was being laid on a sheet, she cried out. With bayonets and rifle butts, the entire band turned on her. In a moment, she was still.

When the family lay in the back of the truck, covered by a tarpaulin, someone discovered Anastasia's small dog, its head crushed by a rifle butt. The little body was tossed into the truck.

The "whole procedure," as Yurovsky later described it, including feeling the pulses and loading the truck, had taken twenty minutes.

David Remnick is editor of the *New Yorker* and author of two books about Russia, as well as *King of the World*, a biography of Muhammad Ali. This piece is drawn from *Lenin's Tomb* (Random House, 1994).

The Forest Coup

On a dreary summer's day, Colonel Aleksandr Tretetsky of the Soviet Military Prosecutor's Office arrived at his latest work site: a series of mass graves in a birch forest twenty miles outside of the city of Kalinin. He and his assistants began the morning digging, searching the earth for artifacts of the totalitarian regime—bullet-shattered skulls, worm-eaten boots, scraps of Polish military uniforms.

They had heard the alarming news from Moscow on television and radio before coming to work that morning: Mikhail Gorbachev had "stepped down" for "reasons of health." The GKChP—the "State Committee for the State of Emergency"—had assumed power, promising stability and order. But what to make of it? Kalinin was several hours north of Moscow by train and a long way off the trail of rumor and information. And so like almost everyone else in the Soviet Union on the morning of August 19, 1991, Tretetsky set to work, an almost ordinary day. The digging in the woods outside Kalinin was a merciless project. A half-century before, at Stalin's direct order, NKVD executioners slaughtered fifteen thousand Polish military officers and threw the bodies into rows of mass graves. The month-long operation in Kalinin, Katyn, and Starobelsk was part of Stalin's attempt to begin the domination of Poland. The young officers had been among the best-educated men in Poland, and Stalin saw them as a potential danger, as enemies-in-advance. For decades after, Moscow put the blame for the killings on the Nazis, saying the Germans had carried out the massacres in 1941, not the NKVD in 1940. The Kremlin propaganda machine sustained the fiction in speeches, diplomatic negotiations, and textbooks, weaving it into the vast fabric of ideology and official history that sustained the regime and its empire. The Kremlin took history so seriously that it created a massive bureaucracy to control it, to fabricate its language and content, so that murderous and arbitrary purges became a "triumph over enemies and foreign spies," the reigning tyrant a "Friend to All Children, the Great Mountain Eagle." The regime created an empire that was a vast room, its doors locked, its windows shuttered.

All books and newspapers allowed in the room carried the Official Version of Events, and the radio and television blared the general line day and night. Those who were loyal servants of the Official Version were rewarded and pronounced "professors" and "journalists." In the Communist Party citadels of the Marxist-Leninist Institute, the Central Committee, and the Higher Party School, the priests of ideology swerved from the dogma at their peril. There were secrets everywhere. The KGB was so keen to keep its secrets that it built its vacation houses in the village of Mednoye near Kalinin, where the Polish officers had been executed and buried in mass graves, the better to keep watch over the bones.

But now something had changed—changed radically. After some initial hesitation at the beginning of his time in power, Gorbachev had decreed that the time had come to fill in the "blank spots" of history. There could be no more "rose-colored glasses," he said. At first, his rhetoric was guarded. He spoke of "thousands" instead of tens of millions of victims. He did not dare criticize Lenin, the demigod of the state. But despite Gorbachev's hesitation, the return of historical memory would be his most important decision, one that preceded all others, for without a full and ruthless assessment of the past—an admission of murder, repression, and bankruptcy—real change, much less democratic revolution, was impossible. The return of history to personal, intellectual, and political life was the start of the great reform of the twentieth century and, whether Gorbachev liked it or not, the collapse of the last empire on earth.

For decades, the massacres at Kalinin, Starobelsk, and Katyn had been a symbol for the Poles of Moscow's cruelty and imperial grip. For a Pole merely to hint that the Soviet Union was responsible for the massacres was a radical, even suicidal act, for it made clear the speaker's point of view: the "friendship of peoples," the relationship between Moscow and Warsaw, was one based on violence, an occupier's reign over its satellite. Even Gorbachev knew that to admit the massacres would be to undermine the Polish Communists. But by 1990, with Solidarity in power, Gorbachev saw little to lose. While General Wojciech Jaruzelski was visiting Moscow, Gorbachev finally conceded Moscow's guilt and turned over to the Polish government a huge packet of files on the massacres at Katyn, Starobelsk, and Kalinin.

Soon after the Kremlin's admission of guilt, the excavations began. Working with Soviet army soldiers and Polish volunteers, Colonel Tretetsky started work in Mednoye on August 15, 1991. Tretetsky, a career officer in his mid-forties with a thin mustache and sunken cheeks, had spent several months uncovering graves in Starobelsk. With every new grave, he felt himself more deceived. He had believed deeply in Communism and the Soviet Union. He served first in the navy and then, after studying law in Ukraine, signed on in the military for life. He served nearly four years in East Germany and even volunteered to be sent to Czechoslovakia in 1968, the year the Soviet Union crushed the "Prague Spring."

"I was dumb," Tretetsky said. "I believed in it all. I would have given my life for the Motherland on a moment's notice."

He petitioned the military for a commission to Afghanistan and served there from 1987 to 1989. Tretetsky came home to Moscow only to get a bitter taste of the real history of the country he knew so little about. He was assigned to the Military Prosecutor's Office, which was conducting massive investigations into the rehabilitations of people who had been repressed over the past seventy years. Slowly, he began to learn about some of the ugliest incidents in Soviet history: the purges, the massacre of the Polish officers, the army's bloody attack on peaceful demonstrators in 1961 at Novocherkassk.

Put in charge of the excavations, first in Starobelsk and now in Mednoye, Tretetsky attacked his work with passion and precision. In Mednoye, he knew perfectly well where to dig and what to look for. He had already interrogated a local man, a retired officer of the secret police, who had helped carry out the orders from Moscow in 1940. Vladimir Tokaryev was blind and eighty-nine years old by the time history caught up with him, but his memory was clear. Sitting with Tretetsky and a video camera, he described how in April 1940 his unit of the secret police shot Polish officers in the woods outside Kalinin—two hundred and fifty a night, for a month.

The executioners, Tokaryev said, "brought with them a whole suitcase full of German revolvers, the Walther 2 type. Our Soviet TT weapons were thought not to be reliable enough. They were liable to overheat with heavy use. . . . I was there the first night they did the shooting. Blokhin was the main killer, with about thirty others, mainly NKVD drivers and guards. My driver, Sukharev, for instance, was one of them. I remember Blokhin saying: 'Come on, let's go.' And then he put on his special uniform for the job: brown leather hat, brown leather apron, long brown leather gloves reaching above the elbows. They were his terrible trademark. I was face to face with a true executioner.

"They took the Poles along the corridor one by one, turned left, and took them into the Red Corner, the rest room for the prison staff. Each man was asked his surname, first name, and place of birth—just enough to identify him. Then he was taken to the room next door, which was soundproofed, and shot in the back of the head. Nothing was read to them, no decision of any court or special commission.

"There were three hundred shot that first night. I remember Sukharev, my driver, boasting about what a hard night's work it had been. But it was too many, because it was light by the time they had finished and they had a rule that everything must be done in the darkness. So they reduced the number to two hundred and fifty a night. How many nights did it last? Work it out for yourself: six thousand men at two hundred and fifty a night. Allowing for holidays, that makes about a month, the whole of April 1940.

"I took no part in the killings. I never went into the execution room. But I was obliged to help them by putting my men at their disposal. I remember a few individual Poles. For instance, a young man. I asked him his age. He smiled like a young boy. I asked him how long he had been in the frontier police. He counted on his fingers. Six months. What had he done there? He had been a telephone operator.

"Blokhin made sure that everyone in the execution team got a supply of vodka after each night's work. Every evening he brought it into the prison in boxes. They drank nothing before the shooting or during the shooting, but afterward they all had a few glasses before going home to bed.

"I asked Blokhin and the other two: 'Won't it take a lot of men to dig six thousand graves?' They laughed at me. Blokhin said that he had brought a bulldozer from Moscow and two NKVD men to work it. So the dead Poles were taken out through the far door of the execution room, loaded onto covered trucks, and taken to the burial place. [The site] was chosen by Blokhin himself. It was near where the NKVD officers had their country homes, near my own dacha, near the village of Mednoye, about twenty miles from Kalinin. The ditches they dug were between eight and ten meters long, each one being enough to hold two hundred and fifty bodies. When it was all over, the three men from Moscow organized a big banquet to celebrate. They kept pestering me, insisting that I should attend. But I refused." On and on the blind man droned, pointing his finger at "the others," denying the importance of his own role, no less a cruel, bland beast than Eichmann in Jerusalem. But Tokaryev was hardly the issue now. Nor were the executioners themselves. Blokhin and three of the others had long ago gone mad and committed suicide. The point was that nearly everywhere they went, historians, prosecutors, archivists, and journalists discovered that the legacy of Soviet power was at least as tragic as everything they had heard from "forbidden voices": Solzhenitsyn's *The Gulag Archipelago*, Varlam Shalamov's *Kolyma Tales*. Now no book, no voice, was forbidden. To regain the past, to see plain the nightmares of seventy years, was a nearly unbearable shock. As the return of history accelerated, television routinely showed documentary films about the slaughter of the Romanovs, the forced collectivization of the countryside, the purge trials. The monthly literary journals, the weeklies, and even the daily newspapers were crammed with the latest historical damage reports: how many shot and imprisoned; how many churches, mosques, and synagogues destroyed; how much plunder and waste. Under this avalanche of remembering, people protested weariness, even boredom, after a while. But, really, it was the pain of remembering, the shock of recognition, that persecuted them. "Imagine being an adult and nearly all the truth you know about the world around you and outside your own country has to be absorbed in a matter of a year or two or three," the philosopher Grigori Pomerants told me. "The entire country is still in a state of mass disorientation. "The men of the Communist Party, the leaders of the KGB and the military and the millions of provincial functionaries who had grown up on a falsified history, could not bear the truth. Not because they didn't believe it. They knew the facts of the past better than anyone else. But the truth challenged their existence, their comfort and privileges. Their right to a decent office, a cut of meat, the month of vacation in the Crimea—it all depended on a colossal social deception, on the forced ignorance of 280 million people. Yegor Ligachev, a conservative figure in the Politburo until his forced retirement in 1990, told me ruefully that when history was taken out of the hands of the Communist Party, when scholars, journalists, and witnesses began publishing and broadcasting their own version of the past, "it created a gloomy atmosphere in the country. It affected the emotions of the people, their mood, their work efficiency. From morning to night, everything negative from the past is being dumped on them. Patriotic topics have been squeezed out, shunted aside. People are longing for something positive, something shining, and yet our own cultural figures have published more lies and anti-Soviet things than our Western enemies ever did in the last seventy years combined."

When history was no longer an instrument of the Party, the Party was doomed to failure. For history proved precisely that: the Party was rotten at its core. The ministers, generals, and apparatchiks who organized the August coup of 1991 met secretly at KGB safe houses outside Moscow many times to discuss the ruin of their state. They talked of the need for order, the need, somehow, to reverse the decline of the Party. They were so deluded about their own country that they even believed they could put a halt to the return of history. They would shut it down with a decree and a couple of tank divisions. The excavations at Mednoye and the other sites of the Polish massacre were no exception. The putschists would try to undermine the work as well as they could. Long before the coup, Valery Boldin, Gorbachev's chief of staff and one of the key plotters in the August coup, tried to control the damage by secretly transferring many key documents on the case from Division Six of the Central Committee archives to the "presidential archive," which he controlled. But that small step did very little. Boldin and the rest of the plotters were now prepared to eliminate everything that aggrieved them. They would end the return of history. They would turn back time. Once more, fear would be the essence of the state.

On the day of the putsch, Tretetsky's men, both the Soviets and the Poles, tried to keep their minds on their work. They dug up old graves and washed the bones and skull fragments in battered bowls. But as the news of the coup reached them, piece by piece, it became harder to concentrate. The soldiers under Tretetsky even heard that the troops deployed on the streets of Moscow were from their own division: the Kantemirovskaya Division. They turned on a television in one of the tents near the work site and saw familiar faces, friends sitting on armored personnel carriers near the Kremlin, outside the Russian parliament, and on the main streets of the capital.

"The weather was wretched," Tretetsky remembered. "It rained nearly all the time, and so to dry the fragments of uniforms, we had to put them in tents, fire up a furnace, and keep the tent open to circulate the air." The team worked until late in the afternoon, when Tretetsky told them all, "The work for today is over." He told them nothing more.

All day long, Tretetsky had been getting calls from the headquarters of the KGB command in Kalinin. The KGB general there, Viktor Lakontsev, warned Tretetsky that the excavation "was no longer necessary," that work should stop and that he must come immediately to headquarters. Tretetsky refused, saying work would go on as planned. He said he would come to KGB headquarters only at the end of the working day. Despite his brave front, Tretetsky was frightened. "I knew there was trouble," he said. That evening Tretetsky was driven under KGB guard to Lakontsev's office in Kalinin.

The work must stop, Lakontsev insisted. "If it does not," he said, "we cannot guarantee your safety or the safety of the Polish workers."

Tretetsky had to laugh. Throughout his work in Starobelsk and Mednoye there had always been KGB men at the sites—"observers," they called themselves. "Our United Nations observers," the workers called them.

Tretetsky would not back down. "Over my dead body," he thought to himself. To Lakontsev, he put the refusal more subtly. He told the KGB general that if it was a question of the Poles, he would take responsibility for their safety. The Poles could live together in the tents with the Soviet army troops instead of in the city.

"The investigation cannot stop," Tretetsky said. "What would I tell the Poles? I need to talk to my own chief. This is not an easy question." All the same, Tretetsky thought, "Lakontsev is a big boss, and who am I?"

When he returned to his camp, Tretetsky called Moscow and was told that there had been no stop-work order. He was relieved. Exhausted, he went to sleep in his tent. But not long after, the commander of the army troops woke him saying that an order had come from Moscow: the soldiers had to return to the Kantemirovskaya base in the town of Naro-Fominsk outside Moscow.

"Listen, Viktor," Tretetsky told the commander, "this is an oral order, isn't it?"

"That's right."

"And to bring your men here, you had a written order."

"Yes, I did."

"So why should you obey?"

The troops stayed where they were. The KGB had tried to trick Tretetsky and they had failed. There never had been an order from the Military Prosecutor's Office in Moscow.

At nine the next morning, Tretetsky went before the men and said, "The work goes on. Let's begin now. Everyone is to work intensively, with enthusiasm. And that's it!"

The KGB sabotaged the tractor the men had been using for the excavation. But by now Tretetsky had connections with people in the area, and a collective farm lent him one of its tractors. The Polish workers were especially grateful and pounded Tretetsky on the back. For two more days, the Soviets and the Poles worked at the graves and listened to the radio reports coming from Moscow. Slowly, the news improved. When the men heard that the coup was on the verge of collapse, they seemed to work even harder. Finally, on the morning of August 21, after the plot had failed and troops had returned in relief and triumph from Moscow to their bases, Tretetsky went before his men. He would not live the lie any longer. He refused to return to the past, except to study its bones.

"The criminal investigation ordered by the president of the Union of Soviet Socialist Republics, Mikhail Sergeyevich Gorbachev, goes on!" he cried out. Then the colonel gave the order and his men began to dig.

Jonathan Sanders was the Moscow correspondent for CBS News, where he reported on Russia and the fall of communism. He is the author of *Russia 1917: The Unpublished Revolution*. This article is excerpted from Sanders's introduction to *The Face of Modern Russia's Political Opposition*, a volume he wrote in collaboration with Heidi Hollinger (Les Editions Intouchables, 1999).

Pictures from the Rubble Patch

The rubble piled high by the implosive collapse of communism buried the familiar faces of *homo sovieticus*, Soviet man. Out from under the broken fragment of a soul-numbing age of stagnation a renewed and liberated kind of photography has begun to emerge. Individualism, sometimes highly idiosyncratic, replaced devotion to socialism's common man. Explicit depictions of life's bad and ugly sides gained an audience. Daring images supplanted rigid socialist prescriptions. In portraiture, especially that of politicians or anyone with "an official face" guardedness, an overreaching sense of concealment, yielded pride of place to a photographic mandate that allowed the capturing of the telling unguarded moment.

Instead of rigid formality came moments of spontaneity. As the rusty borders between East and West, us *vs.* them, began to disappear, Moscow began to link up with communities beyond its crumbling empires. This internationalization occurred across the board, in personnel, in styles, techniques and technology, as well as respect for photography as an art. Russia began to reconnect with its own roots. Instead of its designated role as journalistic servant of the state's mythmaking apparatus, photographic portrait-taking and portrait-making again became experimental, emotional, and independent. As part of a broad cultural renaissance, photography began asserting itself as an independent means of artistic expression. Prompted by visionaries who understood the vibrant and essential role a fine arts photographic culture plays in leading cities, Moscow grew its own galleries, shows, and by 1996, a "Fotobiennale"—the first international month of photography, a city-wide set of nearly one hundred exhibitions. Joyously skylarking through the new Moscow world is a remarkable young Canadian-born woman, Heidi Hollinger. She is a pioneer of a new kind of photographic portrait of Russians.

Camera in hand, Heidi Hollinger explores the underside and the other side of Russia in the 1990s. Her instinctual response to change is contrarian. She looks hard at the overlooked. She brings color, verve and vitality to a portrait tradition long fixed in Soviet memories, as if in cement, by the gray "officialness" of politburo portraits that hung in every office, shack, factory, school, and institution across the old USSR. Heidi's irrepressible playfulness subverts the stodgy trope of airbrushed and lifeless portraiture. By concentrating on the psychological interchange between subject and photographer, she returned picture making to the emotionally powered expressiveness characteristic of the best artists working in Moscow during the first two decades of this century. She brought from the west the empathetic, environmental portrait making of her home continent to an old world long cut off from the photographic mainstream.

Heidi's impulse is to focus on roots, very Russian roots.

She lives more like a Russian than the typical expatriate. Moscow has upwards of a quarter million foreign residents. Heidi lives in the heart of the capital of mother Russia. She is definitely NOT a member of the troubadours-of-capitalism-fife-and-bugle-marching-carpetbagger corps. Unlike most foreigners feeding from a "transitional" economy trough, she is not entranced by the trendy flowerings of Moscow's newly rich set. Of course, she knows them—Heidi seems to know everyone who is anyone or is becoming someone in Moscow. However, it's people on the edges—those whose ego, ids, ideologies, and individuality put them outside the mainstream—who attract her. Initially, instinct brought her to something Slavic: aiming the lens of her Canon at the losers. Political representatives of the hurt and humiliated first received the center-weight of her attention. Heidi's attraction to the minority figures, a visual *menshevism*, gives a unique perspective on Russia's painful struggle to build its own kind of participatory democracy.

With exquisite timing, an intuitive sense of the decisive moment, Heidi moved to Moscow in 1992. She had first come to the capital the previous year to improve her language skills by living with a Russian family. That investment of her time quickly began paying enormous dividends. Soon, when graduate study of politics at Moscow State University proved less intriguing, less relevant, than the swirling, sometimes enraged politics of dissent that engulfed the capital city she abandoned footnotes for footwork and focusing.

Initially, she used her Canon EOS 35mm camera as a prop, a kind of camouflage to get close to politicians. Her approach was charmingly straightforward. On the cold, often angry, but then not particularly mean streets of Moscow, when opponents of President Boris Nikolaevich Yeltsin's regime protested, Heidi would simply show up. She would move towards the head of the crowd and hold up her camera topped by its electronic flash and "*Luminos*" plastic flash bounce diffuser, a device almost as big, but not as shapely as little five foot Heidi. She would tilt this black photographic "mask" aside to say innocently—"hi, you don't mind if I take your picture; my name is Heidi Hollinger." What was there to lose? Most everyone agreed. After all, a little attention was (and is) a wonderful thing as well as rarity for these people.

In August 1991 Boris Yeltsin became the icon of Russian democracy; his portrait in action personified the myth of Russia's latest revolution. Pictured atop a tank in defense of reform, Yeltsin became the "poster boy" for change.

The ex-politbureau member became the ICON for iconoclastic destruction of communism. He helped force the dismemberment of the Soviet Union and the resignation of Gorbachev at the end of 1991. Yeltsin became the most easily recognized figure in the world, a "bulldozer of radical reform" overshadowing those opposed to his new regime.

The losers in this revolution felt forgotten in the waves of triumphant celebration of (self-proclaimed) liberal democracy and (crude) capitalism. As limelight, spotlights, all lights illuminated the advocates of change, the proponents of continuity lingered forgotten in the darkness of defeat. The opposition welcomed the outsider—the effervescent Canadian girl who courted, flirted, flattered and photographed the vanquished. In the early 1990s they were amazingly approachable, especially on the streets. There were no filtering spin doctors, image-making consultants from think tanks, press aids or scrum-forming security thugs to separate the opposition from anyone who cared about such a motley crew of outcasts. Interest was access. A big western camera was obviously a credible identification badge.

Heidi's approach was elementary. She took the opposition seriously as politicians. Conditioned by her academic predilection, political science, she concentrated on leaders. However silly or scurrilous their ideas, she sought to represent them in a non-distorting manner on 35mm film. Heidi worked to make pictures that reflected the politics and personalities of these men (mostly always men with only a few notable exceptions at first) without making value judgments. She got to know many as people, some as friends, all as subjects placed in an appropriate context. Often Heidi looked for a setting that was different from traditional Soviet photographic iconography—no airbrushing, no looming big office or official posturing, no frozen formula for stiff poses— she tried to have something in the background that gave a hint of who the subject is or would like to be. She endeavored to reveal an inner life and to introduce objects symbolic of the sitter's preoccupation or mental universe.

Nowhere did Heidi's ability to gain the trust, even the friendship, of an opposition figure pay greater dividends than when she turned her portrait lens on Vladimir Volfovich Zhirinovsky. The most outrageous political character to emerge from the drained swamp that is post-Soviet Russia, Zhirinovsky catapulted himself onto the world stage late in 1993 as the embodiment of the threat that the ex-super power was "going fascist." He gained fame for bombast (running for President in 1991 as an advocate of more vodka for everyone), but even his opponents feared his populist appeal.

Zhirinovsky was the first Russian with an intuitive grasp of the kind of politics as theater that Abbie Hoffman advocated for the American counterculture in the late 1960s. Part performance artist, part demagogue, part Captain Outrageous ever-ready with a brazen, but eminently quotable, quip. With his promise to resurrect the lost Soviet empire, to put the smug Americans in their place ("we will take back Alaska"), to punish the new corrupt elite while millions wallow in poverty ("lock the borders don't let the bankers out for six months while we see who is honest and who is not") to stop the insidious western commercialism corrupting true Russian values ("smash McDonalds, let its American [actually Canadian] owners shovel cow shit on a collective farm for a couple of years instead of the poison they are pushing on our public") played well to the millions reeling from the disintegration of their predictable and secure Soviet way of life.

In the 1993 election for the Duma, Zhirinovsky shocked the world as the big winner; his party collected 23 percent of the vote. Stunned by Zhirinovsky's success, pundits and politicians everywhere brooded: was Russia going fascist? Others asked seriously, "Russia, have you gone mad?" Many feared Russia returning to rule by its primordial dark forces. Popular culture in the West depicted Zhirinovsky as Darth Vader. When CNN documented his hidden secret, an altered birth certificate buried in a Central Asian archive that proved he had a Jewish father, Volf Edelshtein, it only heightened the "Star Wars" comparison. The image of Zhirinovsky, the demagogic speaker of Russia's "dark side," spread panic. The cunning of his presentations grew each time he addressed a crowd. On the stump—at a protest meeting beside the Latvian Embassy in Moscow, threatening to unleash a wave of radioactivity across the newly independent Baltic state if it refused to rejoin the motherland (or at least respect the rights of the Russian minority now oppressed in this semi-foreign land)—Zhirinovsky entranced a willing audience. After decades of enforced gray conformity in public discourse, Zhirinovsky gave voice to the hurt felt by the losers in Russia. He spoke crudely and rudely. He blamed the usual suspects, Jews, Westerners, disease-bearing black-skinned spreaders of AIDS. He pointed accusing fingers at the Communist elite and the new Kremlin elite around Yeltsin.

Swift of tongue, pithy, caustic Zhirinovsky made himself into a one-man offensive band pounding out insults left, right and center, knowing that his uncouth language would separate him from meaning-murdering politicians trained in the Soviet double speak tradition. Every time he spoke, he cleverly demonstrated that he had broken with the long dominated by gray Orwellian circumlocutions or the coded convoluted syntax of reformers, such as Mikhail Gorbachev. Political incorrectness and peasant plainness quickly got him gobs of attention. By offending polite society Zhirinovsky tapped a huge reservoir of resentment. He loved the surging attention, and built his act on what worked so well for him. Outrage begat outrage. His was the foul mouth that roared as it tilted at taboos. Like the impresarios of western counterculture in the 1960s, he quickly understood that sacred cows make the tastiest hamburgers.

The ultra-nationalist firebrand put on a fierce act in public, but he was not as hysterical as he seemed. Zhirinovsky noticed who was around him. Frequently the crowd of journalists included Heidi. At first he was quizzical, but her perseverance, non-threatening demeanor and seriousness of purpose, her desire to portray opposition figures as themselves, not as monsters, coupled with his amused reaction to having a Canadian girl seriously interested in Russian politics and people, won him over.

Heidi can calibrate her charm setting as quickly as she can adjust her f-stops. It has been said that she can charm the rattle off a rattle-snake—and in four different languages. Zhirinovsky invited her to his weekend retreat, his dacha.

What could be more Russian? In what other setting could Heidi better demonstrate her sympathetic and empathetic understanding of a Slavic soul? She encouraged him to be himself. Even performance artists go off stage sometimes, even if dreams of sensationalist, attention-grabbing antics never completely leave their heads. Heidi captured Zhirinovsky at rest as no one else. But while her bicultural receptors and reputation may have landed her in the right place at the right time, something slightly more universal triggered her breakthrough picture. Her early morning picture of him lounging in his undershorts with his hand dreamily by his crotch became a Heidi (and new Russia) classic. Neither sexy nor warm and cuddly, it was immensely candid. And candidly she explained, "he was trying to come on to me. As a macho man he thought I couldn't resist when he took off his shirt and suggested I put on a bathrobe because of the heat in that part of the dacha. Instead, I decided to take his picture." Zhirinovsky's ego overcame his id. "He didn't seem offended or mad about me making the picture instead of making it, at least at the time," Heidi explained. Impishly, she enjoyed informing those small minded enough to ask that the great defender against western goods coming to corrupt Russian values prefers Calvin Klein briefs.

Heidi's picture, taken at the very time when western journalists, commentators, politicians, and Kremlinologists were demonizing Zhirinovsky as a genuine fascist, a one-man threat to baby Russian democracy, showed a man, a human being, not a trend. But the photograph did not make Zhirinovsky's politics more palatable. In a place where ideology and party platforms maintain a popular respect level only slightly better than the bubonic plague, the personal is profoundly political.

Serge Schmemann has served as a correspondent for the Associated Press in Johannesburg and for the *New York Times* in Moscow, Bonn, Jerusalem, and New York. What follows is the beginning of his book *Echoes of a Native Land: Two Centuries of a Russian Village* (Knopf, 1997).

A Corner of Russia

This is the story of a Russian village, known at different times over its three centuries of recorded history as Goryainovo, Karovo, Sergiyevskoye, and now Koltsovo. It lies by the Oka River in the ancient Russian heartland, 90 miles south of Moscow, near the city of Kaluga. It is a village to which I was originally drawn because before the Russian Revolution it had been part of an estate owned by my mother's family. But the Soviet government's long refusal to let me go there turned my curiosity into a mission. I finally reached Koltsovo only when Communist rule began to wane. I came to know the people; I immersed myself in the local lore; I even bought a log house there. Koltsovo became my little corner of Russia—my entry into the charm, beauty, and romance of that vast northern land, and also its backwardness, cruelty, and suffering.

I first arrived in Russia with my family in 1980, but ten years passed before I reached the village. By then the stern ideological taboos of the Soviet era were lifting, and people in the village were starting to lose their fear of talking to foreigners. Gradually, they opened up their memories and their history: how the women fooled the German occupiers who wanted to chop down the stately larches of the Alley of Love, how the old drunk Prokhor Fomichyov took the church apart after the war to trade bricks for vodka. Some went further back and remembered how in the 1930s the Bolsheviks sent industrious peasants into exile and herded the rest into collectives. A retired teacher even remembered how before the revolution the peasants would stop to listen to the great "silver bell" at the church, and village girls would gape at the bows and smocks of the young mistresses on their way to Sunday worship. The people talked about the present, too—about how youths left the village as soon as they finished school, and only the old people and the drunks stayed on; how the love child of the albino accountant was beaten to death by his son in a drunken brawl; how nobody knew what to make of the new "democracy"; how the collective farm was selling off cattle to pay its mounting debts while the director built himself a big new house.

The first person I met in the village was Lev Vasilievich Savitsky, the retired head of an orphanage that had operated there after the war, and a staunch Communist. He told me how a KGB agent had come out there a few years earlier because some foreign correspondent was trying to visit Koltsovo, claiming that his ancestors came from there. Lev Vasilievich said the agent and the village leaders concluded that the place was too rundown to show a foreign reporter, that he would only write how things had gotten worse under the Communists. And so I learned at last the real reason I had been barred so long from Koltsovo. When I told Lev Vasilievich that I was that inquisitive reporter, he fell silent, and for a while he eyed me with suspicion and unease.

Lev Vasilievich told me that the manor house had burned down in 1923, and all that remained of the old estate was a gutted bell tower, a crumbling stable, and the former parish school. The school had been a teachers' training institute after the revolution and an orphanage after the war; it was now a weekend "rest base" for workers from the giant turbine works in Kaluga, twenty-five miles to the west. The village and the lands were eventually formed into a *kolkhoz*, or Soviet collective farm, named Suvorov after the eighteenth-century Russian military commander. The *kolkhoz* produced milk and meat, though mostly it gobbled up government subsidies without ever turning a kopek of profit. After the Soviet Union collapsed and the collective farms were officially freed of tight government controls, the Suvorov Kolkhoz changed its name to the Koltsovo Agricultural Association and began gobbling up bank loans instead of government credits.

But on my first visit, that was not what I wanted to know. I wanted only to see beauty and romance, to walk where my ancestors had walked, to catch the echoes of a native land. It was the height of summer, I was in Russia on a brief visit, freedom was coming to the land, and the place was beautiful—a timeless Russian landscape of birches, winding rivers, log houses, and vast expanses. Lev Vasilievich's grandson, Roma, his patched pants rolled up Tom Sawyer-style, led me to the places my own grandfather had so lovingly described: the old park planted two hundred years ago with ordered rows of linden trees; the lane of soaring larches known as the Alley of Love, which led past the Round Meadow, a low hill deliberately left wild for honeybees; the icy "Robbers' Spring," whose waters my grandfather had tapped for the house; the steep descent through the oaks and birches of the Zaraza forest, which abruptly opened onto a stunning vista of the Oka River winding through lush flood meadows, bluffs, and forests of birch.

In the evening, I sat under an apple tree outside Lev Vasilievich's house, blissfully drinking in the old stories and gossip with my hot tea. The laughter of children playing in the unpaved street mingled with the summer din of frogs, crickets, and birds. I felt I had been here before, on a glorious day just like this one, a century earlier, which my grandfather Sergei Osorgin described in his memoirs:

In the summer, the windows all open, evening tea would be set on the terrace, and my sister Maria and I would sit on the steps, listening as Mama played my favorite nocturne of Chopin, and the evening bells would be ringing: It is already dark, only a pale-yellow streak remains in the western sky, the continuous thin trill of a small frog rises from the pond by the barn, and from the nearby village of Goryainovo wafts a peasant song, "Oh you day, this my day, finish quickly. . . . " I'm happy, totally happy, but I long for something even more wonderful . . . the sweet, romantic sadness of Chopin, what music! and how Mama plays! The watery trill sounds on, the stars of the Big Dipper grow brighter, the strong aroma of roses, sweet peas, and mignonettes, "Oh you day, this my day, finish quickly. . . . " My God, I thank You that all this was, and that it all still lives in my soul.

It was my grandfather's description of a youth spent here that first prompted me to search for this corner of Russia. When I finally gained access to it I learned that all the extraordinary resources of the world's first police state had failed to eradicate the past. It lived on behind the imposed ideological formulas and slogans, clandestine little truths cautiously stored in closed archives and in the deep recesses of people's memories.

In Koltsovo, the premier repository was Alexandra Nikitichna Trunin. In her seventies when I met her, Alexandra Nikitichna had settled in Koltsovo after the war to work in the orphanage. Her background as a history teacher soon combined with her boundless curiosity to establish her as the unchallenged authority on local lore—what the Russians call a *krayeved*, literally "knower of the region." In the 1960s, Alexandra Nikitichna set up a one-room museum in what was then the orphanage, filling it with photos, poems, and letters from local people who had made a mark in Soviet society. An ardent and honest Communist for most of her life, she earnestly rejoiced in Soviet triumphs and achievements. But there were also things that Alexandra Nikitichna kept to herself—things that could not be put in her museum.

Also in the 1960s, workers dismantling a chimney of the burned-down manor house found an urn full of letters and photos, presumably concealed there by the Osorgins, my mother's family, before they were expelled. There were letters from "the boys at the front" and a postcard from one of the girls to her mother about a suitor she could not shake off. The letters circulated in the village and disappeared, Alexandra Nikitichna said. Only a few photos survived—cracked and faded snapshots of ladies in long gowns and children in a field. In the 1970s, Alexandra Nikitichna's brother was secretly scanning Western shortwave radio broadcasts (a risky but common enterprise in those days) and came upon an interview with an Osorgin in Paris, talking about Sergiyevskoye. He understood that the discussion was of the former estate in Koltsovo and told his sister. In the informal seminars she held on local lore, however, Alexandra Nikitichna toed the official line, that the former landowners had been rapacious feudal exploiters.

Not all pre-revolutionary history was taboo, however. If little was said about the Osorgins, everybody knew about the man who had owned these lands before them, General Kar: a certified villain of Russian history. According to the prevailing legend, Kar was a cruel Englishman in the service of Empress Catherine the Great who was banished to this estate by her for abandoning his command and fleeing before the armies of the rebellious peasant Pugachev. Alexander Pushkin, Russia's greatest poet, immortalized Kar's infamy in his history of the rebellion, and centuries of local embellishments turned the general into a truly evil figure. Exiled to his estate here, it was said, Kar used a barrel of ill-gotten gold to build himself a grand mansion modeled on an English fort. Then he had his serfs burrow a tunnel to the Oka River so he could escape if any of his many enemies came after him. All the serfs who worked on the tunnel disappeared, it was said, and when some local boys found the tunnel in the 1920s, they claimed to have seen crucified skeletons inside. According to Pushkin, Kar met an appropriate end—he was torn apart by enraged serfs. Then his devout and long-suffering widow, a princess born, built a beautiful church on the estate to expiate his sins.

Local legend did not stop there. Kar's estate was eventually inherited by his son Sergei, a sadistic wastrel who was supposed to have taken his pleasure with peasant girls and then killed them and dumped their bodies in the forest. This was why, Alexandra Nikitichna told me, the forest was called Zaraza—Contagion. Sergei went on to lose the estate in a game of cards to Mikhail Gerasimovich Osorgin, a military man who went mad on his very first visit to the property when he realized that Kar's pious mother was buried in the estate church, and so Sergei Kar had in effect gambled away his own mother! A few years ago, Alexandra Nikitichna said, workers digging on the site of the old church came upon a skeleton draped in fine black cloth, with precious rings on the bones of the fingers. The rings disappeared, and local kids were caught playing soccer with the skull.

Of course, there was a buried treasure. Sometime in the 1960s, Alexandra Nikitichna said, a man arrived with two beautiful daughters and settled in the abandoned stable, in the linden park. Every night he dug in the park; then one day they were gone, leaving behind an unfilled hole. Who he was, or what he found, nobody ever learned.

Alas, when I began to research the history of the place I often found that the facts did not measure up to the legend. It turned out that General Kar was of Scottish, not English, descent and he was probably less a coward than a victim of court intrigue. The forest was named Zaraza not because of decomposing maidens but after an archaic meaning of the word, "steep and uneven ground," which it certainly is. But what is truth? The facts of history? The version the Bolsheviks imposed? Or the legends that live among people? In the Soviet Union, "history" as science always bore the stigma of ideology, while the legends at least had the dignity of age.

Gloria Emerson won a National Book Award for her book on Vietnam, *Winners & Losers*. Her first novel, *Loving Graham Greene*, was published in October 2000 (Random House).

After the Oslo Accords in 1993, Gaza was given limited self-rule, ending twenty-seven years of Israeli occupation. Emerson spent a year (1989–90) in Gaza writing about the life of Palestinians. Fierce clashes in the West Bank and Gaza beginning in September 2000 threatened the peace process. Palestinians demonstrated for an end to expanded Jewish settlements in the West Bank and for self-government in a Palestinian state and their right to establish their capital in Jerusalem. These demands were not acceptable to Israel. This excerpt is drawn from her book, *Gaza: A Year in the Intifada: A Personal Account from an Occupied Land* (The Atlantic Monthly Press, 1991).

Goodbye to Rafah

I made a last visit to Rafah in mid-January when the green, white and black flag with the red triangle hung over three streets. Wandering around, a friend of the Palestinian guide led us to a small workplace where two men at sewing machines were making lined children's parkas of Israeli material which they sold wholesale. Glad of a chance to stop and chat, the older man joked about his wife and said we should meet her, really she was something, a woman without fear that one. He again told a little story which the other man at the sewing machine liked hearing again. Besides, they had almost finished the morning's work, their quota was always six parkas a day and sometimes they worked beyond the hour when Palestinians were supposed to stop. They had families to feed but did not love the intifada less.

It went like this: on Friday, December 9, 1989, soldiers in their neighborhood began looking for men to take down the large Palestinian flag hanging from the power lines. They came to the house of the tailor, who was at work, and cornered a thirty-two-year-old male cousin, able-bodied but considered dim-witted. The cousin heard the order. He thought. "No," he said, "I will not do it." Wanting to save the cousin, and fearing for her sons, the wife stepped forward, a volunteer. Five women stayed with her as she marched into the street flanked by those friends.

At my insistence, the tailor cheerfully led us home so his forty-seven-year-old wife might speak for herself. A small, strong-looking woman with a face darkened by the sun, Fatmah had six children and was a little too busy to waste time. So she gave a factual account without embellishments and the proud husband listened with a small smile. On that Friday she found a pole and took down the piece of cloth as an officer and soldiers from the Givati Brigade watched.

What the obstinate woman did next was unforgivable to the men. Taking her time she neatly folded the flag, held it in her hands for a second and lowered her head to kiss it. Only then did she hand it over to the officer.

"A soldier said in Arabic, 'God damn you,'" said Fatmah. "Well, it's our right to kiss the flag." She showed us how she had done it, the ancient sacred kiss, the priest touching the altar with his lips.

Every Gazan knew the penalty for such an act so Fatmah stood, frozen, awaiting the blow. It was useless to run. She thought two of the soldiers were moving in when the miracle happened. A United Nations van driving by suddenly stopped and out stepped a bearded man, a Refugee Affairs Officer from the United Nations Relief and Works Agency, speaking English. He did not know what had taken place, he only saw the soldiers bunching up, and the women standing very still. Smiling, he said to the officer: "It seems you have a problem. What can we do. . . ." It was his job to intervene in such incidents as diplomatically as possible, the welfare of the refugees his concern.

Perhaps it helped that he did not look too Anglo-Saxon, coming from a family of Armenian origin. He was a thirty-nine-year-old industrial psychologist from California named Fred Brauer, but no one knew that when he so skillfully interfered. The soldiers were stymied by the American with his agreeable, patient manner, so the women raced home. The little group around her that day, as she gave her account, agreed that this bearded stranger had been a blessing.

The year sank to its end with more prayers, more pleas for peace, more anger, more prayers, more criticism of the occupation and derision for those who assailed it. The Anglican Archbishop of South Africa, Desmond Tutu, visited Jerusalem, only an hour from Gaza but as remote as Capetown or London, and said a prayer at a memorial, near the Dome of the Rock mosque, for the Palestinian victims of the Sabra and Shatila massacre in Lebanon. His presence worried and disturbed many Israelis, who were not grateful for his earlier remarks in the newspaper, *Ha'aretz*: "I am a black South African and if I were to change the names, a description of what is happening in Gaza and the West Bank could describe events in South Africa."

B'Tselem, the Israeli Information Center for Human Rights in the Occupied Territories, released its first annual report on human rights violations. Its editor Roni Talmor, speaking at the time of publication, said: "If we compare the first year of the intifada to its second with regards to human rights violations in the territories we can say: everything is the same, only more so. There were more people killed, more wounded, more house demolitions, more arrests, more administrative detainees, more places in detention centers, more days under curfew, more restrictions of movement, more limits on freedom of expression, more use of administrative punitive measures."

The Civil Administration was considered an arm of punishment and connected to all the punitive measures used by the security forces.

Deportations were ended. This happened only because the defense establishment "wants to expel immediately without giving the deportee time to petition the High Court of Justice, and the Justice Ministry does not permit this," the editor said. Because the Israeli military believed delayed deportations were ineffective, expulsion orders were no longer issued.

"When they stop hating us they will start to hate each other and that will be the end of it," a thirty-eight-year-old Gazan shoemaker said but it was not a prophecy, only what he needed to believe.

All the flags went up in Rafah, came down and were hoisted again as if no power on earth could prevent this. The woman who kissed the flag knew her own daughters would someday do what she had done. The old pain made them reckless and more persistent.

The third year of the intifada began. The Israeli reservists, in their endless rotations, were jubilant to leave Gaza and did not make known all that had happened when they were home once more. Then, in the summer of 1990, a fresh and diverse disaster startled many nations when, in the Persian Gulf, a tiny, rich kingdom bloated with oil was quickly seized and swallowed by Iraq. The tragic contradictions came soon enough: old allies were new enemies, old enemies were quickly courted and won over. The Iraqi aggressor, once so favored that he was given billions of dollars in loans, was now compared to Hitler.

The peculiar new alliances and ruptures, the oratory from leaders who lacked the gift, the television film of American soldiers in the desert and pilots who could not see where sky, sand or sea began and ended, claimed all our attention. There were thousands of new hostages whose wives began to plead for their release and a multitude of foreign workers, suddenly penniless and stranded, fleeing occupied Kuwait. The United Nations was suddenly useful, even crucial. Everywhere people waited for war and some were hoping for it.

It was a discouraging time for those Israelis who, in the words of Camus, wanted to love their country and love justice. Many, who believed in the right of Palestinians to have their own nation, were repelled by their intense acclaim for an Iraqi despot.

In the Occupied Territories Palestinians did not feel forgotten because Saddam Hussein linked the withdrawal of his troops from Kuwait to an Israeli withdrawal from Gaza and the West Bank. The intifada, which seemed only a minor convulsion with ugly spasms now and then, could no longer be overlooked as the killings increased. Because no other Arab leader spoke so loudly, so harshly on their behalf, it was not surprising that he excited and impressed the Palestinians who for so long felt themselves betrayed and unprotected.

Not everyone believed in him. But in Gaza they knew how to wait, how not to give in to hopelessness. It was as the fisherman put it that summer day when he came home with the shrimp. If it meant two years or ten years before there was a Palestinian state that was all right.

"But it must come," he said. "We have to have this."

William Greider is National Affairs Correspondent for the *Nation*, and author of *One World, Ready or Not* (1997), *Who Will Tell the People* (1992), and *Secrets of the Temple: How the Federal Reserve Runs the Country* (1987), all published by Simon & Schuster. This piece is from *Who Will Tell the People*.

Mock Democracy

In a democracy, everyone is free to join the argument, or so it is said in civic mythology. In the modern democracy that has evolved, that claim is nearly meaningless. During the last generation, a "new politics" has enveloped government that guarantees the exclusion of most Americans from the debate—the expensive politics of facts and information. A major industry has grown up in Washington around what might be called "democracy for hire"— business firms and outposts of sponsored scholars devoted to concocting facts and opinions and expert analysis, then aiming them at the government. That is the principal function of all those enterprises along Washington's main boulevards like K Street—the public-relations agencies, the direct-mail companies and opinion-polling firms. All these work in concert with the infrastructure of think tanks, tax-exempt foundations and other centers that churn out reams of policy ideas for the political debate. Most are financed by corporate interests and wealthy benefactors. The work of lobbyists and lawyers involves delivering the material to the appropriate legislators and administrators.

Only those who have accumulated lots of money are free to play in this version of democracy. Only those with a strong, immediate financial stake in the political outcomes can afford to invest this kind of money in manipulating the governing decisions. Most Americans have neither the personal ability nor the wherewithal to compete on this field.

The contours of this barrier are embedded in the very texture of everyday political debate itself. Citizens have been incapacitated, quite literally, because they do not speak the language. Modern methodologies of persuasion have created a new hierarchy of influence over government decisions—a new way in which organized money dominates the action while the unorganized voices of citizens are inhibited from speaking. A lonely congressman, trying to represent the larger public interest, finds himself arrayed against an army of authorities working for the other side.

Beyond the fact of unequal resources, however, lies a more troubling proposition: that democracy is now held captive by the mystique of "rational" policymaking, narrow assumptions about what constitutes legitimate political evidence. It is a barrier of privilege because it effectively discounts authentic

272

political expressions from citizens and elevates the biases and opinions of the elites.

This mystique, not surprisingly, is embraced and exalted by well-educated citizens of most every persuasion, the people who are equipped with professional skills and expertise, including the dedicated reformers who attempt to speak for the larger public. After all, it is the basis for their own primacy in political action. Yet the premise of rationality, as the evidence demonstrates, is deeply flawed and routinely biased in its applications.

For those who are active every day in the conventional politics of governing, this proposition may not be so easy to grasp. Indeed, it will seem quite threatening to some of them, for it challenges their own deeply held beliefs about how politics is supposed to work and puts in question the meaning of their own political labors. Ordinary citizens, those who are distant from power, will have much less difficulty seeing the truth of the argument—that information-driven politics has become a convenient reason to ignore them.

Jack Bonner, an intense young denizen of K Street, has the squirrelly enthusiasm of a salesman who can't stop talking about his product because he truly believes in it. What Bonner's firm sells is democracy, not the abstract version found in textbooks, but the living, breathing kind that occurs when people call up a senator and tell him how to vote. Bonner & Associates packages democratic expression and sells it to corporate clients—drug manufacturers and the cosmetic industry, insurance companies and cigarette makers and the major banks.

Jack Bonner's firm is an exotic but relatively small example of the vast information industry that now surrounds the legislative debate and government in general. You want facts to support the industry's lobbying claims? It pumps out facts. You want expert opinions from scholars? It has those in abundance from the think tanks corporate contributors underwrite. You want opinion polls? It hires polling firms to produce them. You want people—live voters who support the industry position? Jack Bonner delivers them.

When the Senate was debating the new clean-air legislation in 1990, certain wavering senators received pleas from the grassroots on the question of controlling automobile pollution. The Big Brothers and Big Sisters of the Mahoning Valley wrote to Senator John Glenn of Ohio. Sam Nunn of Georgia heard from the Georgia Baptist Convention and its 1.2 million members. The Easter Seal Society of South Dakota lobbied Senator Thomas A. Daschle. The Delaware Paralyzed Veterans Association contacted Senator William V. Roth, Jr.

These groups and some others declared their opposition to the pending clean-air amendment that would compel the auto industry to improve substantially the average fuel efficiency of its cars. The measure would both conserve energy and reduce the carbon-dioxide pollution that is the main source of global warming. These citizen organizations were persuaded to take a stand by Bonner & Associates, which informed them, consistent with the auto industry's political propaganda, that tougher fuel standards would make it impossible to manufacture any vehicles larger than a Ford Escort or a Honda Civic.

Vans and station wagons, small trucks and high-speed police cruisers, they were told, would cease to exist. The National Sheriffs Association was aroused by the thought of chasing criminals in a Honda Civic. The Nebraska Farm Bureau said rural America would be "devastated" if farmers tried to pull a trailer loaded with livestock or hay with a Ford Escort.

For twenty years, whenever the government has attempted to improve auto safety or environmental protection through new regulation, the auto industry has always made similar groans—satisfying tougher standards would be impossible without dire social and economic consequences. The industry warnings have always proved to be false, but the innocent citizens recruited to speak for Detroit probably didn't know this history.

Jack Bonner was thrilled by their expressions of alarm and so was the auto industry that paid him for them. Bonner's fee, which he coyly described as somewhere between $500,000 and $1 million, was for scouring six states for potential grassroots voices, coaching them on the "facts" of the issue, paying for the phone calls and plane fares to Washington and hiring the hall for a joint press conference.

"On the clean-air bill, we bring to the table a third party—'white hat' groups who have no financial interest," Bonner explained. "It's not the auto industry trying to protect its financial stake. Now it's senior citizens worried about getting out of small cars with walkers. Easter Seal, Multiple Sclerosis—a lot of these people have braces, wheelchairs, walkers. It's farm groups worrying about small trucks. It's people who need station wagons to drive kids to Little League games. These are groups with political juice and they're white hot."

In the textbook version of democracy, this activity is indistinguishable from any other form of democratic expression. In actuality, earnest citizens are being skillfully manipulated by powerful interests—using "facts" that are debatable at best—in a context designed to serve narrow corporate lobbying strategies, not free debate. Bonner & Associates does not start by looking for citizens whose self-interest might put them on the auto industry's side. It starts with a list of the senators whose votes the auto industry needs. Then the firm forages among those senators' constituents for willing bodies.

"We sit down with the lobbyists and ask: How much heat do you want on these guys?" Bonner explained. "Do you want ten local groups or two hundred groups? Do you want one hundred phone calls from constituents or a thousand phone calls?"

Bonner's K Street office has a "boiler room" with three hundred phone lines and a sophisticated computer system, resembling the phone banks employed in election campaigns. Articulate young people sit in little booths every day, dialing around America on a variety of public issues, searching for "white hat" citizens who can be persuaded to endorse the political objectives of Mobil Oil, Dow Chemical, Citicorp, Ohio Bell, Miller Brewing, U.S. Tobacco, the Chemical Manufacturers Association, the Pharmaceutical Manufacturers Association and dozens of other clients.

This kind of political recruiting is expensive but not difficult. Many of the citizens are no doubt flattered to be asked, since ordinary Americans are seldom invited to participate in a personal way in the larger debates, even by the national civic organizations that presumably represent them. In a twisted sense, Jack Bonner does what political parties used to do for citizens—he educates and agitates and mobilizes.

Since members of Congress are not naive, they understand the artificiality well enough. They know that many of the 400 million pieces of mail they receive each year are contrived by interested parties of one kind or another. Hearing authentic voices from the grassroots, however, provides them with a valuable defense on controversial votes, especially when a senator intends to vote with the auto-industry lobbyists and against cleaner air. Public opinion, as every senator knows, is with the air.

"Obviously," Bonner said, "you target senators inclined to go your way but who need some additional cover. They need to be able to say they've heard from people back home on this issue. Or we target people who are genuinely undecided. It's not a good use of money to target senators who are flat opposed or who are already for you."

Corporate grassroots politics, as Bonner likes to emphasize, is really borrowed from the opposition—the citizen "public interest" organizations, especially in the environmental movement, who first perfected the technique of generating emotional public responses with factual accusations. "Politics turns on emotion," Bonner said. "That's why industry has lost in the past and that's why we win. We bring emotion to the table."

The democratic discourse is now dominated by such transactions— information and opinion and scholarly expertise produced by and for the self-interested sponsors. Imagine Bonner's technique multiplied and elaborated in different ways across hundreds of public issues and you may begin to envision the girth of this industry. Some firms produce artfully designed opinion polls, more or less guaranteed to yield results that suggest public support for the industry's position. Some firms specialize in coalition building— assembling dozens or hundreds of civic organizations and interest groups in behalf of lobbying goals.

This is democracy and it costs a fortune. Democracy-for-hire smothers the contemporary political debates and, while it does not always prevail, relatively few Americans have the resources to hire a voice for themselves. David Cohen of the Advocacy Institute, which trains citizens in how to lobby for their causes, recognizes a kind of class system emerging in the political process itself. "We are moving to a system," he said, "where there are two different realms of citizens—a society in which those with the resources are going to have the ability to dominate the debate and outcomes while others are not going to be able to draw on the tools of persuasion." If democratic expression is reduced to a question of money, then those with money will always have more.

In previous times, reformers wrote devastating critiques about the "capture" of government regulatory agencies by the industries they were supposed to regulate. The Civil Aeronautics Board became the puppet of the airlines. The Bureau of Mines was owned by the coal industry. The Federal Communications Commission belonged to the broadcasters. The occasional exposés sometimes produced reforms though the basic problem endured.

Now, however, it is not an exaggeration to say that democracy itself has been "captured." The forms of expression, the premises and very language of debate, not to mention the rotating cadres of experts and managers, are now owned in large measure by relatively few interests, much the way that powerful industries came to own regulatory agencies. Democracy is held captive, not just by money, but by ideas—the ideas that money buys.

America's Funniest Home Videos may be dismissed as the kind of daffy (and irresistible) fluff that network television serves up, except for its revolutionary implications. The show is mostly devoted to ridiculous moments in everyday life—spontaneous, backyard sight gags captured by ordinary people with their own video cameras. But now and then the homemade videotapes reveal something more. Folks not only have their own TV cameras now, but many have learned the higher production values of television—the dramatic arts of staging and editing and narration that make the medium so effective. Given their store-bought equipment, these amateurs are now making quite skillful parodies of the professionals.

It is possible, in other words, to watch *Funniest Home Videos* and imagine America, someday soon, as a nation of TV producers. Citizens making their own messages for broadcast—that's power. Citizens everywhere covering the news for themselves—that's power too, as the Los Angeles policemen discovered when a home video recorded their brutal beating of a black motorist.

Possibly, some enterprising TV syndicate will eventually move beyond the sight gags and invite citizens to tell other kinds of stories about themselves—to send in videotapes that record deeper dramas from their lives or, who knows, even stories that express their own political ideas and aspirations. I can envision an entertaining and meaningful low-budget program that simply airs the most provocative works of America's TV guerrillas—citizen filmmakers who harness the outrage of talk radio to more purposeful content and with less manipulation by the on-air personality.

This sort of possibility is just the beginning of the next liberating revolution—and the new grounds for optimism about democratic possibilities. New technologies are coming into the marketplace that will give individuals more control over the nature of electronic communications. Once the means of creating the message are widely distributed in many hands, invention is sure to follow. The truly original ideas for using video—the techniques for adapting its power to democratic relationships—will not come from the corporate conglomerates that now control broadcasting and publishing. But they might come from someone's backyard.

George Gilder has sketched a most ambitious vision of democratic optimism, based on the emerging developments in microelectronics. Communications grids that decentralize the originating controls, telecomputers and personal data resources that will shift power away from institutions and to individuals—these technologies and others promise to empower citizens, Gilder explained. As this happens, people will be able to liberate themselves from mindless anonymity in the mass audience.

"The force of microelectronics will blow apart all of the monopolies, hierarchies, pyramids and power grids of established industrial society," Gilder declared. "It will undermine all totalitarian regimes. Police states cannot endure under the advance of the computer because it increases the powers of the people far faster than the powers of surveillance. All hierarchies will tend to become 'heterarchies'—systems in which each individual rules his own domain."

Meanwhile, however, in the here-and-now, the pace of change is largely controlled by those corporations that own the equipment and existing franchises—and most of them, for obvious reasons, have a compelling interest in resisting change and preserving the status quo. Like George Gilder, one may assume that profound technological change sooner or later sweeps away the old order, regardless of its political power to resist. But the actual shape of the future still depends crucially on which economic and political forces get to design it.

The unmentionable political issue is who owns the media—unmentionable because neither media nor politicians will bring it up. Ben H. Bagdikian, former dean of journalism at the University of California at Berkeley, bravely explored the question and reached a frightening conclusion:

> The United States, along with other major democracies, is moving swiftly toward media control by a handful of gigantic multi-national corporations. The trend is unmistakable. Leaders in the trend are quite candid: they predict that in a few years a half-dozen corporations will control most of the public information available to Americans.

If that sounds like an extreme forecast, consider the results of Bagdikian's research. When his book, *The Media Monopoly*, was first published in 1983, he counted fifty organizations that controlled most of the business in all major media—radio, television and its derivatives, newspapers, magazines and books. Five years later, when the second edition was published, he found the fifty organizations had shrunk to twenty-nine.

As Bagdikian demonstrated, the great promise of new communications technologies has been thwarted in the past by the commercial self-interest of those who owned them. Cable television, for instance, was heralded twenty years ago as the great liberating innovation that would foster diversity in broadcasting and reinvigorate the public dialogue simply because cable grossly multiplied the number of available channels. On the whole, the promise has not been fulfilled. With rare exceptions, cable TV does not stray from the narrow commercial objectives of its owners—owners who are mostly the same companies that own newspapers, magazines, radio and television stations.

David Fenton, who orchestrated the Alar campaign, sees the problems of democracy rooted in the power of the media to set the agenda for public debate, however randomly they do so. "I agree with the right wing," Fenton said. "Here we have this powerful instrument for political opinion and solving social problems that is completely unaccountable and unwilling to examine itself and against letting itself be used to attack social problems. Citing the First Amendment is not an answer. Nobody wants to appoint politically corrupt bureaucrats to run the media, but maybe it's not so good to leave the media entirely in the hands of people who are only interested in private profit. If we want an environmentally sound economy, that little box can make it happen. Or do we have to leave it to little guerrilla operations like ours?"

The democratic imperative, therefore, is to develop new political and legal doctrine that will challenge the concentrated ownership of communications on behalf of democracy. As individual citizens develop their own communications skills and organize their own computer networks, they will be able to go around the mass media and talk to one another. But they will still be shut out of the mass-audience debate if the owners refuse them access. The proposals to allot free air time for political candidates in campaigns, for instance, are a useful but inadequate reform. The problem is also providing air time for citizens, not just for elections, but in every season.

To produce genuine change, media companies might, for instance, be prohibited from cross-ownership in different sectors of media or limited to some modest share of the overall national marketplace, as Bagdikian has suggested. Media owners usually hide behind the First Amendment when such questions are raised, but the practical effect of media concentration is actually to restrict the "free speech" of everyone else, the voiceless citizenry. Who gets to enter the debate? The choice belongs to reporters and editors and producers and, really, to the companies they work for. Sooner or later, this arbitrary restriction on democracy must be confronted.

Michael Kinsley of the *New Republic* has suggested, for instance, that companies that use their media ownership to promote their own products or political interests might find themselves restricted to the more limited First Amendment privileges accorded to "commercial speech." When NBC broadcasts an account of the success of the nuclear-power industry in France, is it informing the public or selling a product made by NBC's owner, General Electric? In 1990, the NBC Nightly News ran three segments, totaling fourteen minutes, on a new device to detect breast cancer without finding time to mention that the machine is manufactured by NBC's parent corporation. As the control of the major news media becomes still more concentrated, their supposed neutrality, in both commerce and politics, will become more and more suspect.

To take another example of reform, cable franchises, originally envisioned as public utilities, could be broken up into multiple ownerships—commercial and noncommercial, political and nonpolitical. Public-access channels are available for free and inventive expression, but they have no institutional base from which to develop coherent programming and quality. Given the redundancies that now exist in the content of TV broadcasting, nothing would be lost if some channels or blocs of air time were assigned to responsible community institutions (churches or labor unions or even political parties) that are motivated, not by profit maximization, but by the desire to foster social connections.

Public accountability would require a diversity of voices and a rough sense of balance among the competing interests that are given control of the access. Ralph Nader has proposed, for example, an "audience network" in which citizens' groups, depending on their size, could be awarded an hour or so of air time to broadcast programming that originates with the public, not the media corporations. "Given the immense concentration of power and uniformity that characterizes the broadcasting industry," Nader wrote, "leaving the dissemination and content of new information technology to myopic profit formulas runs counter to community sense and historical precedent."

At the very least, while we await the liberating possibilities of the next communications revolution, some new rules of equity need to be developed—rules that spread the costs of political speech among many in order to democratize its availability for everyone. Most individuals cannot undertake this for themselves. Without new institutional arrangements in communications, control of access inevitably will be held by the few.

The media corporations are busy concentrating their market shares and acquiring rivals. The politicians dare not challenge the structure of media ownership, for that would provoke severe retribution from press and television and their corporate owners. The power of corporate politics, as the next chapter makes clear, is the centerpiece in the institutional arrangements that dominate politics.

The debate about media power, therefore, has to come from the people—from the TV guerrillas who want to reach a larger audience with their original messages, from ordinary citizens who are able to envision a more robust democracy. If the people do not raise these questions, they will not be raised at all.

Landon Y. Jones Jr. is the author of *Great Expectations: America and the Baby Boom Generation* (Coward, McCann and Geoghegan, 1980). He is the past editor of the *Princeton Alumni Weekly* (1969–74), *Money* magazine (1984–89), and *People* magazine (1989–97). In this excerpt from *Great Expectations*, he examines how the "baby boomer" generation shaped the economy of the 1950s—and was shaped by it.

The Big Barbecue

In the early 1950s, the huge Census Clock in Washington was clicking like a runaway taxi meter. Every seven seconds the Birth Light blinked off a new baby. Boys were arriving with familiar names like Robert, John, James, Michael, William, Richard, Joseph, Thomas, Steven, and David, making a Top Ten of favorite names that was proudly all-American. Girls were named Linda, Mary, Barbara, Patricia, Susan, Kathleen, Carol, Nancy, Margaret, and Diane. And perhaps thanks to Debbie Reynolds, "Deborah" would have a run all of her own later in the decade.

Like the steel industry, mothering was running at close to 100 percent capacity, and it was harder and harder to keep up. In January of 1952, General Electric decided to celebrate its seventy-fifth anniversary by awarding five shares of common stock to any employee who had a baby on October 15. Some public-relations whiz tried to predict the eventual number of winners by dividing the total of 226,000 G.E. employees by the U.S. crude birthrate. Unfortunately, he forgot that G.E. workers as a population were considerably more fertile than the United States as a whole, since they contained no one under 17 or over 65. In the end, the company's guess that thirteen G.E. babies would be born amounted to underestimation on a grand scale. The workers, true to the thriving surplus economy of the era, came through with no fewer than 189 new G.E. babies that day.

But General Electric was not about to complain. It was investing $650 million in new plants and assembly lines over seven postwar years to prepare for the boom in babies. As early as 1948, *Time* noted that the U.S. population had just increased by "2,800,000 more consumers" (not babies) the year before. Economists happily predicted that the new babies would set off a demand explosion for commodities such as homes, foodstuffs, clothing, furniture, appliances, and schools, to name only a few examples. *Fortune* pronounced the baby boom "exhilarating" and with an almost-audible sigh of relief concluded that the low birthrates of the 1930s were a "freakish interlude, rather than a trend." "We need not stew too much about a post-armament depression," the magazine wrote. "A civilian market growing by the size of Iowa every year ought to be able to absorb whatever production the military will eventually turn loose."

As the economic and baby booms surged on together, the cheerleading became almost feverish. Public-service signs went up in New York City subways reading, "Your future is great in a growing America. Every day 11,000 babies are born in America. This means new business, new jobs, new opportunities." After-dinner speakers began to talk about "Prosperity by Population" and lofted tantalizing guesses of up to five million new babies a year by 1975. Financial magazines editorialized about the joys of "this remarkable boom." "Gone, for the first time in history," announced *Time* in 1955, "is the worry over whether a society can produce enough goods to take care of its people. The lingering worry is whether it will have enough people to consume the goods."

The most euphoric article of all, perhaps, was a story *Life* printed in 1958, at the height of the boom. Three dozen children were crowded onto the cover along with the banner headline: KIDS: BUILT-IN RECESSION CURE—HOW 4,000,000 A YEAR MAKE MILLIONS IN BUSINESS. Inside, the article began with another headline—ROCKETING BIRTHS: BUSINESS BONANZA—and continued chockablock with statistics and photographs about new citizens who were "a brand-new market for food, clothing, and shelter." In its first year, *Life* calculated, a baby is not just a child but already a prodigious consumer, "a potential market for $800 worth of products." Even before returning from the hospital, an infant had "already rung up $450 in medical expenses." Four-year-olds are not just sugar and spice or puppy-dog tails but rather represent "a backlog of business orders that will take two decades to fulfill." A rhapsodic *Life* then clinched its case by visiting Joe Powers, a thirty-five-year-old salesman from Port Washington, New York. He and his wife, Carol, had produced ten children and were buying seventy-seven quarts of milk and twenty-eight loaves of bread a week, just for starters. Faced with examples like that of meritorious devotion to the Procreation Ethic, little wonder that some American mothers felt as if it were their duty to have children. Either they were pregnant or, if not, wondered whether they should be.

The baby-boom kids had kicked off in America a buccaneering orgy of buying and selling that carried all things before it. The only thing like it earlier was the Gilded Age of the post-Civil War 1870s, which the historian Vernon Louis Parrington so aptly dubbed "the Great Barbecue." Here was a feast spread out for an entire nation, and everyone scrambling for it. More food was spoiled than eaten, perhaps, and the revelry was a bit unseemly, but no one minded. Everywhere people were getting rich in a demographic debauch.

The spending boom started, literally, at the bottom. Diapers went from a $32-million industry in 1947 to $50 million in 1957. The diaper services (disposables had not yet arrived) also prospered. Mothers and fathers were paying $5 million annually (twice the preboom business) to have baby's shoes bronze-plated at L. E. Mason, Inc., in Boston. The under-five appetite, which had grown from 13 million mouths to 20 million by 1960, more than one out of every ten Americans, was consuming baby food at a rate of 1.5 billion cans a year in 1953 (up from 270 million cans in 1940).

As the kids grew up, so did the markets. Throughout the 1950s the five-to-thirteen age group grew by an additional one million baby boomers every year. The toy industry set sales records annually after 1940, growing from an $84-million-a-year stripling to a $1.25-billion giant. Sales of bicycles doubled to two million a year; cowboy outfits became a $75-million subindustry; space-science toys claimed another $60 million. Children's clothes became a boom market, and packaging researchers suddenly discovered the troika of "family" sizes—Giant, Economy, and Supereconomy. At its peak, the juvenile market was ringing up a staggering $33 billion annually.

The rain of spending did not fall evenly on society. Rather, it was both a cause and an effect of what amounted to the opening of a new American frontier: the suburbs. Historians had already suggested that America's expansiveness during the nineteenth century was built on the common goal of settling the West. Now there was a new impetus behind the conquering of the suburban frontier: babies. The suburbs were conceived for the baby boom—and vice versa. Here in green garlands around the cities, Americans were creating new child-oriented societies, "babyvilles" teeming with new appetites, new institutions, and new values. Families who were asked why they moved to the suburbs first mentioned better housing and leisure, as if they were conforming to the old goal of a country place that began with the French aristocracy. But then, invariably, they added that they thought suburbia was "a better place to bring up the kids." The common acceptance of this goal united the suburbs. "Instead of the wagon train, where people leaned on one another as they moved across the continent," historian Daniel Boorstin remarked, "Americans in suburbs leaned on one another as they moved rapidly about the country and up the ladder of consumption." Author William H. Whyte found the same communal spirit in his examination of the mythical suburb of Park Forest. Families shared baby-sitters, cribs, lawn mowers, tea services, and baseball equipment. "We laughed at first at how the Marxist society had finally arrived," one suburban executive told Whyte. "But I think the real analogy is to the pioneers."

As an internal migration, the settling of the suburbs was phenomenal. In the twenty years from 1950 to 1970, the population of the suburbs doubled from 36 million to 72 million. No less than 83 percent of the total population growth in the United States during the 1950s was in the suburbs, which were growing fifteen times faster than any other segment of the country. As people packed and moved, the national mobility rate leaped by 50 percent. The only other comparable influx was the wave of European immigrants to the United States around the turn of the century. But, as *Fortune* pointed out, more people moved to the suburbs every year than had ever arrived on Ellis Island.

By now, bulldozers were churning up dust storms as they cleared the land for housing developments. More than a million acres of farmland were plowed under every year during the 1950s. Millions of apartment-dwelling parents with two children were suddenly realizing that two children could be doubled up in a spare bedroom, but a third child cried loudly for something more. The proportion of new houses with three or more bedrooms, in fact, rose from one-third in 1947 to three-quarters by 1954. The necessary *Lebensraum* could only be found in the suburbs. There was a housing shortage, but young couples armed with VA and FHA loans built their dream homes with easy credit and free spending habits that were unthinkable to the baby-boom grandparents, who shook their heads with the Depression still fresh in their memories. Of the 13 million homes built in the decade before 1958, 11 million of them—or 85 percent—were built in the suburbs. Home ownership rose 50 percent between 1940 and 1950, and another 50 percent by 1960. By then, one-fourth of all housing in the United States had been built in the fifties. For the first time, more Americans owned homes than rented them.

We were becoming a land of gigantic nurseries. The biggest were built by Abraham Levitt, the son of poor Russian-Jewish immigrants, who had originally built houses for the Navy during the war. The first of three East Coast Levittowns went up on the potato fields of Long Island. Exactly $7,990—or $60 a month and no money down—bought you a Monopoly-board bungalow with four rooms, attic, washing machine, outdoor barbecue, and a television set built into the wall. The 17,447 units eventually became home to 82,000 people, many of whom were pregnant or wanted to be. In a typical story on the suburban explosion, one magazine breathlessly described a volleyball game of nine couples in which no fewer than five of the women were expecting.

Marketers were quick to spot what amounted to capitalism's Klondike Lode. "Anybody who wants to sell anything to Americans should take a long look at the New Suburbia," marveled *Fortune* in 1953. "It is big and lush and uniform—a combination made to order for the comprehending marketer." It went far beyond toys and diapers. In suburbia's servantless society, labor-saving devices were necessary adjuncts to having children. The number of washing machines sold in America went from 1.7 million in 1950 to 2.6 million in 1960. Sales of electric clothes dryers doubled during one two-year stretch. With a then-astonishing average family income of $6,500 (compared to $3,800 for everyone else), the suburbanites were creating an American way of spending organized around children and the needs they created. Retailers eagerly followed them to the suburbs, opening branch stores by the dozen and clearing the way for the later age of shopping malls.

The settlers of suburbia also brought with them beasts of burden. They had Fords in their Future—and Chevys and De Sotos and Hudsons and Stude-bakers. The car, especially the second car, was the one indispensable suburban accessory. Car registrations soared along with the birthrate: from 26 million in 1945 to 40 million in 1950 to 60 million by the end of the decade. The number of two-car families rose 750,000 a year and doubled from 1951 to 1958. Station wagons, the housewife's version of the Willys Jeep, began criss-crossing the suburbs like water bugs, dropping off husbands, picking up children, stopping by the supermarket. "A suburban mother's role is to deliver children obstetrically once," said Peter De Vries, "and by car forever after." *Time* joked that "if the theory of evolution is still working, it may well one day transform the suburban housewife's right foot into a flared paddle, grooved for easy traction on the gas pedal and brake."

Even in those days, the automobile had seized its central place in the emotional life of the baby boom. It was the first entire generation to be driven before it walked. It was the first generation to grow up in cars, even to seek its entertainment in cars. Back in 1933 a chemicals manufacturer named Richard Hollinshead had turned a parking lot in Camden, New Jersey, into the World's First Automobile Movie Theatre. Fifteen years later, there were only 480 drive-ins in the country. But between 1948 and 1958 the number zoomed to 4,000, equipped with everything from playgrounds for the kids to Laundromats for Mom. For millions of baby-boom parents, a night at the drive-in neatly solved the suburban dilemma of what to do if you couldn't get a baby-sitter. Much later, the adolescent baby boomers would find their own use for the passion pits. Here is Lisa Alther in *Kinflicks*:

> Mixed with the dialogue were the various sighs and gasps and sucking sounds from the front seats and blasts from car horns throughout the parking area as, in keeping with Hullsport High tradition, couples signalled that they'd gone all the way.

Nowhere was the postwar baby-suburb-car symbiosis more symbolically apparent than during the gasoline shortage of July 1979 in the Philadelphia suburb of Levittown, Pennsylvania. There some 75,000 people live on 7,000 acres of suburb. But, for a city of such density, it is served by little mass transportation. Threatened by the loss of their cars, angry young Levittowners staged the nation's first gas riot, burning cars, stoning ambulances, and battling police. Ironically, many of the 195 who were arrested belonged to the same families who had originally settled there during the baby-boom years and who, in 1960, won the Little League World Series for Levittown.

Meanwhile, the suburbs continued to grow and prosper and create a whole new sequence of bench marks for American Studies teachers. In 1956, white-collar workers outnumbered blue-collar workers for the first time. In 1970, the suburbs became the largest single sector of the nation's population, exceeding both central cities and the farms. By 1972, the suburbs were even offering more jobs than the central cities. Everyone was enthusiastically buying "on time" (as it was called then), and the number of Americans who thought installment financing was a good thing increased from 50 percent to 60 percent in ten years.

Sociologists began to pursue the suburbanites like doctors after a new virus. The baby-boom parents were poked and prodded and examined with the kind of fascination hitherto reserved for South Sea Islanders. They were, to be sure, pioneering a life-style (the dread word first came into currency then) that would be predominant in America. Often living in small houses filled with children, they moved outside to their patios and barbecue pits and created a new, rigorously informal style. Lawn and porch furniture sales went from $53 million in 1950 to $145 million in 1960. Hot dog production likewise zoomed from 750 million pounds to more than two billion pounds in the decade. Everyone first-named everyone and no one criticized the neighbor's kids (at least in front of a neighbor). Books of the time began to portray a strange netherworld of rathskellers and dens, of cheese dips and cocktails (the required icebreakers in a highly mobile society), or Kaffeeklatsches and card parties, and of outer-directed husbands and neurotic corporate wives.

Some of these studies no doubt revealed more of the anxieties of the examiners than the examined. (Did ordinary citizens really have "identity crises"?) But, if there was a common message, it was of the *sameness* of suburbia. It was as if the same forces that produced prosperity and fertility also produced homogeneity. Parents had rediscovered the old verities—home, hearth, children, church. But they had also made a faith out of brand names, modular housing, and gray flannel suits. Everywhere were the same drugstores, the same franchises, the same music on the radio. The children, too, were being shaped by a world of repeatable experience. But they were not being molded by their parents or their teachers. Instead, there was another dominant presence in the early lives of the baby boomers. It was one that would forge their unity as a generation. It would mobilize them as a consumer force. It was television. In 1938, E. B. White prophesied that "television is going to be the test of the modern world and . . . in this new opportunity to see beyond the range of our vision we shall discover either a new and unbearable disturbance of the general peace or a saving radiance in the sky. We shall stand or fall by television—of that I am quite sure." In the year White wrote that, barely two percent of American families owned the small, flickering Philcos and DuMonts dwarfed in their elephantine cabinets. But in less than a decade, the age of television swept over us. From fewer than 6,000 sets manufactured at the baby boom's outset in 1946, production leaped almost impossibly, to seven million a year by 1953. Eighty-six percent of American homes had television sets at the end of the decade and, by 1967, 98 percent of all homes had sets, effectively saturating the market. The exponential growth curve of television was steeper than that of any other technological innovation of the century—including the telephone, radio, and automobile.

It was also the most important new child-care development of the century, one that would redefine the environment in which Americans grew up. Some of the oldest baby-boomers remember when the first sets were lugged into their homes. But, for most, television was not an intruder in the home but what Buckminster Fuller called "the third parent," practically a family member itself. These children treated the glowing box not with the awe due a mysterious and wonderful invention but with the unquestioned familiarity of an old armchair or the kitchen sink.

Families wanted to stay home in the 1950s, and television made it easier. Aside from the growth in drive-ins, movies almost withered away during the baby-boom years. In 1946, the first year of the boom, Hollywood had recorded its biggest year ever: 400 features were released and 90 million went to the movies every week. Then in 1947, movie attendance dropped 10 percent as parents stayed home with their babies. By January 1953, when a record 50 million of them watched another baby-boom mother, Lucy Ricardo, have her baby on *I Love Lucy*, movie attendance had been cut to one-half the 1946 level, despite such lures as 3-D movies. (The first was *Bwana Devil* in 1952.) With most of its screens located in emptying downtowns instead of expanding suburbs—in New York City alone, fifty-five theaters closed in 1951—Hollywood lost an audience it would not even begin to reclaim until it squeezed theaters into suburban malls twenty years later.

Television, meanwhile, was giving the baby-boom children a series of vivid images that would color their memories forever. They all sang "M-I-C-K-E-Y M-O-U-S-E" with Karen and Doreen. (In those days, no one noticed that there were no black or Asian or Hispanic Mouseketeers.) They grew up glued to *Howdy Doody*, part of a vast Peanut Gallery in a national Doodyville. Mr. Bluster was a faintly disguised Ike, and as author Jeff Greenfield has observed, Clarabell was the original Yippie. Two decades later, in the aftermath of the Vietnam antiwar strife, Buffalo Bob and Howdy put together a road show that offered a burned-out student generation a return to a childhood myth that somehow seemed more real, or at least comforting, than the 1960s had been.

The baby-boom parents themselves were mirrored in nuclear family dramas like *The Adventures of Ozzie and Harriet*, *Father Knows Best*, and *The Life of Riley*. Yet, on TV at least, the birthrate remained surprisingly low—evidently the bumbling Ozzie Nelsons and Chester A. Rileys were a lot more savvy about some family matters than their children ever could have suspected. (*The Brady Bunch*, with its amalgam of six children by two different marriages, was more of a postboom family that arrived ahead of its time.) Perhaps the prototypical baby-boom family was the Cleavers in *Leave It to Beaver*. Beaver Cleaver could have been penned by Norman Rockwell as a sort of Tom Sawyer relocated in Pasadena. The rumor that the actor who played Beaver, Jerry Mathers, had been killed later in Vietnam seemed cruelly symbolic of the death of the generation's own innocence. (The reality was, if anything, even more appropriate: Mathers had actually gone from selling insurance to real estate, while his klutzy buddy, Eddie Haskell, had really become a cop with the Los Angeles Police Department.)

As the baby boomers grew out of diapers, advertisers looked at the figures and discovered that American mothers had created the biggest market in history. Now technology had produced the tool to move it: television. The earliest ads had been silly jingles about chlorophyll toothpaste and chlorophyll chewing gum. But then a marketing consultant named Eugene Gilbert stumbled on a galvanizing truth: "An advertiser who touches a responsive chord in youth can generally count on the parent to succumb finally to purchasing the product." It was the Relativity Theorem of television: a law that changed everything. Money for commercials flowed like a river as TV went about the business of turning toddlers into consumer trainees. Tests showed that children could recognize the word "detergent" before they could read. They sang "Pepsi-Cola hits the spot / Twelve full ounces, that's a lot" before they knew the national anthem. They were trained to buy. As Joyce Maynard wrote in her autobiographical memoir, published when she was all of twenty, "We are, in the fullest sense, *consumers*, trained to salivate not at a bell but at the sight of a Kelloggs label or a Dunkin' Donuts box." This generation could not be organized socially or politically, Dwight Macdonald argued, because it had already been organized as a body of affluent consumers. Fittingly, the NBC program *Saturday Night Live*, which later drew its audience from the grown-up kids of the fifties, chose as one of its first satirical themes something they knew best: commercials.

Samuel G. Freedman is a professor of journalism at Columbia University. He is the author of *Small Victories: The Real World of a Teacher, Her Students and Their High School* (1990), *Upon this Rock: The Miracles of a Black Church* (1993), and *Jew vs. Jew: The Struggle for the Soul of American Jewry* (2000). The following selection is an excerpt from *The Inheritance: How Three Families and America Moved from Roosevelt to Reagan and Beyond* (Simon & Schuster, 1996).

The Rope Line

On the night of October 20, 1967, only hours before the antiwar movement would besiege the Pentagon, Specialist Fourth Class Tim Carey unrolled his sleeping bag across one of its corridors. Alongside the bedroll he placed his helmet, gas mask, M-14 rifle, .45-caliber pistol, ammunition pouch, and tear gas grenades. As far as Tim could see, his comrades in the 503rd Military Police Battalion similarly ensconced themselves, burying their eyes from the fluorescent lights and wriggling for comfort against the terrazzo floor. Only in the narrow pathway between their collective feet and the far wall could anyone walk, and just as sleep was descending a passing soldier bumped into a hopper used for loading tear gas. Seconds later an acrid fog suffused the air. Farther down the hallway, where the battalion gave way to other units, troops struggled upright and stumbled away, groping behind blinded eyes.

Amid the bedlam, with their nostrils and armpits burning, with tears and mucus streaming, Tim Carey and his buddies merely waited. After all the gas they had inhaled in training, they had grown immune, if not to its effects then to the panic and flight those effects conspired to cause. In just a few minutes, they realized, the worst would subside, leaving their skin tingling as if from after-shave. A few men simply pulled on their masks, rolled back into slumber, and snored through their charcoal filters until morning. The rest congratulated themselves on another test met. This was, after all, the 503rd, "Patton's Palace Guard" in World War II, veterans of the Dominican Republic intervention in 1965. Just four months earlier the battalion had packed its gear, taken its inoculations and executed its wills in preparation for flying into the Middle East war. Only Israel's six-day victory canceled the trip.

For most of the past year, though, the 503rd had been drilling for duty in something closer to civil war, the race riots and political protests kindling across America. Hour by monotonous hour it practiced tactics that harked back in some cases to the Napoleonic campaigns—how to clear a street in a marching wedge; how to leave those being gassed a route of retreat; how to maintain an impassive face against constant provocation. When the battalion held maneuvers Tim got to play a hippie antagonist, donning granny glasses, buckskin jacket, and shoulder-length wig to stir revolution on the imitation corner of Oak and Broad. The 503rd made instructional films for police departments; it demonstrated techniques for the FBI. On this night a brigadier general, Carl C. Turner, visited the men in their hallway to shake hands. The next afternoon, the attorney general, Ramsey Clark, and the secretary of defense, Robert McNamara, would observe their performance from the windows of the Pentagon.

For all the gravity of the assignment, Tim knew only its rudiments. In a briefing, his commanding officer had told the men that an antiwar march was planned, with its terminus outside the Pentagon. There were rumors and threats of an attempt to storm the building. A character named Abbie Hoffman had even vowed to levitate it in an exorcism. "You have to hold your line," the commanding officer had said. "Don't let the people through. Make sure things don't get out of control." Beyond that, neither Tim nor anyone else in the battalion required direction. What was the point of all that training if not to render instruction unnecessary?

Not only did the impending protest seem vague to Tim, so did the larger movement that had organized it. He had never come any closer to antiwar activism than flashing peace signs during the 503rd's riot rehearsals. He was twenty years old, barely months beyond a job installing and repairing oil burners. Even after being drafted, he had never expected to serve, not with his 20/200 eyesight. On the morning he went to Fort Hamilton in Brooklyn for his induction physical, he fully expected to return home for dinner in Crotonville as a 4-F. Instead, he was riding a troop train to Fort Jackson, South Carolina, with only the clothes he was wearing. After basic training, when he was selected for the MPs, he asked a sergeant why. "For the motor pool," he was told. That made sense; Tim had been fixing cars since he was twelve, and no doubt the talent had shown on the army's aptitude test. But, no, he wasn't bound for changing the oil in jeeps. Soon he was policing Fort Bragg in North Carolina, dragging spouses to neutral corners in marital rows, peeling apart the bodies during brawls at the noncommissioned officers' club, and meanwhile being steeled to safeguard his nation against insurrection.

But if Tim and his comrades were supposed to hate their peers across the barricades, or at least to regard them as the enemy, the antipathy had not taken hold. What the men in the 503rd harbored was not fervent anti-Communism so much as a mixture of obligation and inevitability. You got drafted; you went; you went, if you were Tim Carey, just like your father and your uncles and your big brother had gone before you. The domino theory had nothing to do with it, and the idea of enlisting was preposterous, except under the sort of legal duress Michael Carey had known. Most of the MPs in the 503rd hailed from the Northeast, from places like Boston and Philadelphia and Long Island, and they exuded a cosmopolitan cynicism, at least compared to the faction of small-town southerners in the unit. Each kept a calendar with the days left in his hitch marked in descending order. It was called an "F.T.A.," literally the abbreviation for the recruiting slogan "Fun, Travel, Adventure," but more commonly for "Fuck the Army." One guy in the barracks, Eddie Katheder, a would-be folksinger, brought records by Tom Paxton, Bob Dylan, and Joan Baez. When the MPs shot pool in the dayroom, they brayed along with Phil Ochs on "Cops of the World." It drove the southerners crazy, almost as crazy as the sight of Eddie and his crowd smoking a joint.

Tim heard Ochs's song not as an anthem of dissidence, but as an acute comment on a war he saw as absurd rather than immoral. Nobody had even declared it a war. What was that phrase he remembered from studying Korea? "Police action." Was that what you called it when boys were dying and America still kept its biggest guns holstered? The only advice Michael had ever given Tim about the military was to stay in the pack, not call attention to yourself. That meant serving two years and then going home, maybe to take the exam for becoming a New York City cop. Or so Tim Carey thought on the evening of October 20, clucking at soldiers who couldn't handle a little tear gas, envisioning nothing more demanding the next day than glorified guard duty.

Across the Potomac, the leaders of the demonstration understood the import clearly. This event aspired to be the largest in the nation since 100,000 "doves" had massed in Manhattan six months earlier. As important, it marked the transformation of the antiwar movement from protest to resistance, Old Left to New. The sponsoring coalition, the National Mobilization Committee to End the War in Vietnam, consciously welcomed Maoist and Trotskyite sects alongside Quaker pacifists and the suburban bourgeoisie of SANE. From Jerry Rubin and David Dellinger to Dr. Benjamin Spock and the Reverend William Sloane Coffin, the leadership crossed lines of generation and tactics. Few observers could miss the symbolism that the rally preceding the march on the Pentagon would be conducted from the steps of the Lincoln Memorial, the very ground consecrated in August 1963 by Martin Luther King and the March on Washington.

Under the aquamarine skies of Indian summer, weather that normally would have brought touch football to the site, a crowd assembled in the tens of thousands. Some had arrived the previous day for a mass return of draft cards at the Department of Justice; some had lurched stiff-legged out of overnight buses just that morning, bag lunches in hand. They looked not like the hippie caricature Tim had portrayed but the college students they were, clad in tweed coats and flannel shirts and penny loafers, perhaps a paisley bandanna or a serape carried back from a Peace Corps stint. Like delegations to a mock convention, each group bore aloft its sign—"Princeton Seminary,"

"Ethical Culture School," "Rutgers Newark," "B.U.S.D.S." When Pete Seeger soared into the final harmony of "Wasn't That a Time," his listeners applauded earnestly enough for a hootenanny.

The largest banner of all, stretched taut behind the podium, declared in block letters tall as a hedge, "SUPPORT OUR GI'S . . . BRING THEM HOME NOW!" It was a message at least some of the organizers strained to convey, appreciating the precarious path their movement walked between patriotic dissent and wartime disloyalty. Yet even this rally, notable for its good manners above almost all else, frayed at the edges. From a homemade flagstaff, someone flew the Viet Cong colors. A placard proclaimed, "Avenge Che!" "Johnson Bullshit," offered another. From the stage, one performer led a sing-along that surely would have enraged the MPs languishing in a Pentagon corridor. "It takes a real man to say, 'I won't go,'" she caroled. "It takes a real man to say, 'No.'"

By the time the rally ended and the procession to the Pentagon commenced, the serene surface was blistering with confrontation. Among the protesters themselves, arguments erupted over whether to follow the rather circuitous permitted route or advance more directly, inviting a showdown with the authorities. For the moment, moderation prevailed. A gaggle of counter demonstrators, saying they represented the Polish Freedom Fighters, Inc., brandished their own signs about the "Red Clergy" and "Jewish-Red Anarchy." "You're escaping," one shouted at a medical student. "No," the young man insisted, his voice cracking with nerves, "I will go to Vietnam after I graduate." To which the Pole chortled with a derision rich beyond words.

Meanwhile, Tim remained indoors and ignorant. It was Ramsey Clark and Robert McNamara who monitored the march's progress by radio and closed-circuit television. It was they who decided how to deploy the 10,000 men at their disposal. There were federal marshals, many hardened by duty in Montgomery, Alabama, and Oxford, Mississippi, during the civil rights crusade. There were troops from the Eighty-second Airborne, only months removed from service in the Detroit riot. There were Armored Cavalry and National Guardsmen and federal Park Police. Fifteen judges stood ready in Washington to conduct assembly-line arraignments, and 1,500 vacant jail cells had been reserved. Despite all the manpower and all the judicial machinery, the goal of the Johnson administration that day was to "act in a way which holds to the absolute minimum the possibility of bloodshed and injury [and] minimizes the need for arrest," as a planning memorandum put it. Any other outcome would qualify as a public opinion disaster, something a president already astride a divisive war could ill afford.

Shortly after one-thirty, Tim Carey and his companions in Company A of the 503rd were summoned into action. They marched out a basement door, up a flight of concrete steps, and aligned themselves at the front of a raised plaza overlooking a parking lot, where the march was officially to culminate. The full complement of MPs took the shape of an inverted U, cupping the colonnade of the Pentagon's Mall Entrance. Tim himself held a post in the front rank, the most likely scene of a collision with protesters. Before him ran only two ropes, pitched at the levels of knee and waist, the sort of restraint suited to a movie-house concession stand.

Those ropes formed part of the scheme for avoiding strife. So did the assignment of the 503rd. Dressed more like police than soldiers, they would present less provocation, it was thought. On orders, most had left their rifles inside the Pentagon and their pistols unloaded. The task of making arrests belonged to several hundred federal marshals who were situated twenty yards behind the front line, and were wearing business suits augmented by helmets and billy clubs. If all went well, if all subscribed to plan, their efforts would not be required, for the wall of imperturbable MPs would have convinced any protester to reconsider aggression. Perhaps none of the demonstrators would realize most of the MPs were just teenagers, as light as 135 pounds, and for all their training were virgins to genuine crowd control, much less on the scale of some 35,000.

Beneath his helmet and behind his baton, Tim showed a mask of pure opacity. Look straight ahead, he repeated to himself in the mantra of drills. Don't answer. Talk out of the side of your mouth so only the MP next to you can hear. Inwardly, however, the spectacle filled him with awe. Never had he seen a larger crowd than the several thousand who filled the bleachers when Ossining High played Sleepy Hollow in the annual football rivalry. Even Scott Kessler, a more worldly comrade, shared the sensation. He had spent a few New Year's Eves in Times Square and this throng struck him as something vaster, for there were no skyscrapers to interrupt the bodies.

For the moment, the mood indeed seemed celebratory. Pivoting his eyes across the crowd, Tim spotted people drinking beer and smoking marijuana. Farther down the formation of MPs, where they were carrying rifles, a girl placed daisies in muzzle after muzzle. From an unseen stage drifted the choppy rhythms and nasal harmonies of a rock band called the Fugs. Soon they halted in favor of the modal drone of multitudes chanting "Ommmm" in their attempted exorcism. If it worked as Abbie Hoffman had predicted, then any time now the Pentagon would rise three hundred feet aloft, turn orange, and start spinning. And Tim, eyes obediently forward, would miss the whole thing. He could only think it was true what cynics said about these student protesters: They didn't give a damn about politics, they just wanted an excuse to party.

Then he saw the first can fly toward his position. Tomato soup, he noted as it lay dented on the ground; he had stocked plenty in his days at Shopwell. Another missile soon followed, then a third. Anyone who had bothered to lug a case of canned soup a mile and a half from the Lincoln Memorial to the Pentagon, Tim realized, had arrived with assault in mind. But his training forbade any response. He stood rigid as rocks and soda bottles fell in squalls, as faces pressed so close to his own he could feel the breath that carried temptations and taunts. "You're an asshole. . . . Come on over with us. . . . Do you know what you stand for? . . . Just lay down your gun." Two rows into the crowd, an unsleeved arm rose, clasping a draft card that danced with flame. Another hand lifted another card to it, as casually as bumming a light. Then there were four, six, eight cards afire, mocking the conscripts mere feet away.

All around Tim swirled a cacophony. Demonstrators howled, "Hell no, we won't go." Copters chopped the air. A platoon sergeant shouted from behind, "Don't listen to 'em. Keep your place. Keep your space." Then a captain took up the bullhorn: "A Company, hold your ground. A Company. Nobody comes and nobody goes. Just hold your ground." It sounded as much a plea as an order.

Tim never saw the first surge coming. Years later he could only compare the experience to being at Belmar or Seaside, his favorite places on the Jersey Shore, and getting toppled by an unexpected breaker. "Leave us alone," he ordered fecklessly. "Get back." Protesters by the hundred were shredding the line. Some grabbed MPs by the chin strap, spinning them to the ground. Others yanked at the tear gas grenade secured in each man's utility belt. During the tussles many detonated and began spewing gas. The cloud billowed so thick even Tim lost his vision. He pulled on his mask, found no improvement, then tore it off. Bodies banged. Voices grunted. Marshals and sergeants back-pedaled into the defense called a shrinking perimeter, leaving the forward MPs atomized and adrift in the human tide.

If Tim's life to this point had yielded a single truth, if all the drills had underscored a single tenet, it was to protect your own. Squinting into the banks of gas, tightening his fist around his baton, Tim cared nothing for Vietnam or Lyndon Johnson or the army or the Pentagon. He wanted only to find his comrades, Terry Sunkes and Joe Kelleher and the rest. He swung his club into chests and necks, each stroke of wood against bone sounding like a shattering dish. He attacked anything around him not wearing MP green. True to his training, he never lifted his weapon against any foe's skull. No, it was too easy to break a baton that way.

Only when reinforcements poured from the Pentagon, taking gun butt, nightstick, and combat boot to the protesters, did the battle line push safely in front of Tim. With his position now manned by fresh MPs, he staggered back toward the colonnade. Between gasps of breath he asked if everyone was all right. There was word one of the MPs had been injured, but nobody knew whom or how badly. Terry Sunkes, it turned out, had been knocked down and nearly trampled. Joe Kelleher had pushed Scott Kessler out of the path of a kick in the groin, and then Kessler had battered his attacker to the ground. Contained and incensed, the crowd bellowed in sarcasm, "Hold that line! Hold that line!"

Each side fired by bloodshed, the rage built for ninety more minutes. Then, at five-thirty, as day was resolving into dusk, a glory of auburn and lavender, the offensive was launched. A force of demonstrators, easily beyond a thousand, burst through the single line of MPs at the far edge of the perimeter. Immediately ahead lay a secondary entrance, marked simply "Corridor 7." Tim missed the moment of attack, occurring as it did fifty yards diagonally behind him. By the time he turned, he saw the protesters being driven back by the Sixth Armored Cavalry, 638 strong, which had been waiting in the very hallway breached. Bristling with rifles and bayonets, the unit rolled forward until it restored a defensible front. Then came the medics and the marshals, attending to many of the forty-five injuries and 667 arrests the demonstration would ultimately produce.

By mid-evening, only an encampment of two thousand marchers remained, burning picket signs and barricades for heat. Tim Carey finally repaired to his hallway and his sleeping bag.

Dramatic as the day had been, he shared no war stories with the 503rd. His silence was partly a function of professionalism; even handling a car accident or a bar fight at Fort Bragg, he hated to gossip about duty. More important, what he felt now exceeded anything that could be handily reduced to an anecdote. As he relived the experience of the last eight hours, he focused not so much on the soup cans or the exorcism or the blinding gas as on a single phrase borne on the wind. At one point early in the afternoon, the breeze had swiftly changed direction so that it carried sound especially clearly from the stage. Someone was speaking—the comedian Dick Gregory, Tim would later learn—about just who filled up the army. "Poor blacks," Tim was pretty sure he heard, and "dumb whites."

Maybe, Tim told himself now, those words were what had riled the crowd. Or maybe he was crediting Gregory too much. What had been riled, at least these few hours later, was within Tim. Until today, it had never fully struck him how different he was from those people across the ropes, most of them his own peers. He knew a handful of classmates back in Ossining who had gone to college or gotten married for the deferments or finagled a way into the National Guard to avoid combat. But those had seemed like individual decisions, not the pattern etched by privilege. And for young men like Tim who went into the service, basic training set out to destroy any such distinctions as social class. With his shaved head, olive uniform, and standard-issue glasses, Tim gazed into the latrine mirror some mornings unsure if he was seeing himself or the private behind him in line. Then, at Fort Bragg, only one distinction appeared—between the cops, of whom he was one, and the resentful soldiers they policed.

It took Dick Gregory calling Tim Carey dumb to smarten him up. Hardly anyone in his unit, now that he thought about it, had a college education.

Even the officers corps, without enough degreed men from which to draw, was accepting high school graduates. Tim knew that college had plenty to do with class. The schools in Ossining rarely prepared a Crotonville kid to be anything loftier than a mechanic or clerk. College was for the wealthy of Chilmark and Briarcliff, for the middle class of The Hill. Tim hardly begrudged his contemporaries who took ivied sanctuary while he obediently marched, not when "I shoulda gone to college" was a standard barracks refrain. But he could barely contain the disbelief, the near hatred, that those fortunate sons should attack American soldiers, should attack *him*, for bearing the burden they shirked.

What Tim's viscera told him ultimately found confirmation in the emotionless realm of statistics. Eighty percent of American soldiers in Vietnam hailed from poor and working-class homes, calculates Christian G. Appy in his authoritative 1993 book *Working-Class War*. In profiling the four hundred men from Long Island killed in Vietnam, *Newsday* described the vast majority as having been the children of "blue collar or clerical workers, mailmen, factory workers, building tradesmen, and so on." Harvard's graduating class of 1970, in comparison, contained just two veterans among its nearly 1,200 men. This class schism held just as true for the world immediately around Tim Carey. All four sons in his family served during the Vietnam War, with two of them seeing combat and the eldest, Michael, being severely injured in an ambush. The one hundred households of Crotonville sent twenty-three sons into the armed forces during the Vietnam era, bettering the level of participation for America as a whole. With a population of about 24,000, Ossining lost thirteen young men, giving it a per capita death rate twice the nation's. Across the Croton River, in the more affluent and liberal community of Croton-on-Hudson, not a single boy perished. As Tim's mother, Edith, had shouted at the local draft board in 1972, when her youngest son was called, "You've already got three of mine. Go get one from somebody who hasn't given any."

Years would pass, of course, before Tim or anyone else discovered most of this data. As of October 21, 1967, some 18,000 Americans had died in Vietnam, less than one-third of the ultimate total, and both the war and its opposition were escalating rapidly. Within hours of the Pentagon protest, imitative rallies arose in Tokyo and Paris, Oslo and Berlin. Several days later a priest, Philip Berrigan, poured blood into the files of the Selective Service headquarters in Baltimore. The next month the Students for a Democratic Society sent a delegation to Hanoi. One of its members, Cathy Wilkerson, would ultimately join the Weathermen and plunge into hiding after a homemade bomb exploded in her father's Greenwich Village townhouse. Three of the principal organizers of the Pentagon rally—David Dellinger, Jerry Rubin, and Abbie Hoffman—would sit as defendants in the Chicago Eight trial. Norman Mailer, arrested at the Pentagon, would liken the demonstrators to Civil War heroes in *The Armies of the Night*. The day the Pentagon was stormed, as he saw it, was the day the American left threw off its "damnable mediocre middle," its "sterile heart." His friend Jimmy Breslin, writing the morning after in the *Washington Post*, found less to celebrate. After a rally of "taste and human respect" before the Lincoln Memorial, he argued, some three thousand "troublemakers . . . put a deep gash into the anti-war movement."

And into Tim Carey's psyche, it could be added. For years afterward, large crowds riddled him with fear. He turned down free tickets to football and baseball games. He went mute addressing a high school audience during the 1972 presidential campaign. Seized by cold sweats and nausea, he once retreated from an amusement park in the midst of a date. His nightmares of the Pentagon demonstration ceased only when he trained himself not to dream.

Eventually, he mastered his anxieties sufficiently to undertake an extremely public life. And the message that would animate it was also forged that day and night of October 21, 1967. Tim remembered not the peaceable mass but the abusive and violent fringe, the ones who taunted him, the ones he clubbed, the ones who returned to college dormitories while he returned to Fort Bragg. He had not yet heard the phrase "liberal elite." For the first time, however, he understood the concept and recognized its face.

Francine du Plessix Gray is the author of nine books of fiction and nonfiction, the most recent of which is *At Home with the Marquis de Sade: A Life* (Simon & Schuster, 1998). In January 1973, when asked by the *New York Review of Books* to cover the second inaugural of the thirty-seventh president of the United States, she sent the following report. It was later published in *Adam and Eve and the City* (Simon & Schuster, 1987). Her most recent work is a biography of Simone Weil.

Nixonland

When Richard Nixon walked onto the inaugural stand—it was the first time I had seen him in the flesh and I was only twenty yards away from him, in the second row of the press section—I began to weep. I don't know precisely why. Anger for the lives he had wasted? Fear of the enormity of his power? During my brief outburst a women's page reporter near me was talking into her tape recorder: "Pat in green coat with imperial Russian sable collar, Julie in apricot melton wool with sable collar, Mamie Eisenhower in crimson with matching hat, black gloves, no fur." Below the inaugural stand the U.S. Marine Band's mammoth silver-plated tubas brilliantly reflected the white, red, and gold costumes of the players. Members of the Marine Chorus stood farther down, their bodies pressed angularly against each other's, their young faces turned toward the audience with smiles of cherubic innocence, as in a high-school class picture. Above, in the Corinthian-columned portico erected for the inaugural, stood the President and, at his right, Pat, Mamie, Julie.

"Tricia Cox in pink tweed, blue fox collar and matching muff," the women's page reporter continued, "standing behind her sister and a marine banner."

I followed her observations and, as the wind lifted the purple and yellow tassels of the flag, I observed one of the most curious human beings I had ever seen. A creature so pink and white and vaporous, so serene of pose and tranquil of expression, her fixed smile so sweet and yet so abstract, her bundle of blond ringlets so immobile in the wind, that even metaphors about Meissen porcelain or plastic doll are too hard and real. Standing there in her very pale pink coat, her little hands stuffed into her large silvery muff, Tricia Nixon Cox seemed made of marzipan, her veins flowing with peach milk shake. She brought to mind George Eliot's cornflower-eyed Rosamond Vincy, "a lovely little face set on a fair long neck . . . turning about under the most perfect management of self-contented grace."

Yet Tricia lacked any of the reality of Eliot's heroine, for she seemed to belong to that realm of fantasy which does not allow for any pain or suffering, one in which society will be preserved in a state of impeccable prosperity and repose. And watching this inauguration I realized that Richard Nixon had few weapons more powerful in his arsenal than this rose-hued girl and the two other women at his side: that this pristine family was a central triad in that mythology of well-being which it had been Nixon's genius to create in the midst of national crises, and in the illusion of personal irreproachability which he fashioned through more than six crises of his own.

A mirage of the placid society emanated more powerfully from Tricia than from the other two. Julie's round, swift-eyed face is more mercurial. Pat Nixon's fixed features expressed some ecstasy of decorum rather than the solace of prosperity, and her mirthless smile, set in concrete, resembled not so much her daughter's docility as the grimace of a mortuary mask. Tricia, the most conservative member of the Nixon clan, the one said to resemble her father so strikingly in character, had greeted her parents, when they first came to the newlywed Coxes for dinner, with a table decorated with giant lollipops.

Trivial thoughts often come to mind when politicians offer their platitudes: How do they make love, what do they drink, what cassettes do they listen to? Since the Nixons' aseptic sexlessness seemed part of their sedative effect upon the nation, I glossed swiftly over the first question. But even blander facts were increasingly unavailable, for rigorous privacy was essential to preserve the magic of Nixon's secret politics and surprise tactics, and his palace guard had grown increasingly guarded. ("Does the President wear reading glasses?" "Now and then, but don't quote *me*." "Does the President ever catnap?" "Yes, *but get it from somebody else*.") He had recently boasted, however, that he was the first president in our history who had never missed one day of work through illness, and that he had not even had one headache *in his life*. It had also been revealed that his weight has not changed in twenty years; that he had recently made his austere lunch of RyKrisp and cottage cheese even more Spartan by giving up ketchup; and that his sole sport, since he had given up bowling and golf, consisted of the solitary exercise of running two hundred paces in his bedroom in the same spot.

In his inaugural address, as he pronounced his solipsistic question, "What can you do for yourself?" I reflected upon the newly grandiose nature of his metaphors. He saw himself as having spent "those eight years in the wilderness, the way de Gaulle and Churchill were," before returning to power. In his growing isolation he was identifying himself increasingly with the State, through Walter Mitty metaphors of sports and leadership. "The team goes just as fast as the leader, as the quarterback, and coach, and I am both." "*L'Equipe, c'est Moi*."

He ended his address, of course, by asking us for our prayers, rather than our ideas. As he exited after the benedictions, I saw only one mark of aging upon that changeless, perpetually suntanned sixty-year-old face: the deepening of the nose-to-cheek lines have emphasized those traits of self-denial and discipline that both shaped his ascent to power and enabled him, when young, to drive Pat home after her dates with other men. Self-denial. Is it possible that reality is one of the substances which this elusive man, curled over his sense of destiny, has been until now denying himself? That once the great triumph of his reelection was achieved he would open the door a crack? Trying to maintain certain Quaker principles, I don't want to believe in the irreversibility of evil, therefore in the irreversibility of his monstrous isolation.

Later that day as he watched from a glass booth this most expensive of inauguration pageantries—part of his campaign to free us from dread—he brusquely leaned forward, fascinated by a papier-mâché float of the Spirit of '76, and briefly pressed his strangely shaped nose to the glass, looking upon the outside world as a penniless child looks into a pastry shop. The parade he was observing was pigeon-proofed, Pennsylvania Avenue having been sprayed with a special chemical for the occasion.

AMONG a choice of six sites, I picked the Middle Western States Inaugural Ball at the Pension Building because Guy Lombardo was playing there. Like all the other balls it was an utterly disorderly affair. Running the four-million-dollar inaugural "like a corporate enterprise," Inaugural Committee Chairman and Hot Shoppes tycoon J. Willard Marriott did not produce much joy; nor did the daily visits of analysts from a management consultant firm attempting to co-ordinate the work of four thousand inaugural employees divided into thirty-four committees. Instead of dancing, some five thousand persons stood about in disconsolate clusters waiting for a room to pee in, to check their coats, get their free souvenirs (charms and cuff links emblazoned with the presidential seal), to see the President arrive.

There was a surprisingly large number of black people, of young people, of Democrats for Nixon, and droves of men who claimed that they worked for "the biggest company" of this or that kind in the United States. It was a hard-drinking crowd, who drowned their gripes rather than expressed them; and the bars seemed to have been set up accordingly, with drinks available only in coupon sets of six for nine dollars. This was the first time in ten years that I had been in a crowd of over a thousand people that was not a demonstration or a reform-Democrat fund-raising event, with everyone wearing buttons. I recol-lected with nostalgia the slogans of an era past: Republicans for McCarthy, Free the New York Times 21, Stop the War on November 15, Vacuum Hoover, Free the Berrigans, Save Our Constitution. There was only one motto-wearer in sight: a short-haired collegiate who wore on his lapel, as if in echo of Nixon's inaugural address, the words POWER TO THE INDIVIDUAL. Wayne and Jerry Martin of Bloomington, Illinois, had come to the inaugural with Bert and Katie Butler and their daughter, Bonnie. Old friends from neighboring towns, the Martins were Republicans, the Butlers lifelong Democrats until the 1972 elections. ("We want a negotiated peace, not a surrender, and McGovern was asking for a surrender.") They were fiftyish, effusive, offering to buy me drinks by the six-coupon set, and insisted that their names be printed.

"We've been to Europe an awful lot in the past few years," said Mrs. Martin, in brandy-hued Lurex, "and it's obvious that Americans are so hated over there because we've given them so much, too much. It's the same with welfare. When you give people too much they can't possibly respect you. I loved that part of the President's speech."

"Sure," Mr. Martin said. "If you're a man, you work."

"Of course FDR," former Democrat Mrs. Butler said, "I was a hundred percent behind his policies, his measures were needed because that was a time of crisis, but now we're living in such a stable, prosperous time."

"And what about China?" demanded Mr. Butler, a towering man who said he worked for the largest flat-rate construction industry in the world. "You've got to be a genius to pull that off the way Nixon did."

"Marvelous," said Mrs. Butler, rolling her eyes.

"Wizardly," said Mrs. Martin, holding her glass up in a toast.

"That's why I'm against those friends of mine who're still demonstrating," said Bonnie Butler, a graduate of the University of Illinois who verged on Movement style, no makeup, very long straight hair. "Back in sixty-eight, though I never demonstrated myself, I approved of those of my friends who did; but how can you do it now, Nixon has done too many good things."

"And here they are again demonstrating against the bombing when it brought the enemy back to the table," her father rumbled. "They should be ashamed of themselves."

"You haven't asked us what I like *most* about Nixon," Mrs. Butler reproached me. "What I like the most is the dignity and beauty of his family. So much poise. Have you ever seen anyone with so much poise as Pat and those gorgeous girls? They're just . . . "

"I think that's what every president should have," Mrs. Martin interrupted. "A beautiful family like Nixon."

"That's one thing the Kennedys don't have," Mrs. Butler said, waving her finger at me. "A beautiful family. Or poise."

Guy Lombardo was playing "It seems like old times / Doing the things we used to do / Making the dream come true." I talked to a long-haired student from the University of Michigan who had registered Republican for his first vote because "Nixon was a miracle worker." "Look at China," he said. "Look at the trade deal with the Soviet Union. I'm a government major and I know how important these things are. I'm a little disappointed that he didn't find an earlier solution to end the war, but the bombing must have been necessary. Look, it brought them back to the negotiating table."

Guy Lombardo played "Enjoy Yourself, It's Later Than You Think." I found the only persons who objected to the Christmas bombing, two black women from Chicago, sisters, both lifelong Democrats until '72. "We voted for Nixon because of China though he didn't have anything else to offer—and McGovern had nothing to offer." Guy Lombardo played "Boo-Hoo, I'll Tell My Mom on You."

I talked to a red-eyed businessman from Ohio who described Nixon as a "cle worker" for his China trip, loved the President because "everything he does and says has a dynamic, aggressive aspect," and grew apoplectic at the possibilities of reducing penalties for marijuana. "There are two cultures in this country," he bellowed, "the grass culture and the alcohol culture. I'm from the alcohol culture and I'm proud of it. I'm half-Irish and half-German, two fine strong alcohol cultures, and I have a theory that this grass stuff comes from the ethnic groups very different from mine: the Latin, Jewish, Mediterranean stock you could call them, those people you see sitting around Horn and Hardart's drinking coffee, like Bella Abzug, those are the ones who like pot with their coffee."

The alcohol lobbyist loved all the inaugural proceedings. He hoped they would occur every few months, every few weeks:

"Nixon is good at pageantry, that's what America needs more of. Pageantry is an affirmation of our American heritage. It stresses the good, positive, old-fashioned American values at a time when everyone is knocking them and being so negative. Look at England, the changing of the guard every day. We need more of that. . . . "

In stentorian loudspeaker tones, a voice booming from everywhere and nowhere: "Ladies and gentlemen, the President of the United States!" Guy Lombardo strikes up "Hail to the Chief." The Family comes in to ecstatic applause, dressed in the colors of the American flag. Pat in beaded blue. Julie in beaded white. Tricia in shimmering red satin with matching boa, behind which she teasingly hides half of her sweetly smiling face. The President's stance of pockets in hand, his swooping nose, his newfound ease with fun and jokes suddenly remind me of Bob Hope. He tries to make this part of the country, the Middle West, feel more special, more dearly loved than any other region. "I have a special affection for the Middle West. . . . It's always been called the heartland of America and it's led the way, because since the last election the whole nation is the heartland. . . . " (Cheers and roars.) "And of course as you know my dad came from Ohio. . . . " (More cheers.) "And another reason why this is my favorite ball of all, it's the one where my favorite bandleader, Guy Lombardo, is playing!"

Arms outstretched and fingers in the V sign to express boundless admiration. One arm falls heavily on Lombardo's shoulder.

"You know, I remember way back in the forties when Pat, my wife, and I used to go to New York City. That's before I was a household word. . . . " (Laughter.) "We always used to go and hear Guy Lombardo and his Royal

Canadians because even if you were poor he made you feel so good. Why, he's the best bandleader ever. Hey, Guy, if you make more money you'll give me a cut, won't you. . . . " (Big laugh, started by Nixon.) "And now, I'd like to show you how much I love Guy's music by dancing to it. . . . Guy, give me a four beat, will you?"

"I'll Be Loving You, Always," the band softly strikes up. Dick and Pat dance limply to the tune, not quite cheek to cheek, their smiles fixed. In the last reel of the movie *Millhouse*, Nixon stands by Guy Lombardo at the 1969 Inaugural Ball recollecting the end of World War II. "When VJ day came . . . I remember Pat and I . . . saved up our money and went to the Roosevelt Hotel and we danced to the music of Guy Lombardo . . . and I just hope that we are dancing to his music when we end the next war."

The night before the 1973 Inaugural Ball he had said to a crowd at the Kennedy Center, "Well, I've got great news for you. This year, 1973, Bob Hope is going to spend Christmas at home." The same evening the crowd cheered when the Pat Boone family sang "a personal pledge of allegiance to Jesus," and when Roger Williams played "Autumn Leaves," "The Impossible Dream," "I'm Forever Blowing Bubbles." In the privacy of his own automobile, so cassette dealers relate, Richard Nixon listens to more Pat Boone, more Guy Lombardo, and particularly to Lawrence Welk, whose best known hits include "Ain't She Sweet," "I Want To Be Happy," "I'm Always Chasing Rainbows," "Nearer, My God, to Thee," "Bibbidi-Bobbodi-Boo." Nostalgia for old-time religion and for the quiet Eisenhower fifties. Let's forget the sixties: foreign songs, hundreds of thousands of draft resisters underground, an equal number exiled in Canada, fifty-six thousand dead, twenty-five million living under the poverty level, jailed priests, crumbling ghettos, rising crime, drugged veterans, drugged army, drugged kids, troubles. Pack up your troubles in your old kit bag and smile, smile, smile. Bibbidi-Bobbodi-Boo. Is this inaugural a salute to a vanishing America, or is it the *real* America? Who can say?

Back in my hotel room, I read with fascination the names of the Inaugural Committee's VIPs who dominate Washington's social scene throughout the week: Billy Graham cochairs the Symphonic Concert Committee with heavy campaign contributor W. Clement Stone, Chicago insurance tycoon and activist of fundamentalist religion (in 1969, Stone voted to elect Nixon "Churchman of the Year"). Charlton Heston cochairs the Inaugural Concert Committee with Pam Powell, daughter of Dick Powell and June Allyson, Redskins Coach George Allen is a cochairman of the Parade Committee. Mrs. Vince Lombardi is cochairman of the Inaugural Ball Committee. Hamburger tycoon Anthony McDonald, Jr., one of Nixon's largest campaign contributors, is director of Advertising and Promotion. One is struck by the almost total absence of the old guard East Coast Republican establishment. Not an Aldrich, a Dillon, a Lodge in sight at the festivities. These are post–World War II fortunes, many of them from the South and Southwest, heavy in oil; heavy too on sports, old Hollywood, resort hotels, hamburger stands, the stuff our dreams were made of.

Gathered from the *Washington Post*'s society column: W. Clement Stone, who contributed two million dollars to the campaign, is taking riding lessons in hopes that he will be made ambassador to England. The new D.C. inseparables are Spiro Agnew and Frank Sinatra, who is looking for a house in D.C. to live near Spiro. At their frequent dinners together, Frankie sits down at the piano to croon for Spiro: "This Greek, Unique." Nixon does not have Sinatra on records or cassettes. Evans and Novak have observed that the White House's coolness toward Agnew is based in part on Agnew's friendship with Sinatra, whose life style is clearly too racy for our Spartan President. Witness the grimly abstemious palace guard, led by Haldeman and Ehrlichman, heavily Mormon and Christian Scientist, men who will remain as blameless in their private lives as they grow increasingly ruthless in their hiring and firing.

For Nixon's strength is in part based on that very pristine irreproachability of family style that so reassures Mrs. Martin and Mrs. Butler, that softens the edges of any scandals he may have been associated with. Pat and Julie and Tricia are his continuous Checkers speech, veiling the contradictions and crises of his career. "What can I do for myself?" has been a much maligned phrase, the only honest moment of his inaugural address. Avoiding the "unifying" platitudes or Wilsonian idealisms of 1969, it was the most fitting of mottoes for the shady entrepreneurs and real-estate wheeler-dealers who slinked in and out of Nixon's past and present, the backers of the Cuban refugees who would surface in the Watergate break-in. It was an ideal slogan for the secret slush funds, the Hughes loan of 1960, the ITT dealings, the wheat, milt corn, and other scandals which lay beneath the veneer of his fairy-tale family life and whose closely concealed tracks history may at some future date reveal.

But beyond its unintended candor, was that phrase any more dangerous than the jingoism of John Kennedy's upon which it so bitterly played? "Ask what you can do for your country" now evoked the horrors of reckless patriotism. "Ask what you can do for yourself" simply stated the loneliness of the huckster, an apolitical, metaphysical solitude. At the end of a decade bloodied by the most misguided patriotism in memory, in the middle of an administration marked by the greatest corruption we have known, which seemed worse?

SOME twelve thousand persons attended the first of the inaugural activities, a reception for the Agnews at the Smithsonian Institution. The theme of the party—as of all the inaugural events—was The Spirit of '76. Hostesses dressed like Williamsburg belles, pioneer women, and Indian squaws passed around food meant to emulate ancient American values and Republican symbols: Indian pudding, spoon bread, sugar cookies in the shape of elephants. The patience of the guests, as they waited in line for two or three hours to shake the Vice-President's hand, recalled ancient pilgrimages where crowds stood for hours to kiss some precious relic: a fragment of a sandal, of a toenail. Only once did they swerve from the worshiping line to mob the Nixon women during their brief appearance. I retain from that day an image of Tricia swathed in boa feathers, that mysterious smile of abstract innocence fixed on her face as by a spray gun, her palms spread apart as if about to clap, like one of those dolls that one cranks up with a key, from the back, to dance under a little glass dome.

Shortly thereafter Greyhound buses arrived by the hundreds to load the visitors for the next inaugural event—a Salute to the States at Kennedy Center featuring Bob Hope, Lawrence Welk, and the Pat Boone family. Thousands of Americans burst out of the Smithsonian holding plastic glasses stamped with the blue presidential seal. They had ripped them off by the dozens, relics to carry back to Michigan, Texas, Ohio. Sitting alone on the bus in the middle of the boisterous, roaring crowd, I was joined by a sober and sad-eyed California businessman who told me he had never received his tickets to any of the inaugural events although he had sent his money months earlier. He had to pay for them a second time—a matter of several hundred dollars—yet he accepted this fate with placid submission. "The lady at the inaugural office told me that they wouldn't know until early November who was going to win the election," he explained. "That's why they're so disorganized." He expressed a similar attitude when we discussed the recent Christmas bombings, whether they had harmed the President's prestige. "Ah, those people have been bombed for twenty-five years," he said, "first by the French and then by us. What do three months more or less matter?"

The week of the inaugural I had lectured at Amherst College, where over one third of the faculty and the student body had been arrested some months before, in protest against the Vietnam War. Sitting with students afterward, I understood that many of them were feeling, with varying degrees of candor, a strong sense of disorientation about the supposed ending of the war. "First of all most of us don't believe it can end," one student said. "It's been with us for ten years, ever since we can remember." Others expressed not so much their disbelief in the reality of the peace as their fear that a ceasefire would deprive them of the one unifying focus of "the Movement," as if the constant dying of Americans were necessary to keep us whole, as if this cancer were necessary to remind us that we were ill. Now more than ever, it was those most opposed to the war who seemed most terrified by the fairyland of well-being, the mirage of peace that Nixon would attempt to conjure up in his second term. "What's going to keep us together when our side of the war ends," one student exclaimed, "when we have lost the majesty and horror of it?"

Walter Guzzardi has been a foreign service officer, a foreign correspondent for *Time* and *Fortune*, and an assistant managing editor of *Fortune* in New York. He has written several books, and now works as a freelance editor and author. This article comes from *Fortune*, February 1965, when consulting was largely a male occupation.

Consultants: The Men Who Came to Dinner

Consulting firms can render a real service to management. But the best service of all is the one they render to themselves.

One of the most curious industries flourishing in this problem-ridden business age is an industry that specializes in solutions. Capitalizing on the deepening complexity of managerial affairs, the management consultants have moved into the most intimate compartments of business life. As their legion of clients can testify, consultants can often perform useful functions for management—and sometimes they can overreach themselves and finish up in bafflement or failure. But the consultants have been clearly and indisputably successful in creating for themselves a shining world that would awe most clients if they could peer into it. At its best, it is a world of small capital investment and little risk, a world of high profitability, a world free of carping stockholders and decorated with the lovely landscape of an apparently limitless market—a world, in short, where every prospect pleases. To prosper in that world of opportunity the consultant needs some extraordinary capabilities: an understanding of the harassing environment and the psychology of executives, and some knowledge of how to lighten the executive burden in any of a number of business areas.

Let us assume the case of a top corporate executive struggling with a thousand complexities: the mysteries of the computer age, an entry into the Common Market, the intricacies of the new tax law. He is faced with a spate of decisions on matters whose details he cannot possibly know. He does not completely trust either his intuition or his colleagues—one highly fallible, the other probably partial. To cope with his sharded world, he will use any available help that can ease the strain and the loneliness, and can enable him to prove to the boss or the board, if that should be necessary, that he did everything a prudent man could have done. The closest help, the noncompetitive help that can save him time without threatening his sense of security, is proffered by the management consultant, who, as he unfailingly says, "has no ax to grind."

In our instance, the executive's company has a good record of earnings, but he is troubled, let us say, by the loss of some competent young executives from one division. Unsatisfied by the explanation from within the ranks, he calls in a consulting firm of renown to have a look. A senior member of the firm responds, and, in a brief and intelligent preliminary analysis, recommends an executive-compensation study. The executive has entered what more professorial consultants call "the diagnostic phase."

Impressed with the analysis, and with the demeanor and experience of the senior consultant, the executive agrees to the study. The senior partner is seen very little around the company after that, and the youth of the consultants who actually do the work lifts a few company eyebrows, but the study turns out to be very competent. The executive himself could never have taken the time to be half so thorough. The study satisfactorily explains the resignations, and recommends an overhaul of the divisional salary structure. The recommendation is successfully acted upon. The executive has come swimmingly through the therapeutic phase. He stands solidly on the promontory of a solution.

Then a beckon catches his eye. The senior consultant is standing on high ground up ahead, waving. He has found another problem—indeed, in a sense he has created one. His compensation work at the divisional level has thrown the top echelon out of kilter. He would not be doing his duty if he did not point out to the executive that, unless an entire organization study is made, serious imbalances in the compensation structure may result. "This is a fascinating point in the proceedings," says one former consultant. "The consultant has lots of personal charm. The good ones can really weave a spell."

Of course the executive recognizes this as a bid for new business. He may be moved to cite his company's earnings record to prove that his present organization is quite effective. But that divisional change did create a new situation and—well, hasn't he always had a few nagging doubts anyway? As he is certain to be told, times of high profitability are the very times when reorganizations should be carried out. Otherwise, things may not be so good next year. ("Better call in a consultant if business is fabulous!" adjures one management magazine. "If your earnings are far above your expectations and the reason for this is not completely accounted for, you may be headed for trouble.") The executive agrees that the compensation study was successful . . . something useful may come out of this too . . . the board may like to hear that he is taking a fresh look at things. . . . The second study is soon begun.

No part of that account constitutes a denial that general consulting firms can meet and satisfy some of the needs of management. The second consulting study may be just as useful as the first. It may save the company many times its cost. But one thing is certain—consultants can stay around companies for a long, long time.

The Client Is the Giant

The consulting industry points with pride to its recent growth and substantial present stature. Excluding the economics professors and miscellaneous experts who consult in their spare time, as well as those for whom the term consultant is a handy euphemism—a man between jobs, an executive pushed aside—there are 2,500 consulting firms in the U.S. Their vast inventory of services falls into two categories: "the general management consulting services," which cover every management function, and the technical and scientific services. In his general consulting work, the consultant stands ready to carry out organization, marketing, and executive recruitment studies; to recommend to executives how to merge with a new company, or how to reorganize an old one; how to market Pablum in Nigeria or life insurance in Atlanta; and how much to pay old Joe—as well as to explain why old Joe fell down on the job, to bear the onus for firing him, and to locate his replacement.

In many ways the future for consulting looks just as bright as the past. The consultant describes himself as "a problem solver," and in the words of Charles Bowen of Booz, Allen & Hamilton, largest of the consulting companies, "executives are surrounded by a sea of problems. Everybody has problems." Thus consultants have a broad sky to work under. No serious problem can be left unsolved for long, but even solutions bring new problems in their wake. For example, once a company has made an acquisition—thus "solving the acquisition problem," which, by the way, consultants offer to assist in—it can start to work on the newly hatched problems of how to manage the new property, how to staff it, and how to improve its product line. By the time all that is done the parent itself will probably need reorganization—another problem-spawning process. Thus in an endless uncoiling, old problems die and new ones are born. No consultant, therefore, ever worries over the size of the market. "It is simply not a limiting factor," says E. Everett Smith of McKinsey & Co., Inc. The costs and profit levels of consulting firms can be just as appealing as their market. Consulting companies need no large capital investment to start up or to carry on their trade; their significant costs are staff compensation and rent. And well-run, rapidly growing consulting firms like McKinsey have an effective way of ensuring that sales outrun these costs. They keep prosperous by bringing in young staff members who are well paid, but are cheap when related to the price they can be billed out for. The greatest spread between billings and salary comes when such young men are doing the pick-and-shovel consulting work. McKinsey adopts a tough "up or out" policy with its junior members: by the time a man is forty or before, he must be established as a good analyst and, more important, as a good business getter. If he isn't, he usually leaves. Thus the firm maintains its profitability by adding about 15 percent to its staff—with some companies it may be as high as 20 percent—every year at the bottom of the pyramid, and slicing people off along the sides as it goes along.

Consultants also luxuriate in a marvel known as "negative variable costs." When a consulting firm's staff is underemployed—i.e., when it is largely engaged in looking for clients—the firm must pay for the travel and per diem expenses of many of its people. But as the staff approaches full employment, more and more of such costs can be charged to the client. At the moment of full employment, virtually all such costs to the firm, which may then amount to 15 or 20 percent of its gross volume, disappear. So as consultants make more they spend less—which is a phenomenon that adds considerable incentive to their work.

But their compensation is sufficient incentive by itself. With sales going well, after basic costs and salaries are paid, consultants are left with a pool of money that may run as high as 40 percent of gross revenues. Most firms divide up this pool into bonuses and profit-sharing pension plans for the firm's officers and employees. The fraction that is not so divided becomes what one consultant calls "the nut"—the firm's cushion against evil days. Most of the larger consulting firms are incorporated, and since they seek to pay out as little as possible in corporate taxes, they do not habitually squirrel away a very large nut. After all, there hasn't been a really hard winter yet. As a consequence, senior members of the big firms take home huge amounts of money.

When company executives face senior consultants, they appreciate that they are looking at men whose earnings can match theirs stride for stride, or even forge ahead a little. In that thin atmosphere one does not haggle.

Consultants like to say that they take high risks to match their high profitability. They cite as evidence the fact that even a strong consulting firm could not live very long without getting new business. But the point is not conclusive. For one thing, by reducing the compensation of senior members during the season of feast, the consultants could accumulate assets that would enable them to survive a season of famine. Further, in hard times—an eventuality that postulates a market far different from the one now existing—consultants could reduce costs by ridding themselves of the people whom McKinsey's Everett Smith describes as "not self-supporting"—that is, the ones who do not bring in enough new business.

Taps for the One-Man Band

For some consultants, to be sure, life is not all wine and roses.

The big, balanced companies have enough clients to get a steady income from routine kinds of consulting, like market studies, and to avoid dependence on a specialty that may become obsolete or on a client who may become bored. They can vary their services to meet the changing needs and fashions of management—"we can keep our armor bright," as one of them says.

Failure to travel this new organizational road, however, can have mortal consequences. The firm of Robert Heller Associates, Inc., was one of the largest in the industry a few years ago. But the firm's reins were too tightly held by one man, and the process of transfusion and slough off was interrupted. Men who could not move up began to leave. Heller swiftly rushed to the brink. The firm has now undergone a complete corporate overhaul; however, it is not yet restored to its former size and position.

Shrugging off the charges of the traditional houses that accountants are "second-class citizens" unable to bring objectivity to client problems, firms like Arthur Andersen & Co. and Ernst & Ernst are plunging ahead with general consulting work, and they can show just as impressive a list of satisfied clients as anyone else in the business. One strong bank entry in the field has recently been made by Boston Safe Deposit & Trust Co., which has a new and lively consulting division under experienced leadership.

The battle for new clients takes some odd turns. Consultants do not wage the battle by cutting prices: with the more difficult kind of consulting assignment, no two jobs will turn out to be identical, and therefore no precise price comparison is possible. And where accurate estimates of the length of time the job will take can be made in advance, fees of the various firms are likely to be roughly the same. The bulk of the competitive effort comes with the public activities of the consulting firm—the lunches and dinners, for example, at which a consultant talks about some aspect of the management problem, and after which some genteel buttonholing and card dropping takes place. Executive seminars, articles in business reviews, lectures at the business schools— these constitute a kind of intellectual gymnasium where consultants do backflips and daredevil stunts to attract new customers.

Sick Men Need Not Apply

Curiously enough, however, only certain kinds of clients are hospitably received. While consultants love clients, they do not love them all equally. The old adage that consultants specialize in sick companies is so far from the truth that today a company really on the skids might have difficulty finding a reputable consulting firm to take its case. Like the doctor who recently refused to treat a man bleeding of a gunshot wound, management consultants dislike death on the premises—it can be messy, and people may draw conclusions that could be bad for business. Big consultants may also reject applicants whose business is so limited that only one study is likely to be done for them: "We don't like to tie up our people in a dead end like that," one consultant admits.

First place in the consultant's heart is reserved for the prosperous client who may have a laggard division or two, but whose over-all health is excellent. "Our best work is done for the best managements," remarks McKinsey's Everett Smith, and Booz, Allen's Bowen says, "Most of our clients are companies that are doing well—but would like to do better." Even the busiest consulting company burns for the business of an I.B.M. or a DuPont, not so much for the fee that comes from the first piece of work but for the dazzling prospect, as one consultant says, "of rolling from study to study once we get in." For clients with that kind of potential, the consultant will really exert himself on the first study. "We used several partners on our first study for General Foods in 1951," recalls a man from McKinsey. "We made an all-out effort because we knew there were other things in the company that also needed doing." McKinsey has done fifty studies for General Foods since that time.

Much reluctance exists on the part of both consultant and client to discuss case histories. But even those who are sharpest in criticism of the consultant's sales technique do not deny that the consultant can often satisfy his client by doing for him what he cannot do for himself, or could do only at greater cost. McKinsey's long study of the three big dry-grocery divisions of General Foods ended with the recommendation that, in order to adjust the company better to the changing realities in the food business, sales and managerial responsibilities at local levels should be separated. Soon after acting on the advice, General Foods was able to identify savings that far outran McKinsey's fee for service. And General Foods, which has made careful reviews of results since the changes, is convinced, according to its executive vice president, Arthur Larkin, that "our use of manpower is better, and our customers tell us we are doing a better job with their accounts."

"These easy-to-measure benefits serve to head off the client-consultant fatigue that sometimes sets in on long studies," says McKinsey's Richard Neuschel. In a case that cut across more than one management area, William Roberts, now chief executive at Ampex Corp., recalls that when he was executive vice president of Bell & Howell Co. "both the president and I had been in marketing, and we thought that part of the company was going best. We were very much surprised to learn from an Arthur D. Little, Inc., study that where we thought we were particularly strong we were weak. We had allowed the company to get somewhat out of balance."

Perhaps the most indisputable demonstration of consultants' usefulness can be found in the performance of the specialized firms that cater to one industry or specialize in one kind of operation. Kurt Salmon Associates, Inc., a special consultant to the textile trade, has served Salant & Salant, Inc., a textile company with about $55 million in sales for over thirty years—for the eloquently simple reason that, according to the company's executive vice president, Joseph Lipshie, "Salmon saves me money. I look on his work as a piece of equipment, figuring out how much it will cost, how I will amortize it."

THE SEQUEL CAN BE SAD

But all the sequels to consulting are not happy. From the very successful, the spectrum of results can range through the indeterminate, past the band of mediocrity, to positive failures and even to disasters. Much of the controversy about consultants swirls around organization studies, where nothing can be tested and nothing proved, for there is no norm they can be compared to. A few years ago McKinsey did such a study when American Metal and Climax Molybdenum merged. McKinsey's organization plan was adopted, some of its provisions are still in effect. The client paid the fee and made no complaints. But some company people—and, according to one insider, "not just the ones who were hurt"—dissented from McKinsey's proposals. There is no way to prove whether another plan or another consulting firm would have worked better, or even whether the executives of the merging companies could not have done better by themselves. A great many consulting adventures end up in a similar limbo.

Sometimes the company's external problem is so intractable that it will not yield, no matter how hard a consultant shoves. The H. J. Heinz Co. called in a consultant when Heinz was losing its position in the domestic baby-food market to Gerber Products Co. With the consultant's assistance, Heinz hired some people away from Procter & Gamble, a king of the merchandising companies, but still Gerber could not be dislodged. Says one witness to the events: "When a good company has a real franchise in consumer goods, you can't knock them off until they make several mistakes"—something that Gerber has steadfastly refused to do. Other companies have employed consultants without learning very much. American Machine & Foundry paid nearly $100,000 in consulting fees for a study to determine where and how in AMF's heterogeneous organization computer systems should be used. But the consultant's recommendations were disappointingly prosaic. "It cost us a good deal to teach these people about our problem," says an AMF executive. "We were hoping they would come up with a more sophisticated recommendation than the one we got. They did not provide any original wisdom."

In one period before it was finally acquired by Ford Motor Co., Philco Corp. had consultants silting the company with advice. Philco hired Arthur D. Little to study and propose realignment of the company's creaking corporate structure at a time when the company's condition was already critical. A man who was close to the Philco situation says, "If you took A.D.L.'s solution of Philco's problems and submitted it to the Harvard Business School, it would have got a B+ or an A. But in the appliance business it just wouldn't work. Some of their concepts were brilliant, but A.D.L. got over their depth in this kind of merchandising." But all the blame cannot be laid at the door of the consultant. One witness to the events says: "When management consultants have to be called in to tell the management how to stop losing money—this is a confession of the management's ineptitude."

Sometimes the relationship between consultant and client can become almost morbid. For a decade a consulting company has been mapping out reorganizations, doing product and market studies, and sitting close to the principal officers of a big industrial corporation. That corporation now has a good chief executive and a fine earnings and growth record. In the symbiotic nature of their relationship, consultants and company executives might say, lies its justification. Yet the situation has its repellent aspects. Stockholders are largely unaware of the role the consultant has played in company affairs. How much the company might have saved by buying its managers, instead of renting them for so long, is another point that might be examined. And the way to free the company of consultants is to develop managers that someday will need consultants less, and this is not being done.

The consulting industry also faces some thorny ethical problems. Most consultants serve several clients that are in competition with one another, and thus they occupy a position of trust roughly similar to that held by accountants and lawyers.

By the very nature of the business, consultants who serve competitors are forced to play the role of both poacher and gamekeeper. The consultant wants to protect the clients he already has. Yet, for his own personal earnings as well as for the firm, he also wants to bag new ones. No matter how ethical a consultant may be, it would be asking superhuman moral strength to expect him to stress in conversations with a new client that he has lots of information about the client's industry, but unfortunately won't be able to reveal it. He must emphasize his own expertise. But of course, unethical firms may go a lot further than that, since consultants are as susceptible as anyone else to devilish enticements.

THE CULTURE OF THE SECOND COMING

Management consultants, like other special cadres, have created a distinctive culture of their own. That culture can produce work of the highest quality for truly professional reasons. But unfortunately it also has its priggish side. To hear some consultants tell it, their appearance on the scene ranks with the Second Coming. Some of them affect a kind of mock humility.

Within their own group, management consultants are not perpetually engaged in the dispensation of the milk of human kindness. There are plenty of irritants. "It's an exhausting job," one working-level consultant says. "You work like crazy with the firm's partner A on the problems of company B. You finally finish up on Sunday night, worn out, wrung dry, and flung up on the beach. In you go Monday morning, and there you are with partner C and company D, and the first partner and the first company couldn't give a damn if they ever see you again. You're never established, you're never a hero, you're never any better than your next job. That makes us a scratchy, brooding bunch."

One subject of considerable brooding is the departed consultant who left the firm to start his own consulting outfit, more likely than not taking a couple of good clients with him. "As soon as he leaves, the blackening process begins," one man says. "'He really wasn't much good, as a matter of fact we fired him,' that kind of thing." Another recalls with amusement that after he left McKinsey & Co., "They started to tell people that I was a nice guy but that I just couldn't think."

The personal experience of a transplanted consultant is often disillusioning. As one employer of them says, "They lose their ability to range freely around the company and to get information freely. They also lose that confidential relationship and easy access to the top. After a while they don't look so good any more." The senior citizens of consulting do not often enter other businesses, because they make too much money where they are. But a few have tried it. The late Mark Cresap of Cresap, McCormick had a terrible struggle as president of Westinghouse Electric. And John Burns left Booz, Allen to become president of R.C.A., departing after a few years with obvious disappointment on both sides.

ECHOES FROM THE OTHER WORLD

To the omnipresence, elan, and prosperity of the big consulting firm, the business community has reacted in varying ways. The companies that have had the best experience with consultants find the omnipresence bearable, and the fees not excessive, in view of the savings consultants can effect. (This attitude on the part of management has led some consultants to consider whether they should base their fees on the amount of money they saved for the client.) "We have no feeling about the consultants' profits," says Arthur Larkin of General Foods Corp., which has been conspicuously successful in its undertakings with McKinsey. "Whether it's profitable for G.F. to use them— that's our interest."

Some managers are more skeptical. "When you do business with these guys," one company president comments, "you pay a high price for skills purchasable on the open market for much less." Top consultants cannot give much time to any single client's problem; it just isn't economical for them to do so. "If you buy a General Motors car," says one company vice president, "you're pretty sure you're going to get a good car. But if you go to a big consulting firm, you're not buying Booz, Allen, you're buying a guy who comes in and sits down with your people. Booz, Allen has quality-control problems just like you do. You may end up running a turkey farm."

To get the benefits of consulting without some of its concurrent dangers, some big companies have set up their own intramural consulting divisions. General Electric Co. is putting great emphasis on its internal consulting services, which it believes bring G.E. better consulting work at an annual cost, according to one executive, "no greater than we would pay for one or two big outside projects." Consulting firms say these internal consultants cannot take an objective view, because they have to please their bosses; company men reply that outside consultants also have to please the man who hired them. "Even outside consultants can't spit on the flag," one consultant admits. "I would postulate," one chief executive says, "that the broader the consulting effort, the less effective the result." Another adds: "If you know what you want, you can get it. It's like programming a computer—garbage in, garbage out."

Looking ahead, it seems unlikely that the business community will ever free itself from the coils of the management consultants. Even companies that are burned a time or two have to come back. I.B.M. is said to have been advised by a consultant some years ago not to acquire Xerox; it smarted even more when John Burns of Booz, Allen went to work for R.C.A. after having had an intimate association with I.B.M.'s computer work; and today I.B.M. finds many consultants do not suggest I.B.M. equipment because they feel obligated to make a more original recommendation than one to which the client can reply, "That I could have thought of myself!" But despite those grievances I.B.M. recently has had McKinsey doing a compensation study; it has employed Booz, Allen to work in its typewriter division; and it has engaged smaller firms for programming and other technical work.

Not even General Motors is exempt. One man tells the story of how, seated next to Frederic Donner at dinner, he identified himself as a management consultant. Donner promptly announced that G.M. never used consultants. "I told him that as a matter of fact we were doing some work in a G.M. division at that very moment," the consultant recalls. Donner wanted to know which division. But the consultant, with an eye to the tradition of the industry, protected his client's confidence: "I just laughed—and wouldn't tell him."

Jeremy Treglown has served as editor of the *Times Literary Supplement* and is now Professor of English at the University of Warwick, England, where he has founded and chairs a program in writing. This piece is excerpted from a review he wrote for the *New Yorker*, December 18, 1995.

Class Act

Anthony Powell gave the English language a word it needed: Widmerpool—for anyone indefensibly egotistical, farcically ambitious, and unforgivably successful. The name became a byword even among people who had never read Powell's books. A fan tells a story of meeting the novelist on a train and describing his plan for a party to which "everyone would bring his Widmerpool candidate as his guest." Powell got out at the next station, muttering "Widmerpool, Widmerpool, I know now how Frankenstein must have felt."

Kenneth Widmerpool is one of the main characters in *A Dance to the Music of Time*, Powell's comi-tragic diagnosis of English upper-middle-class life from the First World War through the sixties. The twelve-novel sequence, which was completed twenty years ago and has been reissued by the University of Chicago Press in four handsome paperback volumes, follows the ebb and flow (more ebb than flow) of the mid-century bohemocracy as seen through the eyes of one of its members, the self-effacing but sharply observant Nicholas Jenkins. Jenkins's career takes him from Eton and Oxford via the London literary and movie worlds to military service in the Second World War, after which he retreats into a more secluded life of writing and reading. Meanwhile, his despised old school friend Widmerpool rises irresistibly in politics. Between these tides bob artists, activists, drones, and wreckers—people whom we get to know not only as acquaintances but as elements in a loose kind of psychological taxonomy that Philip Larkin compared to Ben Jonson's "humours."

If this sounds like fictional gossip, so it very enjoyably but only partly is. The biographer Hilary Spurling produced a guidebook to the *Dance* sequence which includes full curricula vitae of more than three hundred characters. They have stood up well—the alcoholic charmer Charles Stringham, for example, or his niece Pamela Flitton, sick in the church font as a child bridesmaid, and a havoc-wreaker in most of the marriages she encounters ever after. Widmerpool himself becomes Pamela's husband, and suffers at her hands some of the many humiliations to which *Dance* subjects him.

So the novels are at one level a high-class, upper-class comic soap. They are also a satirical elegy for an era marked by the Second World War, about which

Powell's historical sense is at its clearest and his social sympathies are broadest. But what's less often said is that *Dance* is a quietly audacious experiment. It is a neo-neoclassical novel—an intricate network of allusions to a part-mythological past that is shown, not always comfortably, as endlessly recurrent. To the most admiring members of its original audience, *Dance* seemed like Proust reconceived by P. G. Wodehouse, or like the work of a modern Thackeray. Critics as diverse as Clive James, Alison Lurie, and V. S. Pritchett acclaimed it as one of the subtlest and funniest achievements in postwar British fiction. Philip Larkin had reservations but praised the way *Dance* contrived "pleasures of accumulation . . . effects that depend on the reader's observation and intelligence," and also "sudden uproarious jokes"—such as a cocktail called Death Comes for the Archbishop.

Larkin's doubts were about depth: he thought the characters didn't suffer enough (although *Dance* has its quota of suicides, dead babies, broken relationships, and unfulfilled talents). Another kind of objection—one that is heard more often—is about snobbery. In a 1975 review of the final volume, Auberon Waugh, son of Powell's contemporary and onetime close friend Evelyn, described Powell as "an odious poseur, a ponderous and conceited public school show-off whose ludicrous one-man act can appeal only to the socially and intellectually insecure." The novels, far from being "some sort of Bayeux Tapestry of our times," reminded Waugh of "one of those marvellously ingenious things done with pins and a cotton-reel which used to be called French Knitting. . . . Those who had enough wool and enough patience could make miles and miles of delicately variegated colours in a long worm which could later be trained into table mats, egg baskets and even tea cosies."

"Public school show-off" seems a strange gibe coming from this Tory-anarchist quarter. Private quarrels may have heightened the animosity: in Powell's long career as a reviewer, he had tough things to say about the Waughs. But similar abrasions have been inflicted on his most recent book—*Journals, 1982–1986*, an undeniably feeble account of visits to doctor and dentist, its cantankerousness only occasionally lifted by a gift of claret, a literary prize, or an unexpected genealogical link. At Powell's age (ninety) there is perhaps no reason for his diaries to contain anything more. No reason, either, though, for anyone to want to read them. And among the main objections raised against the *Journals* is the one levelled by Waugh against the rest of his work: that it is obsessed with class.

So, of course, was the world that Powell describes. And part of the point of *A Dance to the Music of Time* lies in its defense of hierarchies. Among the classy things valued in the book are high art and literature. The title itself is taken from Poussin's painting of that name in the Wallace Collection, the most unchanging of London's major galleries. Powell describes the allegory in his opening pages: "Human beings, facing outward like the Seasons, moving hand in hand in intricate measure: stepping slowly, methodically, sometimes a trifle awkwardly . . . unable to control the melody, unable, perhaps, to control the steps of the dance."

The novels' "pleasures of accumulation" are also pleasures of reflection and imagination. Their readers grow used to moving around at their own pace, as if they were in a portrait gallery, noticing where a similar motif occurred before, or stopping to look something up in the guidebook. As one of the characters argues, good writers "don't suddenly steal an indispensable secret that gives complete mastery of the situation, but accumulate a lot of relatively humdrum facts, which when collated provide the picture." But, while Powell has never disguised the amount of toil that has gone into his fiction, he makes few claims for it. To him (and like him), Jenkins is simply the kind of person, rarer now than when the sequence began, who was brought up to think it rude to talk about himself and whose judgments have been formed by the shrewd, minute observation of externals. Besides uniquely communicating a crucial aspect of a certain kind of Englishness, this reverses the cardinal modern Western assumption (including that of Proust) that the inner life is all-important.

Powell regards self-examination as a gross form of post-Freudian, late-Romantic narcissism. His own unforthcomingness is famous, and wasn't breached by four volumes of straight memoirs that he published after completing *Dance*. By now one of very few survivors of his Eton-and-Oxford circle, he was the slowest to write his memoirs. His friends Harold Acton, Cyril Connolly, and Henry Green had each brought out an autobiography by the forties, and Evelyn Waugh had done so by the mid-sixties. Powell's didn't begin to appear until 1976, and is much the least self-revealing of the group. One of the characters in his first novel, *Afternoon Men*, asks "Do you mind if I speak plainly?" The answer—"Yes . . . I do. I should hate it"—is very much the voice of Powell himself. Interviews with him end up looking blank. Almost seventy years as a writer have brought him visits from a lot of journalists, but he likens his technique with them to a soldier's keeping a spare set of kit pressed and polished, always ready for inspection. A piece of this kit is to claim self-ignorance. "Most people have a very clear idea of what sort of person they are, and I never have had," he says. "To this moment I don't really know—for good or ill—what I'm like."

I recently visited Powell at his country home, in Somerset—a Regency mini-mansion called The Chantry, where he and Lady Violet have lived since the early fifties, and where most of *Dance* was written. I asked him whether he had been especially interested in the narrators of other people's novels. His answer turned into an alarmingly complicated cough, followed by "When anybody asks me that sort of question, I can never remember having read a book in my life." Yet he is a deeply literary writer, whose work anticipated some of the philosophical tricks with which Borges and Calvino later bowled over their readers. In Powell's 1939 novel, *What's Become of Waring*, for example, a publisher commissions a life of one of the most successful authors on his list, who has been reported dead; the biographer finds out that every book by his subject, whom he has idolized, was a plagiarism. The name Borges elicited nothing more from Powell than a side-long look of discreet aghastness—whether because he hadn't read him or because he didn't rate him highly isn't clear. He responded enthusiastically, though, to the idea that often what gets acclaimed as new has been done by writers for centuries—that the self-reflexive novel is as old as the Arabian Nights. He has a habit of putting whole sentences in italics, and he did so now: *"Absolutely! You couldn't conceivably have said a truer word."*

It's strange that none of Powell's work has yet been televised—not even the hilarious *From a View to a Death* (1933). Set in the rural England of foxhunting, of village pageants about the life of Charles II, and of a squire who in the privacy of his dressing room puts on a sequinned black gown before settling down to a book on the breeding of retrievers, the novel could have been made for *Masterpiece Theater*. Powell's farces usually have a melancholy undertow, but *From a View to a Death* is pure comedy: "A wild-eyed woman wearing a hat like a beehive was whispering a mass of information—it might have been her memoirs or an epic poem—into the ear of her elder son." His friend and admirer Kingsley Amis said it was his favorite Powell novel.

But it is *Dance* that TV producers in Britain now have their eyes on. An option has been bought by a London-based Canadian director, Alvin Rakoff, and he has signed up an Emmy-bedecked team: Christopher Morahan, the director of *The Jewel in the Crown*, and the dramatist Hugh Whitemore, whose screenplays include *84 Charing Cross Road*.

Powell dreams of connectedness, and it's here that *Dance* may have the most to offer readers in a post-historical age. In *A Dance to the Music of Time* everyone is joined to everyone else, whether through kinship, marriage, acquaintance, or sheer coincidence, and a minor character who is scarcely noticed in one episode will usually turn up again somewhere else. The same laws operate in the book's views of the past and of art. In his fiction, even when life seems to be almost at a standstill it can't stop making small dance steps.

Near the end of my visit with Powell, while his wife was seeing about sherry, and the sun inched across the library windows, he became absorbed in the jacket photograph on *Messengers of Day*, the second volume of his autobiography, which I had brought for him to sign. The picture shows a corner house where he lodged as a young man almost seventy years before in Shepherd Market, a discreet red-light district in Mayfair. A taxi of a vintage hard to connect with a living person waits in the street. For a long time, the author doubled himself over this picture, slowly rubbing a finger on a ground-floor window of the house. Was he thinking of Evelyn Waugh, Henry Green, and of the outlived friends of those remote days? Eventually, he looked up and said, in a deep murmur, "That was my bedroom. Tarts used to come and knock on it." As if on cue, there was a rap at the front door. "There's one now," Lady Violet said brightly. But it was only my taxi, come to take me to the station.

POSTSCRIPT: The television adaptation of *A Dance to the Music of Time* was eventually made, but was not judged a success by the critics. Anthony Powell died in 2000.

John Herbers was, for twenty-four years, a reporter and editor for the *New York Times* and since 1987 has been a freelance writer and lecturer. This piece is excerpted from his book, *The New Heartland: America's Flight Beyond the Suburbs and How It Is Changing Our Future* (Times Books, 1978).

The New American Heartland

The United States, for most of its history, has been a nation of cities, small towns, farms, and wilderness. Not until after World War II did suburbs with their distinct character become major areas where people lived, and it was some years after that, perhaps in the late 1960's, that most suburban rings became predominant over the cities that spawned them. More Americans now live in the suburbs than in the cities, small towns, or rural areas. The impact of this rapid suburban growth is well known. The suburbs have changed the character of the nation—sociologically, economically, and politically—by creating a new form of urban environment. This change has been as extensively documented and analyzed as was the earlier mass movement of people from farms to cities over many decades.

Now, while the suburbs are still evolving, another kind of development is taking place. It, too, is changing the character of America and has the potential for causing further change on the scale of the migrations first from the farms to the cities and second from the cities to the suburbs. Yet it has attracted little attention outside demographic and academic circles. The new development at this writing has no specific name because we have no vocabulary to describe it in simple terms. It is misunderstood because it is usually depicted as a nostalgic return to small-town rural America. But that is misleading. This new development is neither urban, suburban, rural, nor small town. Nor is it megalopolitan, though it usually exists within a megalopolis, the awkward term for the merging of several cities and their suburbs. In a sense, the new development is a mixture of rural, suburban, and small town, yet that is not an adequate description either, because it takes different forms in different places. Basically, it is new population and commercial growth of very low density, lower than the sprawling suburbs that were decried for scattering urban populations. It is growth around small towns and metropolitan areas and over rural areas without destroying the essential character of the landscape. It invariably brings suburban features with it, but its mixed character is making it far different from what most Americans have known in the past wherever they lived. It is tempting to call these developing places the latest American frontier because they are offering adventuresome people the opportunity to carve out new settlements at some distance from the old central cities. But the term "frontier" has been so overused as to be almost meaningless.

For want of a better description, I have chosen to call those places collectively the new American heartland. Most lie within the nation's heartland, usually defined as a central land area, that part of a region essential to the viability and survival of the whole. But it has a deeper meaning, I believe, because many Americans are going back to places in the heartland their forebears left to find economic opportunity in big cities, mostly located along the Atlantic and Pacific coasts and the Great Lakes. Repopulation of the heartland is driven by both economic and psychological forces, but the communities being established are far different from anything most Americans have known in the past.

Much of this new growth is invisible to many, especially in the Northeast, where old urban and suburban development covers much of the landscape. Although the new growth is dependent on the automobile and on freeways, much of it is hidden from the interstate highway traveler, as it is to air travelers who fly from city to city and find lodging in suburban or central city hotels. This growth has produced suburban-type shopping centers, schools, churches, industrial parks, and office buildings but few high-rise buildings, though they, too, are beginning to appear. Some of it has been mistakenly described as an extension of the suburbs or as the revitalization of small towns. Those who have studied it know it is neither of these, nor is it a repopulation of the farms.

To understand the new American heartland, it is helpful to forget about political boundaries and Census Bureau definitions such as rural and urban, metropolitan and nonmetropolitan. Until recently a city or town had boundaries that proscribed fairly dense residential and commercial neighborhoods. Now, however, there are many exceptions. The fast-growing cities of the Southwest, where people from the industrial North are resettling, usually contain vast areas of undeveloped land where the new growth is taking place. Austin, Texas, for example, embraces not only the old city of urban character but also thousands of acres of forested hills where new homes are being hung on rocks overlooking lakes and valleys, all within its city limits. Metropolitan areas as defined by the federal government may contain—in addition to cities, suburbs, and small towns—many square miles of desert, mountains, farmland, or forests where the new growth is taking place.

The new heartland can be seen on the outer fringes of metropolitan areas; around small towns far removed from the large cities; along rivers, coastlines, and reservoirs; near recreation and retirement areas; on marginal farmland; along country roads; and on remote land that is barren except for its physical beauty.

LOOKING BACK to post–World War II developments, it would seem reasonable that such a historic shift in migration patterns would have been predicted much earlier than it was. But planners and demographers, like others, have difficulty forecasting the unexpected or accepting it when it arrives. Ever since the presidency of Thomas Jefferson, Americans had been moving from the country to the cities in larger numbers than were moving in the other direction. Rural areas and small towns were associated primarily with agriculture, even after the vast majority of rural counties had moved to manufacturing, mining, education, or services as the backbone of their economies. Because it was apparent that mechanization of agriculture would continue to require fewer people on the farms, it was assumed rural areas would continue to decline. Government policy was geared to that assumption and thus to continued growth of cities. One of the major domestic programs enacted in the latter days of the Johnson administration was an act to encourage the building of new cities that would be a mix of economic and racial groups and provide a variety of jobs for its residents. It never succeeded, in part because it went against the emerging trend of deconcentration that few detected at the time.

NORTH CAROLINA: THE PROTOTYPE FOR AMERICA'S FUTURE

When dawn breaks over Nash County on the North Carolina coastal plain, the rustic landscape at first seems as remote and as hushed as in years past. On a winter's day the gray sky blends with the wet, slate-colored soil and with the umber woods and meadows. Old tobacco barns made of logs and clay dot the fields and gently rolling hills. By the time the sun is up, however, the network of new blacktop roads that lace the county's 586 square miles is alive with vehicles—sleek new sports cars and imports, wheezy old clinkers, pickups, and the latest creations out of Detroit. They come from the hills and hollows, the towns and villages, old farmhouses, rural subdivisions, mobile home parks, and the assortment of dwellings, old and new, that are strung out along the roads and highways. They have multiple destinations as scattered as the dwellings they leave for the day—textile mills; small factories that make furniture, hospital equipment, safety locks, automobile parts, electrical equipment, and multiple other products; and retail stores, fast-food outlets, and offices in the towns, in shopping malls, and along the highways.

This scene is repeated every workday morning throughout North Carolina with variations befitting the distinct regions contained within the state boundaries that stretch west for more than five hundred miles from Cape Hatteras to the Smoky Mountains. More than any other state, North Carolina pioneered scattered growth away from cities and suburbs, and no other state has retained as much of its older landscape in the process of industrialization and economic growth. Neal R. Peirce and Jerry Hagstrom, in *The Book of America*, describe North Carolina as "the newest megastate," now tenth largest in the nation with a population of about 6 million. A larger percentage of its work force, about 35 percent, is engaged in manufacturing than in any other state.

Yet it has no large cities of the size found in other industrial states. Charlotte, at 350,000, is biggest, but no other is above 200,000. There are, of course, many square miles of suburbs that have, as elsewhere in the nation, obliterated all else in their path. Yet these, too, are less massive than in other urban complexes of similar size, and a traveler notices that they soon give way to scattered development that leaves many farms, forests, villages, and old buildings intact. This is the essence of North Carolina, and some authorities such as John Kasarda, an urban sociologist at the University of North Carolina, believe that is what much of the nation will be like by the twenty-first century. There is much evidence to support his views.

Charles Kaiser is the author of *1968 in America* and *The Gay Metropolis, 1940–1996* (Houghton Mifflin, 1997). This piece is excerpted from *The Gay Metropolis.*

The 1950s

In that era of general good will and expanding affluence, few Americans doubted the essential goodness of their society.

David Halberstam

Undergraduates seemed uniformly committed to playing parts from a fifties script, according to which paternal white men benignly ruled a prosperous country devoid of serious conflict.

Martin Doberman

We are not living in experimental times. . . . We are not producing real tragedy. On the other hand we are not producing real satire either. The caution prevents it, all the fears prevent it, and we are left, at the moment, with an art that is rather whiling away the time until the world gets better or blows up.

Leonard Bernstein, 1953

The fifties was the bad decade.

Gore Vidal

Most Americans who lived through the fifties—the triumphant warriors of World War II and their teeming progeny—remember this decade with affection. Millions of returning GIs (with honorable discharges) received subsidized college educations, good jobs in a growing economy and cheap mortgages for their new houses in the suburbs. Inflation was low, gasoline was cheap—less than thirty-five cents a gallon—and white middle-class American families became the best-fed, best-dressed and best-sheltered bourgeoisie in the history of the world. By the end of the decade, millions of Americans seemed as self-confident as Detroit's consummate symbol of conspicuous consumption: a 1959 Cadillac with four headlights, dual exhaust pipes and towering tail fins.

Mass entertainment was careful to promote the values of what remained a remarkably puritan and (publicly) innocent place. Even after the loosening effects of World War II, sex and death remained unmentionable, abortion was illegal, divorce was difficult for anyone who couldn't afford a quick trip to Nevada, the segregation of public schools was still legal, and the Lord's Prayer was a morning staple in most of those public schools. The suburban family with three children, a barbecue, and a two-car garage was good for business—and almost no one was questioning the notion that whatever was good for

General Motors was also good for the United States. Conformity of every kind was king.

The establishment of the Hays Office in 1934 ensured the strict censorship of Hollywood movies. Every picture needed its seal of approval; without one, filmmakers risked a disaster at the box office because of a boycott ordered by the Catholic Legion of Decency. The code's purpose was clearly stated: "No picture shall be produced which will lower the moral standards of those who see it. Hence the sympathy of the audience shall never be thrown to the side of crime, wrongdoing, evil or sin" and "correct standards of life . . . shall be presented" because "correct entertainment raises the whole standard of a nation. Wrong entertainment lowers the whole living conditions and moral ideals of a race."

"The function of the official censors was to protect us from the truth and to saddle us with comfortable illusions," Gerald Gardner wrote in his history of the Hays Office. The censors would "root out all signs of the disagreeable facts of life, and many of the agreeable facts as well."

Adultery and murder could never go unpunished; drug addiction could never be glamorized (nor the profits emphasized); a child could never be kidnapped, unless returned unharmed; and no film could "infer that casual or promiscuous sex relationships are the accepted or common thing." Furthermore, "Lustful and open-mouthed kissing" was prohibited, and passion had to be "treated in such manner as not to stimulate the baser emotions." Obscenity "in words, gesture, reference, song, joke or by suggestion, even when likely to be understood by only part of the audience" was also forbidden. Abortion could "never be more than suggested," and whenever it was referred to, it had to be condemned.

Banned words and phrases included *chippie, fairy, goose, madam, pansy, tart in your hat* and *nuts.* Even *hell* and *damn* were excised from many scripts until the sixties. And, needless to say, "sex perversion or any inference of it" was strictly forbidden. (When the censors of the thirties ordered Charlie Chaplin to eliminate "the first part of the 'pansy' gag" in *Modern Times,* he immediately complied.)

As the fifties progressed, television gradually supplanted the movies as the dominant form of popular entertainment—and TV was even more puritanical than the cinema. Although network television still featured serious drama and even symphony orchestras in the fifties, producers were pressured to appeal to a steadily lower common denominator. But for everyone who could identify with the flickering black and white images of this exploding new medium—pictures of idealized white suburban families on "Leave It to Beaver," "Ozzie and Harriet," and "Father Knows Best"—the fifties felt like a wonderful time to be alive.

"I Love Lucy" became a gigantic hit, watched by as many as fifty million people by the middle of the decade—but first Lucy had to overcome the vehement opposition of CBS executives in gray flannel suits. The network and its confederates at Philip Morris, which sponsored the show, were certain that the casting of Lucy's real-life Cuban husband would be a catastrophe. They wanted their idea of an all-American man (with an all-American accent) to play that part. No one would believe Lucy could be married to a Cuban bandleader. "What do you mean?" Lucy demanded. "We are married!" Eventually CBS relented, but there was still strong opposition after some top entertainers screened the first pilot in New York. "Keep the redhead but ditch the Cuban," Oscar Hammerstein recommended.

Lucy's real-life pregnancy caused a new crisis at CBS. Ultimately the network permitted her condition to be written into the show, but only after realizing that it wouldn't be practical to keep her hidden behind counters and couches at all times. Nevertheless, the word *pregnant* could never be spoken, even after Lucy was allowed to suffer from morning sickness.

These battles with the bosses at CBS illustrate an essential fact of life in the fifties: in this era the American establishment was uncomfortable with all public manifestations of sexuality, not just homosexuality. The *New York Times*, the daily bible of the liberal elite, was particularly squeamish. The historian George Chauncey considered the decade an "utter anomaly" because a larger percentage of the American population was married than at any other time in the nation's history.

The gap between the carefree comedy served up every week by Lucy and Desi and the reality of their rocky marriage mirrored the gulf between real life in America and the white-bread TV version that Americans gobbled up. Unpleasant realities of any kind—from infidelity to racism—were all unfit subjects for programs designed to sell great American products like Marlboros, Alka Seltzer, Geritol and Johnson's baby shampoo.

According to Lucille Ball, "Half of the nicest girls in Hollywood" were having an affair with her husband. And Desi Arnaz, Jr., remembered learning "to relate to 'I Love Lucy' as a television show and to my parents as actors on it. . . . There wasn't much relationship between what I saw on TV and what was really going on at home. Those were difficult years—all those funny things happening on television each week to people who looked like my parents, then the same people agonizing through some terrible, unhappy times at home."

These postwar tendencies toward conformity and obedience were sharply reinforced by the dreadful morality play staged throughout the decade in congressional hearing rooms and federal courts. In a frightening replay of the Red Scare that had gripped the country after the First World War, Americans in nearly every profession learned that the penalty for even momentary nonconformity could be the termination of their careers—sometimes decades after their alleged indiscretions.

Congressional Republicans—joined by quite a few Democrats—began their anti-Communist crusade in earnest after Mao Tse-tung defeated Chiang

Kai-shek in 1949, and President Harry Truman was accused of "losing China." Ruthless investigators decreed that even the oldest and briefest flirtation with the Communist party should be incapacitating for nuclear physicists and Hollywood screenwriters alike. For members of Hollywood's elite, the cost of continuing their careers often included the annihilation of some of their colleagues—because only those who revealed the ancient party member-ships of their former "comrades" were deemed fit to continue in their chosen professions.

Joseph McCarthy was a Wisconsin Republican who was first elected to the Senate in 1946. A heavy drinker and compulsive gambler, the Senate press gallery named him America's worst senator three years after his election. In February 1950, McCarthy pretended to have a list of 205 Communists work-ing in the State Department and known to the secretary of state. It was the first in a long series of charges for which no serious evidence would ever be forthcoming.

The Communist witch-hunt conducted by McCarthy and his cohorts is the nightmare remembered by most liberals who lived through this period. But a parallel persecution of lesbians and gay men began in 1950, with devastating effects.

Gay life in New York City in the 1950s was by turns oppressive and exhil-arating, a world of persecution and vast possibilities. Plainclothesmen tried to entrap men, even inside gay bars in Manhattan, and uniformed officers ha-rassed women dressed like men because women were legally required to wear at least one article of women's clothing whenever they appeared in public. Knowingly serving a drink to a gay person automatically made a bar disorderly under state law, and it was illegal for two men to be on a dance floor together without a woman present.

DESPITE its many hardships, gay life in New York City in the fifties still offered more possibilities than it did anywhere else. Like San Francisco on the oppo-site coast, the city was a magnet for artists and iconoclasts of all sexual persua-sions, a spiritual safe haven for Americans who felt like strangers in their own land everywhere east of the Bay Bridge or west of the Hudson. During the fifties, New York's cosmopolitan appeal was only enhanced by America's pas-sionate embrace of the conventional.

Gay life acted like a bracing undertow, exerting a powerful opposite pull beneath waves of conformity. Because being a rebel is almost always an essen-tial part of accepting one's homosexuality, it was both especially difficult and especially satisfying to be gay in an age like this. Beneath the prevailing waters there was a thriving world of creativity and indulgence which resembled noth-ing on network television. The sterility of mass culture made the life of an outsider particularly attractive to writers, artists, actors and painters. Stress often feeds the sublimation that produces a vibrant culture, and this synergy was conspicuous in the plays, poems, books, and canvases produced all over Manhattan.

Many gay historians have claimed a connection between homosexual orientation and artistic avocation. However, Edward Sagarin, the first American historian of gay life in the fifties, argued that homosexuals are hardly confined to the arts. He suggested that artists were simply more likely to leave behind hints about their sexuality than "scientists, businessmen, [and] political leaders"—men and women who "not only leave no such evidence," but are forced to engage in "vehement denial and deliberate misinformation."

One reason that lesbians and gay men often make great artists may be that being gay and creating art both require similar strengths: the ability to create an original world of one's own and a willingness to jettison the conventional wisdom in favor of one's own convictions. Sagarin wrote that "homosexual creativity" is "often freed from conventional thought, with imagination unbound and unfettered—and sponsored by the need for perfection to overcome the doubt of oneself." Notable gay nonconformists who struggled against the fifties tide included poets like Allen Ginsberg, Audre Lorde, John Ashbery, and Frank O'Hara; painters as diverse as Paul Cadmus, Jasper Johns, Robert Rauschenberg, and Ellsworth Kelly; the composers Leonard Bernstein, Ned Rorem, John Cage, and Aaron Copland; and playwrights and screenwriters like Gore Vidal, William Inge, Arthur Laurents, Edward Albee, and Tennessee Williams.

Nat Hentoff is a syndicated columnist for the *Washington Times* and contributes as a columnist to the *Village Voice, Legal Times, Editor & Publisher*, and *Jazz Times*. This essay figured in *America and the World at the End of the Century: A Tribute to David A. Morse* (New York Society for International Affairs, 1998).

Jazz: Music Beyond Time and Nations

At Gestapo headquarters in Paris, Charles Delaunay, under suspicion of being a member of the Maquis, was brought in for questioning. Delaunay, an expert on jazz, was the author of the first definitive jazz discography—listings of full personnel on jazz labels.

As the interrogation began, the first thing the German officer said to Delaunay was, "You have the wrong personnel on the 1928 Fletcher Henderson recording." They argued the point for a while, and Delaunay was eventually released after routine questioning. "There are jazz aficionados everywhere," Delaunay, who had a quick sense of irony, told me years later.

In Nazi Germany, jazz was forbidden as a mongrel black-and-Jewish music, but recordings were still played behind closed doors. And in Russia, under the Communists, jazz was declared an enemy of the people, but there too it could not be entirely suppressed. Some of my liner notes for a John Coltrane recording were surreptitiously distributed to jazz lovers in Moscow as *samizdats*.

What is it that makes this music a common language throughout the world—as it so transcends popular fads that recordings made seventy years ago are played again and again, continually beyond the ordinary boundaries of time?

A vivid sense of the jazz experience is a 1998 New York play, *Side Man*, by Warren Leight. This is a key scene, described by Peter Marks in the *New York Times*: "Three musicians . . . sit around a cassette player listening to the tape of a fervent, wrenching trumpet solo. The jazz man on the tape is dead, but his instrument remains feverishly alive."

The essential attraction of jazz throughout time is its "sound of surprise"—a term invented by the *New Yorker*'s critic Whitney Balliett. Because the music is largely improvised, the listener is often startled by a sound, a phrasing, a turn of rhythm that is so deeply emotional that he or she may shout aloud in pleasure.

I was eleven when I first heard jazz. Walking down a street in Boston, I was stopped by the sound coming out of a public address system attached to a record store. I was so exhilarated that I yelled in delight—something I had never done before on the proper streets of Boston. The music was Artie Shaw's "Nightmare."

I was soon working in a candy store and expanded my jazz horizons by buying recordings of Duke Ellington, Billie Holiday, Lester Young, Bessie Smith and blues singer Peetie Wheatstraw ("the Devil's son-in-law").

A few years later, I came upon the very essence of jazz. It was late on a winter afternoon when I walked past the Savoy Cafe, in a black neighborhood of Boston. The club was closed, but the blues coming from inside stopped me. I looked through the glass in the door and saw, as in a fantasy, several of the legends of jazz. Sitting in a chair that was leaning back against a table was a saxophonist with a huge, swaggering sound. It was Coleman Hawkins, who had invented the jazz tenor saxophone. The pianist was Count Basie, whose bands were the very definition of swinging, and he had created a precisely economical way of improvising. Each of his notes was exactly placed to give the big tenor a further lift. And on the drums was Jo Jones, whom his colleagues in the Basie band described as "the man who plays like the wind." Uncommonly subtle, his eyes darting from player to player, Jo's brushes were dancing on the drumhead, punctuated by an occasionally deep sigh from a cymbal.

Every night, in many clubs in many countries throughout the world, this ceaselessly intriguing interplay between improvising musicians creates new patterns of melody, harmony and rhythm for an audience that knows no generational divide. Youngsters are drawn to the depth of feeling that can't be found in popular music and older listeners relive their own musical adventures while learning more about the further dimensions of this music.

There is also the spirit of the jazz musician that attracts lay enthusiasts. Since the music is largely improvised and risk-taking, those qualities also usually define jazz musicians off the stand. They tend to be self- confident, irreverent and unflinchingly independent.

An incandescent illustration of that spirit was Dizzy Gillespie. On one of his trips for the U.S. State Department, he had been scheduled to play at a lawn party in Ankara, arranged by the American ambassador to Turkey. The climax was to be a jam session with Dizzy in charge.

"While I was signing autographs," Dizzy recalled, "I happened to look at the fence surrounding the grounds. A lot of street kids were pressed against the fence. They wanted to come in and hear the music. One of them actually climbed over the fence and a guard threw him right back over it.

"I asked what was going on. 'Why did they do that?' And some official said, 'This party is for select people—local dignitaries and important Americans in the city.' I said, 'Select people! We're not over here for no select people! We're over here to show these people that Americans are all kinds of people!' I had a girl in the band, and almost as many whites as blacks. We had a good mix.

"The ambassador comes over and asks, 'Are you going to play?' I say, 'No! I saw that guard throw a little kid over the fence. Those are the people we're trying to get close to—the people outside the fence.' So the ambassador said, 'Let them in, let them all in!'" That is the spirit of jazz.

Dizzy Gillespie was an original, and so are—and have been—many other conjugators of the forms and feelings of the music. Part of the originality of the music consists of how players have expanded the capacities of their instruments—from the gypsy guitarist Django Reinhardt to the first and never entirely surpassed jazz soloist, Louis Armstrong.

In the early 1930s, a delegation of the leading brass players in the Boston Symphony Orchestra made a journey to Louis Armstrong's dressing room in a theater in the city. They had heard of his almost unbelievable technique and range and asked him to play a passage they had heard in his act. Armstrong picked up his horn and obliged, performing the requested passage and then improvising a dazzling stream of variations. Shaking their heads, these "legitimate" trumpet players left the room, one of them saying, "I watched his fingers and I still don't know how he does it. I also don't know how it is that, playing there all by himself, he sounded as if a whole orchestra was behind him. I never heard a musician like this, and I thought he was just a colored entertainer."

The older players, though very serious about their musicianship and the quality of their instruments, were also entertainers. In the years before there was a reasonably sizable number of jazz admirers, the players worked before all kinds of audiences, and so they had to entertain them between improvisations.

In time, younger musicians, playing by then before musically sophisticated listeners, declined to entertain in the traditional sense. And their music began to reflect their interests outside of music. Max Roach and Julian "Cannonball" Adderley, for instance, composed pieces dealing with the Civil Rights Movement. Duke Ellington, of course, had been writing about black music and culture long before the Civil Rights Movement had begun ("Black Beauty," "Black, Brown and Beige," et al.).

Revealingly, in one of the more dramatic events in jazz history, Louis Armstrong also inserted himself into the struggle for black equality. Before then he hadn't done this explicitly in his music, and there were younger musicians who, accordingly, called him an "Uncle Tom." Armstrong proved them decidedly wrong when, in the 1950s, Governor Orville Faubus of Arkansas defied the orders of the Supreme Court of the United States to integrate the public schools of Little Rock. When then President Dwight Eisenhower delayed and delayed intervening, Armstrong declared: "The way they are treating my people in the South, the government can go to hell! The president has no guts."

In 1965, when Martin Luther King's march on Selma, Alabama, was brutally attacked by local and state police, Armstrong told the nation: "They would beat Jesus if he was black and marched."

At one point Armstrong's manager, the powerful and forceful Joe Glaser, sent an emissary to find Armstrong on the road and order him to stop saying such controversial things, for they would cause him to lose bookings. Louis Armstrong threw Glaser's emissary out of his dressing room. That, too, is the spirit of jazz!

It is an unavoidably personal music. John Coltrane, who created new ways of hearing as well as playing jazz, told me, "The music is the whole question of life itself." Other players have also emphasized that what you live—and how you live—becomes an integral part of what you play each night. Jazz, then, is a continual autobiography, or, rather, a continuum of intersecting autobiographies—one's own and those of the musicians with whom one plays. As the prodigious bassist and bold composer Charles Mingus told me: "I'm trying to play the truth of what I am. The reason it's difficult is because I'm changing all the time."

Then there was Charlie "Bird" Parker, who changed music fundamentally, as Louis Armstrong had before him. Describing Parker, as he evolved into a dominant musician of his time, bassist Gene Ramey was also describing the acute sensitivity of other jazz players to the sounds all around them: "Everything had a musical significance for Bird—the swish of a car speeding down a highway, the hum of the wind as it goes through the leaves. If he heard a dog bark, he would say the dog was speaking. . . . And maybe some girl would walk past on the dance floor while he was playing, and something she might do, or an expression on her face, would give him an idea for something to play on his solo."

And Duke Ellington would tell me how, at a dance, a sigh of pleasure from a dancer would float back to the bandstand and enter into the music. One of his sidemen told me how, after a long, wearying bus trip, the musicians would be regenerated by the dancers: "You're giving them something to move by, but you're giving them something back. You can tell whether you're really cooking by how they move on the floor, and when they groove, they make you groove more."

It's harder for these physical and emotional messages to be sent and received in a concert hall, where more and more jazz is played. But the interactions between musicians and listeners take place there too, because jazz is a music in which both the player and the audience are continually in conversation.

I once asked the flawless pianist Hank Jones whether he agreed with Dizzy Gillespie that music is so vast that no one can get more than a small piece of it. "That's exactly right," Jones said. "That's why every night, I begin again."

Duke Ellington resisted the very idea of ending. Trumpeter Clark Terry said of him, "He wants life and music to be always in a state of becoming. He doesn't even like to write definitive endings to a piece. He always likes to make the end of a song sound as if it's still going somewhere."

And that's the story of jazz.

Lucinda Franks has received a Pulitzer Prize for national reporting, as well as other awards for her coverage of the war in Northern Ireland and for her feature writing for the *New York Times Magazine*. She also writes for the *New Yorker* and *Talk* magazine. This piece was published in the *New Yorker* on May 17, 1999.

Miracle Kid

Max was born with deformities so severe that the hospital thought his parents might choose not to prolong his life. Instead, they fought to give him every chance.

My nephew Max emerged into the world on June 11, 1992: plump, pink, and with an abundance of fair silky hair. Right up to the moment of his birth, my sister Penelope had been relaxed, and laughing at the doctors' jokes. This was her second child, and sonograms had pictured a perfectly normal baby boy. But now, as the baby appeared, the room went quiet. The staff stood frozen, holding the baby up in the light, and didn't seem to hear Penelope when she asked what was wrong. A "Code Blue" announcement came over the loudspeaker, and Penelope thought that there must be a problem with another baby in another birthing room.

Then she heard the slap of paper booties on linoleum and the murmur of voices as white coats bobbed above her. "I don't know what this is, I just don't know," a doctor said plaintively as he put the baby into her arms. Beneath the lush head of hair, the baby's face was like a child's unfinished drawing. He had only one, unnaturally small eye, on the right side of his face. On the other side, there was a concave blankness beneath the brow. His nostrils were separated by a deep cleft, and his nasal ridge was squashed. Penelope took his curled fist and felt for fingers, but none were there. Her husband, Bernard, looked down at her, ashen-faced.

"Bernie, what did we do?" she said.

A doctor who had just arrived, with a leather jacket thrown over his hospital scrubs, began asking questions. Had she taken drugs during pregnancy? Alcohol? Ingested anything unusual? No, she said, unless you counted six chocolate croissants she'd eaten an hour before she went into labor.

The doctor asking these questions was John Graham, the head geneticist at Cedars-Sinai Medical Center, in Los Angeles, and he had seen hundreds of birth defects; as he later told me, he knew that these were severe deformities. He studied the mother's face: fair skin; high cheekbones, Roman nose. Then the father's: tawnier skin and a flat, Slavic roundness. Were they related in any way? Dr. Graham knew that his only hope of saving the baby was to diagnose the syndrome; he left to consult his genetics library.

By this time, the nurses had whisked the baby away to the neonatal intensive care unit for evaluation. Bernard went along, desperate to make himself useful. As the nurses hooked the baby up to heart and lung monitors and took X-rays, Bernard tried to count fingers and toes, unsure of how to classify the little stubs protruding from his son's hands and feet. Finally, with tears running down his cheeks, he shouted, "Five fingers and five toes! That's pretty good, huh?"

Penelope was suffering violent cramps, and the painkillers she had received during labor put her into a troubled sleep. For the past fifteen years, she had worked in theater and film. Now she dreamed that she had left the water running in the bathroom of a theater and couldn't stop the torrent that was washing over the audience.

She awoke to hear someone saying softly, "Low viability." Dr. Graham had returned from his office. "It was nothing you could have prevented," he told her gently. The baby had a very rare genetic disorder called Fraser syndrome, which interrupts the development of a fetus's organs and other body parts. The skin over the eyes often does not split to create eyelids, and the fingers and the toes usually do not separate. Anomalous recessive genes are part of everyone's genetic makeup, but they usually remain undetected for generations. If both parents turn out to have the same wild gene pair, the chances are one in four that they will produce a child with birth defects. The odds against this baby's conception, based on documented cases, Graham explained, were probably a million to one.

Eventually, testing revealed that, although the baby had only one kidney, most of his internal organs were intact. But he had severe hearing loss, and it was assumed that his single, underdeveloped eye could not function. Brain scans suggested that he had no corpus callosum, the nerve pathway between the left and the right side of the brain. Moreover, statistics showed that the outlook for children afflicted with Fraser syndrome was grim.

Over the next few hours, Penelope questioned every doctor she could find. If her baby made it through one night, what were the chances that he would live a second? A week? A month? A year? His childhood? What could be fixed? One frustrated genetics resident finally said, "I can't tell you. We've only seen these babies in a bottle."

Bernard sat on the hospital bed and wept. He was a logical man, good at mapping strategies: he had a small metals-manufacturing business, and had managed to make it flourish in a falling market. But now he had no plan. One nurse felt duty-bound to inform him that in some rural hospitals such babies might be left to die. "This is my son!" Bernard told her, yet he secretly wondered: should the baby survive—blind, deaf, mentally impaired?

Penelope sat beside the incubator, where the baby lay in a cocoon of tubes, needles, and wires, and tried to imagine him as a stranger would. She needed to see him through the eyes of the staff, some of whom took detours to avoid his incubator, and she wanted to understand the distress of one nurse, who had reportedly asked to be transferred from his case. Craniofacial deformities, more than any other birth defect, have been found to profoundly alter the mother-child bonding process. Dr. Graham initially expected Penelope to reject the baby, but since childhood my sister had been a collector of the wounded and the halt. Hairless newborn rodents warmed under her desk lamp; lame puppies roamed our house. She immediately knew that this child was her destiny; she felt a magical confluence of souls.

At the end of the second day, as Penelope was sleepily holding the baby's hand through the incubator porthole, she felt his single, unblinking eye fixed on her. She called for Bernard, and asked him, "Do you see this? Something's rocketing off him, like he's saying, 'I'm in here. Who are you?'" At that moment, Penelope made a pact with God. "If he lives, I can make it through anything," she told Bernard. "But I can't make it through if we lose him—I just can't. We're going to beat this, and we're going to let them know it. Right, Bern?"

Bernard hesitated. He thought about the enormous emotional and financial costs of caring for this baby. They were not wealthy, and Penelope would have to give up her job. But he had always been powerless in the face of her enthusiasms. (She had been, over the years, not only an animal-rights activist but also a scholar of Buddhism and an ice hockey player.) Suddenly, both he and Penelope remembered that Luke, their seven-year-old son, was still with the babysitter. While Bernard went to retrieve him, Penelope kept watch over the baby. Clusters of interns and residents came to look, and she heard some of them referring to him as "it." Finally, Penelope had had enough. "This 'it' is my son, and he wants to be left alone," she said.

Penelope persuaded a reluctant nurse to put the child to her breast, and he began to suck vigorously. The nurse said firmly, "It's only instinct. Any baby will nurse." Then she pointed out another nurse, who was unhooking a plump baby from a ventilator and rushing out the door with him. "That baby has been on life support for months," the first nurse said. "It has been unending agony for the mother, and she's decided to end it. She's waiting in a private room so the baby can die in her arms."

If the staff members at Cedars-Sinai were discouraging, it was because they feared that Penelope might have unrealistic hopes for the child. Doctors have identified hundreds of inherited malformation syndromes in the past three decades, but, even if they know what genes cause these deformities, there is no gene therapy to correct them. Formidable neonatal technology will sometimes save even the most compromised babies, but families can be bankrupted both emotionally and financially in the process, so hospitals have begun to exercise some discretion. "Our bioethics committee asks itself, 'Are we saving a life, or merely prolonging death?'" Graham later explained to me. "In this case, the neonatology division was unsure. Two fetuses with Fraser syndrome had been stillborn at the hospital, but we had never had a live birth." And, he confided, a baby had recently been born with a similar syndrome, Apert, and the parents apparently couldn't cope. "The baby was struggling to breathe," Graham said, "and after much soul-searching we decided to withhold help, and the infant died."

When I arrived from New York three days after the birth, Penny had grown tired of waiting for the hospital to make a decision about her baby, and she enlisted me in a campaign to convince the doctors that this was a whole child, who could see, hear, and feel, not just a jumble of damaged parts. She called in a Catholic priest, and he stood over the incubator with water and baptized the baby Max. She had already found an ally in the night nurse, who agreed that the baby had good muscle tone and was not flaccid and limp, like many neurologically impaired newborns. Together, Penelope and I squeezed squeak toys over the crib and conspicuously praised his responses.

My sister is six years younger than I, and our relationship has not always been a peaceful one. Sometimes we are intensely close. Then some dramatic bit of sibling rivalry—the spoiled, successful firstborn vs. the easily dismissed, often-aggrieved second child—will drive us apart. In fact, we had barely spoken for four years when I got her call from the hospital. But I was amazed by Penelope's extraordinary determination to convince herself and everyone around her that to give Max anything less than immediate and complete treatment would be immoral, even a crime.

Late one afternoon, an ophthalmologist named Yaron S. Rabinowitz was sent in to confirm the diagnosis of blindness. He peered into Max's eye, then ran out and came back with magnifying lamps attached to his forehead. Finally, he turned and said, in a heavy South African accent, "The kiddie sees. This kiddie *sees!*"

Most Fraser-syndrome babies have cryptophthalmos: one or both of their underdeveloped eyes are buried beneath the skin. Max was lucky to have one eye, but without a lid the cornea would soon dry up. Penelope and I began to quiz Dr. Rabinowitz about whether it was possible to reconstruct a lid. He explained that tissue was fused to the cornea, and it would be risky to separate it, the baby's chances of going blind on the operating table were eighty percent. Without the operation, we argued, his chances increased to a hundred percent.

Good news began to trickle in. On June 15th, brain scans revealed that Max did in fact have the nerve pathway that connects the two sides of the brain. The next day, doctors upgraded his chances for survival, and decided to surgically repair his intestinal tract. Another hearing test revealed that Max could discern speaking voices.

During that first week, I became troubled by Max's raspy breathing and alerted a resident, who wearily replied that this would be put on the list of irregularities to check. The next day, a pediatric ear, nose, and throat specialist, Eugene Flaum, examined Max's larynx and trachea, and saw that the upper part of his airway was no wider than a swizzle stick—in a normal newborn, it would be four times that size. According to Penelope, Flaum explained that because he was not Max's doctor he would make a recommendation to the hospital's bioethics committee.

"And if you were his doctor?" Bernard asked.

"I would put a tracheostomy in right away," Flaum replied.

"Then you're our doctor," Bernard said.

"That's all I needed to hear," Flaum replied, and he marched into the operating room. At that moment, Penelope knew that Bernard had joined the fight for their son.

On June 22nd, when Max was eleven days old, the neonatology division called a sombre meeting to discuss his future. A hospital official began by saying that no one could blame a family for exploring all the options, and he mentioned group homes and long-term-care facilities. Penelope bristled, but Bernard hushed her and hauled out a sheaf of notes he had made about Fraser syndrome. Not satisfied with the one-page entry in a standard medical text the hospital had provided, he noted its flaws. He pointed out, for example, that of the approximately one hundred cases of Fraser syndrome documented in the report forty-five of the infants had been stillborn or had died in the first year of life—with most deaths occurring within the first week. The chance of mental deficiency for a Fraser child was put at eighty percent—but that figure was based on data from only twenty-one children. "What kind of a statistic is that?" he now asked the members of the neonatology division. "What about the intelligence of the twenty-four other babies who survived?" Eventually, he and Penelope tracked down several other Fraser-syndrome children, from Louisiana to Germany, and learned that all of them were of normal intelligence.

Penelope jumped in. "We do not intend to warehouse our son," she said icily. "There's only one option we'd like to discuss, and that is aggressive medical intervention."

By late June, Max's eye had become dry and ulcerated. Rabinowitz had been researching and plotting out an experimental operation, but he was pessimistic about it. Nevertheless, on June 28th, he and Norman Shorr, an ophthalmic plastic surgeon who works for both Cedars-Sinai and the U.C.L.A. medical center, performed the first of two procedures to free the eye and create a protective top lid. To the soothing tones of a Mozart sonata, Rabinowitz trained a high-powered microscope on Max's eye, took a razor-sharp instrument, and began to peel away skin and tissue fused to the top portion of the

339

cornea. Using tiny forceps, he removed layer after layer, each thinner than onionskin, while trying to avoid perforating the cornea. "In the middle of the operation, I stopped, thinking I had gone too deep," recalls Rabinowitz, who knew that any puncture could destroy the eyeball. After many hours, he and Shorr finally exposed the cornea without damaging it. "Gee, it looks like this little eye's going to make it," Rabinowitz said. Now they needed to construct an upper and a lower lid, using tissue and membrane harvested from inside Max's mouth. This, too, was laborious and innovative work. When Rabinowitz came out to tell the family that the procedure had been successful, they feared the worst, for he appeared dour and stooped: hunching over Max so tensely for nine hours had hurt his back.

Meanwhile, Dr. Graham had come up with his own innovation, to deal with Max's partially incomplete skull: a polypropylene helmet, which, as Max grew into it, would insure that he would not develop a lopsided head. He would have to wear the helmet all the time, and be fitted for a larger one after six weeks.

On July 4th, Max was discharged. Bernard had convinced the insurance company that home care would be more economical, and their white stucco house, in the hills east of Los Angeles, had been made ready. It was small with two bedrooms and one bath, so the dining room had been furnished with a crib and with shelves of medical supplies. Luke was waiting at the door.

"Wow!" he said when he saw his new brother's helmet, his bandaged eye, and the metal tube from the tracheostomy in his neck. "He looks like a Power Ranger."

Along with Max came enough machines to outfit a spaceship: a generator, with a loud industrial whirr; a suction machine to clean out the fluids in Max's trachea; a big humidifier; and an apnea monitor that regularly emitted high-pitched beeps. In time, Luke got to work the machines, to clean them, and to change the cannula, a little tube that fitted inside the larger tracheostomy tube to catch mucus clots. If Max started to choke, Luke would just pull out the silver cannula, leaving an open passageway for air to come in. Then the cannula was sterilized and reinserted.

At first, Penelope was in a permanent state of anxiety; the doctors had warned her that anything could happen. "Nobody knew—they don't know to this day—why he was doing so well," she told me. "I had this sense that some minor thing, letting his head fall back feeding him too fast—anything or nothing—would cause his body to just implode." She bought emergency breathing equipment and stocked the house with extra cannulas, at two hundred dollars apiece, so that there would always be one in easy reach.

Penelope avoided despair by focussing completely on Max's treatment. She consulted specialists for every part of his anatomy, it seemed, and took him to two or three appointments a day, drafting Luke to help lug the heavy equipment. A steady stream of nurses, vision and hearing experts, technicians to service the machines, and special-needs counsellors paraded through the house, so that Bernard was forced to race from bedroom to bathroom in the morning, and was never sure whom he would run into. Those first few months, he felt invaded, ignored, and scared, and he would flee to the office early every morning.

The original day nurse was fired after Lulu, the babysitter, caught her washing Max's bottles in dirty dishwater. "What's the difference? He's going to be a vegetable," the nurse had said with a shrug. For a while, the family worked in shifts to complete all the daily chores of Max's care: changing surgical dressings, administering antibiotics and ointments. Every two hours, someone had to put on surgical gloves, thread sterile tubing into the tracheostomy, and suction it out. Penny was sometimes frazzled and short-tempered. Max's hair would smell from the helmet, and occasionally, in frustration, she would take it off. Finally, three excellent nurses were found, who lightened the atmosphere in the house by tending to Max with crisp, good-natured efficiency.

One day, Penelope noticed Max raising his eye toward the light. But the eye was still covered with a patch and was stitched shut from the first surgery. She had read that kittens whose eyelids don't open during infancy become blind. She began calling Rabinowitz regularly, pressing him to do the second operation before it was too late. "She was right—we were cutting it close," Rabinowitz recalls. "But we couldn't risk dividing the lid before it had completely healed."

After three weeks, Max was wheeled into surgery and the bandages on his eye were removed. Rabinowitz and Shorr found that the sutured lid had knitted well and the cornea was clear. Now, in a six-hour operation, they divided the lower lid, which had been stretched upward, and used its upper half to give Max a top lid. The new upper lid had no muscles, so he would never be able to close his eye completely, but it provided enough of a canopy to protect his vision.

For the next week, Penelope kept passing colorful objects in front of Max's eye, but got no reaction. Then, one day, Luke took out his baseball glove and idly began throwing a tennis ball into the air. Max, propped in a baby carrier, started shaking his rattle and hissing through his tracheostomy tube—the only sound he could make. Luke saw that Max's eye was following the ball up and down. From then on, Max began tracking people, studying his hands, and bringing his eye up close to a picture of his brother that was taped to the rails of his crib. He was taken to the medical center for new tests, but, to the family's disappointment, the vision in his single eye registered a dismal 20/400—legally blind.

The street that Penelope and Bernard had lived on for more than five years was filled with young families, yet few visited immediately after Max was born. One kind gesture came from the neighborhood children: they signed their names to a poster that read "Welcome Max" and slipped it under the front door. To most neighbors, Max was just a tiny bundle in a white helmet, which they saw being carried from the car to the door. "Aren't you tired of being the new tragedy instead of the new baby?" one of the nurses finally asked. "You know, before Max is able to defend himself, how you treat and feel about him is what others will feel, too," she said. "Let people know he's here to stay, he's waiting to join the world."

Penelope bought Max a new red, yellow, and blue outfit, and took him to a neighborhood block party. The neighbors crowded around in celebration, and Penelope began to feel relaxed, almost happy. Perhaps, she thought, she could even join one of those "baby and me" classes. One woman came over and complimented her on Max's cute clothes, adding that it was good she would dress him up anyway. Penny asked what she meant by "anyway." The woman replied, "Well, you know . . . you know." Penny's cheeks began to burn. After a moment, she handed Max to Bernard and went inside. "I'm kidding myself," she told the nurse tearfully. "We'll never fit in."

Penny was brash and outspoken with Max's powerful doctors, but she began to shrink from the reactions of strangers. She had smoked-glass visors made for Max's helmets, and when the helmets finally came off, at sixteen months, she bought him hats with big brims. In an elevator once, a woman asked playfully, "Who's that behind that hat? Doesn't he have a face?" Finally, the woman flipped up the hat. As she gasped and shrank back, Penny just stared at her.

Bernard had a different attitude. He left the hats at home, and proudly carried Max on his shoulders. "Max just continually amazed me," Bernard said. "He was regularly dragged to the hospital, cut and sewed, and within a few hours of surgery he would be raring to go." Bernard tried to help Penelope cope with the behavior of strangers which so infuriated her. On one occasion, at the Price Club, he noticed a woman watching Max. "This is how you handle these things," he said to Penelope, and walked over to the woman. "Hi, I noticed you were staring at my son," he told her. "Would you like to meet him?" After Bernard had explained Max's syndrome to her, the woman thanked him enthusiastically.

"People are just curious," Bernard told Penelope. "They want to understand."

"I don't give a flying fuck what they want," said Penelope. She knew her own reactions were sometimes extreme, but she didn't like being patronized.

Though Penelope and Bernard frequently clashed over the challenges of raising Max, his birth had brought them closer together after a period of estrangement. "You know that intense bond men have in war? Well, that's what happened to us," Penelope told me. "It was so huge, when you see doctors freaking out, when everything hinges on one little detail of timing, all the petty bullshit evaporates. Then, after each little unexpected victory, you look at each other and think, I got to see your best, I got to see deep inside you. You develop this profound respect for each other." I knew what she meant, because my relationship with Penelope had changed, too. Before Max's arrival, I was the star in our family, and Penelope refused to compete with me. Now there is no question who the real hero is.

IN FEBRUARY, when Max was eight months old, Dr. Myles Cohen, of Cedars-Sinai, performed the first surgery to separate his fingers. First, he put tourniquets on Max's arms to prevent bleeding. Then, taking care not to cut the arteries and nerves crucial to touch, movement, and sensation, he freed Max's thumb and separated the first two fingers from the second two. Skin grafts taken from Max's groin were sutured onto the newly exposed surfaces, and his forearms were encased in bulky plaster casts. When they came off, Max delighted in his ability to pick up and hide various objects, such as his helmet and his mother's glasses. The screen door banged regularly as neighborhood children came through to measure his progress. They regarded Max as their special secret, and they loved teaching him tricks.

One day, Penelope saw Luke making his own chocolate milk—three parts chocolate, one part milk. "I don't think I really noticed until then how much he had changed," she told me. "He had been a typical firstborn, a Caesar accustomed to the instant gratification of his wishes, and almost overnight he had lost his staff, his audience, his whole kingdom. He was just a kid who had to run his own life." Luke had been a colicky baby, and a very thin-skinned, jumpy toddler, who hated to be touched. Yet now he would calmly hold and stroke his brother. "He understood we were in a life-and-death situation, and he became very calm, particularly when I got excited," Penelope said. "Once, when we were replacing the surgical ties on the tracheostomy, Max coughed, and the whole tube popped out. I was fumbling and screaming, and of course Bernard just stood there, being a man. Then we heard Luke's voice in the next room, calmly asking the emergency operator what he should do."

When Max turned one, Dr. Flaum was still concerned about his airway, and insisted that the tracheostomy tube remain in place. Penelope grew frustrated as she watched Max strain to communicate, and she worried that he would miss the opportunity to learn to speak. She decided to master sign language, and enrolled Bernard, Luke, and Lulu in signing school, too.

It was now clear that Max was not retarded. Using the three fingers that had been freed on each hand, he quickly picked up twelve basic word signs. As long as the tracheostomy tube was in place, no one expected him to talk, though one of his nurses had taught him to emit little sounds through his lips by gently blowing and cooing at him. So when Max one day pointed at a lamp and said, "Ike!" Penelope and Bernard didn't react at first. They just looked at him blankly. Max, who was sitting on Bernard's lap, tried again. He pointed to another lamp, and then to the glow of the television set, and said, "Ike, ike, ike!"

"'Light,'" Bernard said, getting up so fast he nearly dropped Max. "My God, he's saying 'light'!"

The sounds that Max uttered were approximations, made in the back of his mouth. Thus he said "Uke" for "Luke" and "Gaa-ee" for "Daddy." He could never muster the air to form an "m" sound for "Mama." But he loved to talk and the neighborhood children competed to see whose name he would learn first.

At ten months, Max had had an ultrasound test to check his single kidney. When the technician had almost completed the scan, Penny pointed to a shadow on the right side of the screen. The technician moved the probe closer to the shadow, then went to get the doctor, leaving Penelope to pray that the dark spot was not a tumor. When the doctor examined the scan, he announced that Max had a second kidney, and further tests found it to be partially functional. It had been missed at birth because it was situated in the middle of the abdomen, where embryonic kidneys begin, rather than lower in the torso.

Also at ten months, Max started walking—six months earlier than his brother had. Penny pushed the furniture to the walls, afraid that Max would bump into things. But he didn't. In fact, he would toddle right through the center of a doorway. Later, he rode a tricycle down the center of the sidewalk—a remarkable feat for a one-eyed child.

By late summer, Max's new upper lid had begun to adhere to his cornea. Surgery was done again, and this time Rabinowitz and Shorr sewed little slices of silicon sponge onto the lid to keep it from sticking. But they were cautious about the long-term results.

In September of 1993, Max underwent surgery to widen his airway. In the embryo, the windpipe begins as a solid cartilage tube, which later hollows out, but Fraser syndrome had interrupted that process. Dr. Flaum took a piece of rib from Max's rib cage, cut open the front part of the trachea and the area near the larynx, then fitted the piece of rib into the cut to widen the opening.

Throughout the second year of his life, Max had surgical procedures every few weeks. Eventually, his medical bills totalled more than half a million dollars, almost all of which was paid by health insurance. Doctors repaired an umbilical hernia, created a new navel, and separated his remaining fingers. Every month or so, Max would have a laryngoscopy-and-bronchoscopy examination. Eight months after his second eye reconstruction, a third was done, because the lids were once again beginning to adhere to the cornea and blood vessels were encroaching on the cornea. He also had a series of operations to correct urological malformations.

In a way, Max's surgeries became a reassuring routine. All children crave rituals, and his involved a mask and gown, and treats conferred by special friends. Each time he took the distressing ride down the corridor to the O.R., he would hold his mother's fingers through the bars of the gurney until the swinging doors pulled mother and child apart. Then, when he emerged from anesthesia, Penelope would be standing at the end of the bed holding balloons or a toy, and Max would gurgle with pleasure. Within days, he would be running after Luke or begging Bernard to swing him around and toss him on the couch.

Max plunged enthusiastically into the terrible twos. If Penelope told him to stop playing the bongo drum, for example, he would simply bang louder, leaving her to wonder whether his hearing had deteriorated or he was just being stubborn. Discipline was tricky with a child who could show his displeasure by throwing up and possibly choking to death. Usually, he got his way. He would stand in the shopping cart and scream "Wan daa!" whenever he spotted a toy fire truck or police car. Back at home, he would put on a fire hat and race his engines across the rug, calling "Put it out! Put it out!" He ate only tortillas and cheese, and drank only ice water. He refused to sleep anywhere but in Bernard's green leather easy chair. When he made mischief, it was hard to know whether or not he'd done it on purpose. One Sunday night, while Penelope was heating a can of SpaghettiOs, there was a knock on the front door. She had on short pajamas, the rugs were strewn with popcorn, and Bernard was away, so she opened the door only a crack—and saw a police officer. "Are you all right?" he asked. Behind him, four members of the L.A.P.D. crouched with guns ready.

"We have a report of a hostage situation here," the officer explained. Max had called 911, and the operator, hearing his raspy breathing, had asked, "Are you being held? Are you a hostage?" Max had replied with a grunt.

THE TRIPOD educational program, in nearby Burbank, teaches deaf and hard-of-hearing children alongside their hearing peers, and it agreed to admit Max despite his other disabilities. Although Max registered a fifty-five-to-sixty-five-decibel hearing loss on tests, he seemed to understand people when they spoke loudly. Dr. Flaum thought that Max had perhaps learned to read lips and found other ways of picking up sound. "Beethoven could hear and write music when he was deafer than Max," Flaum said. "Perhaps he felt the music, and perhaps Max does, too."

Developmental therapists didn't really know how much Max could hear, or see, and they couldn't explain why he made such steady progress even with the constant interruptions of his surgeries. By age three, he was on target in every area except his speech, which was broken, faint, and lacking in consonants. Flaum kept postponing removal of the tracheostomy tube, though, because the airway was still too narrow. Flaum had become Penelope's anchor at Cedars-Sinai, and their relationship was unusually friendly. She teased him for being so stern that he scared the nurses; he chided her for badgering the doctors. Now, however, they were locked in a battle of wills.

Max had virtually stopped signing, because he wanted to be like the hearing children in his Tripod class, even though they didn't always understand his speech. His teachers insisted that Max communicate with the deaf children, too, but Max was adamant, and Penelope feared that he would fall into a crevice between two worlds.

Finally, when Max was three and a half, Flaum pronounced the airway adequate and scheduled a procedure to remove the tracheostomy tube. Penelope was waiting in the recovery room when Max was wheeled out from the operation, and she saw at once that he still had the tube in his throat. When Flaum's eyes met hers, she recalls, he said, "Don't go off the deep end, now. I can take this out, but, you know, I wanted to check with you. It wouldn't hurt if we left it in awhile longer."

Penny remembers that at that moment all her anger at him melted. "I had the strangest sensation that we needed to switch roles for a minute," she told me. "He had gone the whole distance with Max, and it was hard for him to let go. I heard myself saying, 'It's O.K., Gene, it really is. We can do this.' Then he nodded, and very, very gingerly he took the tube out and plugged the hole."

Max loved the sensation of taking in gulps of air and forming sounds. After several weeks, he began talking nonstop, and his long vowels made him sound like a slightly hoarse Southern gentleman. He was also far more mobile without his suctioning equipment. Lulu began to take him on errands, and once, when he saw a boy in a wheelchair, she had to explain to him that the boy was disabled. Max certainly didn't think of himself that way. When he met another Fraser-syndrome child—one of four whom his parents were in contact with— he was bewildered to see that she had no eyes. But he seemed comfortable with the fact that he had only one. At the beach once, he was rubbing beneath his left brow, and Bernard's mother, Ethel, instinctively told him he would get sand in his eye. He laughed and said, "Grandma, there is no eye there."

As it turns out, though, there is. Buried under the skin is a fetal eye the size of an undilated pupil which had stopped developing at eleven weeks. Penelope and Lulu are convinced that the eye can perceive light, but Rabinowitz says that this is very difficult to verify. He does believe, however, that someday a microchip could be implanted and connected to the optic nerves. Luke likes the idea that his brother could have a bionic eye.

When Max became settled in school, Penelope decided to return to work. "I needed the rest—I couldn't sit through one more surgery," she said. She went back to her job in television and film production, and found that Max had changed her profoundly. "I was tougher, calmer, more focussed and analytical," she said. "When you are doing battle every day, you have to keep your head." At first, Bernard took over surgery duty with enthusiasm. But, after four operations, Penelope saw that he was exhausted. The next stage of reconstruction for Max was to fix his nose and eye socket, and sculpt his face. "Let's keep him the way he is, Dad," Luke advised. "He's cool. And some of these things could be useful. His webbed toes will make great fins when he learns to swim."

Bernard agreed that more than fifty-five surgical procedures in five years was enough—that Max needed time to enjoy his childhood. The helmets had succeeded in rounding his head, natural growth had lengthened his jaw, and Coke-bottle glasses obscured the fact that his left eye socket was empty. With the tracheostomy tube, Max's lips had often been fixed in an uncomprehending "O," but now he could smile freely. People didn't shrink from him anymore; they reached out to him. Penny had even put the hats away.

Once in kindergarten, Max made remarkable progress, though his deaf teachers still had to nag him to sign. He would sometimes grow frustrated with his stiff, clumsy fingers, which could not make more intricate sign-language movements, or even grasp a pencil firmly. Despite his best efforts, his handwriting remained shaky. But he rapidly learned to read, using books with large type.

Still, Penelope was anxious when his teachers declared that Max was ready to move on to first grade, and a more mainstream school environment. "Already, his glasses had been broken twice on the playground," she said. "What would happen when he was with older kids? Who could keep him from being teased and hurt?" She worried, too, because Max's social skills had not caught up with his academic achievements. If he wanted to roughhouse, he would simply tackle another child without preliminaries. Or he would barrage classmates with annoying, persistent questions, even when he knew the answers. The Tripod staff assured her, however, that Max would soon become bored if he didn't move on to a regular first grade. "He is so very, very bright that had he full use of his senses he would be labelled a gifted child," said Dr. Anne Galloway, a vision specialist for the Burbank school system, who works with Max. "The tests show that he sees, hears, and even feels tactilely only half of what his intellectual equals do, but his brain fills in the gaps. He is right up at their level, and rising fast."

So the teachers began to drill Max on the social niceties—how to make small talk, to wait his turn, to share, to reach out to others with the offer of a toy, a game, or a little joke. Because he would be going into a special Tripod first-grade classroom, with deaf, hearing-impaired and hearing children, Max had to master these skills in two languages.

That summer, Max joined a children's hockey clinic. The coaches were task-masters, and treated Max like any other child, making him drop to the ice and do pushups. Somehow, Max was able to move the puck across the ice and hit it into the goal, and Penelope entertained visions of his becoming the first deaf-and-blind hockey player.

LAST FALL, almost three months after his sixth birthday, Max reported to George Washington Elementary School, in Burbank, for first grade. He had a new wedge haircut and big blue wire-rimmed glasses, which he had chosen himself, and he wore the school uniform of blue shorts, a white polo shirt, and a monogrammed red sweatshirt. In his backpack were his eyedrops, a reading book, a work folder, and his lunch money. Hundreds of children jostled about in the hallways. Loud bells rang, and Max didn't know what they meant. Twice during the day, he had to negotiate several sets of stairs so that the nurse could put drops in his eye. On one of these trips, Dr. Galloway discovered him pressed against a wall, waiting for a stampede of sixth graders to pass. "So, Max, how do you like your new school?" she asked. He sighed dramatically: "It's an absolute nightmare."

Once he was back in the classroom, though, with his hands folded on his desk, Max "looked for all the world like a professional first grader," Galloway recalled. But Max had been allowed to live without many rules, and at first he rebelled. When something interesting happened in the back of the room, he would turn his chair around in order to see it—and there he would stay. "He is so stubborn, he put up a valiant fight against school discipline," Galloway said. "But when he finally learned how to be one of many, that allowed him to move forward."

The Tripod teachers at Washington Elementary were determined to minimize the special treatment extended to Max. "People at this school care deeply about Max, and some wanted to pamper him—give him less work, and computers to spell for him, and lots of paraphernalia—but the teachers had expectations for Max," Galloway said. "We all knew this was a make-or-break six months for him, and they made him work." Max had only three crutches—an extra-fat pencil, materials with large print, and permission to go up to the blackboard when he couldn't see the writing.

Max now prints legibly within the lines and keeps up with his peers. Though he is taken out of class once a week for mobility therapy, "you would not pick him out of a line as acting, or even looking, much different from anyone else," Galloway said. "The biggest difference I see is his mind. It has an unusual passion and persistence, and a conceptual beauty. His class studied penguins, and afterward Max saw penguin attributes everywhere." Each night, he has to read a book, do math and language drills, and work on memorizing a poem to recite in class that week.

An aide is supposed to spot him on the playground, but Max usually manages to dash off without her. He seeks out and is accepted by the most popular kids, because, as one teacher said, "that is the way he sees himself." He has learned also how to deal with other children's first reaction to him. If they ask, for example, why he has only one eye, he will answer, "That's just the way it is," impatient to move on to more important things, like soccer or kickball.

For years, Max was obsessed with Thomas the Tank Engine. Lately, it has been the comic-book hero Spider-Man, whose face is a blank red-and-black mask with eyeholes. Last Halloween, Max and his best friend wore Spider-

Man hoods, thereby cutting down on some of the confused and unkind reactions that Penelope had got in previous years when strangers saw Max in
costume.

In February, the family celebrated the loss of Max's first tooth. Penelope put
it in a satin ring box under his pillow. Dental X-rays showed that Max's permanent front teeth will come in normally, but they may have no roots. Just for a
moment, "I began to feel sorry for myself, you know, thinking most moms
take their kids to the dentist hoping for no cavities and here I am hoping for
just teeth," Penelope told me.

Everyone who knows Penelope has noticed that she has become both
steadier and more lighthearted than she was. "The truth is that Max has made
me more deeply happy than I have ever been," she explained. "He changes
everyone who meets him. He changes their ideas about beauty, about worth.
He has made every member of our family—immediate as well as extended—
grow up and change their life view in some essential way."

Max has also changed a lot of people at Cedars-Sinai Medical Center. "We
think everyone has to be perfect, physically, mentally," Dr. Flaum said. "It's
easy to write people off, say, 'This one's so abnormal, forget it.' Max has re-
affirmed that you cannot look at a person and know for sure that he has no
ability to learn and be a good member of our society." Many of the protocols
devised to help Max have become standard at the hospital. Dr. Rabinowitz
considers the operations to reconstruct Max's single eye to be some of his most
successful innovations. He and his colleagues have published the results in the
American Journal of Ophthalmology. Rabinowitz has set up a research foundation for birth defects of the eye, is trying to restore the fetal eyes of two other
Fraser-syndrome children, and has plans to help several others. "It is a remarkable story," he said as he played a videotape of one of Max's operations
in his office at the hospital. "The odds were so much against that eye. His
vision is far better than I ever expected. He sees things that the optical tests
can't confirm that he does."

When I visited Max last year, we went after school to the hockey rink to
watch Luke practice with his team, the Bay City Bombers. Luke has become
one of the team's top players, and Max is his biggest cheerleader. I bought Max
a sugar doughnut, and we went to sit in the bleachers. He proudly read a
picture book about firemen, but then pointed out with irritation that stripes
on the firemen's coats were white. In his quest to make a blurry world distinct,
he demands truth in detail, and he knows that the stripes should be yellow.

He asked why the sugar stuck to his face, why I didn't like doughnuts, and
why I was there. "Because I'm your aunt," I said. To which he replied, "Why
are you my aunt?" He wanted to know where I was born, and when I asked
him the same question he said, "In a hospital. It was very scary. I wanted to get
out. There was this machine, and they put a balloon in my mouth. I counted
two, three, four, five. Do you dream, Cindy? I dream a violin got put in my

mouth and somebody plays it with that stick. Then ghosts come, and they're not friendly like on TV. They put Lukey in the garbage."

Just then, Luke came out onto the ice, and Max leaned over the rail shouting, "Go, Lukey, go!" in a husky voice that seemed to come from a megaphone. I became aware of people staring at us and practiced how I would react if someone approached. A boy somewhere behind us kept asking his mother what was wrong with Max. Then I could tell by the trembling of the bleachers that they were coming down. Before I could whisk my nephew away, the woman was kneeling beside him. "It's a privilege to meet you, Max," she said, smiling. "We can see that God made you very special."

"Were you in a bad fire?" her son asked.

"What?" Max squinted up at him, and the boy, looking worried, repeated the question.

"Do you want to come to my house and play?" Max replied. The boy looked doubtful. "Do you like fire trucks?" To this, the boy nodded. "I have eleven—I have twelve fire engines."

"Do they have sirens?"

"They have sirens. They have bells," Max said excitedly. "And I have a real fire coat with yellow stripes."

John McPhee is a *New Yorker* staff writer and author of more than 25 books. Since 1975 he has been a Ferris Professor of Journalism at Princeton, teaching a writing course called *The Literature of Fact*. This piece about Plymouth Rock is in the collection *Irons in the Fire* (The Noonday Press, Farrar, Straus and Giroux, 1997).

Travels of the Rock

Plymouth Rock is a glacial erratic at rest in exotic terrane. When May-flower, an English merchant ship, approached the rock, in 1620, the rock, like the ship, had recently been somewhere else. Heaven knew where. Some geologists have said that the rock is Laurentian granite, from north of the St. Lawrence River (Loring, 1920). Most American geologists have preferred a provenance closer to home: Cape Ann, for example, north of Boston (Carnegie Institution, 1923); or the region of Cohasset, south of Boston (Shimer, 1951); or even the bed of Plymouth Bay (Mather, 1952). Wherever the boulder came from, it was many times larger in 1620 than it is today.

It was also in one piece. In 1774, the rock was split in two, horizontally, like a bagel. There were those who feared and those who hoped that the break in the rock portended an irreversible rupture between England and the American colonies. If so, the lower half was the Tory half, for it stayed behind, while the upper part was moved from the harborside to Liberty Pole Square for the specific purpose of stirring up lust for independence. Scarce was independence half a century old when a new portentous split occurred, in the upper, American, rock. It broke, vertically, into two principal parts, shedding fragments to the side. Eventually, the two halves of the upper part were rejoined by common mortar, containing glacial pebbles from countless sources, and the rock as a whole was reconstructed. The upper part was returned to the waterfront, where a thick filling of mortar was slathered on the lower part, and Plymouth Rock—with its great sutured gash appearing like a surgical scar—was reassembled so that it would be, to whatever extent remained possible, a simulacrum of the landmark that was there in 1620.

In the course of the twentieth century, the mortar did not hold. Pebbles fell out. Chunks. Despite a canopy over the rock (McKim, Mead & White, 1921), water got into the great crack, froze, and wedged against the bonding force with pressures as high as two thousand pounds per square inch. The rock could not stay whole, and on August 7, 1989, in an item disseminated by the Associated Press, the Massachusetts Department of Environmental

Management announced that the oldest symbol of the New World was in dire need of a mason.

IN THE British merchant marine, Mayflowers were numerous. The one that approached the landmark in Plymouth Bay that December was twelve or so years old, and had, for the most part, carried wine to England from Bordeaux. Her new assignment was equally commercial. When she sailed from Devon, she was under instructions to go to the mouth of the Hudson River, where her passengers, under a seven-year contract with investors in London, would warehouse timber, furs, and fish. She was meant to land on New York rock, but she missed. After a crossing of nine stormy weeks, she came upon Cape Cod. She dropped anchor in the cape's sheltered bay and spent a month there while a number of passengers, including William Bradford, went ashore to reconnoitre the cape's resources. In the woods one day, Bradford noticed a sapling bent over like a dancer touching the ground. Acorns were strewn beneath the sapling. Bradford moved close, too close, and "it gave a sudden jerk up, and he was immediately caught by the leg" (Mourt, 1622). The noose that caught him was state of the art by English standards, and so was the rope. In their searches the explorers found stored corn in buried baskets, which they took for their own use. They opened the grave of a child. "About the legs and other parts of it was bound strings and bracelets of fine white beads; there was also by it a little bow, about three quarters long, and some other odd knacks. We brought sundry of the prettiest things away with us, and covered the corpse up again." Before the sun had set four times, "arrows came flying amongst us."

In a small sloop, a scouting party sailed west, into a gale that broke the boat's rudder and shattered the mast. Nonetheless, they found what is now Plymouth Harbor, climbed to the high defendable ground behind it, discovered a sweet brook and deserted fields. This was not the "rockbound coast" that poetry and fiction would claim it to be. The shore was sandy. It was a beach. It was a long strand of wave-sorted till with almost no rocks of any size. A most notable exception was a big boulder of more than two hundred tons, alternately washed and abandoned by the cycle of the tides—a rock so prominently alone that from across water it would have looked like a house.

Bradford, Carver, Standish, Winslow, Howland, and the others—the exploring party—sailed back to Cape Cod to inform the Mayflower company that they had chosen a site for the plantation. They learned that Bradford's wife, Dorothy, had gone over the side of the ship and had drowned. She was one of four who died before the ship reached Plymouth. To get ashore on the cape, the people had to wade in several feet of water. Temperatures were often below the freeze point. Rain and spray formed ice on their clothing. Most of the children as well as the adults had colds, coughs, pneumonic symptoms that plunged into scurvy. On that gray water under gray sky—under wind and through snow—the land around them must have seemed less than promised. Dorothy Bradford was an apparent suicide. There had been a hundred and two passengers in all. One by one, across the next few months, forty-seven more would die.

A few days before Christmas, the ship entered Plymouth Harbor and approached the site near the mouth of the brook, the landmark rock below the foot of the hill. Most of the people lived on the ship until the end of March, routinely coming and going to trap or hunt or work on the initial construction. The brook, entering the bay, had cut a channel in the otherwise shallow water. The channel turned north, paralleled the shore, and ran close to the seaward side of the great rock. For two hundred years, oceangoing vessels would use this channel.

AFTER THE theory of continental glaciation was developed and accepted, in the nineteenth century, geologists reviewing the story of Plymouth took pleasure in pointing out that the rock had travelled, too: "The Pilgrims' Rock is . . . itself an older pilgrim than those who landed on it" (Adams, 1882). "Plymouth Rock is a bowlder from the vicinity of Boston, having accomplished its pilgrimage long before the departure of the Mayflower from Holland" (Wright, 1905, "The Ice Age in North America and Its Bearings Upon the Antiquity of Man").

A headline in the New York *Times* of October 25, 1923, said:

PLYMOUTH ROCK CANADIAN

What followed was a summary of confident assertions emanating from the Geology Department of the University of Rochester. The news caused the Acting Governor of Massachusetts to schedule hearings. The news caused Charles E. Munroe, the chairman of the Committee on Explosives Investigations, of the National Research Council, in Washington, to write a "PERSONAL—Confidential" letter to Robert Lincoln O'Brien, the editor of the Boston *Herald*, seeking his assistance in developing an investigation that would yield "more complete knowledge of the rock" and, fortuitously, "trace its origin to some other locality than Canada, thus greatly relieving the minds and assuaging the feelings of many, not only within New England but without."

What Munroe wanted was a piece of the rock. He wanted to place a hand specimen in the hand of Henry S. Washington, petrologist, geologist, geochemist, of the Carnegie Institution's Geophysical Laboratory. O'Brien, in turn, put the request to Arthur Lord, the president of the Pilgrim Society, in Plymouth. Lord replied that the rock had been studied by geologists and identified as syenite. Syenite? said Munroe to Henry Washington. Where could that be from? Montreal, said Henry Washington. Or half a dozen places in Ontario. He also identified possible sources in Vermont, New Hampshire, Maine, and Massachusetts, including Cape Ann. Cape Ann was the likeliest of this lot. Large boulders glacially transported are seldom moved very far.

When the theory of plate tectonics congealed in the late nineteen-sixties, it opened corridors of thought that have led to a complete revision of the geologic history of New England, where, it now appears, there is enough alien rock to effect the total detonation of the late chairman of the Committee on Explosives Investigations if he were here to hear about it. The short travels of glacial boulders are ignored by these new insights. In present theory, New England's very bedrock has come from overseas.

In Reston. Virginia, not long ago, at the headquarters of the United States Geological Survey, E-an Zen invited me to have a look at a snapshot taken from a space shuttle a hundred and sixty miles above Plymouth. The picture was nine inches high and eighteen wide. It had been made with a Large Format Camera. As with the old view cameras from the era of Mathew Brady, the negative was as large as the print. With a casual glance, you could see at once the region the picture covered. You could see Lake George, in the Adirondacks. You could see Vermont lakes, the Connecticut River, Narragansett Bay, and Cape Cod. But the picture was of such small scale—from eight hundred and forty-five thousand feet—that most of it seemed to the unaided eye a swirl of white patches in varying abstracts of gray. It covered, after all, at least twenty-four thousand square miles. Zen handed me a Hastings Triplet, a ten-power lens that geologists hold close to outcrops and specimens in order to study crystals. He put his finger on the edge of Massachusetts Bay, and said, "Look there." I leaned close to the photograph, as if it were a rock, and saw stripes at the head of a runway at Logan Airport. Moving the lens down the coast, I saw the breakwater in Plymouth Harbor. I saw Town Brook, Town Wharf, State Pier, and Coles Hill. I did not see Plymouth Rock, because of the canopy above it. On the shore of a Vermont lake I saw a small outcrop called White Rock, which I knew from childhood. Zen also had a picture that reached from Montreal to the Maine coast. I saw the house of a friend of mine on Mount Desert Island. I saw a fourteen-acre island in Lake Winnipesaukee, where I fish for chain pickerel in the fall. I saw smoke drifting away from the weather station at the summit of Mt. Washington.

After I put down the hand lens and leaned back, Zen asked if I could discern in the unmagnified pictures variations in texture from one area to another. I said I could. The country east of the Penobscot River, for example, differed from the country to the west as, say, burlap differs from tweed. Most variations were more subtle. On those pictures, from that altitude, the differences were no greater than the differences that sometimes occur on the surface of a calm lake. But the differences were there. New England appeared to consist of several swaths, as much as a hundred miles wide and more or less parallel to the seacoast. Zen was sporting a pleased grin. The large-format photographs seemed to illustrate conclusions he had reached from paleomagnetic, petrologic, structural, and seismic data interpreted in the light of plate tectonics, and in no way refuted by paleontology. Placing a finger on each side of the Penobscot River, he said those differing textural bands were exotic terranes.

As plate theorists reconstruct plate motions backward through time, they see landmasses now represented by Europe and Africa closing together with North America during the Paleozoic Era. These were the assembling motions that produced the great continent Pangaea. Much more recently, western Pangaea split apart to form the Atlantic Ocean, which is young, and is widening still. The ocean that was closed out in the making of Pangaea—the older ocean, the ancestral Atlantic, which used to be approximately where the Atlantic is now—is commonly called Iapetus, since Iapetus was the father of Atlas, and plate theorists, in studied humility, thus record their debt to mythology. The collision, as Zen and others see it in the rock they study and the data they otherwise collect, was not a simple suture of the two great sides. There were islands involved, and island arcs—Madagascars, New Zealands, Sumatras, Japans. "They were large islands in an ocean of unspecified size," he said. "Islands like Newfoundland." Some of them may have amalgamated while still standing off in the ocean. Some not. In one way or another, they were eventually laminated into Pangaea, and slathered like mortar between the huger bodies of rock.

A couple of hundred million years later, as the Atlantic opened, bits and pieces of original America stuck to Europe and rode east. The Outer Hebrides, for example, are said to derive from the northern North American continental core.

HEBRIDES CANADIAN

The converse was true as well. Stuck to North America, fragments of Europe stayed behind. Baltimore, for example. Nova Scotia. A piece of Staten Island. The part of Massachusetts that includes Plymouth and Boston is now understood to derive from overseas. If from Europe, part of New England could be part of Old England, a New Old England in an Old New England or an Old Old England in a New New England. The Mayflower people landed where they left.

AROUND eight one morning in mid-November of 1989, Paul Choquette, of South Dartmouth, Massachusetts, who had been selected only three days earlier as Mason to the Rock, arrived in Plymouth under considerable pressure to get the repair work done well before Thanksgiving, which was eight days away. He showed up in a U-Haul truck with Nebraska license plates and this message emblazoned on the sides: "ONE-WAY & LOCAL/ADVENTURE IN MOVING." Choquette was a trim man in his forties, with green eyes, dense brown hair, a loose, lean frame, and the serious look of a concentrating golfer. There was, as well, resemblance to a golfer in his roomily draped wine-red sweater, in his striped collar hanging free, less so in his bluejeans and his white running shoes. He had with him his entire family and then some. He had Jonathan, Jennifer, Elizabeth, and Tim—his children, twelve to twenty-one. He had his brother-in-law, Richard Langlois, and Richard's six-year-old, Ian, who said, "Why is this important? There's no such thing as Pilgrims."

Mark Cullinan, the chief engineer of the Department of Environmental Management, remarked that Choquette's task would be something like taking the tonsils out of the President of the United States—a relatively minor operation that nonetheless required someone of more than ordinary skill in the art. Moreover, the work would be accomplished with a lot of people watching: the public and the media, not to mention Paul Botelho, Cullinan's assistant chief engineer; Ruth Teixeira, the Region 1 regional engineer; Ronald Hirschfeld, a geotechnical consulting engineer; Chris Green, a landscape architect of the Office of Cultural and Historic Landscapes of the Department of Environmental Management; Peter O'Neil, the departmental press secretary; Shelley Beeby, the deputy commissioner of communications; and Donald Matinzi, of Plymouth, the park supervisor.

This was a day of chilling, intermittently heavy rain, and no one was sorry to be standing inside the McKim, Mead & White portico, which is locally known as the cage. It's a bit like a Bernese bear pit. Granite walls enclose the rock on three sides. The fourth side, through iron grillwork, is open to the sea. The entablature is supported on twelve tall columns, and is six feet thick, or thick enough to block rain. Under it, visitors stand behind iron railings looking down at the rock on its patch of beach.

The rock has become fairly round and has a diameter varying from five and a half to six and a half feet. Early in the eighteenth century, it was measured for purposes of a town plat, with the resulting description that the "Grate Rock yt lyeth below Ye sd Way from ye stone at ye foot of The hill neare the Southerly Corner of John Ward's land is :30: foot in width" (Plymouth Records, 1715–16). What you see now weighs only four tons. The lower, buried part is larger. Spring tides climb into the cage and far up the rock. Nor'easters drive seas against it as well. When trucks go by on Water Street, the rock shakes.

The rock is filled with xenoliths—alien and black. They are stones, cobbles, hunks of older rock that fell into the larger mass while it was still molten or, if cooler than that, sufficiently yielding to be receptive. The xenoliths are like raisins in a matrix of bread. The rock is crisscrossed with very narrow, very straight veins of quartz. At some point in the nineteenth century, it cracked along one or two of these veins.

On the seaward side, the old repair was in particular need of attention. The national treasure looked sorry indeed, like twice-broken crockery. After the news of its condition went out on the A.P., epoxy-makers all over the country offered their expertise free of charge. But Cullinan decided that high-strength epoxy was too much of a high-tech solution. To get rid of it, if that should ever be necessary, you would have to destroy rock.

Mortars can be mixed that look like stone. In other words, despite the fact that the great crack was as wide as a python, an effort could be made to fool the public into thinking it wasn't there. Cullinan rejected that idea, too. The remaining choice—other than leaving the rock alone—was to chip out the old mortar and replace it.

Choquette climbed down into the cage with so many others that they did suggest a surgical team. He had his duckbill chisel, his cold chisels, his brick hammer, his five-pound hammer, his three-pound hammer, his paintbrushes, his wire brushes, his cord, his trowels, his wrenches, and his two sons. His brother-in-law stacked three planks against the iron grillwork on the seaward side and wrapped a rubber sheet around them in anticipation of the rising tide. It was a day of full moon.

Choquette went at the crack with a chisel. Tap. Tap. Ta-tap-tap-tump. He said, "Listen to that void!" Bits of mortar flew away. The opening widened. After a couple of hundred taps, he reached in and pulled seaweed out of Plymouth Rock. It was dry, and looked like twigs and straw. It came out of the interior like mattress stuffing.

He said the old mortar was very hard—"a lot of Portland and not much lime." In replacing it, he would use four parts pulverized stone and four parts aggregate with one part lime (for plasticity). He would clean the crack with Detergent 600. He would put his new mortar in and, twenty minutes later, wash it with a hose and brush it. This would get rid of lime that tends to come to the surface. It would make the mortar darker, and also cause it to blend better into the pores of the rock.

To show to anyone who might be interested, he had a yogurt cup full of the pulverized stone. It came from a quarry in Acushnet, he said. Acushnet, Massachusetts, next to New Bedford, sits on hundreds of feet of long-transport glacial till. It is probable that the shards of rock going into Choquette's mortar came from three or four New England states and much of eastern Canada, and, in turn, from almost any Old World country south of Lapland. If a corner of the Old World was missing in the pulverized till, it might well be represented among the small angular stones that Choquette had brought from his own property, in South Dartmouth, to match the aggregate in the existing mortar. Steadily tapping, he continued to clean out the rock.

From above, someone in the gathering crowd asked him why he was attracted to this sort of specialty.

He said, "It intrigues me. Everything today is fast track. You know—you work it up and say, 'Where's the check?'"

"Are you ready for the Liberty Bell?"

"If you give me a shot at it, I'll try." Tap. Ta-tap-tap tump. "This rock is already eighty percent gone. Even if we can preserve ten percent of it, we should preserve it. What matters is what it means."

The Department of Environmental Management had sought an expert mason who had experience with historic masonry. The Historic Commissions of five states were asked for recommendations. This produced a short list of eight masons, including the restorer of Belvedere Castle, in Manhattan's Central Park, and the restorer of Austin Block, in the Charlestown section of Boston—a three-story granite building made of rock from an island in Boston Harbor. Seven years earlier, Choquette had reached his decision that there had to be more in masonry than trowelling together new buildings. Venturing into restoration as often as he got a chance, he had done the exterior of the Academy of Music Theatre, in Northampton, the exterior of a church in New Bedford, and various lithic antiquities on Nantucket. As masons were evaluated for the Plymouth assignment, they were asked in formal interviews what approach they would take to the problem—to say in detail just how they would think through and plan the work. Among the candidates was one who replied, "You wanta me to fix the crack, right? I do a good job. It take an hour." The finalists were Steve Striebel, of Gill, Massachusetts, and Paul Choquette. The job then went to bids. Striebel's bid was a hundred times as high as Choquette's. So Choquette got the job. He bid a dollar.

IN NOVEMBER and December of 1620, Mayflower people landed (and slept) in half a dozen places before reaching and settling in Plymouth. In the two contemporary accounts of the Plymouth landings—the several landings of the exploring sloop, and the arrival of the ship itself—nowhere is it mentioned, or obliquely suggested, that anyone set foot on a rock (Mourt, 1622; Bradford, 1630–50). Yet by 1820 the rock was set in the diadem of the republic. Daniel Webster, as the principal speaker on Forefathers' Day, on the two-hundredth anniversary of the Plymouth settlement, said, "Beneath us is the rock on which New England received the feet of the Pilgrims." He continued for an hour, his eloquent images provoking tears, and no one seemed to doubt him. The media had long since accepted the story. "The Federalists toasted their ancestors with the hope that the empire which sprung from their labors be as permanent as the rock of their landing" (*Colombian Sentinel*, December 22, 1798). And when Plymouth's first official history was published it said, "The identical rock, on which the sea-wearied Pilgrims first leaped . . . has never been a subject of doubtful designation" (Thacher, 1832). Foreign journalists covering the United States noted in conversations with Americans everywhere what "an object of veneration" the rock had become—a reverence that was growing in inverse proportion to the size of the rock itself. "I saw bits of it carefully preserved in several towns of the Union. . . . Here is a stone which the feet of a few outcasts pressed for an instant, and the stone becomes famous; it is treasured by a great nation; its very dust is shared as a relic" (Tocqueville, 1835).

Inevitably, a shrine was built to enshrine it—a tall four-legged canopy reaching back in time to Trajan and the baldachino and forward to the missile silo. The designer was Hammatt Billings, the illustrator of "Uncle Tom's Cabin," "Mother Goose," and "Little Women." It stood for fifty-three years before it was replaced by McKim, Mead & White. The rock that fitted into this ciborium not only had travelled across an ocean as bedrock and then an unknown distance as a glacial boulder but also had become remarkably mobile in Plymouth. When twenty yoke of oxen were brought to the site to move it, in 1774, pitonlike screws were put into it to assist the operation. The splitting occurred as if in a quarry, and the oxen went off with half a rock. On the Fourth of July, 1834, that upper half was moved several blocks, from the town square to the yard of Pilgrim Hall. In a two-wheeled cart, it was drawn through Plymouth as if it were the bull Ferdinand. It was escorted by the Plymouth Band, the Standish Guards, and half a dozen youths hauling behind them a model of the Mayflower. A story has come down from that parade to the effect that a pin came out of the bed of the cart, causing it to tilt, and—with the whole town of Plymouth looking on—the rock crashed to earth and broke into several pieces. Of the crisscrossing quartz veins in Plymouth Rock, each is a healed crack. The cracking and the healing could be associated with its original cooling (when its temperature got down to about a thousand degrees Fahrenheit), or with tectonic activity (anything from local faulting to pervasive plate motions) that heated it up. In either case, the quartz seams are planes of weakness—quarrymen call them sap streaks—and the break that Paul Choquette would one day be asked to fix followed such a vein. Since the story of the parade accident lacks convincing roots, it is probable that the rock's famous crack was made over years by rainwater, penetrating along a vein, freezing, wedging.

Meanwhile, the lower half of the rock remained at the waterfront, and actually served as a part of the surface of a commercial wharf, with iron-tired carts rolling over it filled with fish or lobsters, timber, coal. In the mud-traceried right-of-way, it bloomed like a plantar wart. It was a few feet from the front step of a grocery. When tourists came to see the rock, the grocer swept it clean, saying that he was "brushing off the cornerstone of the nation," and if anyone wanted a souvenir there was a hammer and chisel near the door. While Billings' canopy was under construction, the lower-half rock was hoisted up and placed to one side. As it sat there for some years exposed, it lost considerable weight. Large pieces were broken off and stolen. Some were rebroken into small pieces that were individually sold or, in one case, used as aggregate in making a concrete floor. A few large hunks went into a pickle barrel to weigh down corning beef. A piece that weighed four hundred pounds became a doorstep.

In 1867, when the lower half of the original rock was placed in its new setting, it did not fit. It was too long and thick for the display purposes the designer had in mind. So the rock was trimmed and planed. Its upper surface was lowered, as chips flew.

In 1880, the halves were reunited. The upper half was hauled downhill and set on top of the piece in the canopy. Together, the two parts were about as stable now as an egg resting on an egg. They were chinked firm by imported rocks of no established pedigree. Into the upper half the date 1620 was chiselled boldly.

At the time of the tercentenary, the Plymouth shoreline was reconfigured, and some thousands of tons of large broken rock were lined up as riprap on the once sandy beach. The old canopy was removed to make way for the new portico. As the national triolith was lifted by a crane, its repaired crack widened and the parts separated. The Obelisk Waterproofing Company, of New York City, was called in to waterproof the rock. This done, Plymouth Rock in its several parts was put on skids and hauled to a warehouse, where it remained until the portico was ready. In 1921, with mortar and trowel, the sculptor Cyrus Dallin reassembled the parts. His standing bronze figure of Chief Massasoit watched from Coles Hill, the high defendable ground above.

I am indebted to Julie Johnson, of Boston, who once studied Plymouth Rock for the Department of Environmental Management and whose specialty is historic preservation, for guiding me to a large part of this research, in the archives of Pilgrim Hall, in Plymouth.

The rock came to Plymouth about twenty thousand years ago. During the past couple of centuries, much of it has continued to travel, and some has recrossed the sea. A trimmed, squared hundred-pound piece long stood on a twenty-foot plinth in the courtyard of an inn at Immingham, in Lincolnshire, where, on the Humberside in 1607, the disaffected Puritans departed for Holland. There are pieces of Plymouth Rock at the Conoco refinery in Hull, Massachusetts. A piece of Plymouth Rock that weighs more than fifty pounds is in the Plymouth Congregational Church, on Schermerhorn Street, in Brooklyn. There is a piece of Plymouth Rock in Los Gatos, California. There is a piece of Plymouth Rock in the Nevada State Museum, in Carson City. In the Smithsonian Institution, in Washington, is a piece of Plymouth Rock about twenty-two inches long and of such craggy beauty that it could serve the art of *suiseki*, in which it would be called a distant-mountain stone. In the nineteen-twenties, the Antiquarian Society of Plymouth sold pieces of the rock as paperweights. There have been tie tacks, pendants, earrings, cufflinks made from Plymouth Rock. In 1954, a patriotic citizen sent President Eisenhower a piece of Plymouth Rock with the message "Now, Mr. President, if there are times when the going is hard and you may be discouraged, just take this little stone in your hand and . . . " Ike wrote back to thank him.

E-AN ZEN, who is approximately as exotic as the rock he studies, was born in Peking in 1928 and came to the United States when he was eighteen years old. Educated at Cornell and Harvard, he has worked primarily in the northern Appalachians. He seems to know every outcrop, contour, brook, and village of New England. Zen is wiry, spare, compact. It is not unimaginable that the term "rock-ribbed" was coined so that it would exist to describe him. He is the editor of the geologic map of Massachusetts (Zen, Goldsmith, Ratcliffe, Robinson, Stanley, 1983). Among his benchmark papers is one that is titled "Exotic Terranes in the New England Appalachians" (1983). When I saw him in Reston, he had recently written a guidebook for the International Geological Congress, laying out a field trip across the complete aggregation of terranes from Saratoga County, New York, through Vermont, New Hampshire, and Massachusetts to the coast of Rhode Island. He showed me the map the field trip followed. Rutland and Bennington, in Vermont, and Williamstown and Stockbridge, in Massachusetts, were all lined up near the eastern edge of the old North American continent. Hanover, New Hampshire, and Brattleboro, Vermont, were in a sliver of country with an average width of scarcely twenty miles that Zen called the Brompton-Cameron Terrane. He said it was not exotic. It seemed to be "a distal part of North America that was pushed onto the continent like a floe in an ice-jam—rammed in." Keene, New Hampshire, Amherst and Springfield, Massachusetts, and much of the Connecticut River lay in a swath about seventy miles wide that he thinks is truly exotic and is a southerly reach of the Central Maine Terrane. "It is from the other side of the ocean," Zen said. Its outer boundary runs through Fitchburg, Massachusetts, where it is welded to the country east of it by the Fitchburg Pluton, a granite batholith. The country east of it was the Massabesic-Merrimack Terrane (Portsmouth and Nashua and Manchester, New Hampshire; Sturbridge, Massachusetts; Storrs, Connecticut), which also came over the Iapetus Ocean. East of that—and including New London, Connecticut, and Worcester, Massachusetts—was a bent, irregular piece of the world as little as two and as much as seventy miles wide, of which Zen remarked, "God knows where it came from. It's a big enigma. It has no fossil control. It could be delaminated basement of the Massabesic-Merrimack Terrane. It is known as Nashoba." And, finally, through Cape Ann, Salem, Lynn, and Boston, nearly as far west as Worcester, and including Newport, Providence, and Plymouth, was New England's "most distinctly and unequivocally exotic terrane," Atlantica.

Atlantica. Seaward of all the voyaging pieces that had collided in sequence, making mountains, Atlantica differed from the others in a clear and puzzling manner: it was not pervasively deformed. You don't crash head on into a continent and take the shock of the tectonics undeformed. The successive collisions that preceded the arrival of Atlantica, which are collectively known as the Acadian Orogeny, had folded, faulted, and profoundly metamorphosed all the other terranes. In Atlantica, by contrast, even the gas cavities in Precambrian volcanic rocks are undeformed. Tiny shards are recognizable in Precambrian ash. In Atlantica, Zen said, Ordovician plutonic rocks are as fresh as the plutonic rocks of the Sierra Nevada, which are four hundred million years younger. In Atlantica, Silurian-Devonian volcanic and sedimentary rocks are undeformed. "In Acadian time, they were not touched."

"So where was Atlantica during the Acadian events?" I asked him.

He said, "I wish I knew. It's entirely conceivable that at the end of Acadian time you could have walked dry-shod from the Adirondacks to Atlantica—to Boston, but not where Boston is now. It would have been some hundreds of kilometres away; my prejudice would be to the south—a prejudice based on paleomagnetic data."

When the Acadian events were over and the mountains stood high, Atlantica, to remain undeformed, must have come sliding in along a transform fault, like southwestern New Zealand along the Alpine Fault, like southwestern California along the San Andreas Fault. Thus arrived Atlantica, from whose bedrock the ice sheet almost surely plucked up what became Plymouth Rock, and where, in any case, the Mayflower landed.

I said, "If you had to make a choice, where would you say Atlantica came from?"

He said, "Africa."

THE ROCK reassembled is not a perfect fit, because so much of it is missing. On the seaward side, the walls of the great crack diverge concavely, like a clamshell. Cleaning out the old mortar, Choquette opened a space deep enough to hide a football. When he worked far inside, his entire forearm was in the rock. Also, he removed rotten mortar from the top of the buried portion—the cushioning mattress beneath the two joined segments that are visible to the visiting public. Sparks jumped from the cutting edge of his chisel. The visiting public, now two and three deep around the railings above, had come to Plymouth to see a cold, silent stone and were watching the trajectories of sparks. A man in a bright-red jacket with an American flag on one shoulder snapped the rock with a Japanese camera and said to his wife, "They're looking for fossils."

Plymouth is a red-brick-and-white-clapboard town that has cheerfully shouldered the burdens of its negotiable antiquity. Outside one store, the words "KARATE CHECHI" appear on an eighteenth-century oval wooden sign. Ye Olde Town Crier is some doors away from Hair Illusions. There are houses that were known to the original people (1640, 1666). The streets are neat, the park is attractive under Coles Hill beside the bay, where the rock in the cage reposes. The Mayflower in replica—a hundred and six feet long, a hundred and eighty-one tons, with a very high and narrow stern—floats at a pier nearby: a gift from the City of Plymouth in Devon. Plymouth, Massachusetts, averages something like three thousand visitors a day—ten thousand on Thanksgiving, and scarcely a slack moment in any part of the year. Ruth Walker, a retired science teacher who works for the state as an interpreter of the rock, once told me some of the questions that visitors frequently ask:

"How did he get all those animals on that boat?"

"Where are the Nina and the Pinta?"

"Why doesn't the rock say '1492'?"

"Where is the sword?"

A man once appeared with a boxer on a leash and asked if it would be all right if the dog "marked the rock."

A descendant will blush modestly, rub one Reebok against another, and announce that his name is Howland. With a glance over a shoulder at the hill above the rock, another man says his name is Coles. His billowing sports shirt cannot drape the fact that since 1620 he has eaten very well. A Soule says hello, he's related to George. Descendants seem to appear by the shipload. In their sneakers, their cowboy boots, their leather jackets and one-way shades, they are Fullers, Winslows, Whites, Brewsters, Billingtons, Warrens, Browns, Aldens, and mixed collaterals. Someone tells the story that as Massasoit watched the ship arrive he said, "There goes the neighborhood."

A great many people are disillusioned when they see the size of the rock. At some level of consciousness they have confused it with Gibraltar. If they are asked what they expected, a high percentage of them will actually mention Gibraltar. The extent of the letdown is this: Gibraltar is thirty million times as large as Plymouth's potato-like boulder. Visitors have called it "the biggest disappointment in New England." When Jim Jenkins, of Greensboro, North Carolina, saw it, he said, "I've turned over bigger rocks than this mowing grass."

Don Matinzi, who grew up in Plymouth, said, "I get very defensive about the rock. People ask, 'What did the Pilgrims do, fall over it?' They say, 'It's a pebble.' And so forth. I'd like to have some of these people experience the privation the Pilgrims did. Instead, they ask, 'Where's the sword?'" Matinzi—young, with rimless glasses and brown shoulder-length hair—is an artist, a photographer, and a graduate of the Art Institute in Boston, and helps to support himself as the park supervisor, watching over the rock.

When I asked him one day if he knew of many other erratics bestrewn through the Plymouth woods, he thought for a while and counted few. The great Laurentide Ice Sheet had not, in this region, been generous with large boulders. There was one on Sandwich Road called Sacrifice Rock. It was sacred to the Wampanoags, of whom Massasoit was chief. Even today, offerings will appear from time to time on Sacrifice Rock—handfuls of pebbles, branches of trees. Its actual name is Manitou Asseinah (God's Rock). It sits by the roadside unfenced. When we went to see it, Matinzi said, with some ambiguity, "This is the only rock that does have a history that relates to the area." The boulder had come to rest six and a half miles from Plymouth Rock. Coarse-grained, with large crystals of pink feldspar, it may have derived from greater depth.

Now in Plymouth, as a rising tide was threatening the efforts of Choquette, Matinzi was saying that an amazingly large percentage of the rock's annual visitors were from other nations. Among all the categories of people who come to Plymouth, non-Americans are an even larger group than retired people, schoolchildren, or Mayflower descendants. The cage at the moment was full of children. By the schoolbusload, kids in great numbers had been coming and going all morning: BEDFORD CHARTER SERVICE, BIDDEFORD SCHOOL DEPT, BOSTON PUBLIC SCHOOLS. Matinzi said, too, that since his own schooldays, in Plymouth, he had seen the rock shrink. "It has shrunk six to ten inches from each end in my lifetime," he remarked. It was Matinzi who had noticed the disintegration of the old patchwork mortar and reported the need for repair.

As Choquette tapped with his chisel, his twelve-year-old, Jonathan, stood with a hand on one end of the rock. He said, "This thing here, Daddy, it's vibrating very much." With a hose, Choquette had from time to time been flushing out the chiselled bed of mortar from beneath the upper half. In his application interview, many weeks earlier, he had told the engineers that he thought the upper and lower halves made such an ill fit that with the rotten mortar gone at least three feet of the upper half would be cantilevered, and now he was proving himself right. He washed out so much mortar that eight inches of space separated a considerable area of the upper rock from the Tory basement. A couple of tons, including the celebrated vertical crack that Choquette was meant to repair, was projecting in air. Jonathan felt the rock rocking. It was obvious now that steel pins or steel staples must be holding the upper part together, for mortar alone could not retain so much suspended weight.

Lest the rock split and crash while the schoolchildren watched, Choquette supported it with riprap from the shore, and refused to continue until the state provided a couple of tons of three-quarter-inch bluestone to pack in as a new bed for the upper rock. The tide was stopping him anyway. Evading the rubber barricade, it came up through the sand. It just developed around his feet and was soon on its way to his knees. Matinzi said that the midday rise the day before had been the highest non-storm tide in years. Today's would be much the same. Choquette climbed out of the cage. By noon, the rock was almost underwater.

ANNE, another merchant ship, arrived in Plymouth in 1623, with something like sixty passengers, one of whom was John Faunce. He remained in Plymouth and raised a family, including a son named Thomas, who was born in

1647. The Old Comers, or First Comers, as the Mayflower people were called, were still very much around, and the young Faunce could not have helped knowing them. Myles Standish died when Thomas Faunce was nine years old, William Bradford when Faunce was ten, John Howland when Faunce was twenty-six, and John Alden when Faunce was forty. By then, Faunce was keeper of the Plymouth Records, a job he performed for thirty-eight years. He also became the ruling elder of Plymouth's First Church. His mother's brother, Nathaniel Morton, was the colony historian. Thomas Faunce was what geologists call autochthonous; that is, he originated in Plymouth and he never moved. He was literally immobile—enfeebled, ninety-four years old—when the day came that the facts of his life assembled here acquired their collective relevance. Someone told Faunce that the big boulder on the harbor shore would soon be buried.

Faunce had himself driven downtown and carried the final distance sitting in a chair. The chair was set beside the boulder. In 1741, this was enough to attract a crowd. Like the countless thousands of historic objects that would be lost forever in coming years, the rock was scheduled to disappear in the foundations of a wharf. Faunce was there to prevent that. He told his listeners not to forget that this was the landing rock of the Old Comers. They would do well to show it appropriate respect.

Faunce had grown up on this story. And history selected him as the earliest person to mention it. In a hundred and twenty-one years, the boulder's role in the American narrative had in no surviving way been reported to the future. The first-rate and firsthand accounts in "Mourt's Relation" (1622) overlooked it. In a hundred and fifty thousand words William Bradford does not mention it—a fact that would carry more weight if Bradford had mentioned the Mayflower.

A couple of centuries of reverence rest on the hearsay of Thomas Faunce. People who believe in the rock say there is no obvious reason that any of his predecessors would mention it. And, besides, it was a Bradford characteristic to be aloof from details. More than twenty times its present size, the boulder was near the edge of the channel; the settlers may have connected it to the shore with planks and used it often. Believers align what few facts they can in a generally positive direction. Skeptics do the reverse. The middle ground does not seem crowded.

The late Samuel Eliot Morison, of Harvard, once Harmsworth Professor of American History at Oxford, and the editor of Bradford's journal (Knopf, 1952), received a letter in 1953 from Rose Briggs, a Plymouth regional historian, asking his help with a monograph she was preparing on the story of the rock. What to say about "the Elder Faunce tradition"? she wrote. "He could have known; he may have been senile. Clearly the town believed him."

By return mail came a note from Morison, written in a hand sufficiently illegible to have qualified him as a physician:

I see no reason to go back on Elder Faunce now. *The American Neptune* chart of P. Hbr 1780 . . . shows a 1-fm. channel coming up to the shore there. The Rock, at ½ tide could have been a convenient place from which to lay logs or hewn planks to high water mark for a dry landing of people and goods—very important in "that could countrie."

I do hope however that you will point out that the Rock as a landing applies only to Mayflower arriving . . . *not* to the Exploring Expedition. . . .

In an address I shall give to naval officers in Jan. I am going to compare the (hypothetical) logs or planks laid from Rock to shore, to the pontoon causeways we had to use on shelving landing beaches in World War II to land vehicles from LSTs.

Sincerely yours,
SEMorison

BY TWO in the afternoon, the tide was in retreat, but the water was slow to leave the cage. It ponded there, higher than the surface of the harbor. Mark Cullinan, in hip waders, went down into the cage to bail out the rock. Paul Choquette, in twelve-inch yellow boots, joined him with another bucket. As they moved about, long microphone booms followed them, sparring over their heads. They were entertaining not only children now but ABC, NBC, CNN, and CBS. One mike was kept in a fixed position close to the top of the rock, not to miss a syllable if the rock had something to say.

When Choquette was able to resume work, he threw coffee into the small cavern he had opened, and watched it drip down the sides. Where mortar remained, the coffee turned the lime green. Choquette went after it with his chisel. Like a dentist doing his best with a split and cavitied tooth, he worked primarily on the inside, where he needed to prepare a clean, dry surface completely free of the old mortar. Jonathan held a flashlight for him, and together they created an odd tableau: a twelve-year-old boy shining a flashlight into the innards of Plymouth Rock while his father knelt beside him with both arms inserted to the elbows.

During this effort far within, the chisel removed a couple of flakes of the rock itself—fractions of an ounce. I asked for the flakes and Cullinan gave them to me. I wanted to take them to geologists at Princeton University and the United States Geological Survey to see what might be learned about the nature and origin of the boulder. In this era, a piece of rock of remarkably small size will serve the purposes of chemical and mineralogical analysis. In 1969, moon rocks as small as pinheads were sent to selected petrologists.

In Princeton, I took a flake to Douglas Johnson, the departmental lapidarian, who removed some crystals and also sawed off a piece of the rock a thousandth of an inch thick. This so-called thin section, mounted on a glass slide and readied for a microscope, was added to a collection of thin sections that Johnson had made from rocks I had gathered in various localities north of Plymouth—Cape Ann, for example, the region of Cohasset, and Kingston, on the edge of Plymouth Bay. Romantically, I hoped for a matchup in the thin sections—for a strong indication of a place or places where the ice sheet could have ripped out the bedrock that it carried to Plymouth, fashioning en route the national boulder.

I sent the entire kit—all the thin sections and a smidgen of Plymouth Rock—to E-an Zen, in Reston. The rock travelled Federal Express. In the morning, Zen looked at it with a hand lens and a microscope, called me on the telephone, and told me what he saw. First of all, Plymouth Rock was granite. It appeared to be Dedham granite, a major component of the Atlantica Terrane. "I'm convinced that it is a piece of the Dedham," he said. "Where the rock is freshest, the feldspar is distinctly pink, which is characteristic of the Dedham. The thin section shows a wedge-shaped crystal that is brownish blood red. That is a crystal of sphene. The blood-red sphene is distinctive of the Dedham. There are two distinct original feldspars. The potassium feldspar is in a form called perthite, and the plagioclase feldspar has become a highly altered saussurite, rimmed by an inclusion-free zone of sodium-rich plagioclase, all of which is also characteristic of the Dedham."

For reasons unfathomable, I had hoped that one of my numerous samples from the plutons of Cape Ann would match up with Plymouth Rock, like two setts of the same tartan. If so, the boulder could be said to have derived from the bedrock of Gloucester and traversed what is now Massachusetts Bay to come to rest in Plymouth. In Zen's lineup, however, all those samples were clear losers. "The Cape Ann granite contains only one feldspar," he said. "Like the Peabody granite and, for that matter, the Quincy granite. Moreover, they are gray granites. You never see pinkish feldspar in the surface of those granites. Plymouth Rock is not one of them."

He said, incidentally, that the quartz in Plymouth Rock had been "deformed very thoroughly."

I recalled his telling me that the Atlantica Terrane was undeformed.

"Atlantica is shot through with local faults," he said. "Plymouth Rock could have sheared along a fault zone. In almost any outcrop of the Dedham, you can see that. Plymouth Rock is a piece of the Dedham that has deformed in the solid state. This is not a pervasive deformation. It's a local fault, a crushing of the rock rather than a plastic deformation. If you go to Minute Man National Historical Park, where the Battle of Lexington was fought, you see Dedham granite that was very much sheared up in the Bloody Bluff Fault Zone. Plymouth Rock is locally sheared more than usual. Almost surely, when the boulder cracked it broke naturally along a weak zone formed by the shears. That is what the mason was repairing."

Looking further into the Plymouth thin section, he discerned that the biotite in the original granite had been recrystallized in the fault zone, becoming sugary and smoky green. There was also a lot of epidote. He said, "Epidote, saussuritized plagioclase, potassic feldspar, and the presence of sphene are distinctive of late Precambrian granitic rocks in the Boston area, of which the Dedham is an example."

So where did E-an Zen think Plymouth Rock derived from?

He said, "Somewhere between Boston and Plymouth Bay, I would guess. The ice direction was south-southeast. So the rock would have come north by northwest."

Within any large body of granite, there are countless minor variations. Compared with Plymouth Rock, the samples I had taken south of Boston from the Cohasset region through Weymouth to Kingston were close in nature but not identical.

I said, "How far northwest?"

"You cannot go beyond Concord and Lexington, because there you leave Atlantica," he said. "There is no rock like this except in Atlantica. It's a very, very distinctive rock."

PLYMOUTH ROCK AFRICAN

The Dedham granite, Zen added, had been radiometrically dated at six hundred and eight million years. That was when, in some far-distant land, the cooling magma froze as rock—a date that could be looked upon as accurate within seventeen million years.

In Plymouth, that week before Thanksgiving, darkness came early and quickly, and it left the television crews with nothing to see. They departed, but the visiting public kept arriving, even after dusk. They had not come to be on television or to witness the master Choquette. They knew nothing about the repair. They were drawn, like everyone else in all seasons, by the stone that is treasured by a great nation, its very dust shared as a relic. They were surprised, all of them, to find so much activity in a place that ordinarily has the aspect of a tomb. I remember particularly a young man from Florida and his companion, a woman from California, who clambered down the riprap to the harbor shore, the better to peer into the cage. The sound of the chisel was as rhythmic as a drum. The flashlight brightened in the growing darkness. The young man from Florida had shoulder-length gray hair. His friend was a waist-length-waterfall blonde and wore a black leather coat that nearly reached her shoes. He was wearing a Christmas-red sweatshirt decorated with large script that said "Dear Santa, I want it all." Apparently, it all was in Plymouth. He was exuberant. "What luck! What luck!" he kept saying. "What luck to find all this going on! My girlfriend wanted to stop here. I didn't. We argued in the car. She insisted that we come. And I said to her, 'It's a rock! Nothing ever happens to it.'"

ACKNOWLEDGMENTS

The editors and the publisher would like to thank the following copyright holders for permission to reprint the pieces in this book.

Jonathan Alter. "Cop-Out on Class," from *Newsweek* 7/31/95; "It's a Wonderful Legacy," from *Newsweek* 7/14/97; "The Era of Bad Feeling," from *Newsweek* 12/28/98. © 1995, 1997, 1998 *Newsweek*, Inc. All rights reserved. Reprinted by permission.

Jeremy Bernstein. "Annie of Corsica." Reprinted by permission of the author.

Malcolm Browne. "Left the Light On, But Nobody Came." © 2000 by *The New York Times*. "The Invisible Flying Cat." © 1981 by *The New York Times*. "At Least the Monsters Survive." © 1980 by *The New York Times*. "Beauty, As Scientists Behold It." © 1980 by *The New York Times*. Reprinted by permission.

Blair Clark. "On Robert Lowell," from *The Harvard Advocate*, Vol. CXIII, n 1 and 2. Reprinted by permission of *The Harvard Advocate*.

Leslie Cockburn. "Looking for Trouble." Reprinted from *Looking for Trouble*, Doubleday, 1998.

Barbara Crossette. "All Sentient Beings," from *So Close to Heaven* © 1995. Reprinted by permission of Alfred A. Knopf, a Division of Random House, Inc.

John Darnton. "Two Deaths—One Then, One Now; On Losing a Father, A Newspaperman." © 1996 by *The New York Times*. Reprinted by permission.

Irving Dilliard. "People and Character." Reprinted by permission of the author.

R. J. Donovan. "Twentieth-Century Odyssey." © 2000 by the Curators of the University of Missouri. Reprinted from *Boxing the Kangaroo: A Reporter's Memoir*, by permission of the University of Missouri Press.

Richard Eder. "Critic's Notebook." © 1999 by *The New York Times*. Reprinted by permission.

Gloria Emerson. *Gaza: A Year in the Intifada*. © 1991. Used by permission.

Lucinda Franks. "Miracle Kid." Originally published in *The New Yorker*. Reprinted by permission.

ACKNOWLEDGMENTS

Samuel G. Freedman. "The Rope Line." Reprinted with permission of Simon & Schuster from *The Inheritance*. © 1996.

Nancy Gibbs. "Massacre at Columbine High School." © 1999 Time, Inc. Reprinted by permission.

Richard Gilman. "Faith, Sex, Mystery." Reprinted by permission of Simon & Schuster from *Faith, Sex, Mystery*. © 1986.

James Gleick. "Manual Labor" and "Maintenance Not Included." Reprinted by permission of the author.

Francine du Plessix Gray. "Nixonland." Reprinted by permission of the author.

William Greider. "Mock Democracy." Reprinted with permission of Simon & Schuster from *Who Will Tell the People*. © 1992.

Charlotte Grimes. "Kathleen, the Country Is at Crisis Point" and "Memo to Conservatives: Family Ties Are the Strongest Values of All." Reprinted with permission of the *St. Louis Post-Dispatch*. © 1993 and 1992.

Walter Guzzardi. "Consultants: The Men Who Came to Dinner." © 1965 Time, Inc. Reprinted by permission.

Nat Hentoff. "Jazz." Reprinted by permission of the author.

John Herbers. Selections from *The New Heartland*. © 1978, 1986. Used by permission of Times Books, a Division of Random House, Inc.

Jim Hoagland. "Two of a Kind," "Truly a Nation," and "A Little Homer at the Beach." © 1999 Washington Post Writers Group. Reprinted with permission.

Landon Y. Jones Jr. "The Big Barbecue." Reprinted by permission of the author.

Haynes Johnson. "The Boat," from *The Bay of Pigs: The Leaders' Story of Brigade 2506*, by Haynes Johnson et al. © 1964. Used by permission of W. W. Norton & Company, Inc.

Charles Kaiser. "The 1950s," from *The Gay Metropolis, 1940–1996*. © 1997. Reprinted by permission of Houghton Mifflin Company.

Larry King. "Driver's Education." Reprinted by permission of the author.

Gina Kolata. "At Last, Shout of Eureka." © 1993 by *The New York Times*. "Scientist Reports First Cloning Ever of Adult Mammal." © 1997 by *The New York Times*. Reprinted by permission.

Jane Kramer. "Joséphine Guezou," from *Europeans*. © 1988. Reprinted by permission of Farrar, Straus and Giroux.

Robert Massie. "Down 23 Steps," from *The Romanovs: The Final Chapter*. © 1995. Reprinted by permission of Random House, Inc.

John McPhee. "Travels of the Rock," from *Irons in the Fire*. © 1997. Reprinted by permission of Farrar, Straus and Giroux.

Karl E. Meyer. "The Forthright Estate," from *Pundits, Poets and Wits*, edited by K. E. Meyer. © 1991. Used by permission of Oxford University Press, Inc.

Roger Mudd. "Code of Ethics." Reprinted by permission of the author.

Victor Navasky. "Saving *The Nation*." Originally published in *The Atlantic Monthly*. Reprinted with permission.

Don Oberdorfer. "A Farewell to Hue." © 1975, *The Washington Post*. Reprinted by permission.

Terrence Rafferty. "L'Atalante," from *The Thing Happens*. © 1990. Used by permission of the author and Grove/Atlantic, Inc.

David Remnick. "The Forest Coup," from *Lenin's Tomb*. © 1993. Reprinted by permission of Random House, Inc.

Harrison Salisbury. "Deus Conservat Omnia." Reprinted by permission of the author's estate.

Jonathan Sanders. "Pictures from the Rubble Patch." Reprinted by permission of the author.

Jonathan Schell. Selection from *The Gift of Time*. Reprinted by permission of the author.

Serge Schmemann. "A Corner of Russia," from *Echoes of a Native Land*. ©1997. Reprinted by permission of Alfred A. Knopf, a Division of Random House, Inc.

David K. Shipler. "Beauty for Ashes," from *A Country of Strangers*. © 1997. Reprinted by permission of Alfred A. Knopf, a Division of Random House, Inc.

Ronald Steel. "When Worlds Collide." © 1996 by *The New York Times*. Reprinted by permission.

Alice Steinbach. "The Miss Dennis School of Writing." Reprinted by permission of Bancroft Press, publisher of *The Miss Dennis School of Writing and Other Lessons from a Woman's Life* (Baltimore, 1997).

371

Richard Stengel. "My Own Vox Pop." © 1996 Time, Inc. "Space Invaders." Originally published in *The New Yorker*. "Stardom? They'd Rather Pass." © 1998 Time, Inc. Reprinted by permission.

Jean Strouse. Introduction to *Morgan, American Financier*. © 1999. Reprinted by permission of Random House, Inc.

Walter Sullivan. "What if We Succeed?" from *We Are Not Alone*. © 1992. Used by permission of Penguin, a division of Penguin Putnam, Inc.

Deborah Tannen. "Gender in the Classroom." Reprinted by permission of the author.

Paul Taylor. "Father of His Country." © 1994, *The Washington Post*. Reprinted by permission.

Stuart Taylor. "Harassment by Kids" and "Workplace Discrimination." © 1999, *National Journal*. Reprinted with permission.

Jeremy Treglown. "Class Act." Originally published in *The New Yorker*. Reprinted with permission.

Milton Viorst. "Meeting Mahfouz," from *Sandcastles*. © 1994. Reprinted by permission of Alfred A. Knopf, a Division of Random House, Inc.

Jonathan Weiner. "From So Simple a Beginning," from *Time, Love, Memory*. © 1999. Reprinted by permission of Alfred A. Knopf, a Division of Random House, Inc.

Lawrence Weschler. "Why I Can't Write Fiction." Originally published in *The New Yorker*. Reprinted with permission.

John Noble Wilford. "Pioneer 10 Pushes Beyond Goals, Into the Unknown." © 1983 by *The New York Times*. "Get Set to Say Hi to the Neighbors." © 2000 by *The New York Times*. Reprinted by permission.

Isabel Wilkerson. "First Born, Fast Grown: The Manful Life of Nicholas, 10." © 1993 by *The New York Times*. Reprinted by permission.

Geoffrey Wolff. "Heavy Lifting." Reprinted by permission of the author.

Christopher Wren. "Lenin Peak." Reprinted by permission of the author.

INDEX

Alter, Jonathan, 131, 133, 134

Bernstein, Jeremy, 170
Browne, Malcolm W., 209, 210, 212, 213

Clark, Blair, 147
Cockburn, Leslie, 36
Crossette, Barbara, 107

Darnton, John, 176
Dilliard, Irving, 72
Donovan, Robert, 22

Eder, Richard, 163
Emerson, Gloria, 268

Franks, Lucinda, 335
Freedman, Samuel G., 289

Gibbs, Nancy, 123
Gilman, Richard, 87
Gleick, James, 216, 218
Gray, Francine du Plessix, 298
Greider, William, 272
Grimes, Charlotte, 99, 104
Guzzardi, Walter, 306

Hentoff, Nat, 330
Herbers, John, 321
Hoagland, Jim, 137, 139, 140

Johnson, Haynes, 11
Jones, Jr., Landon Y., 281

Kaiser, Charles, 325
King, Larry L., 66
Kolata, Gina, 221, 223
Kramer, Jane, 18

Massie, Robert K., 249
McPhee, John, v, 351
Meyer, Karl E., 41
Mudd, Roger, 46

Navasky, Victor, 75

Oberdorfer, Don, 29

Rafferty, Terrence, 166
Remnick, David, 252

Salisbury, Harrison E., 234
Sanders, Jonathan, 259
Schell, Jonathan, 9
Schmemann, Serge, 264
Shipler, David K., 3
Steel, Ronald, 114
Steinbach, Alice, 151
Stengel, Richard, 94, 95, 97
Strouse, Jean, 242
Sullivan, Walter, 225

Tannen, Deborah, 126
Taylor, Jr., Stuart S., 59, 62
Taylor, Paul, 51
Treglown, Jeremy, 316

Viorst, Milton, 156

Weiner, Jonathan, 198
Weschler, Lawrence, 143
Wilford, John Noble, 204, 207
Wilkerson, Isabel, 117
Wolff, Geoffrey, 179
Wren, Christopher, 193